AF758132

Law and Policy for a New Economy

Law and Policy for a New Economy

Sustainable, Just, and Democratic

Edited by

Melissa K. Scanlan

Professor of Law, Associate Dean for Environmental Programs, Director, Environmental Law Center and Co-Founder and Director, New Economy Law Center, Vermont Law School, USA

Edward Elgar
PUBLISHING

Cheltenham, UK • Northampton, MA, USA

© The Editor and Contributing Authors Severally 2017

All rights reserved. No part of this publication may be reproduced, stored in a retrieval system or transmitted in any form or by any means, electronic, mechanical or photocopying, recording, or otherwise without the prior permission of the publisher.

Published by
Edward Elgar Publishing Limited
The Lypiatts
15 Lansdown Road
Cheltenham
Glos GL50 2JA
UK

Edward Elgar Publishing, Inc.
William Pratt House
9 Dewey Court
Northampton
Massachusetts 01060
USA

A catalogue record for this book
is available from the British Library

Library of Congress Control Number: 2016962582

This book is available electronically in the Elgaronline
Law subject collection
DOI 10.4337/9781786434524

MIX
Paper from responsible sources
FSC® C013056

ISBN 978 1 78643 451 7 (cased)
ISBN 978 1 78643 452 4 (eBook)

Typeset by Servis Filmsetting Ltd, Stockport, Cheshire
Printed and bound in Great Britain by TJ International Ltd, Padstow

Contents

Figures

Contributors

Shalanda H. Baker is an Associate Professor, the Faculty Advisor to the Environmental Law Program, and the founding director of the Energy Justice Program at the University of Hawaii at Manoa William S. Richardson School of Law. Professor Baker teaches international environmental law, renewable energy law, sustainable development, administrative law, and related courses in energy and international development. Her research explores large energy and infrastructure project development, including renewable energy projects; indigenous rights; and the effect of development on the environment. She is an Associate Fellow with the New Economy Law Center at Vermont Law School and a 2016–17 Fulbright-García Robles Scholar.

David Bollier is an independent American scholar, activist and blogger whose work focuses on the commons as a new paradigm of economics, politics and culture. He pursues this work primarily as co-founder of the Commons Strategies Group, an advocacy project that works internationally with various commons projects. Bollier has written or edited eight books on the commons, including *Think Like a Commoner: A Short Introduction to the Life of the Commons* (2014) and, with co-editor Silke Helfrich, *Patterns of Commoning* (2015) and *The Wealth of the Commons* (2012). He is an Associate Fellow with the New Economy Law Center at Vermont Law School. He lives in Amherst, Massachusetts, and blogs at Bollier.org.

Catherine Iorns Magallanes is a Reader in the School of Law at Victoria University of Wellington, Aotearoa New Zealand. She works primarily on environmental law, indigenous rights, and statutory interpretation. Professor Iorns is also a national board member of Amnesty International Aotearoa New Zealand and of 350 Aotearoa. She is a member of the International Law Association Committee on the Implementation of the Rights of Indigenous Peoples, a member of the IUCN World Commission on Environmental Law, and is the Academic Advisor to the NZ Council of Legal Education. She holds an LLM from Yale Law School.

Mark James is an Assistant Professor at Vermont Law School and a Senior Research Fellow in the Institute for Energy and the Environment (IEE). Professor James holds an LLM in Energy Law from Vermont Law School and he served as an IEE Global Energy Fellow from 2014 to 2016. His work explores privacy protections for data generated by smart meters and rooftop solar arrays, the SunShot Plug and Play project to commercialize adhered solar PV panel technology, and federal hydro-power production tax credits. He received his JD from the University of Ottawa.

Kevin B. Jones is a Professor of Energy Technology and Policy and the Director of the Institute for Energy and the Environment at Vermont Law School. Professor Jones leads the Smart Grid Project and the Energy Clinic and is co-author of the book from Praeger, *A Smarter, Greener Grid: Forging Environmental Progress through Smart Energy Policies and Technologies*. He is a Senior Fellow with the New Economy Law Center at Vermont Law School and a Lecturer in the University of Vermont's Sustainable Entrepreneurship MBA program.

Janelle Orsi is Co-founder and Executive Director of the Sustainable Economies Law Center (SELC), which facilitates the growth of more sustainable and localized economies through education, research and advocacy. She is a lawyer, advocate, writer and cartoonist focused on cooperatives, land trusts, and the grassroots sharing economy. Janelle has also worked in private law practice at the Law Office of Janelle Orsi, focusing on sharing economy law since 2008. She is author of *Practicing Law in the Sharing Economy* (ABA Books 2012) and *The Sharing Solution* (Nolo 2009). She is a Senior Fellow with the New Economy Law Center at Vermont Law School.

Jedediah Purdy is a Professor of Law at Duke University. He teaches constitutional, environmental and property law and writes in all of these areas. He also teaches legal theory and writes on issues at the intersection of law and social and political thought. He is the author of a trilogy on American political identity, which concluded with *A Tolerable Anarchy* (2009); *The Meaning of Property* (2010), and *After Nature: A Politics for the Anthropocene* (2015). He has published many essays in publications including The Atlantic Monthly, the New York Times Op Ed Page and Book Review, Die Zeit and Democracy Journal, and his legal scholarship has appeared in the Yale Law Journal, University of Chicago Law Review, Duke Law Journal, Cornell Law Review and Harvard Environmental Law Review, among others.

Laurie Ristino is an Associate Professor and the Director of the Center for Agriculture and Food Systems at Vermont Law School. Before Vermont Law School, she was Senior Counsel with the Office of the General Counsel, United States Department of Agriculture (USDA) in Washington, D.C. advising on environmental matters ranging from protection of the northern spotted owl to the BP oil spill in the Gulf of Mexico. She received her law degree from the University Iowa College of Law and a Masters degree in public administration from George Mason University. She is a Senior Fellow with the New Economy Law Center at Vermont Law School.

Melissa K. Scanlan is the Associate Dean of the Environmental Law Program, Professor of Law, Director of the Environmental Law Center, and Co-Founder and Director of the New Economy Law Center at Vermont Law School. Before Vermont Law School, she was the University of Wisconsin Law School's Water Law and Policy Scholar and a lead consultant involved in launching the Center for Water Policy at the University of Wisconsin-Milwaukee's School of Freshwater Sciences. She founded and served as Executive Director of Midwest Environmental Advocates. She earned her law degree and Master of Science in Environmental Science, Policy and Management from the University of California-Berkeley.

Linda Sheehan is Executive Director of Planet Pledge, which advances collaborative investments and grantmaking to reduce greenhouse gas emissions globally. Prior to Planet Pledge, she was Executive Director of the Earth Law Center, where she developed and implemented new legal models that acknowledge the natural world's inherent rights to exist, thrive and evolve. She previously ran California Coastkeeper Alliance, where she successfully advanced legislation, policy and litigation initiatives to improve waterway health, designate marine parks, and create new environmental funding streams. Ms Sheehan earned her BS degree from MIT, and her MPP and JD degrees from the University of California, Berkeley. She is a Senior Fellow with the New Economy Law Center at Vermont Law School.

James Gustave "Gus" Speth is Co-Founder and Senior Fellow of the New Economy Law Center at Vermont Law School. He previously served as a law professor at Vermont Law School and Dean of the Yale School of Forestry and Environmental Studies. From 1993 to 1999, he was Administrator of the United Nations Development Programme and Chair of the UN Development Group. Prior to his service at the UN, he was Founder and President of the World Resources Institute;

Professor of Law at Georgetown University; Chair of the US Council on Environmental Quality in the Carter administration; and Co-founder and Senior Attorney of the Natural Resources Defense Council. He currently co-chairs The Next System Project.

Jennifer Taub is a Professor of Law at Vermont Law School. She researches and writes in the areas of corporate governance, financial market reform, securities regulation and white collar crime. Her first book was *Other People's Houses: How Decades of Bailouts, Captive Regulators, and Toxic Bankers Made Home Mortgages a Thrilling Business* (2014). Professor Taub is also the co-author of *Corporate and White Collar Crime: Cases and Materials*, 6th edn (2017). She has testified before the United States Senate Banking Committee and a United States House Financial Services Subcommittee concerning financial reform matters. Prior to joining academia, Taub was an Associate General Counsel with Fidelity Investments. She received her BA degree, cum laude, from Yale University, and her JD, cum laude, from Harvard Law School. She teaches business law courses, including Contracts, Corporations, Securities Regulation and White Collar Crime. She is a Senior Fellow with the New Economy Law Center at Vermont Law School.

Diana R. H. Winters is an Associate Professor at the Indiana University McKinney School of Law, where she joined the faculty in August of 2012. Previously, she was a Visiting Assistant Professor at Boston University Law School, an Assistant Solicitor General for the New York Attorney General's Office, and an Associate at Hogan Lovells (then Hogan & Hartson). She teaches torts, health law and policy, and food law, and her research focuses on food law and the interaction between different levels of regulatory authority. She received her PhD in the History of the American Civilization from Harvard University, and her JD, cum laude, from New York University School of Law.

Mary Christina Wood is the Philip H. Knight Professor of Law and Faculty Director of the University of Oregon School of Law's Environmental and Natural Resources Law Center. She teaches property law, natural resources law, public trust law, federal Indian law and environmental law courses. She is the Founding Director of the school's nationally acclaimed Environmental and Natural Resources Law Center and is Faculty Leader of the Program's Conservation Trust Project, Native Environmental Sovereignty Project, and Food Resiliency Project. Professor Wood is the co-author of a textbook in natural resources law and one in public trust law, and is the author of *Nature's Trust: Environmental Law for a New Ecological Age* (Cambridge University Press 2013). She has written extensively about climate crisis and is a frequent speaker on environmental issues. She is an Associate Fellow with the New Economy Law Center at Vermont Law School.

Foreword

Jim Salzman*

By many measures, the modern era of environmental law has been impressive in its accomplishments. Looking from today back to the United States of 1970, the air is cleaner, water safer to drink, wetlands better protected, and waste more properly treated and disposed. To be sure, much remains to be done, but overall this represents a success story – glass half full.

At the same time, however, larger trends give real cause for concern. Greenhouse gas concentrations are still on the rise, as are extreme weather events around the world; global deforestation continues; biodiversity loss proceeds; water scarcity has become an ever-greater threat; the nitrogen cycle continues to be disrupted. While the oft-used image of rearranging deck chairs as the Titanic sinks may seem melodramatic, it has a kernel of truth, particularly if climate change models prove accurate.

Increasingly sophisticated and funded, the environmental movement has been remarkably effective in improving air quality, water quality and waste disposal in the United States, yet many of the most important global measures are going in the opposite direction. As Gus Speth has provocatively charged, the environmental movement has fallen short in addressing these larger threats and there is little reason to think that more of the same will make a difference. How have we done so poorly while doing so well?

Something new is needed. But what? It's hard to think of a more important question of our time. More specifically, what would an economic and legal system even look like that meaningfully addressed not only our greatest environmental challenges but also did so in an equitable and socially just manner? Can we make this transition through incremental movements or is transformative change necessary? Should we reframe our whole conception of what constitutes environmental issues?

This book offers a series of vantages into these basic yet profoundly difficult questions. The authors of the different chapters do not share

* James Salzman is the Donald Bren Distinguished Professor of Environmental Law, Bren School of Environmental Science & Management, University of California Santa Barbara, and Law Professor University of California Los Angeles.

a uniform vision of what a New Economy should look like. No shared ideology drives their views. Instead, their contributions offer us the opportunity to conceive of different futures.

Some of the visions work within the current legal system, with separate chapters calling for innovations that would advance crowdfunding, distributed solar power, food policy and agricultural reform. Others are more ambitious, calling for a legal transition to commons-based structures, or from the public trust doctrine to a much more encompassing nature's trust. Other chapters challenge us to think outside our shared experiences and imagine the law and policy of a joyful economy, an Earth-based economy, or an environmentally just economy within the emergent Anthropocene era.

The value of this book lies in forcing us to overcome the false comfort of cognitive dissonance. The current world of environmental law and policy is intentionally myopic, focused on the operation and challenges of a complex, massive legal system. Does the low carbon fuel standard violate the dormant commerce clause? Should "waters of the United States" encompass seasonally dry riverbeds under the Clean Water Act? It is entirely proper that scholars and practitioners focus on these types of questions because they have great practical import. At the same time, however, these efforts risk missing the larger and arguably more important trends.

If one accepts that climate change, loss of biodiversity, and other measures of planetary health are steadily moving in the wrong direction and appear likely to do so under business as usual, then intellectual honesty forces us to accept Gus Speth's charge that something new is needed. Readers will most likely not agree with all the proposals in these chapters. I certainly do not. But I also find myself in the uncomfortable position of not having a good alternative.

Law and Policy for a New Economy is an important book for the simple reason that it takes seriously the cognitive dissonance of the modern environmental movement – working within the system while acknowledging that something new is needed. As you read the chapters that follow, you will enter into an important discussion that is at once provocative, innovative, and sorely needed.

Prologue

Melissa K. Scanlan

At seven my daughter learned in school about how climate change is threatening the future existence of the majestic polar bears. She responded by writing an appeal letter to her school friends to stop burning coal and oil, refrain from buying unnecessary things, and walk to get where you're going. Some weeks later she looked at me with those big clear eyes that only a child has and asked for an honest answer: is it too late to stop this?

As an environmental lawyer and professor, I have spent countless hours discussing and debating these matters with adults. But it was this exchange with my child that brought out for me the glaring failure of environmental law's close to half century of experimentation. While laws are the fundamental infrastructure that undergirds our economic, political and social systems, environmental law is not understood as such. This shortfall starts with environmental law courses, which in the US, typically teach the primary federal environmental statutes, with a focus on the field as a set of rules that establish pollutant limits for specific waterbodies; protect identified species, ecosystems, and natural resources; or direct an industry to use a required technology. Although necessary, these rules do not address the motivating paradigm of our political economy; and as such, they don't address what we can see today as the deep drivers of environmental deterioration.

The most daunting example of failing to tackle these drivers is seen in increasing amounts of greenhouse gases (GHGs)[1] and global climate disruption. A compounding problem is that, in the main, environmental law is oblivious to racial, social and wealth inequalities. While the environmental justice movement has sprouted alongside to correct the course, this is often too little, too late. In order to develop a new economic system that is aligned to provide better results for the climate and for economic justice, we need to rethink what we consider environmental law. We need

[1] GHGs include carbon dioxide (CO_2), nitrous oxide (N_2O), methane (CH_4), Sulphur hexafluoride (SF_6), hydrofluorocarbons (HFCs), and perfluorocarbons (PFCs).

laws that facilitate a new ecologically-sustainable system. And as this book reveals, that goes well beyond just determining how many parts per billion of a pollutant are allowed in a specific water body.

This book addresses the laws and policies needed to support the emergence of a new economy across a variety of major areas – from energy to food, across common pool resources, and shifting investments to capitalize locally-connected and mission-driven businesses. This is not a book that tinkers with current mindsets, arguing about how to set the best standard to protect water, air, or even our climate. If you're looking for that, there are many other books to provide it. Instead, these authors take the approach that the challenges are much broader than setting parameters around pollution, and go to the heart of the dominant global political economy. It explores the values needed to transform our current economic system into a new economy supportive of ecological integrity, social justice, and vibrant democracy.

Many of the chapters in this book discuss ideas about bolstering participatory democracy in response to the indicators of a breakdown in democratic rule making. This is not cabined to democratic governments alone; instead it involves a greater emphasis on subsidiarity, diffusing decision-making to the broadest and lowest possible level of an entity, organization, business or government.

The new economy movement presents an alternative paradigm that the way to address social and climate needs and achieve better, more joyful lives is with an economy powered by renewables and a focus on improving our family relationships, our community and friends, our financial situation up to the point of meeting basic needs, our work, our health, our personal freedom, and our personal values. This paradigm emphasizes quality over quantity. It focuses on reducing gaps between rich and poor. It imagines a different relationship with the natural world, one based on endowing nature with inalienable, enforceable legal rights to exist, thrive and evolve. And it describes the role of government as a trustee with fiduciary duties running to the public.

In Chapter 1, I orient the reader to the need to rapidly reduce GHGs to meet the climate imperative, and the larger system changes that could help facilitate this. I discuss systems thinking and systems change, highlighting leverage points to achieve change, from paradigms to parameters. Here you'll find an overview of the new economy movement that has emerged to provide an alternative. Using a systems lens, I identify the areas where the law needs to evolve to build a more sustainable, equitable, and democratic future. The book then proceeds in two parts: paradigms for an ecological age (Chapters 2–5) followed by practical applications to demonstrate where these changes are already occurring (Chapters 6–12).

Part I begins with a chapter by James Gustave Speth explaining how environmental organizations have gone wrong, such that 46 years after the first Earth Day, we find ourselves on the path to a ruined planet, not one sustained and whole. He makes the case for a new environmentalism that offers hope of finally turning the corner before it is too late. In Chapter 3, Jedediah Purdy writes about environmentalism for the next economy. For environmental law to contribute to a more egalitarian and cooperative economy, it will have to be recast in a way that gives a central place to the organizing concerns of environmental justice: the distributive effects of environmental law and policy, and the constitutive question of which problems count as environmental, and whose conception of a good life in the natural world environmental law advances. This chapter locates that goal within two developments that have shifted the field more generally: the renewed recognition of the depth and importance of inequality and the emergence of "the Anthropocene" as a characterization of a transformed relationship between human beings and the rest of the planet.

Catherine Iorns Magallanes and Linda Sheehan's chapter on Earth Rights reframes rights and responsibilities to prioritize nature. It focuses on three essential elements: the recognition of the intrinsic value of nature, the recognition of inherent rights of nature, and the establishment of a framework of human responsibility for nature. Such a legal framework would entail a paradigm shift; however, adoption of such elements in law can also help achieve such a shift in mindset as well as in practice. To this end, this chapter includes examples of existing and proposed laws adopting these three essential and intertwined elements, with global focus areas that include California and Aotearoa New Zealand.

Also operating at the level of paradigm change, Mary Christina Wood's Chapter 5 focuses on the public trust doctrine. She envisions the government as a trustee with respect to crucial shared commons, such as the atmosphere and climate. Calling this Nature's Trust, she explains that government actors have a legally-enforceable duty to protect and restore nature. Trusteeship stands in contrast to the current model of the iron triangle between corporate interests, lobbyists and legislators/regulators where the public interest and long-term management is subverted to special interests with short-term private aims. A fundamental component of democracy, the Nature's Trust empowers citizens to hold government accountable for ecological protection.

Part II transitions from longer-term paradigm change to practical applications occurring now around the globe. The new economy paradigm influences the types of business structures that should flourish and the role of profit in corporate goal setting. As described by the Democracy Collaborative, some promising business structures for the new economy are: cooperatives; employee stock ownership plan companies (ESOPs); community development financial institutions (CDFIs); social enterprises; municipal enterprises; and hybrid enterprises.[2] These more locally-rooted business structures add to the diversity and self-organizing, adaptive capacity of the economy.

In Chapter 6, Janelle Orsi describes principles for organizations to embed in their legal, financial and governance structures in order to build commons and move beyond the extractive structures of conventional business. "The commons" is emerging as a unifying framework for the creation of sustainable and equitable economies, and organizations everywhere will increasingly ask their lawyers for guidance on how to set up a "commons-based" entity structure. Land trusts, energy cooperatives, water mutuals, worker cooperatives, food cooperatives and housing cooperatives will all require that lawyers approach legal structural design with a mindset that decisively rejects business-as-usual. These principles emerge from practice and are designed to be immediately applicable in any organization.

Taking this commons theme further, David Bollier's chapter on reinventing law for the commons provides historical roots of commoners seeking to use law to decriminalize their sharing and secure legal recognition for their self-organized management of shared wealth – "commoning". He describes a variety of creative initiatives attempting to reinvent law for the commons in disparate settings – indigenous, subsistence, digital, urban, local and organizational, among others – which are part of an emerging effort to legitimate the commons as a generative social form.

New economy advocates look to transform the corporation from an enterprise designed primarily to provide profits for shareholders to one concerned about a broader set of values and stakeholders. Such a shift ideally would help us prioritize people, place and planet. Perhaps those who bring leadership to businesses that focus on social and environmental concerns – social entrepreneurs – can answer the call by reorienting the corporations they create. Such localized efforts to transform individual firms could inspire widespread change. Diversifying local businesses is an important counterweight to the monopolizing, homogenizing influence of Wall Street corporations. Yet, capitalization of businesses that are not traded on the stock market is a bottleneck to their expansion.

There are a variety of barriers to investors who want to direct their funds towards local businesses. However, US security law changes may

---

[2] Marjorie Kelly, Steve Dubb and Violeta Duncan, *Broad-Based Ownership Models: As Tools for Job Creation & Community Development*, The Democracy Collaborative (January 2016).

alter this dynamic. In Chapter 8, Jennifer Taub focuses on investing locally. She argues that new laws facilitate funding socially-minded enterprises. Entrepreneurs have promising new options available for broadly soliciting like-minded investors and organizing their business enterprises to include social goals. In the US, those seeking to fund an enterprise can forgo a complex, time-consuming full federal registration process with the Securities and Exchange Commission (SEC) while still reaching out to solicit a wide group of potential investors. This general solicitation can include advertising online through crowdfunding portals. Taub's chapter provides background on securities laws in the US and then details how recent legal developments at the federal and state levels can aid the startup or expansion of social, community, and environmental business enterprises.

Shifting to the two areas of the economy that hold the greatest potential to rapidly reduce GHGs and meet the climate imperative, Chapters 9 through 12 discuss energy and food systems and highlight exemplars that show how to redesign these systems to also enhance democracy and address wealth inequalities. Kevin Jones and Mark James's chapter and Shalanda Baker's chapter on community solar explain how new business forms of owning energy will speed the transition to renewables, and will open up renewable options and increase resiliency for low-income communities. These chapters focus on solar power because it is booming, as the costs fall and interest in clean and distributed energy grows. Jones and James's chapter explores trends in renewable energy development and how clean distributed energy may disrupt the current utility model. The chapter discusses US state and federal policies for solar development and how they can be used to promote meaningful community ownership: a model that supports the local economy while reducing carbon emissions. The chapter concludes by exploring strategies for scaling up Vermont's community solar model to support the goals of a new economy.

Shalanda H. Baker describes the battle over the future of net energy metering in the US, and posits that energy justice lies at the heart of the debate, but is missing from the discourse. She underscores the importance of creating authentic opportunities for participation in renewable energy generation by low-income communities to alleviate inequality and vulnerability. She argues that community energy programs can address inequality by providing communities an opportunity to generate, own and distribute renewable energy.

In Chapters 11 and 12, Diana Winters and Laurie Ristino examine the food system, taking up the tensions between centralizing and localizing food regulations and legal design to expand access to legal tools, respectively. In Winters's chapter she discusses food regulation, and explains how a system that permits decentralized policymaking, such as the American one, can be a leverage point for change. She provides several examples of recent sub-national government's laws to address gaps in and perceived problems with federal food policy. Despite, or perhaps because of, their transformative potential, these actions on food policy raise questions about where lies the proper balance between the uniformity and predictability of a national system and the flexibility and responsiveness of local regulation.

The book ends with Laurie Ristino's chapter, in which she argues that as taught and practiced law has been made socially irrelevant, undermining its potential to generate and sustain paradigm-shifting change. Although the legal academy has adopted a more practice-ready pedagogy, the fact remains that legal education and its substance is stubbornly unchanged, divorced from other disciplines and communicated in a traditional parlance intended only for other legal professionals. The result is that most people do not understand the value of the law in their daily lives because the barrier to legal information is too high. The antidote she prescribes is legal design and transdisciplinary collaboration. Legal design requires that legal solutions are designed with the end user in mind. Moreover, legal design integrates the law into social products. She describes this as "Legal Democracy" because the law and the empowerment it represents is made broadly available. Using the food movement as an example of legal democracy in action, Ristino highlights legal products created by the Food and Agriculture Clinic of the Vermont Law School. Finally, she explains how this approach to the law has the capacity to scale healthy food systems and support vibrant local and regional economies through cataloging and disseminating innovative legal and policy solutions.

Part II's exploration of practical applications of changes to the legal rules defining incentives, punishments, and who gets to participate in ownership in the economy flow from Part I's unpacking of the upper level paradigm changes about an economy that is a tool for shared prosperity, ecological balance, and strong democracy. Taken together, the book presents options for system change aimed at speeding our transition to a new, more joyful, economy. With both clarity about the daunting challenges we face and audacious optimism about the possibilities at hand, it provides an answer: it is *not* too late.

Table of cases

Table of constitutions, legislation, and regulations

CONSTITUTIONS

LEGISLATION

New Zealand

United States

REGULATIONS

OTHER AUTHORITIES

1. Climate change, system change, and the path forward

Melissa K. Scanlan

I. INTRODUCTION

The law must grow to meet evolving societal concerns, sometimes leading, sometimes lagging, but always there to identify and provide the new guidance and norms that are needed. And so it is now as we face the reality of our current system of political economy, which is characterized by large externalized environmental costs, a GDP growth fixation, rapidly widening income inequality, and runaway consumerism, to mention but a few of the major dimensions. Today's system is misaligned to meet the global imperatives to rapidly reduce greenhouse gases, to share wealth more equitably, and to encourage broader more inclusive participatory democracies.

Amidst the signs of system breakdown, the new economy movement has emerged to provide an alternative approach where ecological balance, wealth equity, and vibrant democracy are central to economic activity. But how does law and policy encourage the current economic system to evolve into the new economy the planet needs? And where does one even begin to intervene to leverage changes within the window of time necessary?

This chapter starts with an orientation to the conflict between the climate imperative and our current global GDP growth goals. The chapter then discusses systems thinking and various approaches to systems change, identifying paradigm change as one of the most powerful change agents. Then it explains the new economy paradigm that has emerged as an alternative to the current global political economy. Using a systems lens, the chapter explores areas where law and policy needs to evolve to facilitate a truly green and equitable economy, built on democratic principles.

II. COLLISION COURSE: THE CLIMATE IMPERATIVE AND THE GLOBAL ECONOMY

In taking the pulse of the planet, one could assess a vast array of different system trends (that is, world population, urbanization, water usage, marine fish capture, domesticated land and so on); many prominent scientists have done so and have sounded the alarm that we have left the Earth's known stable conditions of the Holocene Era.[1] As detailed in Speth's chapter, although we recognize environmental improvements in the US and Europe related to problems associated with industrialization, such as rivers that do not catch fire, air in major cities that is cleaner, lead out of gasoline, and a ban on DDT, it is far from enough progress. There is much more to be done in the US to meet long-established goals: restore damage to major ecosystems; ensure people are not just breathing cleaner air, but healthy air; and provide waters that are clean enough to support healthy fish populations and drinking water for people.

Significantly, three-quarters of the world population lives in countries where these primary environmental problems persist. Coupled with these environmental problems is the number of people living in poverty despite reductions in the percentage of people living in poverty.

> The percentage of the world's population living in extreme poverty (less than US$1/day) fell from 28 percent in 1990 to 21 percent in 2001, unevenly around the world. Yet, over the long haul, the number of people living at the barest subsistence level has not declined in more than two hundred years. In 2007 close to 3 billion people . . . lived on less than US$2/day.[2]

On top of these persistent global problems of poverty and traditional pollutants, we face the most significant and intractable environmental

---

1 Press Release, Int'l Geosphere-Biosphere Programme, "Planetary Dashboard Shows 'Great Acceleration' in Human Activity Since 1950" (15 January 2015), available 13 January 2017 at http://www.igbp.net/news/pressreleases/pressreleases/planetarydashboardshowsgreataccelerationinhumanactivitysince1950.5.950c2fa1495db7081eb42.html; Will Steffen et al., *Planetary Boundaries: Guiding Human Development on Changing Planet*, 347 Sci. 6223 (2015) (showing 4 of 9 boundaries have been crossed). According to one of the authors, Professor Steve Carpenter, "[i]t might be possible for human civilization to live outside Holocene conditions, but it's never been tried before. We know civilization can make it in Holocene conditions, so it seems wise to try to maintain them." WiscLimnology, *Planetary Boundaries, Nutrient Pollution, and Human Civilization*, YouTube (15 January 2015), available 13 January 2017 at https://www.youtube.com/watch?v=_8MUcaNPbL0.

2 Peter A. Victor, Managing Without Growth: Slower by Design, Not Disaster 49 (Edward Elgar 2008).

threat to the world: climate disruption. Increasing human pressures on the environment, fueled by excessive consumerism in wealthy countries and an expansion of fossil fuel usage by rapidly growing populations in low-consuming countries, has brought us to the climate cliff. Climate change has revealed a fundamental weakness in environmental law, national and international: in the current system the law is doomed to be a weak antidote to correct the global economy's vast externalization of environmental costs. Ultimately, the law should be aimed at supporting the emergence of a new economic system deploying accurate measures of prosperity and progress and fully aligned with sustainability, wealth equity, and vibrant participatory democracies.

Societies tend to aim towards what is measured. For at least the last 50 years, the primary measure of prosperity, to the exclusion of all other considerations, has been the Gross Domestic Product (GDP). In the most simplistic of terms, GDP growth is seen as good and anything that impedes GDP growth as bad. For a measure that is simply the calculation of "the total unduplicated value of the goods and services produced in the economic territory of a country or region during a given period" to have achieved this level of shorthand for "progress" underlies some of the major problems the world faces with climate change and wealth inequity.[3]

"If we understand progress to mean an improvement in well being, then GDP is a poor measure. It includes many items that grow when things are or might be getting worse":[4] for example, medical bills to treat cancer, building infrastructure that encourages people to use cars, cleaning up toxic waste, and home security, police forces and military expenditures. As far as GDP is concerned, it does not matter if a society invests more in prisons than education, the dollars are tallied the same way.

The elevation of such a crude and misleading measure to the role of the leading benchmark for progress is part of the reason environmental protection laws are less muscular than they need to be. Whenever the environment or better wages for the working class is pitted against GDP growth, the latter usually wins. As will be explained, GDP growth is now on a collision course with what countries around the world need to do to meet the climate imperative, which underscores the urgent need to use a measure of progress that tells us more about the well-being of the earth and the people who call it their home.

Economist Peter Victor explains in *Managing Without Growth* how to direct policies towards "far more specific economic, social, and

---

[3] *Id.* at 9.
[4] *Id.*

environmental objectives" – the triple bottom line – than the predominant GDP fetish currently allows.[5] He argues for making the kinds of transitions contemplated in this book through a deliberate and thoughtful slowing of the rate of economic growth in rich economies rather than transitions driven by scarcity and high prices.[6]

While an in-depth analysis of climate change and its wide-ranging destructive and disruptive impacts is beyond the scope of this chapter, the major elements are outlined. The focus is on the long-term levels of atmospheric carbon dioxide and its stillborn baby, ocean acidification. The ocean absorbs carbon dioxide, and as levels of atmospheric carbon dioxide increase, the ocean absorbs more, thus changing ocean chemistry, making it more acidic.[7] As acidity increases, it removes chemicals that are the basic building blocks of shelled organisms, corals, and more. Damage to such organisms poses a major risk to the marine food web. Such damage will have a global human impact, as currently more than a billion people rely on high-protein food from the ocean.[8] According to the US National Oceanic and Atmospheric Administration:

> Estimates of future carbon dioxide levels, based on business as usual emission scenarios, indicate that by the end of this century the surface waters of the ocean could be nearly 150 percent more acidic, resulting in a pH that the oceans haven't experienced for more than 20 million years.[9]

Thinking in geologic time does not come naturally to many; so to put this into context, humans did not exist on earth 20 million years ago. So again, we are moving well beyond the conditions known to support human life.

The long-term trends in global temperature, carbon dioxide, and pH levels (a measure of acidity) in the oceans are shown in Figures 1.1 and 1.2.

Not shown in the temperature graph in Figure 1.1 is the most recent data: Each of the last 14 months prior to July 2016 has been the hottest month ever recorded and atmospheric carbon dioxide has exceeded 400 parts per million.[10] In response to our clear departure from long-term trends, moving

---

[5] *Id.* at 25.

[6] *Id.* at 69.

[7] Ocean Acidification, Pac. Marine Envtl. Lab., U.S. NAT'L OCEANIC AND ATMOSPHERIC ADMIN., available 13 January 2017 at http://www.pmel.noaa.gov/co2/story/Ocean+Acidification.

[8] *Id.*

[9] *Id.*

[10] Robinson Meyer, *Not Doomed Yet: The Can of Fanta in the Marina Trench*, ATLANTIC (28 July 2016), available 13 January 2017 at http://www.theatlantic.com/science/archive/2016/07/the-hottest-land-temperature-ever-recorded/493436/.

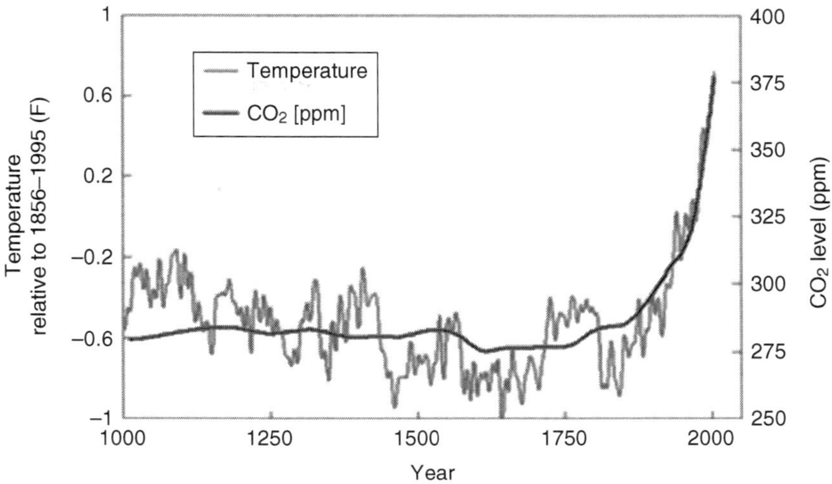

Notes:
Data sources for CO_2: Vostok ice core, Law Dome ice core, and Mauna Loa air samples.
Data source for temperature: Vostok ice core.

Source: EDF, http://blogs.edf.org/climate411/2007/06/29/human_cause-3/.

Figure 1.1 Temperature and CO_2 for the last 1,000 years

beyond levels of greenhouse gases (GHGs)[11] that are known to support human life and ocean pH levels known to support diverse marine life, the international community created the Paris Agreement.

Finalized at COP21 in Paris in December 2015, international leaders agreed to a goal of limiting global warming "to well below 2°C above pre-industrial levels and to pursue efforts to limit the temperature increase to 1.5°C above pre-industrial levels".[12] World leaders recognized the Kyoto Protocol framework was inadequate to deliver on this global goal.[13] So they negotiated the new Paris Agreement, which will apply from 2020 onward.

---

[11] GHGs include carbon dioxide (CO_2), nitrous oxide (N_2O), methane (CH_4), Sulphur hexafluoride (SF_6), hydrofluorocarbons (HFCs), and perfluorocarbons (PFCs).

[12] Framework Convention on Climate Change, *Paris Agreement*, art. 2(1)(a), U.N. Doc. FCCC/CP/2015/L.9 (Dec. 12, 2015), [hereinafter Paris Agreement], available 13 January 2017 at http://unfccc.int/resource/docs/2015/cop21/eng/l09r01.pdf.

[13] INT'L ENERGY AGENCY, KEY TRENDS IN CO_2 EMISSIONS EXCERPT FROM: CO_2 EMISSIONS FROM FUEL COMBUSTION, xi (2015), [hereinafter CO_2 EMISSIONS FROM FUEL

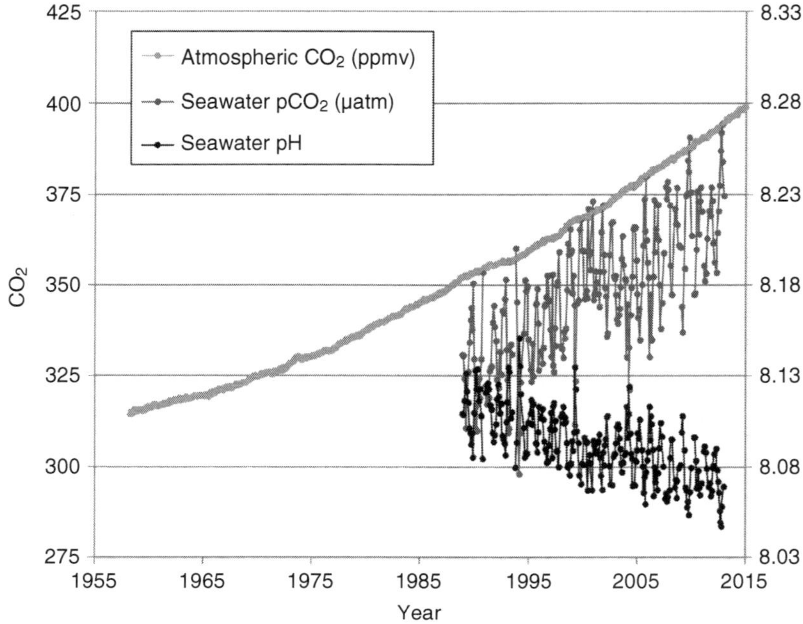

Note: This graph shows the correlation between rising levels of carbon dioxide (CO_2) in the atmosphere at Mauna Loa with rising CO_2 levels in the nearby ocean at Station Aloha. As more CO_2 accumulates in the ocean, the pH of the ocean decreases. (modified after R. A. Feely, Bulletin of the American Meteorological Society, July 2008).

Source: NOAA, http://www.pmel.noaa.gov/co2/story/Ocean+Acidification.

Figure 1.2 Ocean acidification and CO_2 over 60 years

It bears emphasizing that even at current levels of GHGs, the earth is experiencing the hottest temperatures ever recorded; in July 2016, land temperatures in both Iraq and Kuwait registered 54 degrees Celsius (129 degrees Fahrenheit).[14] Given the current situation, it is beyond undesirable to imagine living in a +2°C world. The problem is that at current GHG emission rates, societies will in just a few short years exhaust the emissions quota standing between today and a 1.5°C warmer world. In other words, although all the warming has not yet been "realized", we have for all practical purposes already committed the planet to +1.5°C.

COMBUSTION], available 13 January 2017 at http://www.iea.org/publications/freepublications/publication/CO2EmissionsTrends.pdf.

[14] Meyer, *supra* note 10.

However, for discussion purposes, we will use the Paris Agreement goal. In order to keep warming to +2°C this century, there is debate about how to achieve this, but there is recognition that global GHGs need to peak before 2020, with global emissions in 2050 being 50 to 60 percent below 1990 levels.[15] A logical approach is to focus on the largest sectors of emissions and figure out how to rapidly transform those systems to reduce their GHG contributions. In the US, the two largest sectors for GHG emissions are energy (83.6 percent of 2014 total) followed far behind by agriculture (9 percent of 2013 total).[16]

The US numbers are consistent with a global assessment of where to focus attention for greatest reductions. The UN's 2014 Emissions Gap report identifies sectors and rates their overall emission reduction potential as well as the barriers to implementation. Renewable energy and sustainable agriculture are two sectors that have some of the higher emission reduction potentials globally.[17]

But even with that targeted focus on energy and agriculture, what does this mean for business as usual, and in particular, the function and goal of our current global economy? Before beginning to answer that question, one needs to understand the relationship between carbon dioxide emissions and economic growth, as measured by GDP. The graph in Figure 1.3 helps to show the troubling correlation.

According to the International Energy Agency, the combined growth in population (35 percent) and in per capita GDP (60 percent) led to a dramatic increase in global carbon dioxide emissions (56 percent) between 1990 and 2013.[18] The global economy doubled since 1960 and is projected to quadruple by mid-century. Our current economic system is very good at producing

---

15 Some argue we need to reach net zero emissions by 2050. The Paris Agreement leaves this open to interpretation: "Parties aim to reach global peaking of greenhouse gas emissions as soon as possible (. . .) so as to achieve a balance between anthropogenic emissions by sources and removals by sinks of greenhouse gases in the second half of this century, on the basis of equity, and in the context of sustainable development and efforts to eradicate poverty." Paris Agreement, art. 4.

16 U.S. Envtl. Prot. Agency, Inventory of U.S. Greenhouse Gas Emissions and Sinks: 1990–2014 3-1 (2016), available 13 January 2017 at https://www3.epa.gov/climatechange/Downloads/ghgemissions/US-GHG-Inventory-2016-Main-Text.pdf; U.S. Envtl. Prot. Agency, Inventory of U.S. Greenhouse Gas Emissions and Sinks: 1990–2013 ES-23 (2015), available 13 January 2017 at https://www3.epa.gov/climatechange/Downloads/ghgemissions/US-GHG-Inventory-2015-Main-Text.pdf.

17 United Nations Envt. Programme, The Emissions Gap Report 2014: A UNEP Synthesis Report tbl. 4.1 (2014), available 13 January 2017 at http://www.unep.org/publications/ebooks/emissionsgapreport2014/portals/50268/pdf/EGR2014_LOWRES.pdf.

18 CO_2 Emissions from Fuel Combustion, supra note 13, at ix.

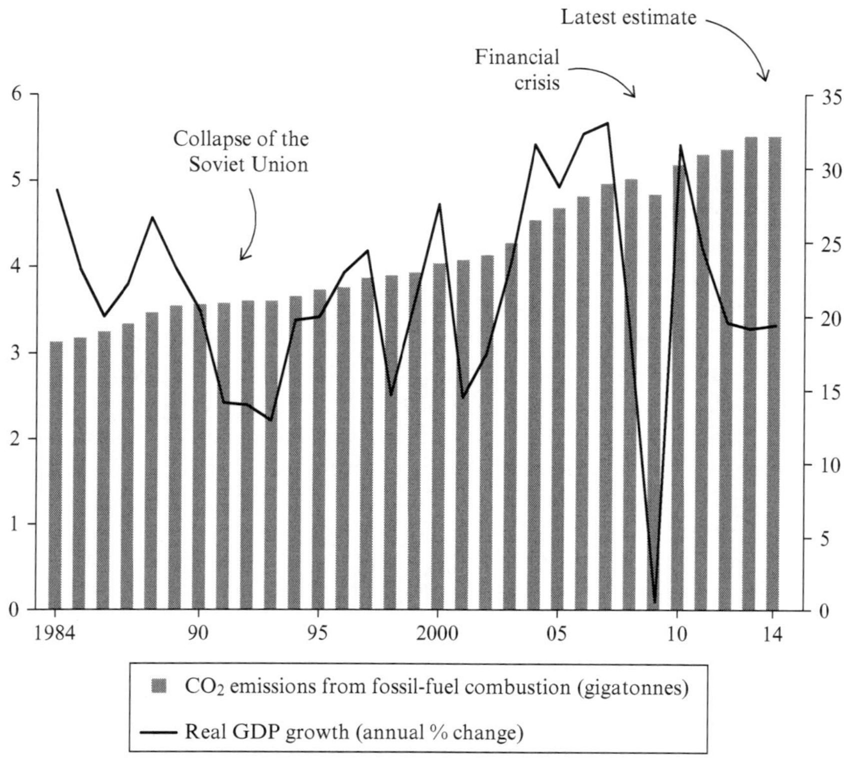

Note: Based on International Energy Agency data from CO_2 Emissions from Fuel Combustion © OECD/IEA [2015], www.iea.org/statistics, License: www.iea.org/t&c; as modified by Yale Climate Connections, *Economic Growth Without An Increase In Global Emissions,* (June 2015), http://www.yaleclimateconnections.org/2015/06/economic-growth-without-an-increase-in-global-emissions/.

Sources: IEA; Thomson Reuters Datastream.

Figure 1.3 Global GDP and CO_2 emissions 1984–2014

GDP growth. However, as shown in Figure 1.3, since 1984 carbon dioxide emissions have generally risen with growth in GDP and population.

If the global economy is growing 5 percent per year, carbon intensity of the economy needs to decline dramatically to meet the Paris Agreement goals: some argue convincingly that the decline must be 9 to 11 percent per year until 2050.[19] While there are those who do not think this level of

[19] *See, e.g.,* James Gustave Speth, America the Possible: Manifesto for a

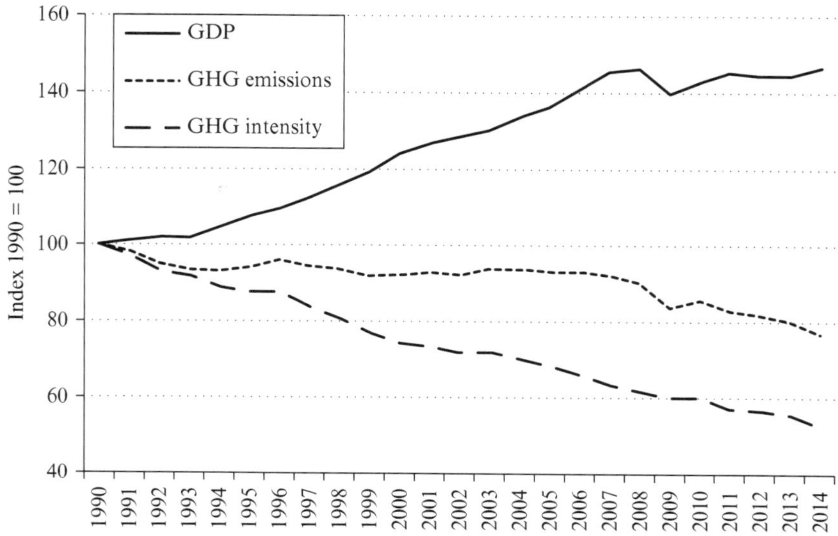

Source: *Report of the Commission to the European Parliament and the Council on Climate Action Progress*, at fig. 2, COM(2015) 576 final (18 November 2015), http://eur-lex.europa.eu/legal-content/en/TXT/?uri=CELEX:52015DC0576, © European Union, http://eur-lex.europa.eu/, 1998-2016.

Figure 1.4 European GDP and GHG emissions 1990–2014

carbon intensity reduction can be sustained while keeping the priority on GDP growth, others urge that global GDP growth can continue if we can successfully "decouple" carbon dioxide emissions; this means that emissions decline while GDP grows, as opposed to emissions growing but less than GDP.

Figure 1.4 shows that in the past decade the EU appears to have experienced a decoupling of carbon emissions from economic growth, with rising GDP alongside falling emissions. The EU economy grew by more than 46 percent between 1990 and 2014, while emissions fell by 23 percent. As a result, GHG emissions intensity in the EU (ratio of emissions per unit of GDP) was reduced by almost half. So does the EU experience provide a path forward?

Unfortunately, this decoupling may not be an accurate portrayal of what's occurring in the EU with GHGs. Some argue the apparent

---

NEW ECONOMY 52–65 (Yale University Press 2012) (finding that carbon intensity = quantity of emissions released to produce USD$1 economic output).

decoupling was only possible because the fossil fuel-based manufacturing and contingent energy use needed to fuel the consumption part of the EU's GDP growth was taken on by other countries, such as China.[20] The way in which emissions are counted towards a country's total support this argument. Emissions are counted for the country where a good is produced and not where it is consumed.[21] Also emissions accounting does not attribute any emissions from the international shipment of goods to any country, and transport-related emissions have grown 90 percent (international aviation bunkers) and 64 percent (international marine bunkers) from 1990 to 2013.[22] These factors allow de-industrializing, yet high consuming, wealthy countries to show emissions reductions even though they are importing those goods for consumption in their country. "As customers and consumers, we are tied to industrial production for our computers, PDAs, cars and trucks, and flat-paneled televisions. And we are dependent on the energy required to make them work, over 70 percent of which comes from burning fossil fuels, as it has for the past 150 years."[23] This is why we need to address consumerism in wealthy countries if we are going to begin to meet the climate challenge to rapidly reduce GHGs.

Furthermore, according to Speth's calculations, the annual rate of GHG emission reduction achieved by the EU between 1990 and 2014 (1.1 percent) is roughly a fourth of the rate needed to reduce EU emissions by 90 percent for the period 1990–2050, an estimate of the desired reduction for rich countries.[24] In other words, the EU may have decoupled GHG emissions growth from GDP growth but at a rate far, far too slow to meet the climate imperative.

Despite the uncertainties about the extent of effective decoupling of emissions and GDP growth in the EU, a move in the right direction is that

---

20 Fiona Harvey, *Global Emissions Stall in 2014 Following Slowdown in China's Economy*, GUARDIAN (13 March 2015), available 13 January 2017 at http://www.theguardian.com/environment/2015/mar/13/global-emissions-stall-in-2014-following-slowdown-in-chinas-economy.

21 CO_2 EMISSIONS FROM FUEL COMBUSTION, *supra* note 13, at 10. *See also* BAPTISTE BOITLER, WORLD INPUT-OUTPUT DATABASES, CO_2 EMISSIONS PRODUCTION-BASED ACCOUNTING VS CONSUMPTION: INSIGHTS FROM THE WIOD DATABASES (2012).

22 CO_2 EMISSIONS FROM FUEL COMBUSTION, *supra* note 13, at xii, Table 1.

23 PETER M. SENGE, ET AL., THE NECESSARY REVOLUTION: HOW INDIVIDUALS AND ORGANIZATIONS ARE WORKING TOGETHER TO CREATE A SUSTAINABLE WORLD 7 (Doubleday 2008).

24 Calculation based on needed exponential rate of decline annually to reduce 23% in 24 years (minus 1.1%) and to reduce GHGs 90% in 60 years (minus 3.9%). (1.1 is 28% of 3.9.) Gus Speth email to author, 10 September 2016 (on file with author).

for the first time global emissions of carbon dioxide related to energy have remained flat for 2014 and 2015 while the global economy grew about 3 percent in each of those years. In the past, whenever emissions flattened or declined there was an associated economic downturn (see Figure 1.3). However, now electricity generated by renewables appears to have played a key role in this positive development.[25]

Yet simply doing more of what has worked to keep energy-related emissions flat will not get us to the level of reductions per year needed to meet the Paris Agreement goals. Is the amount of needed decoupling between emissions and GDP growth achievable without deeper transformation of the political economy? It seems highly doubtful that societies can reduce GHG emissions at needed rates while giving top priority to high and steady growth in GDP and corporate profitability and to regular increases in income and consumption among the already well-to-do. And given that equity in GHGs puts a heavier burden of emissions decline on affluent countries, it is even clearer that the old economic priorities must yield to new economic thinking.

At the Earth Day 2016 signing of the Paris Agreement on climate change, the UN Secretary-General Ban Ki-moon stated, "We are in a race against time . . . The era of consumption without consequences is over."[26]

The stark reality is that even with the Paris Agreement, the commitments for national reductions will not meet the less than +2°C climate goal of the signatories.[27] The United Nations Environmental Programme (UNEP) analysis of the "carbon gap" concludes that current pledges "are most consistent with scenarios that limit global average temperature increase to below 3.5°C until 2100 with a greater than 66 percent chance."[28]

---

[25] *Decoupling of Global Emissions and Economic Growth Confirmed*, Int'l Energy Agency (16 March 2016), available 13 January 2017 at https://www.iea.org/newsroomandevents/pressreleases/2016/march/decoupling-of-global-emissions-and-economic-growth-confirmed.html.

[26] Doyle Rice, '*175 Nations Sign Historic Paris Climate Deal on Earth Day*', USA Today (22 April 2016), available 13 January 2017 at http://www.usatoday.com/story/news/world/2016/04/22/paris-climate-agreement-signing-united-nations-new-york/83381218/. In addition to signing the agreement, each country must ratify it. The agreement will be in force after 55 countries representing at least 55% of global GHG emissions have formally ratified it. Once in force, countries set their own targets for reducing GHGs and these are not binding. *Id.*

[27] *Id.* The difference between what the individual countries have committed to do, if fully implemented, and what is required to keep the Earth under at least 2°C is referred as to Carbon Gap.

[28] United Nations Envtl. Programme, The Emissions Gap Report 2015: Executive Summary, available 13 January 2017 at http://uneplive.unep.org/media/docs/theme/13/EGR_2015_ES_English_Embargoed.pdf.

Thus, even with the Paris Agreement in place, much more is needed than the status quo to meet the climate imperative. We need to rapidly transform our energy sources from fossil fuels to renewables, reduce consumption levels in wealthy countries, make our food system more local and resilient and less carbon intensive, and reverse the trend in numbers of people living in poverty and the rapid growth of wealth inequality. At the core of these transformations, we need new measures of a prosperous society that do not rely on GDP as the sole measure of success. Modern society has been so fixated on GDP growth, that we have ignored critical factors like over-exploiting resources, climate impacts, and the gap between rich and poor.

Moreover, these changes require a different set of values, as described in Speth's chapter; and that people view nature as a commons and a partner rather than property to be commodified, as developed in Chapter 4 by Iorns and Sheehan. People across the world are realizing the extent of these global problems and starting to see that we are on the cusp: at the end of one age and the beginning of another. According to systems thinker Peter Senge,

> Just as the Iron Age didn't end because we ran out of iron, the Industrial Age isn't ending because of the decline in opportunities for further industrial expansion. It is ending because individuals, companies, and governments are coming to the realization that its side effects are unsustainable.[29]

The great challenge of our time is to change the operating instructions of our political economy so economic activity serves the common good. This level of change on the time scale needed (GHGs peak by 2020) calls for strategic systems analysis and rapid transitions.

III. SYSTEMS THINKING AND ITS IMPLICATIONS FOR BUILDING A NEW ECONOMY ALIGNED WITH THE CLIMATE IMPERATIVE

To solve these seemingly intractable problems will require system change because poverty, inequality, viewing nature as a commodity, and climate change are "deeply rooted in the fundamentals of our political-economic system".[30] There are different theories of system change upon which one can draw, and many decades of analysis across the disciplines. Since the

---

[29] SENGE ET AL., *supra* note 23, at 8.

[30] JAMES GUSTAVE SPETH, 'NEXT SYSTEM PROJECT, GETTING TO THE NEXT SYSTEM: GUIDEPOSTS ON THE WAY TO A NEW POLITICAL ECONOMY' 3 (2015), 3 avail-

1950s, people have incorporated systems theory into biology, physics, cognitive science, management, business,[31] public health, evaluation,[32] public schools[33] and economics.[34]

People attracted to systems change sometimes misconceive that systems thinking makes things predictable and controllable, but "self-organizing, nonlinear, feedback systems are inherently unpredictable".[35] Problems, such as the need to move our energy sources from fossil fuels to renewables or reducing the gap between the wealthiest and the poorest, are sometimes called "wicked problems" because they have numerous causes and no clear solutions, involve multiple stakeholders, and require lots of people, organizations, and even governments, to shift their mindset and behavior.

Systems theory is not a panacea; it is a lens through which to see the world. Like other lenses (microscopes, reading glasses, telescopes), it provides access to different perspectives.[36] In order to look through this lens, one needs to look beyond the short-term to long-term behavior and structure of a system.[37]

Of the various systems thinkers, this chapter returns to Donella Meadows' thinking, popularized and criticized since her 1970s *Limits to Growth*, because it is still suitable to the challenge before us. She explains simply that a "system" is a "set of things – people, cells, molecules, or whatever – interconnected in such a way that they produce their own pattern of behavior over time".[38] These behaviors are often known as a system's function or purpose and although a crucial determinant of a system, are often obscured.[39] Purpose comes from behavior, not from simply stating the goals.[40] The set of things in a system or its elements can change with very little impact on the overall system, but if the purpose

---

able 13 January 2017 at http://thenextsystem.org/wp-content/uploads/2015/10/GettingToTheNextSystem.pdf.

31 Senge et al., *supra* note 23.

32 Margaret B. Hargreaves, Mathematica Policy Research, Inc., Evaluating System Change: A Planning Guide 13 (2010).

33 John Kania and Mark Kramer, *Collective Impact*, 9 Stan. Soc. Innovation Rev. 36 (2011).

34 Donella Meadows, Thinking in Systems: A Primer (Diana Wright (ed.), Chelsea Green Pub 2008).

35 Donella Meadows, *Dancing with Systems*, Donella Meadows Inst., available 13 January 2017 at http://donellameadows.org/dancing-with-systems/.

36 Donella Meadows, *supra* note 34, at 6.

37 *Id.* at 87. News is event level understanding, not behavior level understanding, unless it puts the event in a historical context. *Id.* at 88.

38 *Id.* at 2.

39 *Id.* at 2, 188.

40 *Id.* at 14.

changes or the interconnections between the elements, this can result in major system change.[41]

The clear-thinking Peter Senge similarly asserts that "how people see the world, what they value, how society defines progress and organizes itself, and how institutions operate" open the possibility to large-scale system change.[42] In other words, Senge is talking about paradigm change. This builds on one of the significant contributions Meadows has made to systems thinking in her *Leverage Points: Places to Intervene in a System,* which she describes as a distillation of years of working on systems.[43] In it she provides a list (in increasing order of effectiveness) of leverage points to change systems, with paradigm change at the highest level of potential leverage.

12. Constants, parameters, numbers (such as subsidies, taxes, standards).

    Meadows identifies parameters as the least powerful intervention for system change. What she includes in "parameters" are things like setting air quality standards, electing new representatives, even changing campaign finance rules. She estimates that 99 percent of our attention goes towards changing parameters, but concludes there is not much leverage in them. Much of what we teach in US law schools regarding environmental law is focused on this level of change. "After decades of the strictest air pollution standards in the world, Los Angeles air is less dirty, but it isn't clean."[44]

    However, she observes that parameters can become leverage points "when they go into ranges that kick off one of the items higher on

---

[41] *Id.* at 17. One exception to this is changing an element (person) who is a top leader (Bush to Obama), especially if that person has the power to change the purpose. *Id.* From their grounding in soft system methodologies and system dynamics, Foster-Fishman provide complimentary observations that system change happens through: "(1) understanding different perspectives concerning the problem situation [drawing the system boundaries]; (2) locating root causes to systemic problems by identifying system parts and their patterns of interdependency that explain the status quo; and (3) using this information to identify leverage points that will cultivate second-order change [paradigm shift]." Pennie G. Foster-Fishman, et al., '*Putting the System Back into Systems Change: A Framework for Understanding and Changing Organizational and Community Systems*', 39 Am. J. Community Psychol. 197, 201 (2007).

[42] Senge, et al., *supra* note 23, at 5.

[43] Donella Meadows, *Leverage Points: Places to Intervene in a System*, Donella Meadows Inst., available 13 January 2017 at http://donellameadows.org/archives/leverage-points-places-to-intervene-in-a-system.

[44] *Id.*

this list. Interest rates, for example, or birth rates, control the gains around positive feedback loops. System goals are parameters that can make big differences."[45] Electing an individual who has the power to move the mindset of a population would move this action towards the top of the effective leverage points hierarchy.

11. The sizes of buffers and other stabilizing stocks, relative to their flows.

    You may be able to stabilize a system by increasing its buffer. Think here about the use of forests and fields as carbon sinks. These may act as buffers against climate change, but action here is relatively low on the list of effective measures for system change. These buffers will buy time so they are very important and we need to pursue them, but they are not transformative.

10. The structure of material stocks and flows (such as transport networks, population age structures).

    This is often the slowest and most expensive kind of system change, and some structures are unchangeable (for example, populations age at a set rate, or once the ice sheets of Greenland or Antarctica melt sea level rises). Physical structures are not usually leverage points for change once they are designed so the leverage point is at the design stage or in the case of melting glaciers, at the prevention stage.

    Technological change is something that can speed up the rate of adjustment in a system, but because the world's physical capital (factories, roads, boilers, and so on) does not change instantly, technological advances are lower on her list of leverage points.[46] What Elon Musk and others have done to build an electrified transportation network in the US, however, challenges this concept of the rate of change possible with technology. In less than a decade, charging stations for electric vehicles have proliferated, with almost 30,000 electric vehicle charging stations and 681 Tesla Supercharger stations in the US in July of 2016 (compared to 168,000 gas stations for a technology that has existed since Henry Ford).[47] Given the increased rate

---

45 *Id.*

46 *Id.*

47 CHARGEPOINT, https://www.chargepoint.com; *Supercharger*, TESLA, https://www.tesla.com/supercharger (both available 13 January 2017).

of technological change possible today, this may be a much stronger leverage point for system change than Meadows thought.

9. The lengths of delays, relative to the rate of system change.

"Delays in feedback loops are critical determinants of system behavior. They are common causes of oscillations. If you're trying to adjust a system state to your goal, but you only receive delayed information about what the system state is, you will overshoot and undershoot."[48] GHGs present a significant information delay problem in that the climate disrupting effects of emissions are not immediately known, and by the time harm is manifest it may be too late to stop. Given long delays, foresight and applying the precautionary principle is essential.[49]

8. The strength of negative/balancing feedback loops, relative to the impacts they are trying to correct.

When a "stock" grows or declines quickly, there is likely a control mechanism influencing this. These mechanisms, which create consistent behavior, operate through feedback loops.[50] "A negative feedback loop is self-correcting; a positive feedback loop is self-reinforcing."[51] Systems have numerous negative/balancing feedback loops, many of which are not often used because they only exist to allow the system to self correct when needed.[52] For example, the human body sweats to cool off and regulate body temperature.

One needs to strengthen negative/balancing feedback controls to improve a system's self-correcting abilities. Two significant balancing/negative feedback loops are democracy and the market. In an ideal democracy, "people, informed about what their elected representatives do, respond by voting those representatives in or out of office". To function properly as a balancing feedback, democracy relies on "free, full, unbiased" information between the voters and elected officials.[53] So policies that promote that flow of information are critical to a functioning democracy. In an age of curated news

---

48 Donella Meadows, *supra* note 43.
49 Donella Meadows, *supra* note 34, at 104–5.
50 *Id.* at 25.
51 Donella Meadows, *supra* note 43.
52 *Id.*
53 *Id.*

and media consolidation along with lack of effective restrictions on financing political campaigns, this feedback mechanism is undermined. In *People Get Ready, The Fight Against a Jobless Economy and a Citizenless Democracy*, McChesney and Nichols call the current state of the US a "citizenless democracy" because "core political and economic decisions are made by the wealthy few for the wealthy few".[54] The issue of strengthening democracy at multiple levels, from government to businesses and other organizations, is critical to laying the foundation for changing the political economy.

The market is another balancing feedback system with incredible potential for self-correction if the price is clear, timely, and truthful. The more the price fails to reflect the externalities of something, the more problematic it is in leading people to make decisions that are not in their or society's best interest. So the leverage point is getting the price right. This has been the subject of intense study and debate since Adam Smith wrote *The Wealth of Nations* in 1776.

Pollution taxes provide a negative feedback in response to externalized public costs of private benefits, but the tax needs to be set at a level that it can improve the market's ability to correct the externality. Carbon taxes could be a powerful component of correcting the market and aligning the economy with the imperative to rapidly reduce GHGs, if set at the right level. But there are so many conditions that must exist for prices to convey accurate information, such as homogeneity of products, numerous participants, and no externalities to name a few, that prices usually fail.[55] With small economies and minor environmental impacts this is not a big limitation. But with a global economy, massive climate disruption, and growing wealth inequality, the fact that prices – even with taxes and subsidies – are "seriously incomplete and misleading" means that this is not the strongest leverage point to drive needed system change.[56]

7. The gain around driving positive feedback loops.

The more a positive feedback loop works, the more it gains power to continue working. These feedback loops are sources of a system's growth, explosion, erosion, and collapse. These loops can be virtuous

---

[54] Robert W. McChesney and John Nichols, People Get Ready, The Fight Against a Jobless Economy and a Citizenless Democracy 151 (Nation Books 2016).

[55] Victor, *supra* note 2, at 39–46.

[56] *Id.* at 46.

or vicious.[57] A food and agriculture example of a positive feedback loop is soil erosion. "The more the soil erodes, the less vegetation it can support, the fewer roots and leaves to soften rain and runoff, the more soil erodes."[58] If this positive feedback loop continues unchecked or speeds up rapidly, it may lead to chaos and the system collapses. In reality, this is rare, and a negative feedback loop will kick in to self-correct.

Economic growth and population are positive feedback loops. Meadows asserted that "[p]opulation and economic growth rates in the world model are leverage points, because slowing them gives the many negative loops, through technology and markets and other forms of adaptation, all of which have limits and delays, time to function".[59] Controlling rapidly growing positive feedback loops involves slowing down their growth rates.[60]

In addition to this hierarchy of leverage points for system change, Meadows gives us an analysis of system traps and opportunities that are useful here: these are situations that indicate system problems and places where change is possible and important.[61] One such trap involves positive feedback loops that lack effective negative/balancing feedback loops and Meadows calls this "success to the successful". This is a situation where people use wealth, privilege, special access or information to create more of the same for those who have it. One finds this trap whenever "the winners of a competition receive, as part of the reward, the means to compete even more effectively in the future".[62]

A readily known example of "success to the successful" is the game of Monopoly. Another common example is compounding earnings on stock investments. To use an agricultural example, we see this in the consolidation of farms into fewer and larger entities. The acceleration in income inequality also results from this system trap:

---

57 Meadows, *supra* note 34, at 30.

58 Meadows, *supra* note 43.

59 *Id.*

60 "The time it takes for an exponentially growing stock to double in size, the 'doubling time,' equals approximately 70 divided by the growth rate (expressed as a percentage). Example: If you put $100 in the bank at 7% interest per year, you will double your money in 10 years (70/7 = 10). If you get only 5% interest, your money will take 14 years to double." Meadows, *supra* note 34, at 33.

61 *Id.* at 6.

62 *Id.* at 126–7.

> Because the poor can afford to buy only small quantities (of food, fuel, seed, fertilizer), they pay the highest prices. Because they are often unorganized and inarticulate, a disproportionately small part of government expenditure is allocated to their needs. Ideas and technologies come to them last. Disease and pollution come to them first. They are the people who have no choice but to take dangerous, low-paying jobs, whose children are not vaccinated, who live in crowded, crime-prone, disaster-prone areas.[63]

Countering the "success to the successful" trap may come from diversification (for a business), by putting in feedback loops that prevent monopolies (for an industry), and by periodically leveling the playing field by rewarding success in a way that does not bias the next round of competition.[64]

For income inequality there are many ways to break this cycle and create balancing feedback loops: progressive tax, charity, welfare, labor unions, universal high quality health care and education, and inheritance tax are some of the common responses.[65] Although these policies are beyond the scope here, Purdy's chapter discusses the accelerating gap in wealth inequalities – this "success to the successful" trap, and its implications for environmentalism. He calls for environmental justice to be fully integrated into environmentalism, which will reorient environmental law and policy priorities. Further, Orsi's chapter provides examples from her law practice on how to rethink organizational structures, management, compensation, and ownership, towards more environmentally favorable and wealth equalizing outcomes, thus building in balancing mechanisms to counter the "success to the successful" trap. Lastly, Baker's chapter on making renewable energy ownership available to low and moderate-income people provides insight into the need for the law to break the success to the successful trap as we make this historic and necessary transition to renewables.

6. The structure of information flows (who does and does not have access to information).

Sharing information can create important feedback loops. The US Toxic Release Inventory and National Environmental Policy Act, or

---

63 *Id.* at 129.
64 *Id.*
65 *Id.* at 130.

California's Prop 65, among other public disclosure laws can impact behavior quickly. The lack of crucial information in a feedback loop can cause a system to malfunction. To be effective, however, the timing and form of the information are important factors to consider and design into a system.

This does not have to come in the form of publishing an environmental impact report, but can be built into the structural design of a system. Imagine if the law required a factory's water intake pipe to be placed directly downstream from its waste discharge pipe: those producing the waste would know exactly what was going into the water they would very soon be taking back into the factory for reuse and would have a greater incentive to modify the content of the effluent.[66]

Provision of information plays a role in bounded rationality, the concept that people make rational decisions based on the information they have, and when the information is quite limited this can lead to very negative outcomes.[67] The tragedy of the commons is an example of this.

Commons tragedy may occur when there is a commonly shared resource that is limited and erodible when overused, the users of the resource have reason to increase use, and people lack information about the condition of the commons (that is, there is delayed feedback).[68] One way to get out of the tragedy trap, according to Meadows, is to regulate.

The regulation option essentially creates a feedback loop between regulators and users about the condition of the commons; success here depends on regulators with the expertise to monitor, assess, and enforce restrictions, with the benefit of the whole as their goal.[69] In essence, the regulators should act as trustees for current and future generations of users of the commons. "[I]t's not enough to inform all the users of an aquifer that the groundwater level is dropping. That could initiate a race to the bottom. It would be more effective to set a water price that rises steeply as the pumping rate begins to exceed the recharge rate."[70]

This has important implications for a wide variety of proposals to reform the political economy. Setting and adjusting a carbon tax to provide important information flows to inform economic activity, for

66 Meadows, *supra* note 43.
67 Meadows, *supra* note 34, at 106–7.
68 *Id.* at 116–17.
69 *Id.* at 119–21.
70 Meadows, *supra* note 43.

instance. Establishing a trustee relationship to protect the climate is another where paying attention to information flows and setting an effective regulatory structure for this commons are crucial. Wood's chapter on the public trust doctrine explains the trust relationship and legal features in more detail. Of course, regulation is not the only counter to the tragedy trap. Bollier's chapter provides a wide variety of examples of how people are coming together in a diversity of commons without resort to state-generated regulations.

5. The rules of the system (such as incentives, punishments, constraints).

The rules of the system can be absolute and unchangeable by society, such as the law of gravity, or the rules can be human-created and normative, such as constitutions, statutes, regulations, court opinions, agency guidance, and private contracts. The rules of the system can be a powerful leverage point, as they influence human behavior.

"If you want to understand the deepest malfunctions of systems, pay attention to the rules, and to who has power over them."[71] When the rules of a system result in the "success to the successful" trap – as exemplified by rapidly growing income inequalities – there is a strong indicator of a breakdown in the democratic system of rule making. Many of the chapters in this book explore ideas about bolstering participatory democracy in response to the many indicators of a breakdown in democratic rule making. Part of that involves a greater emphasis on subsidiarity, diffusing decision-making to the broadest and lowest possible level of an entity, organization, or government.

4. The power to add, change, evolve, or self-organize system structure.

Along the lines of subsidiarity, Meadows explains: "Self-organization means changing any aspect of a system lower on this list – adding completely new physical structures, such as brains or wings or computers – adding new negative or positive loops, or new rules."[72] Meadows sees this as a powerful point of change, not because it is centrally controlled and directed towards a pre-determined end, but precisely because it is not. She advocates for experimentation, variability and diversity in a system.

---

71 *Id.*
72 *Id.*

This aspect of system change is more abundant when we have diverse and thriving local economies with business organizations that enhance democratic participation. Winters's chapter (Chapter 11) delves into this interplay between centralized and localized decisions, as reflected in law, related to food systems. Orsi's chapter (Chapter 6) gives ideas and examples of lawyers working in partnership with clients to diffuse power and decision-making. Ristino's chapter (Chapter 12) shows how legal design makes law and policy more accessible and interactive to many. And Taub's chapter (Chapter 8) explains how new rules facilitate connecting socially-minded investors to capitalize the proliferation of local business ventures, which increases variability and diversity in the economy.

3. The goals of the system.

The goals of the system are powerful leverage points that influence the lower ranked leverage points. Although there are intermediate goals for different pieces of a system, it is important to identify the hard to see goals for the whole system. Although Meadows identified electing individuals as a less powerful leverage point (she called it changing a parameter and ranked it last), she argues that some individuals have such a powerful position to set the goals of the system that these elections are strong leverage points. US President Ronald Reagan's push for a limited government demonstrates the "high leverage of articulating, meaning, repeating, standing up for, [and] insisting upon new system goals".[73] Speth's chapter (Chapter 2) highlights Reagan's leadership as a pivotal time for the environmental movement, one that was not met with an adequate counterweight, which he argues has influenced where we are today.

In 2016, the Brexit vote in the United Kingdom and the US presidential election provide a contemporary example. The goals that will be set by a UK that no longer automatically follows the EU's environmental laws or a US led by Donald Trump will reverberate widely. Already in early 2017, the election of President Trump is showing itself to be a significant leverage point in changing the goals of the system; he has identified cabinet members to lead key agencies with an influence on climate change who have financial ties to the fossil fuel industry, deny the existence of climate change, a history of litigating against the agency they will lead, or all three.

---

[73] *Id.*

A trap related to system goals is "policy resistance", which arises when multiple entities are pulling a system towards different goals, and any new policy pulls the system in one direction resulting in the other entities pulling harder in the opposite. The policy resistance trap is evident in the policy gridlock we see today in the US on climate change and litigation challenging the Obama Administration's primary policy tool to address it: the Clean Power Plan. Meadows argues that the way out of the policy resistance trap is to step out of the push and pull to seek mutually satisfactory goals.[74] The current situation with lack of alignment of goals between globalized capitalism and rapidly moving off of fossil fuels is an example of the policy resistance trap. Can we articulate aligned goals that move us out of this resistance dynamic? Are we seeing that occur with the rapid development of renewables and community solar in particular? or in the rise of the local food movement across America?

Another goal-related trap is "seeking the wrong goal".[75] A common mistake in setting goals is confusing effort with results. Using GDP as a measure of economic health and prosperity falls into this trap. Since GDP measures all consumption, it lumps together the good with the bad, fails to reflect income distribution, and does not show environmental degradation. Growth in GDP can be driven by building roads instead of public transportation: GDP is agnostic about the type of activity it measures. GDP is simply a measure of throughput (flows of stuff made and purchased in a year).[76] So more resource use, fueled by consumerism, results in improvements to GDP. But as seen above, this directly conflicts with the climate goals of the Paris Agreement because over time GDP growth has correlated with growth in GHGs.

What if instead of GDP growth, the goal was:

- the highest per capita stocks of wealth with the lowest throughput of resources,
- the smallest gap between rich and poor,
- the rapidity with which an economy decarbonizes, and
- the country with the happiest people.

The key here is to define goals that articulate real societal wealth and prosperity and to use indicators that measure results towards those goals instead of simply activity level.[77] The ideal is to define the

---

74 Meadows, *supra* note 34, at 115–16.
75 *Id.* at 138.
76 *Id.* at 139.
77 *Id.* at 140.

correct goals in this way with an eye towards alignment rather than policy resistance.

2. The mindset or paradigm out of which the system – its goals, structure, rules, delays, parameters – arises.

Meadows identifies paradigms about the world (that is, people "own" land) as the source of the systems. Whether it was Copernicus and Kepler showing that the earth is not the center of the universe, or Einstein hypothesizing that matter and energy are interchangeable, or Adam Smith postulating that the selfish actions of individual players in markets wonderfully accumulate to the common good, people who have managed to intervene in systems at the level of paradigm have hit a leverage point that totally transforms systems.[78]

Paradigm change is one of the hardest changes to achieve, but one of the most powerful. The path towards paradigm shift for a society, according to Meadows, is to emphasize repeatedly the failures of the old paradigm, while making people in the new paradigm highly visible to the public and in positions of power. Like Meadows, cultural theorists agree that significant system change takes hold and is sustained over time only by altering underlying beliefs and values that direct daily practices and behaviors.[79]

The current paradigm, which shapes values and our overall policy orientation, is that the way to address social needs and achieve better, happier lives is to expand the economy as measured by GDP growth. "Productivity, wages, profits, the stock market, employment, and consumption must all go up. Growth is good. So good that it is worth all the costs."[80]

If meeting the Paris Agreement climate goals means reducing growth in these parameters of the global economy, it will not be seen as worth it and there will be continued and mounting policy resistance. Speth sketches the current political economy of American capitalism as a linked and mutually reinforcing system. He argues the primary features of this system are an:

> unquestioning society-wide commitment to [GDP] economic growth at any cost; powerful corporate and banking interests whose overriding

---

[78] Meadows, *supra* note 43.

[79] Foster-Fishman, et al., *supra* note 41, at 205.

[80] James Gustave Speth, The Bridge at the Edge of the World 144 (Yale University Press 2008).

> objective is to grow by generating profit, including profit from avoiding social and environmental costs and keeping wages low; a government beholden to corporate interests and thus not strongly inclined to curb corporate abuses; . . . a rampant consumerism spurred endlessly on by sophisticated advertising . . . [and a focus on projecting national military power].[81]

What would an alternative paradigm look like? The new economy movement articulates such an alternative, the major contours of which are described in the next section.

1. The power to transcend paradigms.

Ultimately, Meadows asserts that we should recognize that no paradigm is “true”. It is simply a limited understanding of an immense universe.

IV. THE NEW ECONOMY PARADIGM AND A FUTURE WORTH BUILDING

The new economy movement is advancing a transformative paradigm to the current dominant economic system, one focused on an overall goal of increasing the quality of life now and into the future and moving to an economy that truly sustains and restores human and natural communities. The new economy is one where ecological balance, wealth equity, and vibrant democracy are central.[82]

In this new paradigm the way to address social and climate needs and achieve better, happier lives is with an economy powered by renewables, with resilient and vibrant local and regional food systems, and a goal of improving and strengthening our family relationships, our community and friends, our financial situation up to the point of meeting basic needs, our work, our health, our personal freedom, and our personal values.[83] This paradigm emphasizes quality over quantity. It focuses on reducing gaps between rich and poor. It imagines a different relationship with the natural world, one based on endowing nature with inalienable, enforceable legal

---

[81] SPETH, *supra* note 30, at 3, 7–8.

[82] *About*, NEW ECON. COAL., available 13 January 2017 at http://neweconomy.net/about.

[83] SPETH, *supra* note 80, at 135, (citing RICHARD LAYARD, HAPPINESS: LESSONS FROM A NEW SCIENCE (rev. ed., Penguin 2011).

Table 1.1 Comparison of current economy to green economy

Current economy	Green economy
GDP growth: more economic activity the aim	'Beyond GDP': prosperity the aim
Focus on the near future (short-termism)	Long-termism
Maximisation of return	Safeguarding of long-term incomes
Shareholder value	Stakeholder value: benefit to society
Extraction of natural resources	Management of natural resources
Linear production systems	Circular production systems
Short-life products for sale	Long-life services: the 'performance economy'
Efficiency measured in monetary terms (e.g. cost-benefit analysis, CBA)	Multidimensional efficiency (e.g. multi-criterion analysis, MCA)
Micro- and macrorationality highly divergent	Micro- and macrorationality highly congruent

Source: Eva Alfredsson and Anders Wijkman, *The Inclusive Green Economy, Shaping society to serve sustainability – minor adjustments or a paradigm shift?* (April 2014), Table 1 at 7, http://mistra.org/download/18.2f9de4bl4592al589dl72e2/1473225485133/Mistra_Prestudy_TheInclusiveGreenEconomy_April2014+%281%29.pdf

rights to exist, thrive and evolve. And it describes one role of government to serve as trustee with fiduciary, enforceable duties running to the public.

The movement has a clear emphasis on changing the economic system, and although exactly what "change" means is contested, there are consensus points: "an economy that is increasingly green and socially responsible, and one that is based on rethinking the nature of ownership and the growth paradigm that guides conventional policies."[84]

Table 1.1 highlights nine areas that contrast the current with the new economy to help provide shape to this paradigm shift.[85]

This Table shows a wide gap between the current and new economy.

[84] Gar Alperovitz, *The New-Economy Movement: A Growing Group of Activists and Socially Responsible Companies Are Rethinking Business as Usual*, NATION (25 May 2011), http://www.thenation.com/article/new-economy-movement/.

[85] Eva Alfredsson and Anders Wijkman, *The Inclusive Green Economy, Shaping society to serve sustainability – minor adjustments or a paradigm shift?* (April 2014), Table 1 at 7, available 13 January 2017 at http://mistra.org/download/18.2f9de4b14592a1589d172e2/1473225485133/Mistra_Prestudy_TheInclusiveGreenEconomy_April2014+%281%29.pdf.

In a complementary explanation of envisioning the next system, Speth emphasizes common values that help define alternative systems as we move out of the Industrial Age. He focuses at the level of paradigm, the top of Meadows's hierarchy for change, but the hardest to achieve:

- ENVIRONMENT: sustainable, regenerative, resilient, stewardship
- PLACE: appropriate scale, decentralized, subsidiarity
- COMMUNITY: solidarity, caring, sharing, local and global
- COMMON GOOD: economic democracy, cooperative, maximize not growth but well-being, sufficiency
- JUSTICE: fairness, equality, human dignity, diversity
- DEMOCRACY: deliberative, participatory, people empowered[86]

Speth outlines transformations on the path to the next system in major subsystems such as: the market, the corporation, economic growth, money and finance, social conditions, indicators, consumerism, communities, dominant cultural values, politics, and foreign policy and the military.[87] In Speth's chapter (Chapter 2), he calls for a new environmentalism that tackles systems change instead of relentlessly focusing on changes in parameters, changes that fall short in delivering a sustainable environment with broadly shared prosperity.

The new economy paradigm, which Speth calls the "Joyful Economy", describes a post-growth, conserver society that respects ecological limits and promotes its protection, that is democratic, and values tighter gaps between rich and poor. This requires a paradigm shift towards ecological sustainability and social well-being as fundamental requirements, and the economy is seen as a tool to get there and not an end in itself.[88] This is a shift from the goal of GDP growth to the goal of development.[89]

But when we focus on development, do we ignore the rest of the natural world? What is the relationship between human development and ecological sustainability in a climate-constrained world? In order to ensure the economy is a tool that protects ecosystems, we need a paradigm that recognizes the inherent rights of the natural world to exist, thrive and evolve.

---

[86] Speth, *supra* note 30, at 4.

[87] *Id.* at 11–12.

[88] Alfredsson and Wijkman, *supra* note 85, at 5; TIM JACKSON, PROSPERITY WITHOUT GROWTH: ECONOMICS FOR A FINITE PLANET (Earthscan 2009).

[89] New Econ. Found., Growth Isn't Possible: Why We Need a New Economic Direction (2010), available 13 January 2017 at http://b.3cdn.net/nefoundation/f19c45312a905d73c3_rbm6iecku.pdf.

In our current paradigm, which is heavily focused on private ownership and talks about nature as "assets", "services" and "resources", we lack the vocabulary and related legal instruments to adequately protect collective, long-term and ecological interests in the commons, from groundwater to birds to global climate. In the next economy development needs to be fully aligned with ecological sustainability of the natural world while making opportunities for human development more equitable, and it is essential to develop legal instruments for this.

V. CONCLUSION: THE PATH FORWARD

"The real issue is whether it is possible to challenge the 'growth-at-any-cost' model and come up with an alternative that is environmentally benign, economically robust and politically feasible."[90] Some would argue the path to a new economy is daunting or out of reach, as reflected in this quote. But, if we don't chart a new path, we will follow the same worn path that has led us here. And as we take steps to build legal infrastructure to support a new economy, we are finding that what was previously unimaginable, starts to take shape.

Although some of the concepts discussed here strike chords that sound aspirational or like academic idealism, the chapters to come in this book include real-life examples to demonstrate where these fledgling transitions are starting to take place. Major shifts in the world are often unimaginable until they happen: recall the fall of the Berlin Wall in November 1989 that marked the end of the Cold War and the opening of Eastern Europe to the West or the stock market crash in October 1929 followed by US President Franklin D. Roosevelt's New Deal in the 1930s. When the game changer happens that will mark the end of the Industrial Age and the current global fossil-fueled economy and the beginning of the new economy, this book aims to provide guidance about the new paradigm, goals, and rules that will help us achieve a more sustainable, equitable, and democratic future.

---

[90] Larry Elliot, *Can a Dose of Recession Solve Climate Change?*, GUARDIAN (24 August 2008), available 13 January 2017 at https://www.theguardian.com/business/2008/aug/25/economicgrowth.globalrecession.

PART I

Paradigms for an ecological age

2. The joyful economy: rising up from the devastation of people and nature

James Gustave Speth

I. INTRODUCTION

In his 1976 book, *The Joyless Economy*, Tibor Scitovsky saw environmental neglect as part of a very American pattern of "putting the earning of money ahead of the enjoyment of life".[1] Four decades later, his observation remains valid.

In this chapter, I explore the transition from a Joyless Economy to a Joyful one. In the Joyful Economy, the goal of economic life is to sustain, nourish and restore human and natural communities, so that the material and non-material blessing of life are available to all. It is a new economy that gives true and honest priority not to profit, production and power but rather to people, place and planet. One of its values is caring – caring for each other, for the natural world and for the future. I will argue that promoting the transition to such a new economy must be the central task of a new environmentalism.

To guide us, we do desperately need a new dream – one where the pursuit of happiness is sought not in more getting and spending but in the growth of human solidarity, devoted friendship and meaningful accomplishment; where the average person is empowered to achieve his or her human potential; where the benefits of economic activity are widely and equitably shared; where democracy and civic participation flourish at all levels; where the environment is sustained for current and future generations; and where the virtues of simple living, community self-reliance, good fellowship and respect for nature predominate. These traditions do not always prevail today, but they are not dead. They await us, and indeed they are today being awakened.

"More than a little utopian," some may be thinking. Yes, but a utopian

---

[1] TIBOR SCITOVSKY, THE JOYLESS ECONOMY: THE PSYCHOLOGY OF HUMAN SATISFACTION 210 (rev. ed. Oxford University Press 1992).

vision is precisely what today's situation requires. Things are much too bad for pessimism, it has been noted. And as Richard Flanagan asked recently, "What reality was ever created by realists? . . . What we cannot dream we can never do."[2]

Before I get to the dream of the Joyful Economy, however, I reflect on the history of the US environmental movement, in which I've been actively working in one or another role since the late 1960s. I explain why it has failed by many measures, and certainly on the biggest issue we face, global climate change. I call for a new environmentalism that tackles system change and embraces the big issues that effect environmental outcomes as part of a core agenda. I articulate the motivating values that are center to a new system of political economy, and then explain what a Joyful Economy would look like, and finally offer my theory of how we begin the transition.

II. AN ENVIRONMENTALIST'S TALE AND NEED FOR A NEW ENVIRONMENTALISM

There are many areas of public concern that can frame the case for this economic and political transformation.[3] This chapter presents the environmental one.

Almost a half-century has flown by since a group of us launched the Natural Resources Defense Council (NRDC). Over that period NRDC and other mainstream US environmental groups have racked up more victories and accomplishments than we can count. One shudders to think what our world would be like had they not.

Yet, despite those accomplishments, a specter is haunting American environmentalism – the specter of failure. All of us who have been part of the environmental movement in the United States must now face up to a deeply troubling paradox: Our environmental organizations have grown in strength and sophistication, but the environment has continued to go downhill. The prospect of a ruined planet is now very real. We have won many victories, but we are losing the planet.

---

[2] Richard Flanagan, The Narrow Road to the Deep North (Alfred K. Knopf 2015).

[3] As I reported in 2012 in America the Possible, among the 20 most well-to-do democracies, the United States ranks last or close to it in 25 major indicators of national well-being. The measures span economic, social, and political performance, just not environmental. James Gustave Speth, America the Possible: Manifesto for a New Economy 1–2 (Yale University Press 2012) [hereinafter America the Possible].

Climate change is coming at us very hard. A great tragedy is now likely. Around the world, we are losing biodiversity, forests, fisheries and agricultural soils at frightening rates. Fresh water shortages multiply. Toxics accumulate in ecosystems, and in us.[4]

Even in the country where we first advanced environmental law, major domestic problems persist. Over a third of the fresh water bodies in the US still do not meet the goal of "fishable and swimmable" set in the 1972 Clean Water Act.[5] A third of Americans suffer from unhealthy air that fails to meet regulatory standards. A third of US fish, amphibian and flowering plant species are threatened with extinction, as well as 15–20 percent of birds, mammals and reptiles. And these estimates do not take into account the full impacts of climate change.

Something is terribly wrong. Indeed, all we have to do – to destroy the planet's climate, impoverish its biota and toxify its people – is to keep doing exactly what we are doing today, with no growth in the human population or the world economy. Just continue to release greenhouse gases at current rates, continue to degrade ecosystems and release toxic chemicals at current rates, and the world in the latter part of this century won't be fit to live in. But human activities are not holding at current levels – they are accelerating, dramatically. It took all of human history to grow the USD$7 trillion world economy of 1950. Now, we grow by that amount in a decade, even with today's slower growth rates. The potential for huge environmental losses is very real.

To chronicle how we arrived at this place, it is useful to begin with Frederick Buell and his valuable book, *From Apocalypse to Way of Life*. He writes:

> Something happened to strip the environmental [cause] of what seemed in the 1970s to be its self-evident inevitability . . . In reaction to the decade of crisis, a strong and enormously successful anti-environmental disinformation industry sprang up. It was so successful that it helped midwife a new phase in the history of US environmental politics, one in which an abundance of environmental concern was nearly blocked by an equal abundance of anti-environmental contestation.[6]

---

4 *Id.* at 52–66.

5 The data presented on the US are from JAMES GUSTAVE SPETH, THE BRIDGE AT THE EDGE OF THE WORLD: CAPITALISM, THE ENVIRONMENT, AND CROSSING FROM CRISIS TO SUSTAINABILITY 73–78 (Yale University Press 2008) [hereinafter THE BRIDGE AT THE EDGE OF THE WORLD], and so may have changed in minor ways over the past decade.

6 FREDERICK BUELL, *From Apocalypse to Way of Life: Environmental Crisis in the American Century* 3–4, 10 (Routledge 2004).

Nowhere has this disinformation campaign been more important – and successful – than with climate change, all brilliantly chronicled in Naomi Oreskes and Erik Conway's book, *Merchants of Doubt*.[7]

The disinformation industry that Buell notes was part of a larger picture of reaction. That reaction can perhaps be dated from Lewis Powell's famous 1971 memo to the Chamber of Commerce urging business to fight back against environmental and other regulations. Powell, then a corporate attorney who would become a Supreme Court justice, urged corporations to get more involved in policy and politics. Since then, well-funded forces of resistance and opposition have arisen. Especially since Reagan became president, virtually every step forward has been hard fought. It is not just environmental protection that has been forcefully attacked but essentially all progressive causes, even the basic idea of government action in the interests of the people as a whole.

The entire story of the conservative assault on environmental protections has now been well told in Judith Layzer's important 2012 book, *Open for Business*. Here is her summary:

> Since the 1970s, conservative activists have disseminated a compelling antiregulatory storyline to counter the environmentalist narrative, mobilized grassroots opposition to environmental regulations, and undertaken sophisticated legal challenges to the basis for and implementation of environmental laws. Over time, these activities have imparted legitimacy to a new antiregulatory rhetoric, one that emphasizes distrust of the federal bureaucracy, admiration for unfettered private property rights and markets, skepticism about science, and disdain for environmental advocates. By employing arguments rooted in this formula, conservatives have been instrumental in blocking efforts to pass major new environmental legislation or increase the stringency of existing laws, despite the emergence of scientific evidence suggesting serious new problems and growing risk from previously identified concerns.[8]

A constantly building opposition is the obvious, immediate reason for our mounting environmental failure. But this exercise of power and control is merely the surface political manifestation of deeper systemic imperatives.

Before turning to these deeper issues, let me state the biggest mistake I believe we environmentalists made. As federal environmental laws and programs burst onto the scene in the early 1970s, we eagerly pursued the

---

7 Naomi Oreskes and Erik M. Conway, Merchants of Doubt: How a Handful of Scientists Obscured the Truth on Issues from Tobacco Smoke to Global Warming (Bloomsbury Press 2010).

8 Judith Layzer, Open for Business: Conservatives' Opposition to Environmental Regulation (MIT Press 2012), 4.

important goals and avenues those laws opened up. There, the path to success was clear. But in doing so we left by the wayside the more difficult and deeper challenges highlighted by leading environmental thinkers of the 1960s and 1970s – Barry Commoner, Paul Ehrlich, Donella Meadows and others.[9] Their overall point was that we should strike at the root causes of environmental decline. They saw that doing so would require us to seek fundamental changes in our prevailing system of political economy – to seek a new paradigm to guide our economic and political life.

Most of us ignored these calls for systemic change. In particular, we should have revisited these deeper issues when our momentum stalled after 1980, especially in light of the anti-environmentalism of the Reagan years. What happened instead was that the 1970s' successes locked us into patterns of environmental action that have since proved no match for the system we're up against. Those successes were made possible in large measure by US Senator Edmund Muskie and his monumental clean air and water legislation. These new laws created major opportunities for advocates to make large environmental gains. But in doing so, we were drawn ever more completely inside the Washington, DC Beltway. Once there, inside the system, we were compelled to a certain tameness by the need to succeed. As Washington became more conservative, mainstream environmentalists became more cautious. In sum, we opted to work within the system of political economy that we found, and we neglected to seek transformation of the system itself.

The central precept has been that the system can be made to work for the environment. America has now run a 46-year experiment testing whether this is true. The results are in, and we have learned that the prevailing system of political economy does not work well, to put it mildly, when it comes to the environment.

System change is essential because our environmental problems are actually rooted in defining features of our current political economy. An unquestioning society-wide commitment to economic growth at virtually any cost; a measure of growth, GDP, that includes not only the good but also the bad and the ugly; powerful corporate interests whose overriding objective is to generate profit and grow, including profit from avoiding the social and environmental costs they create; markets that systematically fail to recognize these costs unless corrected by government; government

---

[9] See JAMES GUSTAVE SPETH, ANGELS BY THE RIVER: A MEMOIR 136–37 (Chelsea Green Publishing 2014) and the works cited there for a discussion on the leading environmental thinkers of the 1960s and 1970s. *See also*, THE BRIDGE AT THE EDGE OF THE WORLD, *supra* note 5, at 116–17.

that is subservient to corporate interests and the growth imperative; rampant consumerism spurred endlessly by sophisticated advertising; social injustice and economic insecurity so vast that they paralyze action and empower false claims that needed measures would cost jobs and hurt the economy; economic activity now so large in scale that its impacts alter the fundamental biophysical operations of the planet – all these combine to deliver an ever-growing economy that is undermining the ability of the planet to sustain human and natural communities.

It's clearly time for something different – a new environmentalism. And here is the core of this new environmentalism: It seeks a new economy, a joyful one. And to deliver on the promise of this new economy, we must build a new politics. New environmental leaders will learn from the ideas of the 1960s and early 1970s, rediscover environmentalism's more radical roots, and step outside the system in order to change it before it is too late.

We must ask again the basic question: What is an environmental issue? Air and water pollution, of course. But what if the right answer is that environmental issues include anything that determines environmental outcomes. Then, surely, the creeping plutocracy and corporatocracy we face – the ascendancy of money power and corporate power over people power – these are environmental issues. And more: The chartering and empowering of corporations as artificial persons to do virtually anything in the name of profit; the fetish of GDP growth as the ultimate public good and the main aim of government; our runaway consumerism; our vast social insecurity with half of US families living paycheck to paycheck. These are among the underlying drivers of environmental outcomes, yet they rarely appear on the agendas of mainstream environmental groups.

The agenda of the new environmentalism should embrace a profound challenge to consumerism and commercialism and the lifestyles they offer, a healthy skepticism of growthmania and a redefinition of what society should be striving to grow, a challenge to corporate dominance and a redefinition of the corporation and its goals, a commitment to deep change in both the functioning and the reach of the market and a powerful assault on the materialistic, anthropocentric and contempocentric values that currently dominate.

Environmentalists must also join with social progressives in addressing the crisis of inequality and deprivation now unraveling America's social fabric and influencing global insecurity. Similarly, environmentalists must join with those seeking to reform politics and strengthen democracy. In the US a vicious circle has emerged: income disparities shift political access and influence to wealthy constituencies and large businesses, which further imperils the potential of the democratic process to act to correct the growing income disparities. This is an archetypal "success to the successful" system trap Donella Meadows described.[10] The way out of this trap is public financing of elections, new anticorruption ethical restrictions on legislatures, defending the right to vote, tougher regulation of lobbying and the revolving door of government officials taking jobs at industries they previously regulated, nonpartisan Congressional redistricting and other political reform measures. Environmentalists need also to support Constitutional amendment to ensure that "corporations are not people and money is not speech".

The new environmentalism must work with a progressive coalition to build a mighty force in electoral politics. This will require major efforts at grassroots organizing, strengthening groups working at the state and community levels, and both supporting and fielding candidates for public office. It will also require developing motivational messages and appeals. Our environmental discourse has thus far been dominated by lawyers, scientists and economists. Now, we need to hear a lot more from the poets, preachers, philosophers and psychologists.

Above all, the new environmental politics must be broadly inclusive, reaching out to embrace the concerns of union members and working families, minorities and people of color, frontline communities, religious organizations, the women's movement and other communities of complementary interest and shared fate. Much stronger alliances are needed, alliances powerful enough to overcome the "silo effect" that separates the environmental community from those working on domestic political reforms, a progressive social agenda, gender equality, racial justice, international peace, consumer issues, world health and population concerns, and world poverty and underdevelopment.

The final goal of the new environmental politics must be, "Build the movement". Environmentalists are still said to be part of "the environmental movement". We need a real one – networked together with other progressives, protesting, demanding action and accountability from governments and corporations and taking steps as consumers and communities to realize sustainability and social justice in everyday life.

III. SYSTEM CHANGE

In my books I have endeavored to make the case for driving systemic changes so deeply that we build a new system of political economy, one

---

[10] Donella H. Meadows, Thinking in Systems: A Primer 126–30 (Chelsea Green Publishing 2008).

programmed to routinely deliver good results for people, place and planet. I know that the idea of a new political economy is too big to swallow whole. So I have broken it down. System change can best be approached through a series of interacting, mutually reinforcing transitions – transformations that attack and undermine the key motivational structures of the current system, while replacing these old structures with new arrangements needed for a flourishing of human and natural communities.

I believe the following transitions hold the key to moving to a new and joyful political economy. We can think of each as a progression from today to tomorrow. In each of these areas, there are currently laws and policies that shape today's realities. Collectively, we can think of these laws as the law of today's corporatist, consumerist capitalism. What we should be moving toward is the law of the new economy. In the end, I think we will need new regimes of corporate law, property law, tort law, Constitutional law and more – a reconceptionalization of environmental law.

- *The market*: from near laissez-faire to powerful market governance in the public interest; from dishonest prices to honest ones and from unfair wages to fair ones; from commodification to reclaiming the commons, the things that rightfully belong to all of us;
- *The corporation*: from shareholder primacy to stakeholder primacy, from one ownership and profit-driven model to new business models beyond the profit motive, to economic democracy, and to public participation in major investment decisions;
- *Economic growth*: from growth fetish to post-growth society, from mere GDP growth to growth in social and environmental well-being and growth focused squarely on democratically determined priorities;
- *Money and finance*: from Wall Street to Main Street, from money created through bank debt to money created by government; from investments seeking high financial returns to those seeking high social and environmental returns;
- *Social conditions*: from economic insecurity to security; from vast inequalities to fundamental fairness; from racial, religious and other invidious discrimination to just and tolerant treatment of all groups;
- *Indicators*: from GDP ("grossly distorted picture") to accurate measures of social and environmental health and quality of life;
- *Consumerism*: from consumerism and affluenza to sufficiency and mindful consumption, from more to enough;
- *Communities*: from runaway enterprise and throwaway communities to vital local economies, from social rootlessness to rootedness and human solidarity;

- *Dominant cultural values*: from having to being, from getting to giving, from richer to better, from isolated to connected, from apart from nature to part of nature, from near-term to long-term;
- *Politics*: from weak democracy to strong, from creeping corporatocracy and plutocracy to true popular sovereignty and empowerment of marginalized groups;
- *Foreign policy and the military*: from American exceptionalism to America as a normal nation, from hard power to soft, from military prowess to real security.

The good news is that we already know a great deal about the policy and other changes needed to move strongly in these directions.[11] Even better, we are already seeing the proliferation of innovative actions along many of the lines sketched here, particularly at the local level: sustainable communities, transition towns, solidarity and local living economies, sustainable and regenerative agriculture, new regional and organic food systems, locally owned and managed renewable energy; and community development and investment institutions. We are also seeing the spread of innovative business models that prioritize community and environment over profit and growth – including social enterprises, for-benefit business, worker-owned and other co-ops and local credit unions – as well as numerous campaigns for fair wages, worker rights and pro-family policies.[12] Many of these examples are the subject of the chapters that follow. Together with new community-oriented and earth-friendly lifestyles, these initiatives provide inspirational models of how things might work in a new political economy devoted to sustaining human and natural communities. Practical utopians at work and play, bringing the future into the present!

---

[11] *See, e.g.*, AMERICA THE POSSIBLE, *supra* note 3.

[12] *See generally About*, YES! MAGAZINE, AVAILABLE 13 JANUARY 2017 AT www.yesmagazine.org/about (reframing today's issues to provide information and resources for a path forward); *About C-W*, DEMOCRACY COLLABORATIVE, available 13 January 2017 at www.community-wealth.org (providing information for "the expansion of community wealth-building institutions). *See also* GAR ALPEROVITZ, WHAT THEN MUST WE DO? STRAIGHT TALK ABOUT THE NEXT AMERICAN REVOLUTION (Chelsea Green Publishing 2013); GAR ALPEROVITZ, AMERICA BEYOND CAPITALISM: RECLAIMING OUR WEALTH, OUR LIBERTY, AND OUR DEMOCRACY (Wiley 2005).

IV. VALUES AND A NEW CONSCIOUSNESS

In describing these transitions, and elsewhere in this chapter, I have stressed the centrality of new values and the evolution to a new consciousness. I would never say that no progress can be made until the globally dominant culture has been transformed. But I do believe that we won't get far in addressing our major challenges unless there is a parallel, ongoing transformation in values and culture.

To elaborate, our dominant culture should shift, from focusing on today to tomorrow, in the following ways:

- Instead of viewing humanity as something apart from nature, and nature as something to be transcended and dominated, we will see ourselves as part of nature, as offspring of its evolutionary process, as close kin to wild things, and as wholly dependent on its vitality and the services it provides.
- Rather than seeing nature as humanity's resource to exploit as it sees fit for economic and other purposes, we will see the natural world as holding intrinsic value independent of people and having rights that create the duty of ecological stewardship.
- We will no longer discount the future by focusing so intently on the short term, but instead take the long view and recognize our duties to human and natural communities well into the future.
- Instead of today's hyperindividualism and social isolation, we will reward those who foster a powerful sense of community, conviviality and social solidarity, in all venues from local to cosmopolitan.
- Violence will no longer be glorified nor wars easily accepted. The spreading of hate and invidious divisions will be frowned on and will no longer be a launching pad for careers in broadcasting and politics.
- Materialism, consumerism and the primacy of ever-more possessions will give way to a culture that grants priority to family and personal relationships, learning, experiencing nature, service, spirituality and living within Earth's limits.
- Rather than tolerate gross economic, social, gender, racial and political inequality, we will demand and work for a high measure of equality in all of these spheres.

Here's an often-overlooked fact: We don't need to wait on these changes but can bring them about. "The central conservative truth is that culture, not politics, determines the success of a society", Daniel Patrick Moynihan remarked. "The central liberal truth is that politics can change a culture and save it from itself."[13]

We actually know important things about how values and culture can change. One sure path to cultural change is, unfortunately, the cataclysmic event – the crisis – that profoundly challenges prevailing values and can delegitimize the status quo. The Great Depression is the classic example. I think we can be confident that we haven't seen the end of major crises, but they will drive events in the right directions only if we are prepared and actively engaged.

Two other key factors in cultural change are leadership and social narrative. Harvard's Howard Gardner has written:

> Whether they are heads of a nation or senior officials of the United Nations, leaders . . . have enormous potential to change minds . . . and in the process they can change the course of history.
>
> I have suggested one way to capture the attention of a disparate population: by creating a compelling story, embodying that story in one's own life, and presenting the story in many different formats so that it can eventually topple the counter stories in one's culture . . . The story must be simple, easy to identify with, emotionally resonant, and evocative of positive experiences.[14]

Bill Moyers, a powerful force for good in our country, has written, "America needs a different story . . . The leaders and thinkers and activists who honestly tell that story and speak passionately of the moral and religious values it puts in play will be the first political generation since the New Deal to win power back for the people."[15]

There is some evidence that Americans are ready for another story. Large majorities of Americans, when polled, express disenchantment with today's lifestyles and offer support for values similar to those urged here.[16]

Another key source of value change is social movements. Social movements are all about consciousness raising and, if successful, they can help usher in a new consciousness.

Another way forward to a new consciousness lies with the world's

---

13 Lawrence E. Harrison, The Central Liberal Truth: How Politics Can Change a Culture and Save it from Itself xvi (Oxford University Press 2006).

14 Howard Gardner, Changing Minds: The Art and Science of Changing Our Own and Other People's Minds 69, 82 (Harvard Business School Press 2006). *See also* James MacGregor Burns, Transforming Leadership: A New Pursuit of Happiness (Atlantic Monthly Press 2003).

15 Bill Moyers, *For America's Sake* (5 January 2007), available 13 January 2017 at https://www.thenation.com/article/americas-sake-2/.

16 The Bridge at the Edge of the World, *supra* note 5, at 163. Of course, respondents do not always act on the high-minded sentiments expressed to pollsters.

religions. Mary Evelyn Tucker has noted that "no other group of institutions can wield the particular moral authority of the religions".[17] The potential of faith communities is enormous, and they are turning more attention to issues of social justice, peace and environment. Spiritual awakening to new values and new consciousness can also derive from the arts, literature, philosophy and science. Consider, for example, the long tradition of "reverence for life" stretching back to the Emperor Ashoka more than 2,200 years ago and forward to Albert Schweitzer, Aldo Leopold, Thomas Berry, E. O. Wilson, Terry Tempest Williams and others.[18]

Education, of course, can also contribute enormously to cultural change. Here one should include education in the largest sense, embracing not only formal education but also day-to-day and experiential education as well as the fast-developing field of social marketing. Social marketing has had notable successes in moving people away from bad behaviors such as smoking and drunk driving, and its approaches could be applied to these themes as well.

A major and very hopeful path is seeding the landscape with innovative, instructive models. As noted, there is a proliferation of innovative models of community revitalization and business enterprise. Local currencies, slow money, alternative Genuine Progress Indicators, locavores – these are bringing the future into the present in very concrete ways. These actual models will grow in importance as communities search for answers on how the future should look, and they can change minds. Seeing is believing.

In sum, cultural transformation won't be easy, but it's not impossible either.

The fundamental importance of these changes in values and culture is underscored by the findings of the relatively new field of positive psychology. Studies that compare levels of happiness and life satisfaction among nations at different stages of economic income find that the citizens of

---

17 MARY EVELYN TUCKER, WORLDLY WONDER: RELIGIONS ENTER THEIR ECOLOGICAL PHASE 9, 43 (Open Court 2003).

18 *See* BRUCE RICH, TO UPHOLD THE WORLD: A CALL FOR A NEW GLOBAL ETHIC FROM ANCIENT INDIA (Beacon Press 2010); ALBERT SCHWEITZER, OUT OF MY LIFE AND THOUGHT: AN AUTOBIOGRAPHY (H. Holt 1933); ALDO LEOPOLD, A SAND COUNTY ALMANAC (Random House 1966) (1949); THOMAS BERRY, EVENING THOUGHTS (Mary Evelyn Tucker (ed.), Sierra Club Books 2006); E. O. WILSON, THE CREATION: AN APPEAL TO SAVE LIFE ON EARTH (Norton 2006); TERRY TEMPEST WILLIAMS, REFUGE: AN UNNATURAL HISTORY OF FAMILY AND PLACE (Vintage Books 2001). *See also* STEPHEN R. KELLERT and JAMES GUSTAVE SPETH, THE COMING TRANSFORMATION: VALUES TO SUSTAIN HUMAN AND NATURAL COMMUNITIES (Yale School of Forestry & Environmental Studies 2009).

wealthier countries report higher levels of life satisfaction. Yet, the correlation between income and life satisfaction is rather poor, and it is even poorer when factors such as quality of government are statistically controlled. And this positive relationship virtually disappears when one looks only at countries with GDP per capita over USD$10,000 per year. In short, once a country achieves a moderate level of income, further growth does not significantly improve perceived well-being.[19]

Even more challenging to the idea that well-being increases with higher incomes are extensive time-series data showing that throughout almost the entire post–World War II period, as incomes skyrocketed in the United States and other advanced economies, reported life satisfaction and happiness levels stagnated or even declined slightly. The consistency of this finding across a broad range of societies is impressive.[20] After reviewing the new evidence, Richard Easterlin and Laura Angelescu conclude that "there is no significant relationship between the improvement in happiness and the longterm rate of growth of GDP per capita".[21]

But that is not all. Ed Diener and Martin Seligman, two leaders in positive psychology, note:

> Even more disparity [between income and well-being] shows up when ill-being measures are considered. For instance, depression rates have increased 10-fold over the same 50-year period, and rates of anxiety are also rising . . . There is [also] a decreasing level of social connectedness in society, as evidenced by declining levels of trust in other people and in governmental institutions.[22]

You may have heard the joke: "Those who say money can't buy happiness just don't know where to shop!" But the truth is that the data indicate

---

[19] Ed Diener and Martin E.P. Seligman, *Beyond Money: Toward an Economy of Well-Being*, 5 Psychol. Sci. in the Pub. Int. 1, 3–5 (2004); Avner Offer, The Challenge of Affluence: Self-Control and Well-Being in the United States and Britain Since 1950 15–38 (Oxford University Press 2006). See The Bridge at the Edge of the World, *supra* note 5, at 126–46 for reproduced diagrams.

[20] *See* Jonathon Porritt, Capitalism as If the World Matters 54 (Earthscan 2005) (discussing the United States); Nick Donovan et al., Life Satisfaction: The State of Knowledge and the Implications for Government 17 (Cabinet Office 2002) (discussing the United Kingdom); Bruno S. Frey and Alois Stutzer, Happiness and Economics: How the Economy and Institutions Affect Human Well-Being 9 (Princeton University Press 2002) (discussing Japan).

[21] Richard A. Easterlin and Laura Angelescu, Inst. for the Study of Labor, Happiness and Growth the World Over: Time Series Evidence on the Happiness-Income Paradox 9 (2009), 9, available 13 January 2017 at http://ftp.iza.org/dp4060.pdf.

[22] Diener and Seligman, *supra* note 19, at 3.

that money cannot buy joy or satisfaction in life among the more affluent. Study after study show that there is a sharply declining marginal utility to extra income. As Diener and Seligman put it:

> Economic growth seems to have topped out in its capacity to produce more well-being in developed nations . . . Efforts and policies to raise income in wealthy nations are unlikely to increase well-being and might even undermine factors (such as rewarding social relationships or other cherished values) that have higher leverage for producing enhanced well-being.[23]

If incomes are such weak generators of well-being in our more affluent societies, what are the things that really do produce happiness and well-being? The answer is somewhat complicated, but when a founder of the field of positive psychology was asked to state briefly the lessons of positive psychology, his answer was: "Other people".[24] We flourish in a setting of warm, nurturing and rewarding interpersonal relationships, and within that context we flourish best when we are giving, not getting.

V. THE JOYFUL ECONOMY

Envisioning a better alternative is the first step in realizing it. Can we begin to envision the contours and texture of daily life in the Joyful Economy? We can certainly draw on what numerous communities are striving to do today, and there is an extensive literature on transition towns, intentional communities, new enterprise forms and more.[25] Pointers can also be

---

[23] *Id.* at 10.

[24] MARTIN E. P. SELIGMAN, FLOURISH: A VISIONARY NEW UNDERSTANDING OF HAPPINESS AND WELL-BEING 20 (Free Press 2011).

[25] *See, e.g.*, JULIET SCHOR, PLENITUDE: THE NEW ECONOMICS OF TRUE WEALTH (Penguin Press 2010); DAVID C. KORTEN, THE GREAT TURNING: FROM EMPIRE TO EARTH COMMUNITY (BERRETT-KOEHLER/KUMARIAN PRESS 2006); DUANE ELGIN, VOLUNTARY SIMPLICITY: TOWARD A WAY OF LIFE THAT IS OUTWARDLY SIMPLE, INWARDLY RICH (Harper 2010); DAVID WANN, THE NEW NORMAL: AN AGENDA FOR RESPONSIBLE LIVING (St Martin's Griffin 2010); THOMAS PRINCEN, TREADING SOFTLY: PATHS TO ECOLOGICAL ORDER (MIT Press 2010); BILL MCKIBBEN, DEEP ECONOMY: THE WEALTH OF COMMUNITIES AND THE DURABLE FUTURE (Times Books 2007); JAY WALLJASPER, ALL THAT WE SHARE: HOW TO SAVE THE ECONOMY, THE ENVIRONMENT, THE INTERNET, DEMOCRACY, OUR COMMUNITIES AND EVERYTHING ELSE THAT BELONGS TO ALL OF US (New Press 2010); JANELLE ORSI AND EMILY DOSKOW, THE SHARING SOLUTION: HOW TO SAVE MONEY, SIMPLIFY YOUR LIFE & BUILD COMMUNITY (Nolo 2009); FRITJOF CAPRA and HAZEL HENDERSON, INST. FOR CHARTERED ACCTS. IN ENG. AND WALES, QUALITATIVE GROWTH (2009), available 13

drawn from the findings of positive psychology and our understanding of global, national and local needs in many areas. When all this is pulled together, we can see that life in the Joyful Economy will tend strongly in these directions:

Local life. Economic and social life will be rooted in the community and the region. More production will be local and regional, with shorter, less-complex supply chains, especially but not only in food and energy supply. Enterprises will be more committed to the long-term well-being of employees and the viability of their communities and will be supported by local, complementary currencies and local financial institutions. People will live closer to work and walk and bike more. Energy production will be decentralized, typically with local ownership and management, and overwhelmingly renewable. Socially, community bonds will be strong; neighbors and genuine, unpretentious relationships important; civic associations and community service groups plentiful; support for teachers and caregivers high. Personal security, tolerance of difference and empathy will be high. Local governance will stress participatory, direct and deliberative democracy. Citizens will be seized with the responsibility to manage and extend the commons – the valuable assets that belong to everyone – through community land trusts and otherwise.

Scale and resilience. Building on an emphasis on local life, society and economy and the enterprises within them will not be too big to understand, appreciate or manage successfully. Key motivations will be to maintain a human scale and resilience – the capacity to absorb disturbance and outside shocks without disastrous consequences.

Glocalism. Despite the many ways life will be more local, and in defiance of the resulting temptation to parochialism, people will feel a sense of citizenship at larger levels of social and political organization, even at the global level. In particular, there will be a deep appreciation of the need to bring political accountability and democratic control to the many things that can be done only at national and international levels.

New business models. Locally owned businesses, including worker-, customer- and community-owned firms, will be prominent. So too will hybrid business models such as profit/nonprofit and public/private hybrids. Cooperation will moderate competition, and the profit motive

---

January 2017 at https://www.icaew.com/~/media/corporate/files/technical/sustainability/qualitative%20growth.ashx. *See also* INSTITUTE FOR LOCAL SELF-RELIANCE, https://ilsr.org; NEXT SYSTEM PROJECT, thenextsystem.org; BEAUTIFUL SOLUTIONS, https://solutions.thischangeseverything.org; TRANSITION UNITED STATES, www.transitionus.org; THE U.S. SOLIDARITY ECONOMY NETWORK, https://ussolidarityeconomy.wordpress.com; BALLE, https://bealocalist.org (all available 13 January 2017).

will become secondary and often fade entirely. Investments, frequently promoting import-substitution, will be locally sourced. Global trade will be based on values of fair exchange rather than exploitation. Business incubators will help entrepreneurs with arranging finance, technical assistance and other support. Enterprises of all types will stress environmental and social responsibility.

Plenitude. Consumerism will be supplanted by the search for abundance in things that truly bring happiness and joy – family, friends, the natural world, meaningful work. Recognition will go to those who earn trust and provide needed services to the community. Individuals and communities will enjoy a strong rebirth of re-skilling, crafts and self-provisioning. Overconsumption will be considered vulgar and will be replaced by new investment in civic culture, natural amenities, ecological restoration, education and community development.

More equality. Because large inequalities are at the root of so many social and environmental problems, measures will be implemented to ensure much greater equality not only of opportunity but also of outcomes. Because life is simpler, more caring and less grasping, and people are less status conscious, a fairer sharing of economic resources will come naturally. Livelihoods will be secure.

Time regained. Formal work hours will be cut back, freeing up time for family, friends, hobbies, household productions, continuing education, skills development, caregiving, volunteering, sports, outdoor recreation and participating in the arts. Life will be less frenetic. Frugality and thrift will be prized and wastefulness shunned. Mindfulness and living simply with less clutter will carry the day. As a result, social bonds will strengthen. The overlapping webs of encounter and participation will exist, and trust in each other will be high.

New goods and services. Products will be more durable, versatile and easy to repair, with components that can be reused or recycled. Applying the principles of industrial ecology, the negative impacts of products throughout their life cycles will be minimized, and production systems will be designed to mimic biological ones, with waste eliminated or becoming a useful input elsewhere. The provision of services will replace the purchase of many goods, and sharing, collaborative consumption and community ownership will be commonplace. Fewer people will own, and more will prefer to lend and lease.

Resonance with nature. Energy will be used with maximum efficiency. Zero discharge of traditional pollutants, toxics and greenhouse gases will be the norm. Green chemistry will replace the use of toxics and hazardous substances. Organic farming will eliminate pesticide and herbicide use. Prices will reflect the true environmental and social costs of the products we consume. Schools will stress environmental education and pursue "no child left inside" programs. Nearby natural areas and zones of high ecological significance will be protected. Environmental restoration and cleanup programs will be focuses of community concerns. There will be a palpable sense that all economic and social activity is nested in the natural world. Biophilic design will bring nature into our buildings and our communities.[26]

GDP off, children on the pedestal. Growth in GDP and its local and regional variants will not be seen as a priority, and GDP will be seen as a misleading measure of well-being and progress. Instead, indicators of community wealth creation – including measures of social and natural capital – will be closely watched. Special attention will be given to children and young people. Their education and receipt of loving care, shelter, good nutrition and health care, and an environment free of toxins and violence will be our measures of how well our nations are doing.

It is important to remember that there are many visions of successful new economies and next systems. To frame the Joyful Economy, one cannot do better than to quote from the remarkable John Maynard Keynes. He was also thinking about possible futures in his 1933 essay "Economic Possibilities for Our Grandchildren". There, he envisioned the day when the economy could provide a decent standard of living for all. Then, he wrote that humans will be faced with the real and permanent problem of how to use leisure time wisely when "the accumulation of wealth is no longer of high social importance . . .". He continued:

> I see us free, therefore, to return to some of the most sure and certain principles of religion and traditional virtue – that avarice is a vice, that the exaction of usury is a misdemeanour, and the love of money is detestable, that those walk most truly in the paths of virtue and sane wisdom who take least thought for the morrow. We shall once more value ends above means and prefer the good to the useful. We shall honour those who can teach us how to pluck the hour and the day virtuously and well, the delightful people who are capable of taking direct enjoyment in things . . . Chiefly, do not let us overestimate the importance of the economic problem, or sacrifice to its supposed necessities other matters of greater and more permanent significance.[27]

---

26 *See, e.g.*, BIOPHILIC DESIGN: THE ARCHITECTURE OF LIFE, available 13 January 2017 at www.biophilicdesign.net. *See also* STEPHEN R. KELLERT ET AL., BIOPHILIC DESIGN: THE THEORY, SCIENCE, AND PRACTICE OF BRINGING BUILDINGS TO LIFE (Wiley 2008); DAVID W. ORR, THE NATURE OF DESIGN: ECOLOGY, CULTURE, AND HUMAN INTENTION (Oxford University Press 2004); WILLIAM MCDONOUGH and MICHAEL BRAUNGART, CRADLE TO CRADLE: REMAKING THE WAY WE MAKE THINGS (North Point Press 2002).

27 John Maynard Keynes, *Economic Possibilities for Our Grandchildren, in* ESSAYS IN PERSUASION 358, 365–73 (Classic House Books 2009) (1931).

VI. CONCLUSION: HOW MIGHT WE TRANSFORM THESE SYSTEMS?

In thinking about the need for transformation, I have had to develop a "theory of change" – how transformative change can happen. The theory embraces the seminal role of crises in waking us from the slumber of routine and in shining the spotlight on the failings of the current order of things. It puts great stock in transformative leadership that can point beyond the crisis to something better. The theory adopts the view that systemic changes must be driven both bottom-up and top-down – from communities, businesses and citizens deciding on their own to build the future locally as well as to develop the political muscle to adopt system-changing policies at the national and international levels. And it sees a powerful citizens' movement as a necessary spur to action at all levels.

Here is how it might all come together. As conditions continue to decline across a wide front, or at best fester as they are, ever-larger numbers of people lose faith in the current system and its ability to deliver on the values it proclaims. The system steadily loses support, leading to a crisis of legitimacy. Meanwhile, traditional crises, both in the economy and in the environment, grow more numerous and fearsome. In response, progressives of all stripes coalesce, find their voice and their strength, and pioneer the development of a powerful set of new ideas and policy proposals confirming that the path to a better world does indeed exist. Demonstrations and protests multiply, and a powerful movement for pro-democracy reform and transformative change is born.

At the local level, people and groups come together to take control of their communities' futures and thus plant the seeds of change through a host of innovations that provide inspirational models of how things might work in a new political economy devoted to sustaining human and natural communities. Sensing the direction in which the current is moving, our wiser and more responsible leaders, political and otherwise, rise to the occasion, support the growing movement for change, and frame a compelling story or narrative that makes sense of it all and provides a positive vision. It is a moment of democratic possibility.

One sure sign that the search for a new political economy has begun is the way that constituencies have formed around new concepts of the economy – including the solidarity economy, the caring economy, the sharing economy, the restorative economy, the regenerative economy, the sustaining economy, the commons economy, the resilient economy, the economy for the common good and, of course, the new economy. There is ongoing discussion of the need for a "next system" and a "great transition" and for a "just transition" rooted in racial, gender and class justice. In 2012 the most searched words on the Merriam-Webster website were "capitalism" and "socialism".[28]

Under whatever names, the needed transformations require institutions to promote them. Existing institutions in the US like the Democracy Collaborative, the Institute for Policy Studies, the Tellus Institute, *Yes!* magazine, the Capital Institute, Friends of the Earth, National People's Action, the Labor Network for Sustainability, Jobs with Justice, the National Domestic Workers Alliance, Chelsea Green Publishing, the Institute for Local Self-Reliance, among others, have taken up the cause, as have organizations strengthening new types of businesses such as the Business Alliance for Local Living Economies, the American Sustainable Business Council and B Lab.

Joining them are new entities seeking to bring the many "new economy" issues and organizations together, including the New Economy Coalition (at this time, 140 organizations have already joined the New Economy Coalition) and the Next System Project that I co-chair. Finally, there are a number of impressive new economy groups with a focus on the law. Here, I would mention the Sustainable Economies Law Center, the Community Environmental Legal Defense Fund, the Earth Law Center and the New Economy Law Center at the Vermont Law School that I co-founded. This is important work and it is a privilege to be involved in it.

Whether driven by climate and fossil fuel insults; poverty, low wages and joblessness; deportation of immigrants and other family issues; treatment of women; or voter suppression, movements are now challenging key aspects of the system, seeking to drive deep change beyond incremental reform and offering alternative visions and new paths forward.

There are groups that are marching in the streets, state capitals and local congressional offices. Others are starting to run people for office around alternative agendas. There are places where the needed research is occurring, and new coalitions are bringing diverse groups together. These are among the grounds for hope, the reasons to believe that real change is possible.

I hope today's young people will not worry unduly about being thought "radical" and will find ways to short circuit the long and tortuous path I took. If it seems right to you, embrace it. A wonderful group of leaders and activists who are trying to change the system for the better are building new communities in which we can all participate.

---

[28] Press Release, Merriam-Webster, 2012 Word of the Year (5 December 2012), available 13 January 2017 at http://www.merriam-webster.com/press-release/2012-word-of-the-year.

3. Environmentalism for the next economy

Jedediah Purdy

I. INTRODUCTION

Modern environmental politics emerged in the radical ferment of the early 1970s; activists committed to a more secure, egalitarian and cooperative economy were suspicious from the outset of its easy mainstream appeal and its elite constituency. The same doubts persist today. The venerable Nature Conservancy's close partnerships with corporations and focus on "ecosystem services" that can be monetized are just one reminder that environmentalism's institutional mainstream fits comfortably with neoliberalism.

Consumerist appeals to eco-consciousness (think of the local-sourcing policies and the prices of anti-union Whole Foods) suggest that environmentalism is about image and market choices. Despite decades of talk about environmental justice, the American movement remains disproportionately white, elite, and motivated by romantic attachment to high mountains, old forests and charismatic animals. Even treating climate change as an "environmental" question obscures issues of global justice – the ways that the world's rich are much more responsible for, and less vulnerable to, the problem than the poor.

For environmental law to contribute to a more egalitarian and cooperative economy, it will have to be recast in a way that gives a central place to the organizing concerns of environmental justice: the *distributive* effects of environmental law and policy, and the *constitutive* question of which problems count as environmental, and whose conception of a good life in the natural world environmental law advances. This chapter locates that goal within two developments that have shifted the field more generally: the renewed recognition of the depth and importance of inequality and the emergence of "the Anthropocene" as a characterization of a transformed relationship between human beings and the rest of the planet.

The chapter begins with a discussion of the project of constructing a new environmentalism and tensions with our approaches to nature, egalitarianism and economic growth as measured by Gross Domestic Product (GDP). The chapter probes the question of what is an environmental issue. Then it asks whose problems are environmental and reviews the history of environmental justice. Finally, the chapter gleans lessons to develop the next stage of environmentalism and law.

II. CONSTRUCTING A NEW ENVIRONMENTALISM AND EGALITARIANISM FOR THE NEXT ECONOMY

What would an environmentalism suited to a new economy look like? It would first of all have to change its attitude to "nature". Rather than the unique political voice of nature, environmentalism is the youngest generation of a long-running politics of nature. This politics pivots on contested visions of nature's value, humanity's place in it, and what, in fact, "nature" even is. From the preservationist movement that helped create national parks and wilderness areas to the awareness of ecological interconnection that inspired the anti-pollution laws of the 1970s, the politics of nature has often been democratic and creative in advancing the notion of the living world as part of a human ecology. But the politics of nature has also been an anti-politics, appealing to "nature" to shut down democratic debate.

Theories of nature justified the expulsion of Native Americans, who were accused of ignoring their "natural duty" to develop the continent. Theories of nature rationalized US President Theodore Roosevelt's often progressive, but also undemocratic technocracy, which treated the natural and social worlds as problems requiring expertise rather than political contestation. The Romantic visions of nature that powered the creation of national parks and wilderness areas also elevated WASP[1] elites as nature's privileged interpreters. From Midwestern farms to pristine suburbs to public acreage, American landscapes are a monument to a history of inequality, hierarchy and exclusion. And they are informed at every point by moral and political conceptions of the natural world – often undemocratic in origin and effect – whose advocates tended to deny that they were political at all. "Nature" has often meant what comes before politics and sets its limits, and environmentalism has sought to speak for nature in these terms.

The first task for environmentalists is to own up to this history and ask how today's green mainstream still lacks, or even blocks, democratic

---

1 White Anglo-Saxon Protestant.

and egalitarian projects. Such an environmentalism would insist that, as the joint product of natural forces and human activity, the planet's inequalities are everyone's responsibility. Turning that idea into more than a slogan might begin with linking rich-world concerns about food sourcing and healthfulness to questions of sovereignty over food systems raised by, for instance, hundred-year contracts reserving food production on traditionally communal African lands for Chinese consumption. It might mean making visible the links between the new natural gas–powered bus lines being touted as "clean" by mayors across the US and the environmental destruction caused by fracking to obtain that gas. In other words, it could begin by exposing – and questioning – the distributive logic and concealed violence of the exploitation of the world.

The conceptual anchor of such politics might be an update on a very old idea – that the world originally and essentially belongs to everyone, and that this common heritage may be divided into property only in ways that the dividers can justify on moral and political grounds. This idea that the earth is a kind of common gift converges with a more recent one, that the built world – the world that we make – is a shared product of human labor and intelligence, and its fruits should therefore be distributed justly. An egalitarian environmentalism would bring the two together: the world is both given and made, and in both respects it should be presumptively common.

A. Natural Limits to Growth or Political Limits to Sharing and Restraint?

Maybe the most vexed meeting point between environmentalism and egalitarian economics tradition is the problem of natural limits to economic growth. A strand of green politics has always embraced the material limits of the natural world and worried about how to deal with inequality in the face of them. Traditional egalitarians have instead mostly sought emancipation through growth. But there is no getting around the planet's finitude. Although technological change usually blindsides any specific prediction of crisis, the overall logic remains: economic growth increases the per-person pressure on energy sources, food systems and the global atmosphere. Over the next two centuries, barring science-fiction innovations that essentially decouple human survival from natural resources, people will either find ways to reduce their total demand on the planet or face severe distributive conflict, even resource wars. Easing the demand for growth – as hard as this might seem today – might be the only path to a less divided and more habitable world.

Reformists like John Stuart Mill and John Maynard Keynes once expected economic growth to slow spontaneously. When material needs were met, they argued, people would turn to relationships, self-improvement and other intrinsic goods, and economies would stabilize. This has not happened. From the United States to China, GDP growth remains the hallmark of economic success and political legitimacy.[2]

Perhaps this is because we live in an economic order that drives the demand for growth by actively producing insecurity and dissatisfaction. Contra Mill and Keynes, an increase in wealth can redouble a sense of unsatisfied desire. Cars bring less joy when roads are crowded. In a hyper-competitive and stratified economy, an arms race of credentialing means years of higher education are pursued as instrumental prerequisites for a decent job. Total wealth is much greater, but the fight over its benefits, which are ultimately ways of pursuing good lives, means that much wealth and effort go into running to stand still, so as not to fall behind. Anti-union laws, opposition to universal health care, the end of affordable public higher education and "pension reform" all make the economy more fearsome and workers more fearful. Without economic security and social provision, the world becomes an unsafe place, a place in which you can never have too much protection, that is, too much wealth. So insecurity produces insatiable demands on nature.

Here is where environmentalist and egalitarian projects meet. Only an economy with greater security is likely to produce political forces to limit GDP growth because only a secure economy would make an economic slowdown politically tolerable. A world of heightened insecurity and competition is politically unlikely to square economic life with ecological health. Yet, to note the obvious, everyone needs both.

If environmentalism is to be more than a taste in vacations, environmentalists must insist on limits to material progress and offer ways of thinking about both economics and human lives generally that encourage satisfaction within limits. But if it pursues this effort as an individual aesthetic or spiritual conceit, environmentalism will remain a way of escaping or even rationalizing inequality. Focused instead on how we can build a world worth inhabiting – for everyone – environmentalism offers an expanded picture of democratic life for an age when we have finally acknowledged that political choices shape not just the economy but nature itself.

Sorting out all these questions is beyond the scope of this chapter. Instead, the focus will be on one topic that has considerable potential to advance the above themes: This is environmental justice. Specifically, this

---

[2] See Scanlan's Chapter 1 and Speth's Chapter 2 for critiques of GDP as a measure of well-being.

chapter will think about the place that environmental justice might occupy in an environmentalism that could contribute to the goals of an egalitarian and cooperative economy. Such an environmentalism would be deeply shaped by at least two themes, economic inequality and the concept of the Anthropocene. Indeed, each of these contributes an aspect of what *justice* might come to mean for environmentalism.

B. Economic Inequality

A new history of economic inequality has emerged in the last decade-plus, most visibly in Thomas Piketty's *Capital in the Twenty-First Century*.[3] Piketty and his collaborators show that inequality of both income and wealth has been growing in the developed world since the early-to-mid 1970s. They also find that economic inequality generally grew from the late eighteenth century until World War One. Other than the generalized disasters of two global wars, the major exception was the three decades following World War Two, when economic inequality shrank across the North Atlantic democracies and remained relatively low until a dramatic resurgence began in the 1970s. This latest era of inequality has been especially marked by the concentration of income and wealth in the very highest echelons of distribution.[4]

Much of the response to Piketty's work has aimed at theoretical and empirical accounts of how inequality arises and grows, and at recasting research and policy agendas to give the problems of inequality a new prominence.[5] Besides these important efforts, the new history of inequality opens another, less-noticed front: an opportunity to understand certain patterns of thought and practice in our time as the products of an anomalous but massively influential period when economic inequality was widely believed to be a problem of the past, or at least to have become tractable.[6] This view of the problem had obvious importance for thinking about the sources of injustice and the kinds of principles and policies that justice

---

[3] THOMAS PIKETTY, CAPITAL IN THE TWENTY-FIRST CENTURY (Arthur Goldhammer trans., Belknap Press 2013).

[4] John Cassidy, "Piketty's Inequality Story in Six Charts," THE NEW YORKER (26 March 2014), available 16 January 2017 at http://www.newyorker.com/rational-irrationality/pikettys-inequality-story-in-six-charts.

[5] *See, e.g.*, David Grewal, *The Laws of Capitalism*, 128 HARV. L. REV. 626 (2014) (reviewing PIKETTY, CAPITAL IN THE TWENTY-FIRST CENTURY).

[6] *See, e.g.*, David Grewal and Jedediah Purdy, *Legal Scholarship and the Great Exception*, THEORETICAL ISSUES IN L. (forthcoming 2016); Jedediah Purdy, *Wealth Inequality, Revisited*, NOMOS (2016).

might require. It seems to me that this is as true of environmental justice as it is in other areas.

C. The *Anthropocene*

The *Anthropocene* is a portmanteau term for a new geological "age of humanity" in which human beings have become a force – perhaps the dominant force – in shaping the planet.[7] The term "Anthropocene" has been put to many uses, not all of them mutually consistent, very few of which would be straightforwardly implied were it officially approved by the Stratigraphy Commission. Most compelling of these is the implications of the idea that we live in Anthropocene conditions.

The first implication is that environmental law is a form of world-making, a choice among material futures across a set of dimensions, from the chemistry of the global atmosphere to the mix of species in existence to the pattern of landscapes. That last includes, for instance, the American Midwestern checkerboard of commodity crops, timbered-over national forests and adjacent wilderness areas, and the coal-producing region of central Appalachia, whose topography and hydrology have been irreversibly transformed by mountaintop-removal mining.

Second, because what we still tend to call "the natural world" is a joint production of human activity and non-human forces, traditional baselines of "wild", "primeval" or "unpolluted" nature are either obsolete or fictional, and the benchmarks of environmental policy must rely on explicit value judgments. In practice, this is not so much a new fact as a way of foregrounding a fact that has often been obscured by naturalizing ways of describing and imagining law and policy; most natural resources lawyers would not be unsettled by the fact that "wilderness" is a legal category implementing a cultural and aesthetic ideal.

Third, the boundaries of what is "environmental" are not straightforward. Because natural systems – from weather to waterways – are partly human creations, and interact with the built environments (neighborhoods, infrastructure, and so forth) that have traditionally belonged to fields such as urban planning and public health, no simple criterion offers to identify environmental questions without controversy. Surely energy and agricultural policy are environmental questions. Are food deserts also?[8] What do

---

7 Shalanda H. Baker, *Adaptive Law in the Anthropocene*, 91 CHI.-KENT L. REV. 563, 565–66 (2014).

8 Tess Feldman, *Re-Stocking the Shelves: Programs and Policies in Food Deserts*, 16 PUB. INT. L. REP. 38, 39 (2010) (defining a food desert as "a large geographic area that has no or only distant mainstream grocery stores").

we call a heat wave intensified by climate change in a neighborhood built with poor air circulation, limited or no air conditioning, and little safe and accessible outdoor space? If the last might be a question of environmental justice, why not neighborhood health generally, in light of recent research suggesting that "toxic" neighborhoods are associated with significant harm to life outcomes, some perhaps mediated by bodily conditions such as stress and trauma? It might seem a bit fetishistic, or at best simplistic, to insist that an issue becomes environmental when trees, soil, or weather are involved – a law of the horse, one might say, for the planet. Surely, as argued in Gus Speth's chapter (Chapter 2), environmental issues include anything that determines environmental outcomes; but the category of environmental outcomes is itself a capacious and contested one.

III. THE EMERGENCE OF ENVIRONMENTAL JUSTICE

A. The Development of the Environmental Justice Movement

Environmental justice is usually narrated as a counterpoint to the "mainstream environmentalism" that is associated with the shaping and passage of major US environmental statutes between 1970 and 1977, and with the advocacy organizations that emerged in that period, such as the Natural Resources Defense Council and Environmental Defense Fund. Environmental justice stood for the recognition that environmental law and the advocates who shaped and claimed it had a set of blind spots.

Mainstream environmentalists of the 1970s and 1980s were insufficiently attentive to the distributive dimension of environmental law: where the burdens of pollution and other environmental hazards and harms were concentrated, and how this distribution tracked other patterns of disadvantage, notably race and poverty. One of the canonical documents of environmental justice is *Toxic Waste and Race in the United States*, a 1987 report by the Commission for Racial Justice of the United Church of Christ. The report presented evidence that hazardous waste facilities were disproportionately located in minority communities, and called this pattern "a form of racism".[9] Nearly three decades of follow-on research have see-sawed on the existence, degree, and sources of racially dispro-

---

[9] Comm'n for Racial Justice, Toxic Waste and Race in the United States ix–x (1987), available 16 January 2017 at www.nrc.gov/docs/ML1310/ML13109A339.pdf.

portionate hazards siting, but more refined methods have generally found correlation and grounded intriguing evidence on causation.[10]

A second mainstream blind spot was in the very definition of "environmental" issues. This is what I will call the *constitutive* dimension of environmental justice. Protecting the environment, along with protecting people from a compromised environment, was often presented as a national mission and civilizational crisis between 1962, when Rachel Carson's *Silent Spring* appeared, and the mid-1970s.

Congress passed the major environmental statutes of that period by margins usually reserved to platitudinous resolutions, and for a period in the early 1970s both President Nixon and leading liberals imagined the issue as a new point of unity for a divided country. But mainstream uses of the term "environment" tended to omit or downplay other hazards: workplace exposure to toxins, for instance, or vulnerability to lead paint in the built environment of poor people's homes and neighborhoods. The consequences of these omissions were both practical and symbolic: they expressed operational priorities in pollution control and protection of public health, but also placed certain problems – and certain people's problems – within the nimbus of a core public commitment, while leaving others outside.

This intersection of two questions – which problems are environmental and whose problems are environmental – has been especially important. For instance, Rachel Carson's influence established pesticides as a paradigm environmental problem, but it remained for mostly Latino farm workers in California to agitate against pesticide exposure as a question of workplace safety and labor rights. Environmental concern about pesticides, it seemed, had an implicit view about the position from which one experienced the problem: as one of the innocent suburban or small-town bystanders of Carson's *Silent Spring*, who emerge onto their lawns one morning to a world without birdsong.

No one doubts that coal presents an environmental question when its burning contributes to acid rain or global warming, or when the aftermath of mining acidifies streams to the point where they can no longer support life; but is it also an environmental question when miners' lungs are impregnated by coal dust or silica? When children in mining communities suffer disproportionate asthma from the same causes?

In posing these questions, environmental justice presented a mix of

---

[10] See Paul Mohai and Robin Saha, *Which Came First, People or Pollution?*, 10 ENVTL. RES. LETTERS 115008 (2015) for a valuable assessment of this literature and argument for an integrated view of the causal factors.

structural and cultural criticisms of mainstream environmental law and politics. On the structural side, environmental concern distributed protection and preservation unevenly, in ways that tracked and amplified other dimensions of inequality. On the cultural side, mainstream environmental concern disproportionately expressed the experience and concern of middle-class and professional white Americans – not only the hazards that were salient to them, but their ideas about why the natural world matters and what kind of relation to it human beings should cultivate.

The emergence of environmental justice claims is often traced to two developments in the late 1970s and 1980s: the toxics movement and the identification of environmental racism. The discovery that some 22,000 barrels of discarded toxic waste had entered the soil and water supply of residential neighborhoods and a public school in Love Canal, New York, visiting high rates of leukemia, miscarriages and chromosome damage on mostly working-class residents, proved to be a grim paradigm for the grassroots anti-pollution politics that became known as the toxics movement.[11] Although they eventually drew the support of the Carter Administration and helped to spur the passage of Superfund legislation, Lois Gibbs and her Love Canal neighbors were largely ignored by local officials and the Hooker Chemical Company during years of grassroots investigative work into pervasive and unexplained illness.[12] Love Canal's catastrophe became emblematic as communities around the country confronted the buried, often conveniently half-forgotten, legacy of several decades of largely unregulated chemical waste disposal that followed World War Two.

At the same time, new regimes for dealing with hazardous waste and ordinary municipal trash presented siting decisions: Where to put the bad stuff? These decisions, all too predictably, seemed to follow the familiar lines of least political and economic resistance. In 1982, another emblematic confrontation arose, this one in Warren County, North Carolina, a rural, poor and majority-black county in the state's coastal plain. North Carolina's government had selected a tract of state-owned land in Warren County for disposal of soil contaminated by the illegal roadside dumping of 31,000 gallons of PCB-contaminated oils. The owners of the oils had

---

11 *See, e.g.*, Sedina Banks, *The "Erin Brockovich Effect": How Media Shapes Toxics Policy*, 26 Environs Envtl. L. & Pol'y J. 219, 224–27 (2003); *see also Love Canal*, Ctr. for Health, Env't & Justice, available 16 January 2017 at http://chej.org/about-us/story/love-canal/.

12 Nathalie Schils, *Love Canal Residents Campaign for Clean Environment, New York, USA, 1978–1980*, Global Nonviolent Action Database (22 June 2011), available 16 January 2017 at http://nvdatabase.swarthmore.edu/content/love-canal-residents-campaign-clean-environment-new-york-usa-1978-1980.

flushed it along some 240 miles of state roads rather than dispose of it in an approved facility.[13] County residents did not stop the landfill, but they drew national attention with protests that included blocking dump-trucks with their bodies. Five hundred and fifty were arrested for peaceful protest, eliciting comparisons to the Civil Rights movement.[14]

Both episodes saw popular mobilization arise outside the arrangements of official decision-making and unofficial but well-established advocacy (such as the Natural Resources Defense Council and the Environmental Defense Fund) that had emerged from the 1970s irruption of environmental lawmaking and activism. The movements' working-class and African American makeup sharply distinguished it from what the 1987 United Church of Christ report would call mainstream environmentalism's "white middle and upper class" constituency.[15]

Environmental justice advocates were also distinct from more familiar forms of environmentalism in several other ways. Their motives were local, defensive and immediate, a result of their having come to the issues for quite urgent and concrete reasons: because they were being poisoned, or felt themselves in danger of being, and their formal requests for official attention had been ignored. While mainstream environmentalism had always blended jeremiad and eulogy, dire warnings with praise for the places, species and harmonies that could still be saved, the new environmental justice movements mainly omitted the second, more poetic appeal. William Cronon's great corrective essay on environmentalists' tendency to idealize wild places and ignore ordinary ones, "The Trouble with Wilderness", might have been even sharper had it considered the race-and-class perspective implicit in environmental justice demands.[16]

Mainstream environmentalists have been able to make a great deal of everyday poetry with campus farms, farmers' markets, backyard gardens, and a sometimes overdone appreciation of the aesthetics of decay; but the poor, run-down and toxic places that have produced the environmental justice movement have not drawn so much love.

---

13 Kathleen Onorevole, *Warren County, NC: Birthplace of Environmental Justice*, UNDERTHEC BLOG (15 January 2016), available 16 January 2017 at https://underthecblog.org/2016/01/15/warren-county-nc-birthplace-of-environmental-justice/.

14 *Environmental Justice History*, DEPT. OF ENERGY, available 16 January 2017 at http://energy.gov/lm/services/environmental-justice/environmental-justice-history.

15 COMM'N FOR RACIAL JUSTICE, TOXIC WASTE AND RACE IN THE UNITED STATES xi (1987), available 16 January 2017 at www.nrc.gov/docs/ML1310/ML13109A339.pdf.

16 William Cronon, *The Trouble with Wilderness; Or, Getting Back to the Wrong Nature*, *in* UNCOMMON GROUND: RETHINKING THE HUMAN PLACE IN NATURE 69 (Norton 1996).

Nor did environmental justice activists appeal mainly to the costs-and-benefits balancing version of social rationality that came to matter so much to some mainstream environmentalists and to agency decision-makers. The environmental justice argument was closer to the people impacted. Whatever process had led to the dumping, concealment or siting decision that immediately jeopardized them, it was suspect because of its fruits: an immediate threat that, typically, fit a pattern of social vulnerability and official indifference.

The most visible federal law achievement of the environmental justice movement has been President Clinton's 1994 Executive Order 12,898, which directs all federal agencies to "make achieving environmental justice part of [their] mission by identifying and addressing . . . disproportionately high and adverse human health or environmental effects . . . on minority . . . and low-income populations".[17] It hardly needs saying that EO 12,898 is in itself a rather small victory, especially because the courts have held that the disparate impacts, to which it draws agencies' attention, do not form the basis of individual causes of action under Title VI of the Civil Rights Act.[18]

The idea of environmental justice has, nonetheless, gained a significant foothold across environmental policy and politics. No environmental group or agency will profess indifference to environmental justice, and groups such as EarthJustice and Natural Resources Defense Council have made significant commitments to it. These commitments involve both substantive choice of cases and the procedures of attorney-client relations. The latter change involves their reforms to be more responsive to and collaborative with local communities than an older model of "swooping down with an agenda".[19]

Now claims of environmental justice form part of the lexicon of mainstream advocacy, from mobilizing constituents and organizations to getting media attention. Anecdotal evidence suggests that such claims have made a difference in more siting and funding disputes than a thorough review of the *Federal Register* would reveal. Environmental justice is now a part of environmental law and politics. Its practical consequences, however, have been somewhat uncertain and slow-moving, while its import for the field as a whole remains ambiguous: is it a supplemental consideration mainly relevant to implementing familiar goals or a challenge to the identity and priorities of environmental law and politics generally?

---

[17] Exec. Order No. 12,898, 3 C.F.R. § 859 (1995).

[18] *Alexander v. Sandoval*, 532 U.S. 275, 305 (2001).

[19] *See, e.g.*, Jedediah Purdy, *Environmentalism's Racist History*, New Yorker (13 August 2015), available 16 January 2017 at http://www.newyorker.com/news/news-desk/environmentalisms-racist-history.

B. A Mobilized Challenge to the Statutory and Institutionalized Priorities of Mainstream Environmentalism

Both critics and celebrators of modern environmental law have often emphasized its disruptive elements: the sense of crisis in which it was born, amid warnings of mass poisoning and even the extinction of life on earth; the widespread perception that it represented a challenge to a modern worldview described variously as technological, rationalist or economic; and the linked call for new forms of governance and new forms of consciousness. Viewed in full, however, mainstream environmentalism presents a blend of radical and complacent elements: radical about the scope of the threat the environmental crisis presented, but complacent, or at least self-confident, about the adequacy of largely familiar legal tools to answer the threat. It was also radical in the challenge to familiar human relations to the natural world that environmental reformers claimed to see, but self-confident that the path to a different worldview was clear.

Then the environmental justice movement emerged and, among other things, diagnosed the blind spots of this specific marriage of alarm and self-confidence among the creators of environmental law.

There were blind spots in both the constitutive and the distributive dimensions of environmental justice. On the constitutive side, early spokespersons for the environmentalist perspective were confident that they knew what it meant to speak for nature. On the distributive side, they tended not to concern themselves with unintended but systemic inequities in the distribution of environmental benefits and – especially – harms because they believed, in keeping with the defining assumptions of the mid-twentieth century, that problems of inequality had basically been sorted out: that the economy did not tend to produce intolerable or accelerating levels of inequality and that, where it might, the state would step in to redistribute appropriately.

Here is an opening example. The famous proposal of the dissenters in *Sierra Club v. Morton* that "trees should have standing". They drew this from Christopher Stone's famous 1972 article arguing for standing for natural entities. This was a colorful legal fiction addressing the idea that certain advocacy groups, notably the Sierra Club, should have automatic standing to assert what they regarded as the interests of rivers, forests, species and so forth.[20] Justice Blackmun's unremembered dissent made

---

[20] *Sierra Club v. Morton*, 405 U.S. 727, 736 (1972); *see also* Christopher D. Stone, Should Trees Have Standing? – Toward Legal Rights for Natural Objects (W. Kaufmann 1974).

this explicit, arguing that such groups should have automatic standing as representatives of the "public interest" in conservation, a position that some lower courts, notably the Second Circuit, had adopted in environmental litigation.[21] What is striking in the standing argument is that a unified idea of the public's interest in conservation presupposes a homogeneous public, at least in its attitudes toward the natural world. With that presupposition in place, the image of litigation in the name of nature fits perfectly within the legal-liberal idea that procedural advocacy can complete a pluralist scheme of political representation by inserting the voices of the under-represented into official decision-making processes – here, the voices of literally voiceless natural entities. But, of course, the thought makes sense only if one knows what, so to speak, the voiceless would wish to say.

Reformers in the early period of modern environmental law thought they knew, because they tended not to encounter contradiction. Indeed, Jaffe's 1976 report on the Ford Foundation's involvement in public-interest law responded to the question, "Are there substantial interests in the community that do not get represented adequately because of the way in which public interest law firms tend to choose their clientele?" with the following reassurance: "[M]ost of the time public interest law firms represent established and well-informed groups or organizations. The environmental . . . cases are the best examples of this."[22] The report had already praised the environmental firms' litigation review boards as stabilizing forces. In other words, he defined environmental public interest by reference to a consensus-oriented elite establishment, partly drawn from existing groups such as the Sierra Club whose Legal Defense Fund, along with other mainstream environmental groups, Ford funded. Some may have seen this tight circle of insiders as cause for worry, but in this report it served as evidence that the public interest is properly conceived and represented in environmental litigation.

The consensus-oriented environmentalism being described here, and the broader consensus of which it was a late representative, were always under more pressure than the confident self-narration of Ford Foundation reports suggests. These were, after all, the decades of the Goldwater campaign (1964) and the violence-wracked Democratic National Convention in Chicago (1968). By the early 1970s, left-leaning writers in the *New York Review of Books* were denouncing environmentalism as a pastoral politi-

---

[21] *Sierra Club v. Morton*, 405 U.S. 727, 757–58 (Blackmun, J., dissenting).

[22] Sanford M. Jaffe, *Public Interest Law – Five Years Later*, 62 A.B.A.J. 982, 985 (1976).

cal sedative, while President Nixon, who had prominently tried to seize the environmental mantle, vetoed the 1972 Clean Water Act, which was re-passed in a congressional override.

Between 1975 and 1980, any impression that consensus environmentalism stood astride the field – as Jaffe's report had suggested, describing environmental public-interest firms as moving from litigation to cooperative regulation-writing with welcoming officials – became much harder to sustain. The Sagebrush rebellion broke out in Western states, announcing a wave of agitation against post-1970 environmental laws, often around their application to grazing, logging, and mining concessions on public lands, and in 1980 presidential candidate Ronald Reagan pronounced himself a "Sagebrush rebel" and set the New Right wing of the Republican party on a populist-plus-extractivist course of conflict with environmentalists.[23]

As a challenge to mainstream environmentalism, the environmental justice movement was, in certain ideological and demographic respects, symmetrical to the right-wing rebellion: a mobilized denial that the statutory and institutionalized priorities of consensus environmentalism captured the questions closest to the interests and experience of major constituencies. It was, then, part of a larger decline in influence of a particular formulation of the public interest, its scope, and the identity of its authoritative representatives.[24]

The themes to which the environmental justice movement draws attention are the ones that will demand attention from any environmentalism able to achieve full relevance in circumstances where the contingent certainties of its origin-place no longer hold: that decisions always have distributive dimensions, and that they also have participatory dimensions in that they express one view rather than another of which problems are environmental and who has those problems.

---

[23] *See, e.g.*, Robert L. Fischman and Jerimiah I. Williamson, *The Story of Kleppe v. New Mexico: The Sagebrush Rebellion as Un-Cooperative Federalism*, 83 U. Colo. L. Rev. 123, 158–62 (2011).

[24] See Jedediah Purdy, After Nature: A Politics for the Anthropocene 228–55 (Harvard University Press 2015) for more depth on the historical moment of the early 1970s, in which a fleeting but generative view of the nature and stakes of environmental law left its mark on both statutes and institutions before being fragmented by dissenters left and right.

C. What is an Environmental Question? What is a Question of Justice?

As discussed, this chapter orients itself amidst those arguing that the planet has entered the Anthropocene, a new geological era in which human activity has become a force in the Earth's development.[25] Various earth scientists and historians emphasize different threshold events in proposing borderlines ("golden spikes", in the parlance) for the Anthropocene: the Columbian encounter, the Industrial Revolution, the so-called "great acceleration" in global resource use and concomitant ecological footprint following World War Two, and the detonation of the atomic bomb. This chapter is less focused on the geo-stratigraphic question of what criteria should establish a geological era than on a theoretical point that discussion of the Anthropocene implies there is no longer a stable boundary between what is natural and what is made. The world we inhabit will be, in substantial part, the world we have helped to make, from the chemistry of the atmosphere and the oceans to patterns of land use and biodiversity.

It is important to recognize that human conversations about "nature" are very frequently displaced conversations about politics, economic order, justice and identity. They probe questions of what dispensation of power is natural, who belongs to a continent (and to whom it belongs), what kinds of cooperation may arise spontaneously, and so forth. This recognition is logically and historically independent of stratigraphic arguments. It is very clearly established in the work of Thomas Hobbes, who drew it from the Renaissance revival of Lucretius's Epicurean thought. John Stuart Mill developed the argument rigorously, and modern feminist and critical race scholarship have brought it to the central categories of social life.[26] Much of the generation of environmental history and environmental studies that emerged with and has grown from Cronon's "Trouble with Wilderness" has explored this theme.[27] To be made useful, it has to be brought into a rather more particular cultural and political context – and at that point "the Anthropocene" can as well drop out.

The contemporary discussion of environmental justice takes place in just such a context. As noted in the first part of this Chapter, the "environmental" in environmental justice can be traced to a quite particular moment, roughly the 1960s in the United States, when a set of

---

[25] *See generally Id.* (discussing the interrelatedness of humans and the environment).

[26] *See, e.g.*, John Stuart Mill, The Subjection of Women (1869); John Stuart Mill, On Nature (1904).

[27] *See, e.g.*, Uncommon Ground: Rethinking the Human Place in Nature, *supra* n 16.

problems were newly grouped together under the label *environmental*: pesticides and other toxins (but more as they affected "third parties" than in their effects on agricultural workers), nuclear fallout (but not other side-effects of geopolitical conflict, such as the global proliferation of inexpensive automatic weapons), litter (but not the decrepit condition of public institutions in neglected neighborhoods), urban congestion and sprawl (but not the prevalence of asthma – and, if asthma, then not diabetes – in poor communities), biodiversity (but not yet the diversity of crops in agriculture and their relation to larger patterns of ecological health), and the management of public lands (but not the condition of public infrastructure). Although these "environmental" questions exhibit a certain family resemblance and make up a perfectly usable category, it is much less clear that they reflect a classification that would command any particular sense of coherence outside the historical constellation of concerns in which "the environment" moved to the center of American public concern.

Today, the "environmental" category has experienced a spontaneous expansion that threatens (or promises) to leave it without much use inasmuch as it is defined by a set of substantive concerns. Climate change is surely the environmental problem *par excellence*; but to address it is to address infrastructure, energy, agriculture and transport. Meanwhile, its effects implicate geopolitical conflict, urgent questions of global distributive justice and national responsibility, and refugee policy.

Even apart from their bearing on climate change, agricultural food systems and energy have moved to the forefront of concern among people who think of themselves as working on environmental issues. Each of these developments is well-founded, and they add an emerging appreciation that the collective human metabolism with the planet's cycles (hydrological, carbon, nitrogen, etc.), as mediated through our built environments (our fertilized, irrigated, and tiled farmlands; our energy grids; our highways and cities) is environmental if anything is environmental.

What, then, is not environmental? Surely genetic engineering is environmental, for it will shape both agriculture and biodiversity; the patterns of investment and research into energy technologies are hugely important environmental questions, as environmentalist college graduates indicate when they light out for Silicon Valley start-ups; bitcoin is an environmental problem, for the data processing connected with this entirely immaterial, non-sovereign currency turns out to be terrifically energy-intensive – and in that respect only one of many superficially disembodied aspects of the twenty-first century economy whose effects are massively material and straightforwardly environmental. What is excluded?

The question looks even more vexed when we turn to the effects of environmental conditions – that which surrounds or *environs* us, in the old sense of the world – on human beings. Intensified awareness of inequality has brought sharpened attention to what one might call the human ecology of unequal life-prospects: the ways that the neighborhood or town in which one finds oneself shapes one's life expectancy and prospects for mobility in income and education, holding constant the income or wealth of one's family.[28] Some public health scholars have begun to explore the role of socially induced trauma – exposure to violence, bigotry and deprivation at an early age, for instance – in producing later behavioral pathologies that, in turn, make physical ailment or injury more likely.[29] Are these ways that people's setting infiltrates their bodies and shapes their lives not environmental? Are they not, as much as droughts caused by climate change, a matter of how a setting formed from a blend of natural and made elements shapes the health and capabilities of those who inhabit it?

If one is inclined to say that these are not environmental problems, what would make the difference? Would it be enough to introduce the question of access to public parks, exposure to lead, or availability of healthy food? Wouldn't this be just making a criterion from a familiar habit of thought – that we know an issue is environmental because of the presence of a well-recognized pollutant, or the role of soil or a glimpse of a tree somewhere in the problem? Is that really more than a fetish doing double duty as a definition? Have we reached a point where "environmental justice" is another way of saying "public health", and vice-versa? What, then, is the former category doing for us?

What we call "environmental justice" is quite historically particular. In its most familiar version, it follows other aspects of the civil-rights revolution in pointing to the exclusions and blind spots of the twentieth-century liberalism that produced modern environmental law. Environmental justice mostly follows the substance of received ideas about what it is for a problem to be "environmental". In more probing versions, it pushes the idea of what is "environmental" toward the limits of coherence and tends to merge "environmental" concerns with those of public health. It emerged with the modern, familiar, and now troubled category of

---

28 See, e.g., Raj Chetty, et al., *The Effects of Exposure to Better Neighborhoods on Children: New Evidence from the Moving to Opportunity Project*, 106 Am. Econ. Rev. 1 (2016).

29 *Adverse Childhood Experiences*, Ctrs. for Disease Control and Prevention, available 16 January 2017 at http://www.cdc.gov/violenceprevention/acestudy/ (last updated 1 April 2016) (reviewing research on "adverse childhood experiences" and their long-term effects).

"environmental", and may be following that category into some combination of dissolution and reconstitution in new form.

None of this is intended in a spirit of hostility or debunking; quite the contrary. It does suggest, however, that "environmental justice" thinking cannot rely very far, into the future or in the scope of issues, on unquestioned definitions of either *environmental* or *justice*. That both of these are historical and contested categories seems to me an encouraging rather than a disheartening conclusion. There are at least two ways that environmental justice, as it has developed until now, might serve as a basis for generative engagement with both categories.

Call the first approach methodological and the second substantive, if only to fix ideas. Methodologically, previous environmental justice work has drawn attention to the distributive dimensions of policies that had not been mainly cast in distributive terms: air pollution laws and siting waste facilities, for instance. In this respect, environmental justice makes explicit and debates the distribution of things that, to put it perhaps a bit too cutely, we had not known (or acknowledged) that we were distributing. This insight applies at many scales, from global climate change to local food systems.

This methodological concern is particularly apposite because, as research on the contribution of neighborhood and municipality to lifespan suggests, what is being distributed may often not show up in a standard list of resources eligible for transfer, such as income supplements or job training. Aggregate health and capability may emerge from too many factors, too subtly related, for a straightforward accounting given present levels of knowledge. Yet it is very clear that in the social ecology of institutions, infrastructure, markets and so forth that people inhabit together, their health or suffering, capability or constraint, emerges. In making one another's worlds, we make one another's lives. One might regard this as an ecological way of thinking about the substance of justice generally: that the question of distributive justice is, in good part, the question whether we create a world in which people can live well.

The methodological prompt from environmental justice thus moves in two directions: it poses distributive questions to regimes of system design and management where these questions might otherwise be omitted. And it contributes to questions already recognized as problems of distributive justice by emphasizing that what is to be distributed sometimes cannot be reduced to a list of resources and rights to which an individual may claim – primary goods, to use Rawls's term – but must be understood as a matter of the features of an institutional and social ecology. The first point might be summarized in the claim that managing the environment is always a matter of justice, the latter in the claim that justice is frequently a matter of the character of one's environment. Seen in this way, the many specific problems and conflicts that have produced today's environmental justice practice are instances of more general intersections between justice and environment, and invitations to think of these systematically.

This discussion so far has focused on what I called at the opening of this chapter the distributive dimension of environmental justice. The constitutive dimension also matters here. The earlier historical discussion of environmental justice themes emphasized that the shaping and management of the human relation to the natural world have always picked out, promoted, and naturalized *somebody*'s nature, culturally specific, paradigmatic encounters, experiences and uses of the non-human world at the center of their concerns. That history alerts us to the constitutive dimension of environmental justice going forward: *whose* actual and ideal relations with the natural world figure in policy-making to shape cities, landscapes, and global ecology?

It is all too easy, though not less important for that reason, to point out cases of sharp disparity: climate change notoriously jeopardizes coastal and small-island communities and lives on marginal arable and grazing lands, even as the communities most vulnerable to these changes tend to be ones that have made the least contribution to, and benefited least from, the fossil-fuel based high consuming countries that are transforming the global atmosphere. Revivals of artisanal farming dot the Hudson Valley, pockets of Northern California, and the Piedmont near Charlottesville and Chapel Hill, which are often staffed by scions of prosperous families and the products of elite education. Meanwhile, the industrial-scale hog farms of North Carolina and fruit and vegetable operations of the Imperial Valley of California are worked by immigrant (primarily Latino) populations who, a generation ago, might have been working at small-scale agriculture that has since disappeared in competition with the same industries that now employ them.

The general question is a political one with environmental consequences: whose world do we make? Acknowledging that arguments about the meaning and value of "nature" have always been entangled with cultural politics, with the assertion and counter-assertion of aesthetics, practices, and other aspects of identity, could lead to a comprehensive disenchantment, a determination to treat the natural world as simply a standing reserve of resources to be put to entirely instrumental uses. Alternatively, it could lead to a determination, not to shut down the cultural and political argument about the meaning and value of the non-human world, but to recognize it as a thoroughly human argument, in which transparency, voice and other values of participation matter as they matter elsewhere in collective life. In this respect, the constitutive dimension of environmental justice points to the questions of whose vision is being woven into a half-made world; who chose that vision, and how; and which possible future visions it might foster or foreclose.

Both the distributive and the constitutive dimensions of environmental justice, as described here, would be at the very heart of a version of environmentalism that could serve the transition to, and flourishing of, a new economy.

IV. CONCLUSION

The world is the product of both natural forces and human activity. Thus, egalitarian environmentalism would view the world as presumptively common because it is both given and made, making the world's inequalities everyone's responsibility. Environmentalism should fully incorporate environmental justice in order to advance the goals of both the egalitarian and a cooperative economy. Such an environmentalism would be deeply shaped by economic inequality and the concept of the Anthropocene.

The modern environmental movement should see that managing the environment is always a matter of justice, and that justice is frequently a matter of the character of one's environment. Seen in this way, the many specific problems and conflicts that have produced today's environmental justice practice are instances of more general intersections between justice and environment, and invitations to think of these systematically.

4. Reframing rights and responsibilities to prioritize nature

Catherine Iorns Magallanes and Linda Sheehan

I. INTRODUCTION

The legal framework for the global economy is one based on private property, particularly property over nature. This property framework sees humanity's relationship with nature as one of command and control, whereby humans are separate from and above nature, and are entitled to use it as a resource for our own need and greed. The first three chapters outlined how we need to change our economy to one that recognizes and fosters a different set of relationships. We need an economy that better serves the needs of the Earth and the humans on it, rather than the other way around; one that allows for humans acting in community with others, rather than solely as competing individuals; and thus one where ecological integrity, social justice, and a vibrant democracy are central.

If we want to encourage the emergence of such a new economy, then the legal framework that supports it will need to change. Moreover, this change will need to reflect or embody a very different mindset or paradigm, if we are to achieve the kind of economy that is envisaged in this book. It will have to move from an exclusionary system based on human property rights over nature, to one based on responsibilities for nature that includes respect for all life forms and systems. It will need to abandon the fiction that we are all separate from and independent of nature, to recognize we are all part of and completely dependent for our survival on the Earth and its systems.

As Meadows writes, changing society's "great big unstated assumptions" about how the world works is one of the most effective ways to ensure lasting, meaningful change. Such assumptions include "[g]rowth is good", nature is merely a "stock of resources", and "[o]ne can 'own' land".[1] These anthropocentric paradigms underlie our existing environmental laws

[1] Donella Meadows, The Sustainability Inst., Leverage Points: Places

today, and are the primary reason for their failure to reverse environmental degradation. Only such a paradigmatic shift in mindset can support the Earth-centered laws and economic systems we need in order to live in harmony with nature.

This chapter outlines the essentials of a legal framework that arises from a paradigm that recognizes the importance of nature and re-prioritizes humans' place within it. We focus on three essential elements: the recognition of the intrinsic value of nature, the recognition of inherent rights of nature, and the establishment of a framework of human responsibility for nature. Such a legal framework would entail a paradigm shift; however, adoption of such elements in law can also help achieve such a shift in mindset as well as in practice. To this end, this chapter includes examples of existing and proposed laws adopting these three essential and intertwined elements.

First the chapter discusses the recognition of the intrinsic value of nature, providing some examples of laws and policies which do this. Then it discusses the adoption of legal rights for nature, again with examples. Finally, it addresses laws that establish human responsibility for nature, providing examples from Aotearoa[2] New Zealand. Adoption of these legal elements can produce a law and policy framework that better serves the Earth community, both people and nature flourishing together. This can help us build thriving, relationship-based communities and correct our currently upside-down ordering within the dominant global political-economic system, of economy first, then human and then nature's well-being.

II. RESPECT FOR THE INTRINSIC VALUE OF NATURE

One of the first and most fundamental aspects of an ecocentric approach is to recognize in law the intrinsic value of the environment. Nature exists and has value for its own purposes, not just for human use. Being part of a world community of all life entails respect for all life, for its own sake. This does not mean that humans can never use the environment. It does mean that we have to assume that there is value in nature existing, and that human uses and desires won't consistently shunt nature aside.

TO INTERVENE WITHIN A SYSTEM (1999), available 23 January 2017 at http://donellameadows.org/archives/leverage-points-places-to-intervene-in-a-system/.

[2] This is the Maori term for New Zealand.

International and domestic laws worldwide are increasingly referring to the intrinsic value of nature. For example, the 1992 Convention on Biological Diversity refers in its preamble to the "intrinsic value of biological diversity".[3] The World Charter for Nature asserts that we humans are "a part of nature and life depends on the uninterrupted functioning of natural systems".[4]

A key example of the recognition of intrinsic value is contained in the Earth Charter.[5] While it is not a binding agreement, it provides an excellent example of a holistic, ecocentric approach to a legal framework. The very first principle of the Earth Charter recognizes "that all beings are interdependent and every form of life has value regardless of its worth to human beings".[6] The Earth Charter illustrates that, once we recognize the intrinsic value of nature and our interdependence on it, we can more easily open the way for increased protection of all life. It similarly more easily leads to duties of human responsibility for nature's care,[7] such as through the adoption of concepts such as guardianship.

More recently, the United Nations has adopted several resolutions and reports on Harmony with Nature. The stated driving ethos for the Harmony with Nature program has been respect for nature: "Nature and her intrinsic value must be revered and honoured."[8] Recent reports and UN General Assembly resolutions stress the need to move away from an anthropocentric approach to our relationship with the Earth – or "Mother Nature" – toward a more ecocentric approach.[9] As a 2015 report has

---

[3] United Nations, Convention on Biological Diversity (1992), available 23 January 2017 at https://www.cbd.int/doc/legal/cbd-en.pdf.

[4] G.A. Res. 37/7, (28 October 1982), available 23 January 2017 at http://www.un.org/documents/ga/res/37/a37r007.htm.

[5] Earth Charter Initiative (2000), available 23 January 2017 at http://earthcharter.org/.

[6] *The Earth Charter, Principle I*, Earth Charter Comm'n, available 23 January 2017 at http://earthcharter.org/discover/the-earth-charter/.

[7] *See, e.g.*, India Const. Art. 51A(g) ("It shall be the duty of every citizen of India . . . (g) to protect and improve the natural environment including forests, lakes, rivers and wild life, and to have compassion for living creatures").

[8] Harmony with Nature, Rep. of the Sec'y-Gen. on its Sixty-Fifth Session, U.N. Doc. A/66/302, at ¶ 79 (2011).

[9] *See, e.g.*, "It is therefore essential to go beyond the anthropocentric vision that has led us to live in a state of crisis in all the three dimensions of sustainable development environmental, social and economic. It is necessary to start thinking and designing a world where human and natural interests are balanced by greater respect for the Earth." Interactive Dialogue of the General Assembly on Harmony with Nature, Harmony with Nature United Nations, available 23 January 2017 at http://harmonywithnatureun.org/dialogues.html; *see also* Harmony with

noted, "our current worldview that the Earth is our exploitable property needs to move towards an Earth-centred worldview in which respect towards the Earth can grow."[10] One aspect of this is the need for Earth-centred laws – or Earth jurisprudence – to form the basis of any human governance or regulatory system, in order for it to be in true harmony with nature.[11] In 2015, the UN requested a report from Earth jurisprudence experts internationally to help guide implementation of its Sustainable Development Goals.[12] It released this expert report in August 2016,[13] with updates to follow.

The Earth jurisprudence, or Earth Law movement, is a movement dedicated to advocating for adoption and implementation of these principles in the world's legal systems.[14] While it is a modern movement, the worldview it espouses arises from ancient influences as confirmed by modern science, such as the understanding that we are part of and dependent upon the natural world, not separate or above it.

Our legal and governance systems typically state that they recognize our integration with the natural world, such as through a stated recognition of our dependence on ecosystem "services" and thus our need to protect them in law and policy. However, Earth jurisprudence takes the next step by attempting to recognize in law and governance the two-way essence

---

NATURE UNITED NATIONS, available 23 January 2017 at http://harmonywithnature un.org/.

[10] Harmony with Nature, Report of the Secretary-General on its Seventieth Session, U.N. Doc, A/70/268, at ¶ 32 (2015) (quoting Dr Robin Wall Kimmerer, Presentation at Interactive Dialogue of the General Assembly on Harmony with Nature (27 April 2015)).

[11] *See, e.g.*, *Rights of Nature Law and Policy*, HARMONY WITH NATURE UNITED NATIONS, available 23 January 2017 at http://harmonywithnatureun.org/rightsof nature.html; *see also* Sustainable Development: Harmony with Nature, Report of the Second Committee on its Seventieth Session, U.N. Doc A/70/472/Add.7, at 5 (2015) (deciding to initiate a dialogue in 2016 with "experts on Earth jurisprudence worldwide").

[12] G.A. Res. A/RES/70/208, ¶ 2 (17 February 2016).

[13] Harmony with Nature, Note by the Secretary-General on its Seventy-first Session, U.N. Doc, A/71/266 (1 August 2016).

[14] See Catherine Iorns Magallanes, *New Thinking on Sustainability* 13 N.Z.J. PUB. INT'L L. 1, 9–12 (2015), for a summary of the principles and application of Earth jurisprudence. The movement has also been referred to by the term 'Wild Law'. CORMAC CULLINAN, WILD LAW: A MANIFESTO FOR EARTH JUSTICE (Chelsea Green Pub 2002). This term is still used, particularly in the UK. *See, e.g.*, EXPLORING WILD LAW: THE PHILOSOPHY OF EARTH JURISPRUDENCE (Peter Burdon (ed.), Wakefield Press 2011); WILD LAW – IN PRACTICE (Michelle Maloney and Peter Burdon (eds), Routledge 2014). More recently, 'Rights of Nature' has been growing in use as a label for the movement, especially in the USA.

of our relationship with the Earth – one not where humans exercise their "rights" to nature and its services, but where we exercise reciprocal obligations and duties to ensure the well-being of all. Instead of anthropocentric dominance and control, it suggests that we need to adopt an ecocentric approach to law and governance if we are to maintain an appropriate natural balance for all life on Earth. As the Earth is the source of (natural) laws which govern all life upon it, the Earth law movement argues that our human community accordingly must recognize and comply with Earth's laws. It thus works to embed this broader worldview of relationships in our legal and other institutions.

The key principles of Earth jurisprudence are well articulated in cultural historian Thomas Berry's writings, such as *The Great Work*.[15] The key foundational principle, as described by Berry, is that the universe is the primary source of law; human laws and legal and governance systems are only derivative. Berry describes the universe as a "communion of subjects" rather than a "collection of objects", and argues that nature has inherent value and an inherent right to exist. Berry further directs that humans must live in accordance with the relationships and principles that constitute the Earth community, and therefore "that human governance systems at all times must take account of the interests of the whole Earth community".[16]

These fundamental principles of Earth jurisprudence parallel those of indigenous societies, where guardianship and stewardship of – and relationship with – nature is emphasized as part of treating the natural world with more respect and even reverence. Implications of these fundamental principles include requirements that humans must:[17]

- determine the lawfulness of human conduct by whether or not it strengthens or weakens the relationships that constitute the Earth community;
- maintain a dynamic balance between the rights of humans and those of other members of the Earth community on the basis of what is best for Earth as a whole.

A suggested implication is that all laws and legal systems must "recognise all members of the Earth community as subjects before the law, with the right to the protection of the law and to an effective remedy for human acts that

---

15 Thomas Berry, The Great Work: Our Way into the Future (Bell Tower 1999).

16 Cormac Cullinan, *History of Wild Law*, *in* Exploring Wild Law 12, 12–13 *supra* note 14.

17 *Id.*

violate their fundamental rights".[18] The rights of any single being in turn "are limited by the rights of other beings, to the extent necessary to maintain the integrity, balance and health of the communities within which it exists".

III. LEGAL RIGHTS OF NATURE[19]

In our current, rights-based legal systems, respect and responsibility are acknowledged through legal rights. Therefore, one method for reordering the priority between humans and the environment is to recognize in law the inherent rights of nature. Berry suggests that, within the rights-oriented paradigm within which human societies have ordered themselves,[20] "Rights come with existence. That which confers existence confers rights."[21] The logic of inherent human rights extends to the natural world with which we co-evolved. Recognition of nature's inherent rights to exist, to have habitat, and to "fulfil its role in the ever-renewing processes of the Earth community" is essential for us to build the relationships with the natural world we have been ignoring.[22] Recognition in law and policy of inherent rights can build healthy relationships with and within society, by correcting our error of ignoring those rights in the past.

Christopher Stone made arguments for recognition of the rights of nature in his seminal "Should Trees Have Standing", released in 1972.[23] Stone listed four elements as necessary to recognize effectively the rights of an entity in law:[24]

---

18 *Id.*

19 See Linda Sheehan, *Implementing Rights of Nature Through Sustainability Bills of Rights* 13 N.Z.J. Pub. Int'l L. 89 (2015), for a more detailed discussion of this topic. Some parts of this are reused here with permission.

20 The members of the United Nations Committee drafting the Universal Declaration of Human Rights were asked if they were creating new human rights. They responded that human rights do not come from the committee, or a king, or a Parliament. Rather, rights come from existence. As the drafting committee wrote, "the supreme value of the human person . . . did not originate in the decision of a worldly power, but rather in the fact of existing." *History of the Document*, United Nations, available 23 January 2017 at http://www.un.org/en/sections/universal-declaration/history-document/.

21 Thomas Berry, *Every Being Has Rights*, *in* Twenty-Third Annual E.F. Schumacher Lectures (Hildegarde Hannum, ed., 2003).

22 Thomas Berry, Evening Thoughts: Reflecting on Earth as a Sacred Community 149–50 (Sierra Club Books 2006).

23 Christopher D. Stone, *Should Trees Have Standing? – Toward Legal Rights for Natural Objects*, 45 S. Cal. L. Rev. 450, 453–56 (1972).

24 *Id.* at 458–9.

- rights must be subject to redress by public body;
- the entity must have standing to institute legal actions on its own behalf (a guardian can stand in for the entity as needed);
- redress must be calculated for the entity's *own* damages; and
- relief must run to the benefit of the injured entity.

Stone emphasizes first and foremost that rights must be enforceable by a public body. Merely observing that nature has rights will not provide the effective force of law; enforcement must be included. As to this point, if our actions damage an ecosystem, the restitution needs to go back to the ecosystem. We do not simply write a cheque to the person who claims to own the ecosystem and then leave it in waste. We actually must try to help restore the damage to the extent we can, just as we would if we had injured another person. Where the damage is not fixable, as is the case for extinct species and permanently destroyed habitats, restorative justice and actions in other areas as appropriate should be undertaken, in a long-term process to rebuild our relationship with the Earth.

A. Nature's Rights in the Constitution of Ecuador

In one recent application, the people of Ecuador voted to amend their Constitution in 2008. Included in these amendments was the first constitutional language in the world to recognize the rights of nature, in light of the perceived need to better protect "Pachamama". Pachamama, analogous to the concept of Mother Earth, is commonly used to represent nature throughout the Andes. Notably, the term embodies not only the physical aspects of the natural world but also its spiritual aspects as well, which require deeper respect than the laws had allowed. Several constitutional provisions address the inherent rights of nature, particularly Articles 71–72. Article 71 states:

> Nature or Pachamama, where life is reproduced and exists, has the right to exist, persist, maintain itself and regenerate its own vital cycles, structure, functions and its evolutionary processes.
>
> Any person, people, community or nationality, may demand the observance of the rights of the natural environment before public bodies . . .

Article 72 addresses restitution, stating that "[n]ature has the right to be completely restored". This language illustrates how the work of scholars and advocates for nature's rights, both in South and North America, has built over time. Article 71's language about rights of nature to maintain and regenerate its "evolutionary processes" also mirrors Berry's thoughts on nature's right to participate in the "ever-renewing processes of the

Earth community". Echoes of Stone's observations can be seen in Article 71's language on enforcement by "any person" before "public bodies". We can also see Stone's influence in Article 72's language regarding relief running back to the injured natural system.

One example of the application of these provisions involved Ecuador's Vilcabamba River. Debris from road construction was pushed into the river, channelling the stream flow and creating flooding downstream. Local landowners sued under the constitutional provisions, asserting violations of the river's right to flow. The Court agreed in an early 2011 decision that the river's constitutional right to flow had been violated, noting that the landowners had standing as a result of Article 71 even if they did not prove damage to themselves. The judge ordered the Provincial Government to restore the ecosystem through measures specified by the Ministry of Environment.[25]

Numerous other judicial and administrative actions have been taken in Ecuador to implement the constitutional provisions relating to nature's rights. A recent study of such actions found examples such as:[26]

- Constitutional law action over biodigestors (2009, initiated by citizens): Constitutional Court identified potential violations of the rights of nature even though citizens had not raised them, and ordered creation of a commission to audit and monitor biodigestors to ensure that the rights of nature were protected. The ruling is significant in that the court acknowledged its right to invoke constitutional articles regarding rights of nature, even when claimants did not specifically assert such rights.
- Administrative and constitutional law actions over shrimping in ecological reserves (2011, initiated by government): Constitutional Court found the rights of nature affect all other rights, and ordered the lower court to re-try the administrative action with nature's rights included in the deliberation.

---

[25] *Vilcabamba River v. Provincial Government of Loja*, No 11121-2011-0010, Judgment (Provincial Justice Court of Loja, 30 March 2011). *See also* Natalia Greene, *The First Successful Case of the Rights of Nature Implementation in Ecuador*, THE RIGHTS OF NATURE, available 23 January 2017 at http://therightsofnature.org/first-ron-case-ecuador/.

[26] CRAIG KAUFFMAN AND PAMELA MARTIN, TESTING ECUADOR'S RIGHTS OF NATURE: WHY SOME LAWSUITS SUCCEED AND OTHERS FAIL," Paper Presented at the International Studies Association Annual Convention (Atlanta, GA, 18 March 2016), available 23 January 2017 at http://www.harmonywithnatureun.org/wordpress/wp-content/uploads/Papers/Testing%20Ecuador%E2%80%99s%20RoN_16_04_20.pdf.

- Criminal action over shark finning (2015, initiated by NGO): Found the rights of sharks had been violated, sentenced captain and crew to prison, and ordered the destruction of the fishing vessel.
- Criminal action over condor killing (2014, initiated by government): Found that killing even one condor violated the species' right to exist because of their endangered status, and ordered the perpetrator to prison.
- Criminal action over jaguar killing (2014, initiated by NGOs and government): Found that killing amounted to a "crime against Nature", and ordered the perpetrator to prison.
- Administrative action over logging (2011, initiated by government): Ordered an indigenous community to pay to restore an area they had illegally logged, citing both the constitutional rights of nature provisions and the Forest Law.

B. The Universal Declaration of the Rights of Mother Earth

Ecuador's leadership was quickly followed by Bolivia and the larger international community.[27] In 2010, in reaction to the widely-perceived failure of the 2009 UN climate change talks in Copenhagen, Bolivia sponsored a World People's Conference on Climate Change and the Rights of Mother Earth in Cochabamba. Upwards of 35,000 people from 140 nations attended. These attendees debated and then approved a Universal Declaration of the Rights of Mother Earth.[28]

Parallel to the structure of the Universal Declaration of Human Rights, the Universal Declaration of the Rights of Mother Earth recognized the "inherent rights of Mother Earth"[29] to the natural world's "life, liberty and security of person".[30] These include the rights of the Earth and all beings to "life and to exist", to "wellbeing" and to "identity and integrity".[31] The Declaration added that those rights, like human rights, "arise from the same source as existence".[32] Like the Declaration of Human Rights, the Universal Declaration of the Rights of Mother Earth

---

[27] PLURINATIONAL STATE OF BOLIVIA [CONSTITUTION] 2009, arts 33–34, 108; *see also* Law of the Rights of Mother Earth (Bol.).

[28] *Rights of Mother Earth*, WORLD PEOPLE'S CONFERENCE ON CLIMATE CHANGE AND THE RIGHTS OF MOTHER EARTH (April 2010), available 23 January 2017 at https://pwccc.wordpress.com/programa/.

[29] *Id.* at art. 1(4).

[30] G.A. Res. 217 A (III), at art. 3 (1948).

[31] *Rights of Mother Earth*, *supra* note 28, at art 2.

[32] *Id.* at art. 1(4).

protects the rights holder – here, the natural world – from the excesses of the state and of humans generally.

C. Rights of Nature in International Agreements

Ecuador, Bolivia and others carried forward this concept of nature's rights to the ongoing UN negotiations around the 20th anniversary of the "Earth Summit", the 1992 UN Conference on Sustainable Development in Rio de Janeiro. The UN anniversary event, or 2012's "Rio+20",[33] referenced nature's rights in the final UN Outcome Document. This formal agreement states that "planet Earth and its ecosystems are our home" and notes that "some countries recognize the rights of nature in the context of the promotion of sustainable development".[34] While limited in its direct implementability, this provision in a unanimously adopted UN agreement starts to build rights of nature language into international debates. The Final Declaration of the parallel Rio+20 People's Summit went further, calling on "governments and people of the world to adopt and implement the Universal Declaration of the Rights of Mother Earth".[35]

Another example arises from the International Union for the Conservation of Nature (IUCN). The IUCN is a worldwide NGO with thousands of partner experts offering scientific, legal and other expertise, and it holds official UN observer and consultative status. In its quadrennial meeting in 2012, the IUCN adopted a resolution recommending that the IUCN incorporate rights of nature consideration into "all levels and in all areas of [IUCN] intervention", create a "strategy for . . . advocacy concerning the Rights of Nature" and begin the development of and promote a "Universal Declaration of the Rights of Nature" as a "first step towards reconciliation between human beings and the Earth as the basis of our lives, as well as the foundations of a new civilizing pact".[36] The IUCN committed to implementation of this resolution in

---

[33] United Nations Conference on Sustainable Development, Rio+20, available 23 January 2017 at https://sustainabledevelopment.un.org/rio20.

[34] G.A. Res. 66/288, U.N. Doc. A/Res/66/288, at ¶ 39 (27 July, 2012).

[35] *Declaration: Peoples' Summit at Rio +20 for Social and Environmental Justice in defence of the Commons, Against the Commodification of Life*, Facilitation Committee of Civil Society for Rio+20 (29 June 2012), available 23 January 2017 at http://rio20.net/en/propuestas/final-declaration-of-the-people%E2%80%99s-summit-in-rio-20/.

[36] Int'l Union for the Conservation of Nature, WCC-2012-Res-100, Incorporation of the Rights of Nature as the Organizational Focal Point in IUCN's Decision Making 2 (2012), available 23 January 2017 at https://portals.iucn.org/library/sites/library/files/resrecfiles/WCC_2012_RES_100_EN.pdf.

its 2017–2020 Programme of work priorities, which "aims to secure the rights of nature".[37] Such action by a global entity as respected worldwide as the IUCN heralds well for future rights of nature discussion at the international level. More recently, the IUCN's World Commission on Environmental Law proposed formal adoption of a Declaration on the Environmental Rule of Law, which provides that "all life has the inherent right to exist".[38]

D. Rights of Nature in Local Laws: Facing down Threats to Community Well-Being

Recognition of the rights of nature in law is also occurring at the local community level. In the United States, about three dozen municipalities have passed local laws to recognize the rights of nature.[39] Virtually all of these laws to date have been passed in response to specific local threats such as proposed coal mining, hydro-fracking, groundwater extraction and other risks to the health and well-being of the communities. These local laws generally ban the destructive activities and reject the corporate rights that support them. They also recognize the rights of nature to be protected from such harms, and so acknowledge in law that nature is an important part of their community to be safeguarded and respected. The laws recognize that the community's well-being depends on a strong relationship with the natural world.

The largest United States city so far to pass such a law is Pittsburgh, Pennsylvania. Their 2010 law bans proposed hydrofracking operations and states that corporations do not hold rights to hydrofrack against the will of the people. The law includes specific provision upholding the rights of natural communities and gives citizens enforcement rights. The key provision reads:[40]

---

[37] Int'l Union for the Conservation of Nature, IUCN Programme 2017–2020 (2016), available 23 January 2017 at https://portals.iucn.org/library/node/46366.

[38] World Envtl. Law Congress, Int'l Union for Conservation of Nature, World Declaration on the Environmental Rule of Law 3 (2016), available 23 January 2017 at http://welcongress.org/wp-content/uploads/2016/06/World-Declaration-on-the-Environmental-Rule-of-Law.pdf. The final text is expected to be voted on at the WCEL meeting in August 2016.

[39] See *Earth Community*, Earth Law Ctr., available 23 January 2017 at http://www.earthlawcenter.org/earth-community, for a map and summary of most of these local laws.

[40] Pittsburgh, Pa., Code ch. 618, art. I, § 618.03(b) (2010) (emphasis added).

> Natural communities and ecosystems, including, but not limited to, wetlands, streams, rivers, aquifers, and other water systems, possess inalienable and fundamental rights to exist and flourish within the City . . . *Residents . . . shall possess legal standing to enforce those rights* on behalf of those natural communities and ecosystems.

Based on data through the end of 2014, although Pittsburgh is surrounded by hydrofracking operations, it has remained free of them and their associated impacts.[41]

With such laws, Pittsburgh and similar communities are beginning to knit together a movement for nature's rights and human democratic rights. Another step forward involves implementing the provisions of such laws into policymaking. This step is being explored actively in Santa Monica, California.

E. Using Local Rights of Nature Laws to Implement our Responsibilities toward Nature

Santa Monica, a sizeable city with a popular beachfront in Southern California, provides a holistic and assertive model for the implementation of nature's rights. Santa Monicans proactively sought out the protection of a rights of nature ordinance in response to the United States Supreme Court's 2010 decision in *Citizens United*, which significantly expanded corporate rights, especially in relation to funding political campaigns.[42] The chief concern raised by City residents was that corporations might insist on the right to act contrary to the wishes and adopted plans of residents for a sustainable Santa Monica.[43]

The City's Task Force on the Environment worked with local citizens, Earth Law Center and others to draft a proposed law to address this concern. It sent to the City Council in late 2012 a proposed ordinance that recognized the rights of Santa Monicans to a healthy environment, and the rights of natural systems themselves to health. The City Council approved the final ordinance unanimously in April 2013.

Santa Monica's Sustainability Rights Ordinance pushes back on corporate claims of superior rights, declaring that "Corporate entities . . .

---

41 Chris Amico, et al., *Shale Play: Natural Gas Drilling in Pennsylvania*, Nat'l Pub. Radio, available 23 January 2017 at http://stateimpact.npr.org/pennsylvania/drilling/.

42 *Citizens United v. Federal Election Comm'n*, 558 US 310, 339–40 (2010).

43 City of Santa Monica, Sustainable City Plan (2014), available 23 January 2017 at https://www.smgov.net/uploadedFiles/Departments/OSE/Categories/Sustainability/Sustainable-City-Plan.pdf.

do not enjoy special privileges or powers under the laws that subordinate the community's rights to their private interests".[44] The ordinance protects the rights of human residents, stating that Santa Monicans possess "fundamental and inalienable rights" to self-governance, as well as rights to: clean water from sustainable sources; a sustainable food system that provides healthy, locally grown food; sustainable energy future based on renewable energy sources; and other rights.[45]

The Sustainability Rights Ordinance also recognizes the integration of citizens with the natural world, stating that "[n]atural communities and ecosystems possess fundamental and inalienable rights to exist and flourish in the City".[46] In another echo of Christopher Stone's work, the ordinance additionally provides for broad enforcement powers, stating that: "To effectuate those rights on behalf of the environment, residents of the City may bring actions to protect these natural communities and ecosystems."[47] The City, for its part, is required to report on implementation of the ordinance and bring the report to a public hearing for resident input.

The City's law defines natural or native ecosystems as "groundwater aquifers, atmospheric systems, marine waters, and native species within the boundaries of the City".[48] Accordingly, one area of Ordinance application that the City and stakeholders are currently examining is control over groundwater extraction. While local "police powers" or the power of the City to protect residents' health, safety and welfare, allow the City to oversee groundwater withdrawals, the state's long history of not regulating such extractions[49] make that task challenging. The Sustainability Rights Ordinance reinforces the City's authority to regulate groundwater extraction, which is important given the aquifer is the City's primary water source and the state has been mired in a multi-year drought. The Ordinance, which protects the rights of the aquifer to flourish, allows the City to potentially enact stronger groundwater extraction controls than would have been called for under current law, which focuses only on human needs. That is, the City can thus establish stronger precautionary controls on use of the aquifer than might have been warranted solely based on police powers. This allows for better long-term management of

---

44 Santa Monica, CA, Municipal Code ch 4.75, § 4.75.040(c) (2013).

45 Id. at § 4.75.040(a).

46 *Id.* at § 4.75.040(b).

47 *Id.*

48 *Id.*

49 California adopted its first statewide groundwater extraction law. Cal. Water Code pt. 2.74 (West 2016).

the aquifer's use, benefitting both people and nature. One way the city has applied this Ordinance is by setting a city goal to become 100 percent self-sufficient for its water supply by 2020.[50]

The Santa Monica ordinance provides a model to consider as we move forward from what we say "no" to (such as hydro-fracking and coal mining) to what we say "yes" to (such as water self-sufficiency). Rights-based laws on paper are important, but a way of life that recognizes the rights of nature is inspiring and necessary. As described in more detail below, we need to envision what society looks and acts like under a system of law that recognizes the inherent rights of nature. As a result, we need more pilot efforts around the world to both build these laws and implement them toward lives in harmony with the Earth. Such pilot efforts will help illustrate how to take this movement up in other communities.

F. Implementing the Rights-Based Approach with Earth-Centred Practice

The legal human rights framework arises out of an individualistic, anthropocentric frame. We recommend in this chapter that we reframe our relationship with the Earth to be eco- or Earth-centered. This involves more than simply "adding rights of nature to the catalogue of the rights of humans".[51] The approach of according legal rights for nature, even to recognize the inherent rights of nature to exist and regenerate, is important, but it must be more than merely a "'quick legal fix', which like many other legal solutions, precludes the deep questions necessary for genuine world change".[52] Rights, including human rights, arose out of the anthropocentric mindset we are trying to change. Thus, even though enacting rights of nature in law is necessary and contributes to a revolution in legal imagination and relationship building, it is insufficient on its own to force a paradigm shift if the rights remain paper-bound.

We can shape this trajectory toward an Earth-centric frame by emphasizing that adoption of the rights of nature in law and economic policy is an important tool, but not the end goal. In its favour, recognition in law of nature's rights is essential to correcting our fundamental error of

---

[50] KENNEDY/JENKS CONSULTANTS, SUSTAINABLE WATER MASTER PLAN: FOR THE CITY OF SANTA MONICA, WATER RESOURCES DIVISION ES-1 (2014), available 23 January 2017 at http://www.smgov.net/uploadedFiles/Departments/Public_Works/Water/SWMP.pdf.

[51] Klaus Bosselmann, *Environmental and human rights in ethical context*, *in* RESEARCH HANDBOOK ON HUMAN RIGHTS AND THE ENVIRONMENT 531 (Anna Grear and Louis Kotze (eds), Edward Elgar 2015).

[52] *Id.*

providing extensive rights for humans, but providing none for the Earth's other living systems and species. Adopting rights for nature thus enables people imbued with the individualistic, anthropocentric approach to think of nature in a different way, while using a rights-oriented language and concept already understood and accepted.

Enacting nature's rights in law helps us move in a stepwise fashion toward a new *relationship* with nature, which is in fact our end goal. Implementing nature's rights in practice is vital to creating the ecocentric worldview so essential to the long-term well-being of people and planetary systems. Legal rights and the practice of responsibility go hand in hand. This is especially true because separateness between humans and nature runs throughout our Western environmental legal system. We cannot simply embed nature's rights in this system without exercising our responsibility toward nature. It is the daily practice, which becomes ingrained in our minds, hearts, and bodies, that will guide the necessary paradigm shift. While many indigenous peoples understand this and appropriately emphasize the practice of responsibility, our dominant legal and economic systems do not; hence the importance of recognizing nature's rights formally in law, and the even greater importance of emphasizing responsibility along with rights, as discussed next.

IV. LEGAL RESPONSIBILITY FOR NATURE

If we are to truly respect the inherent rights of nature and our appropriate place within nature, law needs to recognize – if not be based around – our responsibilities towards it. Respect for the intrinsic value of all life has been discussed thoroughly and is an important part of any framework for a future economy. It is frequently discussed in the context of – and as a basis for – a rights-based approach,[53] but it has also been applied more broadly to the advancement of an eco-centric approach, including in international environmental agreements. It is critical to explicitly recognize human responsibility for nature in a way that emphasizes our partnership, guardianship and trusteeship roles, as opposed to the false human construct of our having rights over nature.

---

[53] See, e.g., MYRES S. MCDOUGALL, ET AL., HUMAN RIGHTS AND WORLD PUBLIC ORDER (Yale University Press 1980) (arguing for respect as a universal human rights principle that would protect the rights of all forms of life, including non-human).

A. Legal Statements of Human Responsibility for Nature

The advocation of the adoption of human responsibilities for nature is not new.[54] However, it has most often been seen as a supplement to an anthropocentric human rights system. For example, in the international sphere, most discussion of duties toward the environment has been in relation to the duties necessary to ensure that human rights are fulfilled, as part of the adoption of a liberal world order and philosophy of human rights. States' international law duties to protect the environment today have primarily arisen out of a focus on human rights, especially those of future generations. For example, the movement toward recognizing a human right to a healthy environment at the international level is often used to emphasize the duty to protect the natural world, but it does so for the stated sake of humans and their rights.[55] Similarly, climate change is framed as a problem of intra-generational and intergenerational justice – that is, between people – even as other species are lost worldwide, every year.[56] There is no adoption of species-centric rules such as laws of ecocide, for example, to criminalize the wholesale destruction of other species.

At the domestic level, David Boyd observes that there are a range of environmental duties and rights that appear in countries' constitutions and laws, but the most common are governmental duties.[57] In contrast, the least common form of right or responsibility is an individual responsibility

---

[54] See Samuel Moyn, *Rights vs. Duties: Reclaiming Civic Balance,* BOS. REV. (16 May 2016), available 23 January 2017 at https://bostonreview.net/books-ideas/samuel-moyn-rights-duties, for a brief summary of the philosophical history of duties, See Holmes Rolston, III, *Rights and Responsibilities on the Home Planet*, 18 YALE J. INT'L L. 251 (1993) for related legal comments; *see also* Bosselmann, *supra* note 51, at 8.

[55] See *Special Rapporteur on Human Rights and the Environment*, OFFICE OF THE HIGH COMM'R, UNITED NATIONS HUMAN RIGHTS, available 23 January 2017 at www.ohchr.org/srenvironment for more information on current developments on a human right to a healthy environment.

[56] See, e.g., LIVING PLANET REPORT 2014, WORLD WILDLIFE FUND 4 (2014), available 23 January 2017 at http://assets.worldwildlife.org/publications/723/files/original/WWF-LPR2014-low_res.pdf?1413912230&_ga=1.65965544.770441611.1469908292 (finding that "[p]opulations of mammals, birds, reptiles, amphibians and fish have declined by 52 per cent since 1970."); s*ee also* LIVING BLUE PLANET REPORT 2015. WORLD WILDLIFE FUND (2015), available 23 January 2017 at www.worldwildlife.org/publications/living-blue-planet-report-2015.

[57] DAVID R. BOYD, THE ENVIRONMENTAL RIGHTS REVOLUTION: A GLOBAL STUDY OF CONSTITUTIONS, HUMAN RIGHTS, AND THE ENVIRONMENT 52 (UBC Press 2012).

for environmental protection,[58] although this is perhaps explained at least partly by the function of a constitution being directed at government power.[59] However, it is the human right to a healthy environment that is being adopted in laws and constitutions at an increasing rate worldwide, and is the fastest that has been seen: "No other human right has achieved such a broad level of constitutional recognition in such a short period of time."[60]

While repeated emphasis that our human rights come with individual and government responsibilities is necessary, this supplemental approach, with an increasing emphasis on rights over responsibilities, is insufficient to achieve a paradigm shift toward Earth-centred – rather than human-centred – responsibility. Law needs to go further and acknowledge our collective and individual duties or responsibilities for protecting nature, for its own as well as our sakes.

An illustration of an eco-centric approach to responsibility is provided in the Earth Charter. The Earth Charter identifies human responsibility toward the environment as the foundational principle and framework. Principle 2(a) provides that "with increased freedom, knowledge, and power comes increased responsibility to promote the common good", including the good of natural systems. This responsibility then lays a framework for recognizing rights of nature as well as of people.

B. Maori Concepts of Responsibility for Nature in New Zealand Law

Traditional indigenous views of the environment consider humans as being part of nature and acknowledge and reflect humankind's interdependence with nature. Importantly, these indigenous cultures' connection with nature are so deep that the nature is imbued with personality and viewed as kin – it is regarded as a true living ancestor of the people. This view corresponds with responsibilities to protect nature as guardians, as they would in respect to a family member. The adoption of an indigenous perspective within a legal system can provide a set of responsibilities to nature from an eco-centric approach. An example of this exists in Aotearoa New Zealand, where the guardianship relationship of the indigenous Maori with the environment has been recognized and protected in law.[61]

---

58 *Id.* at 67. See INDIA CONST. art. 51A(g), for an example of such a provision.

59 *Id.* at 68.

60 *Id.* at 76.

61 See Catherine Iorns Magallanes, *Maori Cultural Rights in Aotearoa New Zealand: Protecting the Cosmology that Protects the Environment*, 21 WIDENER L. REV. 273, 273–327 (2015) (hereinafter *Maori Cultural Rights in Aotearoa*

Maori relationships with the natural world have been incorporated or upheld in New Zealand environmental law through judicial decisions and through legislation, as well as through local, regional and national policy. For example, courts have required the Maori spiritual relationship with the environment to be considered by government in making water management decisions, even when the legislation did not specifically provide for this.[62] Another judicial decision held that "the relationship of Maori with their ancestral land"[63] needed to be given greater recognition in government's environmental decision-making, and even "primacy" as a matter of national importance when balancing competing factors.[64] Since 1986, New Zealand has made the need to consider Maori culture and the principles of the Treaty of Waitangi[65] a core part of the development of all national legislation; and it has become part of policy development requirements within the executive.[66]

The primary environmental statute in New Zealand is the Resource Management Act of 1991. Its overriding purpose is "to promote the sustainable management of natural and physical resources", which is widely defined.[67] Significantly, "matters of national importance" which all decision-makers under the Act must "recognise and provide for", include "the relationship of Maori and their culture and traditions with their ancestral lands, water, sites, *waahi tapu* [sacred sites], and other *taonga* [treasured things]".[68] In addition, all decision-makers must "have

---

New Zealand), for more detailed information on the various different ways that New Zealand law has recognized Maori cosmology in law. See Catherine Iorns Magallanes, *Native American Values and Laws of Exclusion*, *in* ENVIRONMENTAL LAW AND CONTRASTING IDEAS OF NATURE: A CONSTRUCTIVE APPROACH 200, 201 (Keith H. Hirokawa (ed.), Cambridge University Press 2014), for more information in a US context.

62 *See, e.g., Huakina Dev. Trust v. Waikato Valley Auth.* [1987] 2 NZLR 188 (HC).

63 Town and Country Planning Act 1977, s 3(1)(g) (N.Z.).

64 *Envtl. Def. Soc'y, Inc. v. Mangonui Cty. Council* [1989] 3 NZLR 257 (CA).

65 The Treaty of Waitangi is the Treaty between the British Crown and the indigenous Maori that was agreed to in 1840 in order to enable British settlement of New Zealand. *The Treaty of Waitangi/Te Tiriti O Waitangi*, NEW ZEALAND MINISTRY OF JUSTICE, available 23 January 2017 at http://www.waitangitribunal.govt.nz/treaty-of-waitangi/.

66 PHILIP JOSEPH, CONSTITUTIONAL AND ADMINISTRATIVE LAW IN NEW ZEALAND 82 ¶ .4.9.4. (4th edn, Brookers 2014). *See also* Cabinet Manual 2008, s 7.60-61 (NA) (N.Z.).

67 Resource Management Act 1991, s 5(2) (N.Z.).

68 *Id.* s 6 (emphasis added). See Catherine Iorns Magallanes, *The Use of 'Tangata Whenua' and 'Mana Whenua' in New Zealand Legislation: Attempts at*

particular regard to" "*kaitiakitanga*," which is defined in the Act as "the exercise of guardianship by the *tangata whenua* [tribe from an area] of an area in accordance with *tikanga Maori* [Maori protocol] in relation to natural and physical resources; and includes the ethic of stewardship".[69] Finally, the Act requires all decision-makers to "take into account the principles of the Treaty of Waitangi".[70]

These provisions upholding responsibility to the environment occur within the anthropocentric, mainstream environmental legal system. However, the application of these provisions has successfully resulted in the consideration, recognition, and even protection of Maori relationships with the natural world in decisions under the Act relating to the use, development and protection of New Zealand's natural and physical systems. This has produced positive protection for such interests in some cases, from their accommodation during the planning and development process to being upheld by courts in reviewing decisions made against such interests. For example, it was decided early on that, where Maori had an ancestral relationship with a natural system, then before any permit ("resource consent") could be issued, decision-makers must recognize that ancestral link, provide for the maintenance of that relationship, and provide for the tribe's guardianship – in accordance with Maori culture – over that natural system for the future.[71]

The protection has thus ranged from the need to consult with relevant Maori over the impact of a development proposal on their interests,[72] to rejection of development proposals because they interfere with Maori values and their spiritual relationship with the site proposed to be developed. Cases rejecting such interference have concerned a wide range of matters, including the discharge of sewage effluent into the sea,[73] the location of a road being too close to old burial sites,[74] a television aerial being too close to and thereby interfering with Maori metaphysical relationships with a

---

Cultural Recognition, 42 VICTORIA UNIV. WELLINGTON L. REV. 259 (2011), for a discussion of the use of Maori terms in legislation.

[69] Resource Management Act 1991, ss. 7, 9 (emphasis added).

[70] *Id.* s 8.

[71] *See, e.g.*, *Haddon v. Auckland Reg'l Council* [1994] 3 NZRMA 49 at 52, 5758 (PT).

[72] *See, e.g.*, *Mason-Riseborough v. Matamata-Piako Dist. Council* [1997] 4 ELRNZ 31 (EC).

[73] *See, e.g.*, *Te Runanga o Taumarere v. Northland Reg'l Council* [1996] NZRMA 77.

[74] *Te Runanga o Ati Awa ki Whakarongotai, Inc. v. NZ Historic Places Trust* [2002] 8 ELRNZ 265 at 272 (EC).

battle site,[75] and a wind farm being too close to – and interfering with Maori metaphysical relationships with – a mountain of spiritual significance.[76]

Again, the inclusion of these elements respecting Maori culture and spiritual relationships with nature has occurred within an anthropocentric legal framework; they have not yet created a whole new, Earth-centred framework. Yet this is the helpful beginning of adopting a structure of responsibility, through upholding the indigenous Maori view of nature as an ancestor and devising legal frameworks for better protecting its interests. Indeed, since the 1980s there have been many such examples upholding responsibility. For example, co-governance arrangements have been established between Maori and the government with the express purpose of restoring lakes, rivers, and other aspects of nature, in line with respect for them as ancestors.[77] Most recently and most significantly, natural features have been accorded legal personality, with human guardians appointed to protect their interests.

New Zealand has recently adopted a novel method for upholding human responsibility for nature: it has recognized elements of nature as a legal person and appointed a guardian to protect each of their interests. There are two current examples: a river and a forest. Both were adopted in order to settle long-standing grievances between the New Zealand government and the indigenous peoples who considered themselves the rightful guardians of these areas. Indeed, the indigenous tribes considered that the river and the forest were their respective ancestors, such that the tribes had the burden and privilege of responsibility of care for them as kin. These examples are discussed in turn.[78]

1. Te Awa Tupua: Whanganui River Settlement Agreement

The Whanganui River flows through the traditional territory of the Whanganui Maori. The river is said to be "central to the existence of Whanganui Iwi and their health and wellbeing", providing "both physical and spiritual sustenance to Whanganui Iwi from time immemorial".[79] The

---

75 *TV3 Network Servs. Ltd. v. Waikato Dist. Council* [1998] 1 NZLR 360 at 363–4 (HC).

76 *Outstanding Landscape Prot. Soc'y, Inc. v. Hastings Dist. Council* [2007] NZRMA 8 (EC).

77 *See, e.g.*, Waikato-Tainui Raupatu Claims (Waikato River) Settlement Act 2010 (N.Z).

78 See Catherine Iorns Magallanes, *Maori Cultural Rights in Aotearoa New Zealand, supra* note 61, for more detailed information on and discussion of these examples.

79 WHANGANUI IWI AND THE CROWN, RURUKU WHAKATUPUA – TE MANA O TE IWI O WHANGANUI cl.1.4 (2014) (hereafter referred to as TE MANA O TE IWI O

river is seen as the ancestor of the Whanganui tribes,[80] and the concept that the people are inseparable from the river "underpins the responsibilities of the *iwi* [tribes] and *hapū* [subtribes] of Whanganui in relation to the care, protection, management and use of the Whanganui River in accordance with the *kawa* and *tikanga* [protocols]" of the tribes.[81] It is this that has given rise to the Whanganui saying "*Ko au te awa, ko te awa ko au*", which means "I am the river and the river is me."

Many activities of the New Zealand government over the years from the 1800s breached not only the guarantees given to the Whanganui iwi by treaty but also violated what they view as the life force or spirit of the river.[82] The New Zealand courts have agreed that such violations of Maori cosmology violated the Whanganui tribes themselves, and prevented them from exercising their duties of guardianship over the river.[83] Throughout the breaches, the Whanganui tribes have maintained that they are still the rightful guardians of the river and of its life force, and that the right to control its management should be returned to them. An agreement in resolution of these grievances[84] – between the tribes and the government over future joint management of the river – was reached in 2012,[85] finalized in 2014,[86] and the legislation to implement the agreement was introduced

---

WHANGANUI), available 23 January 2017 at http://nz01.terabyte.co.nz/ots/DocumentLibrary/140805RurukuWhakatupua-TeManaOTeIwiOWhanganui.pdf.

80 See *Id.* cls. 2.1–2.25, for the Whanganui iwi account of the origins and the significance of the river to them. This account includes tribal lore about the river's supernatural guardians and their relationship to the people. *Id.* cls. 2.19–2.20.

81 *Id.* cl. 3.2 (italics added).

82 WAITANGI TRIBUNAL, TE IKA WHENUA RIVERS REPORT (1998), available 23 January 2017 at https://forms.justice.govt.nz/search/Documents/WT/wt_DOC_68382633/Te%20Ika%20Whenua%20Rivers%201998-compressed.pdf.

83 *Ngati Rangi Trust and Ors v Manawatu Whanganui Regional Council* [2004] NZEnvC 172 at ¶ 318.

84 See Catherine Iorns Magallanes, *supra* note 14, for a summary of a range of modern reparations settlement agreements. See the Office of Treaty Settlements, www.ots.govt.nz/ (accessed 23 January 2017), for more information on settlement of historical Treaty of Waitangi claims. *See* TREATY OF WAITANGI SETTLEMENTS (Nicola Wheen and Janine Hayward (eds), 2012).

85 The 2012 agreement, entitled *Tutohu Whakatupua*, was signed on August 30 between the Whanganui Iwi and the Crown. WHANGANUI IWI AND THE CROWN, TUTOHU WHAKATUPUA (New Zealand Law Foundation 2012), available 23 January 2017 at http://nz01.terabyte.co.nz/ots/DocumentLibrary/WhanganuiRiverAgreement.pdf.

86 The 2014 Deed of Settlement comprises two documents: TE MANA O TE IWI O WHANGANUI (*supra* note 79) (including the main elements of the settlement: apology, recitation of the history of the grievances and claims, and all the elements of the settlement; and RURUKU WHAKATUPUA – TE MANA O TE AWA TUPUA,

into Parliament in May 2016.[87] Significantly, this agreement incorporates the personification of the river held by the indigenous tribes – according it the title Te Awa Tupua – creates a new legal entity for Te Awa Tupua, and upholds the tribes' spiritual relationship with it.

The Whanganui River agreement recognizes the indivisible unity of the river and its metaphysical status as a living being and adopts the genealogical approach to describing the river, emphasizing the connection of people to the river. These various aspects are reflected in a set of overarching "intrinsic values",[88] described also as "the natural law and value system . . . which binds the people to the River and the River to the people":[89]

> *13 Tupua te Kawa*
> Tupua te Kawa comprises the intrinsic values that represent the essence of Te Awa Tupua, namely—
> . . .
> (a) *Ko te Awa te mātāpuna o te ora:* the River is the source of spiritual and physical sustenance:
> Te Awa Tupua is a spiritual and physical entity that supports and sustains both the life and natural resources within the Whanganui River and the health and wellbeing of the iwi, hapū and other communities of the River.
> . . .
> (b) *E rere kau mai te Awa nui mai te Kahui Maunga ki Tangaroa: the great River flows from the mountains to the sea*
> Te Awa Tupua is an indivisible and living whole from the mountains to the sea, incorporating the Whanganui River and all of its physical and metaphysical elements.
> . . .
> (c) *Ko au te Awa, ko te Awa ko au:* I am the River and the River is me:
> The iwi and hapū of the Whanganui River have an inalienable interconnection with, and responsibility to, Te Awa Tupua and its health and wellbeing.
> . . .
> (d) *Ngā manga iti, ngā manga nui e honohono kau ana, ka tupu hei Awa Tupua:* the small and large streams that flow into one another and form one River:

(hereinafter referred to as Te Mana o Te Awa Tupua), available 23 January 2017 at http://nz01.terabyte.co.nz/ots/DocumentLibrary/RurukuWhakatupua-TeManaoTeAwaTupua.pdf (including the agreed *Te Awa Tupua* framework for the status and management of the Whanganui River). See Office of Treaty Settlements, *supra* note 84, for more information and the relevant documents, including a summary of the Whanganui River Deed of Settlement.

87 The Te Awa Tupua (Whanganui River Claims Settlement) Bill 2016 (129-1) (N.Z.) (hereinafter Te Awa Tupua Bill). At the time of writing the Bill was still under consideration by the NZ Parliament.

88 *Id.* cl. 13; Te Mana o Te Awa Tupua, *supra* note 86, cl. 2.6.

89 Te Mana o Te Awa Tupua, *supra* note 86, at 6.

> Te Awa Tupua is a singular entity comprised of many elements and communities, working collaboratively to the common purpose of the health and wellbeing of Te Awa Tupua.[90]

To uphold this in law, the legislation recognizes the river as a legal person: "Te Awa Tupua is a legal person and has all the rights, powers, duties and liabilities of a legal person".[91] This is expressly intended to "reflect the Whanganui Iwi [tribes'] view that the River is a living entity in its own right and is incapable of being 'owned' in an absolute sense" and to "enable the River to have legal standing in its own right".[92]

An official guardian for Te Awa Tupua is being established by the 2016 proposed legislation.[93] This guardian will "act and speak for and on behalf of Te Awa Tupua" and uphold "the Te Awa Tupua status" and intrinsic values, "promote and protect the health and well-being of Te Awa Tupua", and perform other necessary functions for it, including participating in relevant statutory processes and holding property or funds in the name of Te Awa Tupua.[94] Importantly, the guardian "must act in the interests of Te Awa Tupua and consistently with Tupua te Kawa" (the intrinsic values, above).[95]

The guardian, Te Pou Tupua, will consist of two persons "of high standing",[96] one appointed by the Crown and one appointed collectively by all tribes with interests in the river,[97] where each person must have "the mana, skills, knowledge, and experience to achieve the purpose and perform the functions of Te Pou Tupua".[98] Underneath Te Pou Tupua is a 3-person advisory group.[99]

---

90 *Id.* cl. 2.7.

91 Te Awa Tupua Bill, *supra* note 87, cl. 14(1).

92 Tutohu Whakatupua, *supra* note 85, cl. 2.7.

93 This guardian will be called Te Pou Tupua. Te Awa Tupua Bill, *supra* note 87, cl. 14(2).

94 *Id.* cl. 19(1).

95 *Id.* cl. 19(2).

96 Te Mana o Te Awa Tupua, *supra* note 86, cl. 3.8; Tutohu Whakatupua, supra note 85, cl 2.20.4. The high standing is so as to recognize "both the importance of the role and the need to interact with Ministers and other interested parties at a leadership level". *Id.*

97 Te Mana o Te Awa Tupua, *supra* note 86, cl. 3.9; Tutohu Whakatupua, *supra* note 85, cl. 2.19. See Te Mana o Te Awa Tupua, *supra* note 86, cls. 3.9–3.19, for more details of the appointment process, term, and conditions. See *Id.* cls. 3.20–3.40, for the administrative and advisory support for Te Pou Tupua in carrying out its role.

98 Te Awa Tupua Bill, *supra* note 87, cl. 20. "*Mana*" is best translated here as moral authority or standing.

99 The advisory group is called *Te Karewao*. Te Awa Tupua Bill, *supra* note 87, cls. 27–28.

A key interest of the river is its health and well-being. This is specifically addressed through the development of a "Whole of River Strategy",[100] which will be designed "to address and advance the environmental, social, cultural and economic health and wellbeing of the Whanganui River".[101] To this end, the agreement defines the goals, status and parameters of a strategy to identify and address such issues of health and well-being, including recommending actions to address the identified issues.[102] It establishes a strategy group of up to 17 members representing various different organizations with interests in the river,[103] to "act collaboratively" to develop the strategy[104] and monitor its implementation.[105] Local government and other decision-makers will be required to consider and take into account the strategy in relevant decisions. It has been noted that the group and the strategy are intended to provide "strategic direction and the lens through which the River is viewed, not day to day management".[106]

In order to "support the health and wellbeing" of the river, a fund will be established with a Crown grant of NZD 30 million.[107] This is not limited to implementation of the strategy, but may be allocated "on a contestable basis" upon application.[108]

2. Te Urewera: Tūhoe Settlement Agreement

Until recently, Te Urewera National Park was the largest national park in the North Island of Aotearoa, New Zealand. It is all virgin, original forest or bush, but was created from most of the traditional lands of the Tūhoe

---

[100] TUTOHU WHAKATUPUA, *supra* note 85, cl. 2.23. This strategy is called *Te Heke Ngahuru*, in the Bill. Te Awa Tupua Bill, *supra* note 87, cls. 35–36.

[101] TE MANA O TE AWA TUPUA, *supra* note 86, cl.4.1; *see also* TUTOHU WHAKATUPUA, *supra* note 85, cl. 2.24. In the 2014 agreement this Strategy is called *Te Heke Ngahuru*. See TE MANA O TE AWA TUPUA, *supra* note 86, cls. 4.1–4.23.

[102] *Id.* cl. 4.2.

[103] This group is called *Te Kopuka*. Te Awa Tupua Bill, *supra* note 87, cls. 29–32.

[104] TE MANA O TE AWA TUPUA, *supra* note 86, cl. 5.3.

[105] *Id.* cl.5.4. See *Id.* cls. 5.1–5.47, for functions, membership matters, procedures meetings, decision-making, and support. See *Id.* cl. 5.45, stating that the Crown will support it financially.

[106] Press Release, New Zealand Government, Whanganui River Deed of Settlement Initialled (26 March 2014), available 23 January 2017 at http://www.scoop.co.nz/stories/PA1403/S00514/whanganui-river-deed-of-settlement-initialled.htm.

[107] The fund is called *Te Korotete*. Te Awa Tupua Bill, *supra* note 87, cls. 57–58.

[108] *Id.* cl. 59.At earlier stages of the negotiation, this money was described as a clean-up fund for the river.

people. This taking was the subject of grievance against the Crown, [109] and Tūhoe have argued continuously for the need to exercise their spiritual authority over the land through guardianship for it.[110] In 2013, Tūhoe and the New Zealand government agreed on a settlement to this grievance whereby legal personality would be established for the park, and Tūhoe could exercise their guardianship responsibility over it. The lands would remain protected, as they are in a national park, but it would maintain its own separate identity and be governed through a co-governance arrangement with Tūhoe. Legislation to implement this agreement passed in July 2014.

A fundamental aspect underlying this agreement is the importance placed on the intrinsic value of nature itself.[111] The Act explicitly identifies the "intrinsic worth" of Te Urewera,[112] as well as protection of its interests.[113]

The key means of upholding the Tūhoe view of Te Urewera as an ancestor is to declare it to be its own legal entity, with "all the rights, powers, duties, and liabilities of a legal person".[114] It will accordingly hold title to its own land (i.e., title to itself), where that land is inalienable.

Responsibility for the guardianship of Te Urewera is given to the Te Urewera Board, "to act on behalf of, and in the name of, Te Urewera" and "to provide governance for Te Urewera".[115] Membership of the Board is currently half Tūhoe and half New Zealand government-appointed.[116]

---

[109] Tūhoe Claims Settlement Act 2014, cl 9(36)–(37) (N.Z). The detailed Crown acknowledgements of its actions in § 9 and the apology in § 10 provide excellent background to this settlement.

[110] *See, e.g., Id.* cl. 9(36).

[111] Te Urewera Act 2014, s 4 (finding "[t]he purpose of this Act is to establish and preserve in perpetuity a legal identity and protected status for Te Urewera for its intrinsic worth, its distinctive natural and cultural values, the integrity of those values, and for its national importance, and in particular to—

(a) strengthen and maintain the connection between Tūhoe and Te Urewera; and

(b) preserve as far as possible the natural features and beauty of Te Urewera, the integrity of its indigenous ecological systems and biodiversity, and its historical and cultural heritage; and

(c) provide for Te Urewera as a place for public use and enjoyment, for recreation, learning, and spiritual reflection, and as an inspiration for all.").

[112] *Id.* ss. 3(8), 4.

[113] *Id.* s. 18(1)(g).

[114] *Id.* s. 11(1).

[115] *Id.* s. 17.

[116] *Id.* s. 21. After three years the Board will increase to nine members, six of which will be appointed by Tūhoe trustees, so that Tūhoe will have a majority.

The Act contains an extensive list of powers and obligations of the Board, including the ability to make by-laws and to grant activity permits with Te Urewera.[117] Yet the overriding notion is human responsibility for the protection of Te Urewera.

It is too soon to tell how the guardianship regime will operate in practice, including how the interests of Te Awa Tupua or Te Urewera will be defined, and how well they will be protected. Yet this combination of formally legislating for a natural feature as a legal person and upholding its interests for its own sake suggests to all – not just to its Maori descendants – that it is more than just a resource to be exploited, even for relatively benign use, such as low-impact recreation.

The Maori New Zealand examples show that responsibility can be articulated in legislation and that guardians can be established to uphold duties of care for nature. Respect for the rights of indigenous peoples, including redress for wrongs suffered and maintenance of their culture, can result in laws that treat the environment in a way that reflects the kind of paradigm needed for a new economy.

V. CONCLUSION

This chapter illustrates three key elements necessary for any paradigm shift toward an eco-centric legal basis for a new economy: respect for the intrinsic value of nature, recognition in law of the fundamental rights of nature, and establishment and implementation of legal responsibility of humans for nature. At the moment, the various examples discussed are insertions into mainstream anthropocentric legal frameworks. They have not yet constituted a true revolution. However, they are revolutionary in that they arise from a completely different worldview, one that reflects the paradigm that is needed for an economy that respects our relationship with the Earth and its natural systems.

While in Aotearoa New Zealand the examples have depended upon the existence of the indigenous Maori people and the recognition of their human rights, the other examples show that this need not be the case. Indeed, it could be said that the rights of nature examples take ancient concepts of interconnectedness and translate them into a modern, liberal legal system of rights. What is important is to not forget that with all human rights come responsibilities. We must make an extra effort to implement the rights of nature to realize our endpoint of a worldview and

---

117 *Id.* s. 20.

life upholding respect and responsibility for our actions toward the non-human world. Laws on paper alone will not achieve that; we must practice them to push past the boundaries of our existing cultural limitations and legal systems.

Enactment in national and local legislation makes this alternative worldview much more visible, with the potential of eventual normalcy in the eyes of the mainstream. Therefore, adopting such provisions and requiring us to act in accordance with them will start to change our thoughts. Such actions also can re-engender in others the fellow-feeling for other life forms and the understanding that we are all connected to the natural world. This interconnectedness might in turn revive the beliefs in kinship bonds, sacredness and respect which is so sorely needed in a world where nature has very few rights or other protections.

Therefore, perhaps this can offer us that "socio-psychic" element of an alternative paradigm, a new "myth" and "consciousness", "felt as well as intellectualized".[118] Perhaps such recognition in law will help encourage us all to realize, as our forebears did, that our relationships with the natural world are crucial to identity and survival.

118 Stone, *supra* note 23, at 489.

5. The Nature's Trust paradigm for a sustaining economy

Mary Christina Wood[1]

I. INTRODUCTION: HOW ENVIRONMENTAL LAW DESTROYS NATURE AND ENABLES A RUINOUS ECONOMY

The commonly invoked "jobs versus environment" rhetoric over-simplifies a complex problem: our current environmental regulatory system lacks an economic approach that offers hope of prosperity consistent with ecological protection. Though it purportedly aims to control harm inflicted by the industrial economy, environmental statutes actually prop up that same economy by authorizing permits to pollute and destroy. When resources reach the point of collapse, the regulatory hammer finally comes down without an opportunity for planned economic transition towards benign productive enterprise.

Serious endemic flaws exist across the system as a whole. Developers, industrialists, and huge corporations exert relentless pressure on governmental officials to allow exploitation of natural resources, calculated to bring them enormous profit while diminishing the community commons. This pressure, constantly applied, erodes the will on the part of government officials to carry out the protective mandates of the law. Agencies fall prey to political capture and continue to issue permits until resources reach the point of near collapse. A new economy requires a new legal paradigm.

This chapter discusses the climate emergency and how the law must respond with a legal framework called Nature's Trust, conceived to reconstitute environmental law in countries throughout the world in response to the exigencies of the modern ecological age. It builds from an ancient duty

---

[1] Parts of this chapter are adapted from the author's book: MARY CHRISTINA WOOD, NATURE'S TRUST: ENVIRONMENTAL LAW FOR A NEW ECOLOGICAL AGE (Cambridge University Press 2013).

embodied in the public trust doctrine, a legal principle that, in some form, has flowed through countless forms of government since time immemorial and remains vibrant in legal systems throughout the world. At its core, the doctrine declares public rights originally and inherently reserved to the people through their social contract with government. The trust remains an attribute of popular sovereignty that cannot be alienated by any legislature. This principle designates government as trustee of crucial natural resources and obligates it to act in a fiduciary capacity to protect and restore natural commonwealth for the beneficiaries of the trust, which are present and future generations of citizens. The public trust already exists in the law, "on the shelf", ready to be used. It offers the possibility of a new pressure point in climate crisis.

II. HOW THE LAW MUST RESPOND TO THE CLIMATE EMERGENCY

Any effort to bring about a new economy must first respond to the climate imperative – a planetary emergency in which only a narrow window of time remains to prevent catastrophic climate disruption. The global challenge of CO_2 emissions reduction finds unprecedented urgency due to Nature's own "tipping points" – dangerous feedback loops capable of unleashing uncontrollable, irreversible, "runaway" heating. The opportunity for slow, progressive change has long since closed, since already some feedback loops are underway. The challenge is to find leverage points in the law that respond to this short-term urgency while at the same time moving society and its legal systems forward towards a full paradigm shift that ripples across law, politics, culture and the economy.

The search for levers will be aimless without a clear understanding of the ecological reality facing the world, as explained by the best available science. Restoring climate equilibrium requires reducing atmospheric carbon dioxide levels to 350 parts per million (ppm). A global prescription developed by NASA's then chief climate scientist, Dr James Hansen (in collaboration with an international team) aims to achieve atmospheric balance at 350 ppm by the end of the century.[2] It presents two core requirements: emissions reduction and atmospheric drawdown of carbon dioxide.

[2] James Hansen et al., *Assessing "Dangerous Climate Change:" Required Reduction of Carbon Emissions to Protect Young People, Future Generations, and Nature*, 8 PLOS ONE 1, 4 (2013) [hereinafter *Climate Prescription*], available 23 January 2017 at http://www.plosone.org/article/fetchObject.action?uri=info:doi/10.1371/journal.pone.0081648&representation=PDF.

A. Emissions Reduction

The prescription presents a "glidepath", of global annual CO_2 emissions reduction towards an ultimate goal of near-zero emissions. If reduction begins in 2016, the amount annually necessary is 8 percent. However, if reduction is delayed until 2020, the required emissions reduction jumps to 15 percent a year – which may be too drastic for global society to accomplish. Leading scientists emphasize that the future survival of humanity hangs in the balance of rapid CO_2 reduction, stating: "[D]elay in undertaking sharp reductions in emissions will undermine any realistic chance of preserving a habitable climate system . . .".[3]

To confront this climate emergency, a legal strategy must aim to both force governments worldwide to immediately reduce carbon dioxide emissions according to the prescription (or best available science) and divest corporations of their existing property rights to fossil fuel reserves. The strategy, called Atmospheric Trust Litigation (ATL), is underway and described below.

B. Atmospheric Carbon Dioxide Drawdown

Emissions reduction alone is no longer adequate to restore climate equilibrium. The Hansen team made clear a need to remove much of the carbon dioxide that has already accumulated in the atmosphere. Accordingly, the second part of the team's prescription calls for natural "drawdown" of 100 Gigatons of carbon dioxide through massive reforestation, improved agricultural measures, and mangrove and wetlands restoration.

Such drawdown becomes feasible through a global Atmospheric Recovery Plan (ARP) that would coordinate restoration projects around the world. Such projects would have co-benefits boosting employment, supporting food supplies, and creating resilience against climate catastrophes. A legal strategy is underway to develop a cooperative sovereign framework of global restoration and financing through natural resource damage actions brought against the "carbon majors" – dominant fossil fuel companies that are both culpable for the planetary emergency and capable of funding its relief.[4]

The measures described above address only climate mitigation to stave

---

[3] Amici Curiae Scientists Brief at 15–16, *Alec L. ex rel. Loorz v. McCarthy*, 561 Fed. Appx. 7, No. 13–5192, 2014 WL 3013301 (D.C. Cir. June 5, 2014).

[4] Mary Christina Wood and Daniel Galpern, *Atmospheric Recovery Litigation: Making the Fossil Fuel Industry Pay for Damages to the Atmosphere from Carbon Emissions*, 45 ENVTL. L. 259, 306 (2015).

off runaway heating from which there is no plausible recovery. In a world under ecological siege, all remaining natural resources carry a premium for human survival and welfare. A legal strategy, then, must be versatile and broad enough to protect the functioning of all remaining ecosystems.

III. THE NEED FOR A PARADIGM SHIFT: THE NATURE'S TRUST BRIDGE FROM THE INDUSTRIAL ECONOMY TO A SUSTAINING ECONOMY

Beyond responding to the climate emergency, a new legal paradigm must accomplish four main objectives if democracy and civilization have a chance of surviving into the future. First, in an era of collapsing ecosystems brought on by climate chaos, government must allocate crucial resources to the public rather than to private corporations – that is to say, the law must prevent monopolization. The current trend, however, is otherwise, as multinational corporations increasingly gain property rights to scarce water supplies. Second, the legal system must free democratic governments from corporate coercion exerted through campaign contributions. Absent that, leaders will continue to make decisions out of their own self interest to benefit their corporate funders rather than citizens. Third, the law must re-envision the character and decision making latitude of corporations. Fourth, and most fundamentally, environmental law must re-orient to the non-negotiable laws of Nature. These laws determine, for example, climate tipping points and extinction vortexes. Modern environmental law has drifted far from Nature's reality.

Speth writes, "[W]e now approach the fork ahead . . . Beyond the fork, down either path, is the end of the world as we have known it. One path beyond the fork continues us on our current trajectory . . . the abyss . . . But there is the other path, and it leads to a *bridge across the abyss*."[5]

A bridge presents the right image for our task. New paradigms do not magically materialize. They build from established footings in the law recognizable to society and its institutions. A leap too large will not be attempted by a legal system defined by adherence to precedent. At the same time, constructing a bridge towards a new paradigm does not mean merely reforming the law around the edges.

---

5 James Gustave Speth, The Bridge at the Edge of the World: Capitalism, the Environment, and Crossing from Crisis to Sustainability 236–37 (Yale University Press 2008).

The public trust doctrine compels sovereign stewardship of crucial natural resources. Characterizing such resources as a trust for present and future generations of citizens, it designates government as a fiduciary charged with obligations to protect the resources from damage as well as monopolistic privatization. Roots of the trust are found in the Justinian Code of Roman Law, which declared that there can be no private exclusionary rights to *res communes*: "By the law of nature these things are common to all mankind—the air, running water, the sea, and consequently the shores of the sea."[6]

The doctrine rests on a civic and judicial understanding that some natural resources remain so vital to public welfare and human survival that they should not fall exclusively to private property ownership and control. The public trust doctrine reserves such resources to the people as a whole as a common endowment to be sustained by government through the ages. Even in the United States, with its highly libertarian private property rights culture, the public trust sets limits on human activities affecting ecology. The concern of the public trust is both intra-generational and inter-generational.[7] It poses an anti-monopolization mandate, keeping crucial resources open for access to the public. It also secures ecological rights for children and future generations, aiming towards intergenerational justice.

Deriving from property law, the trust forms a counterweight to existing private property rights and government's discretionary police power, both of which now drive much natural resource destruction. As trustee, government must promote the interests of the citizen beneficiaries and ensure sustained resource abundance necessary for society's endurance. The US Supreme Court declared in *Geer v. Connecticut*: "[I]t is the duty of the legislature to enact such laws as will best preserve the subject of the trust, and secure its beneficial use in the future to the people of the state."[8] This duty arises as a limitation on government, an expectation embedded in the popular sovereignty held by the people. Long predating any statutory law, these public rights rank so fundamental that some scholars describe them as natural rights or human rights.

Although longstanding in a variety of countries, advocates have largely overlooked the doctrine in favor of environmental statutes. Passed in the 1970s in the US, these statutes produced thousands of implementing

---

6 J. Inst., 2.1.1. (T. Sandars trans., 4th edn. 1867).

7 John Davidson, Address at Vermont Law School Climate Legacy Initiative Research Forum: *Taking Posterity Seriously: Intergenerational Justice*, (January 2008).

8 *Geer v. Connecticut*, 161 U.S. 519, 534 (1896).

regulations that obfuscate the public trust. Most agency regulators have never heard of the public trust, familiar only with their statutory discretion to allow ecological damage through the permit system.

Recently, lawyers, citizens, judges and regulators have begun to unearth these principles and apply them to environmental controversies. Revived in modern bureaucracy, the trust would introduce an old-but-new limitation on government as it acts through statutory structures. The legal force of the public trust occurs through the fiduciary standards to which government trustees are held to account for their actions.

A. *Res Communes*

The trust *res* consists of natural bounty protected by restrictions designed to serve the trust's purpose. The trust "*res*" consists of "*res communes*", which are, in their Roman law origins, "things owned by no one and subject to use by all: things (as light, air, the sea, running water) incapable of exclusive ownership".[9] Subject to government fiduciary duties of protection and restoration, the *res communes* must sustain future generations. Courts consistently look to the needs of the public when defining the scope of the trust *res*, applying a "public concern" test from the landmark US Supreme Court case, *Illinois Central Railroad v. Illinois*. That 1892 case involved a legislative conveyance of Chicago's waterfront along Lake Michigan to a private railroad company. At the time, lakebeds served a vital role for fishing, navigation and commerce. The Supreme Court declared the grant void, stating: "The ownership of the navigable waters of the harbor and of the lands under them is a subject of public concern to the whole people of the State."[10]

The "public concern" rationale has led courts to greatly expand the scope of the trust to meet modern exigencies. As the New Jersey Supreme Court observed, "we perceive the public trust doctrine not to be 'fixed or static,' but one to 'be molded and extended to meet changing conditions and needs of the public it was created to benefit'".[11] Various courts now recognize biodiversity, wildlife habitat, aesthetics and recreation as purposes of the trust. Aimed toward protecting these modern concerns, the doctrine now reaches well beyond its traditional scope to assets such

---

[9] Res Communes, MERRIAM WEBSTER DICTIONARY, http://www.merriam-webster.com/dictionary/res%20communes (accessed 23 January 2017).

[10] *Ill. Cent. R.R. Co. v. Ill.*, 146 U.S. 387, 455 (1892).

[11] *Matthews v. Bay Head Improvement Ass'n,* 471 A.2d 355, 365 (N.J. 1984). *See also* Melissa Scanlan, *Shifting Sands: A Meta-Theory for Public Access and Private Property Along the Coast*, 65 S.C. L. REV. 295, 325–27 (2013).

as groundwater, wetlands, dry sand beaches, parks, non-navigable waterways and, most recently, air and atmosphere.

Leading public trust cases have recognized the intrinsic connections between different parts of Nature and have expanded the trust *res* to protect ecological function. The Hawaii Supreme Court, for example, held that groundwater must be considered part of the trust *res* because of its inseparability from surface water, stating, "Modern science and technology have discredited the surface–ground dichotomy."[12] While a few courts still cling to an antiquated notion of navigability to define the scope of the public trust *res*, a recent court in Washington state held that the air and atmosphere were part of the public trust, noting that to separate air from recognized streambed trust resources would be "nonsensical".[13]

A Nature's Trust paradigm extends the rationale of these cases to recognize public rights in protecting the full tapestry of Nature. The paradigm rejects the conceptual fracturing of resources that typifies environmental law, instead building from the recognition that Nature's various systems and elements operate in constant interaction to support life, welfare and community prosperity. A Nature's Trust paradigm moves the existing public trust from a state-by-state iteration of public trust assets to the concept of a full "*ecological res*", encompassing waters, wildlife, soils, vegetation, forests, air, atmosphere, oceans, streambeds, wetlands, aquifers and natural landscapes – no matter where or in what jurisdiction they happened to be located. The Nature's Trust paradigm strives to match the reality of Nature's laws. Building on public trust jurisprudence that already recognizes human survival and welfare as dependent on Nature, the Nature's Trust paradigm expands the trust's legal sanctuary to the entire ecological web of life.

B. The Fiduciary Duties

Fiduciary duties form the core of any trust construct. The public trust imposes restrictions and obligations on government actors when managing trust resources. Environmental statutes give agencies tremendous authority to allow damage to natural resources, and they provide few (if any) enforceable mandates to act affirmatively in face of threats. The trust, by contrast, imposes duties on government trustees apart from

---

[12] *In re Water Use Permit Applications*, 9 P.3d 409, 447 (Haw. 2000). *See also id.* at 457 (the trust demands "the maintenance of ecological balance").

[13] *Foster v. Wash. State Dep't of Ecology*, No. 14-2-25295-1 SEA, slip. op. at 8 (Wash. Nov. 19, 2015).

statutory standards. As the Idaho Supreme Court stated in *Kootenai Environmental Alliance v. Panhandle Yacht Club, Inc.*, "[M]ere compliance by [agencies] with their legislative authority is not sufficient to determine if their actions comport with the requirements of the public trust doctrine. The public trust doctrine at all times forms the outer boundaries of permissible government action with respect to public resources."[14]

The fiduciary duties are both substantive and procedural.[15] The substantive duties below have received frequent mention in public trust cases. However, the procedural duties have been largely overlooked until recently when a plurality of the Pennsylvania Supreme Court comprehensively iterated them in *Robinson Township v. Pennsylvania*.[16]

The substantive fiduciary duties require a public trustee to:

(1) Protect the subject of the trust (the *res*) from "substantial impairment". This is an active duty applicable to both direct and indirect action. Such duty therefore includes adaptive management.[17]
(2) Conserve resources for future generations. Because "the beneficiaries of the public trust are not just present generations but those to come", a trustee must protect the *res* to sustain future beneficiaries.[18]
(3) Maximize the societal value of natural resources by following three principles: (a) do not allow squander of the resource; (b) dedicate the resource to its highest public purpose; and (c) do not allocate public resources primarily to serve the interests of private parties.[19] Polluting uses of public trust assets characteristically violate one or more of these mandates.
(4) Restore the trust *res* where it has been damaged.
(5) Affirmatively seek to recover natural resource damages (NRDs) from third parties that harm or destroy public trust assets and use the financing for restoration.

---

14 *Kootenai Envtl. All., Inc. v. Panhandle Yacht Club, Inc.*, 671 P.2d 1085, 1095 (Idaho 1983).

15 For a full discussion of these duties, with supporting citations, see Mary Christina Wood and Gordon Levitt, *The Public Trust Doctrine in Environmental Decision Making, in* Decision Making in Environmental Law (LeRoy C. Paddock, Robert L. Glicksman and Nicholas S. Bryner (eds), Edward Elgar 2016).

16 *Robinson Twp. v. Commonwealth of Pa.*, 83 A.3d 901, 957 (Pa. 2013) (plurality opinion).

17 *See, e.g.*, Melissa K. Scanlan, *Implementing the Public Trust Doctrine: A Lakeside View into the Trustees' World*, 39 Ecology L.Q. 123, 135–7 (2012).

18 *In re Water Use Permit Applications*, 9 P.3d 409, 455 (Haw. 2000).

19 *Id. at* 450–1.

(6) Refrain from alienating (that is, privatizing) the trust, except when doing so furthers the "primary purpose" of the trust and does not "substantially impair" the public's interest in remaining trust assets.[20] Privatization may not occur where the primary purpose is to benefit a private party.

The procedural fiduciary duties require a public trustee to:

(1) Maintain uncompromised loyalty to the beneficiaries and avoid all conflicts of interest that give rise to even the *possibility* for any temptation towards self-dealing. Enforced against government trustees, this principle could counter the corruptive influence of campaign contributions from industries that expect favorable regulatory treatment in return. While the *Citizens United* decision would still allow massive campaign contributions, courts enforcing this trust duty could void and remand tainted decisions, thereby draining the incentive behind campaign financing.
(2) Do not favor one class of beneficiaries over the other: "[T]he trustee has an obligation to deal impartially with all beneficiaries."[21]
(3) Adequately supervise agents. In the public trust context, this duty requires legislative oversight of executive branch agencies delegated with the power of trust management.
(4) Exercise good faith and reasonable skill in managing the assets. A trustee must employ the same vigilance that they would in managing their own affairs. This duty requires agencies to apply their expertise and authority to further the public's interest. Decisions made on political grounds violate this duty.
(5) Use caution in managing the assets and avoid entering into risky ventures. This standard would invoke the precautionary principle in managing natural systems.
(6) Provide a trust accounting and furnish information on trust management and asset health to the beneficiaries.

Viewed in aggregate, these obligations present a necessary paradigm shift for environmental law, forcing a phase-out of legalized destruction through permits and compelling a full-scale restoration program financed by industries that have polluted or destroyed resources. The challenge becomes injecting these obligatory duties of a trustee into a bureaucratic

---

20 *Ill. Cent. R.R. Co. v. Ill.*, 146 U.S. 387, 453 (1892).
21 *Robinson*, 83 A.3d at 959.

structure imbued with statutory permission to destroy Nature. A constitutional underpinning becomes necessary.

C. Constitutional in Nature

Modern scholars and judges increasingly recognize the constitutional force of the public trust doctrine.[22] In *Robinson Township*, a plurality of the Pennsylvania Supreme Court described the trust as embodying the "inherent and indefeasible" rights of citizens reserved through their social contract with government.[23] A similar approach was taken in a Washington case, leading that court to declare a constitutional right to a healthy climate system. Most recently, a magistrate judge in a pending federal atmospheric trust case in Oregon found a federal constitutional public trust duty embodied in the Due Process Clause of the Fourteenth Amendment of the US Constitution, stating: "The doctrine is deeply rooted in our nation's history and indeed predates it."[24] The constitutional nature of the public trust empowers courts to overturn statutory provisions that violate a legislature's fiduciary obligations towards its present and future citizens.

D. Macro in Focus

Statutory law splinters management of natural resources among a multitude of agencies, designating each with a particular facet of responsibility. Statutory enforcement typically amounts to micro claims directed at just one agency and just one type of violation – often a procedural violation. Judicial remedies for these statutory transgressions fail to solve problems that have reached systemic levels of dysfunction across several agencies. Public trust claims allow a macro approach to modern ecological problems by focusing on the natural system (or element) as a whole and its core functioning needs. This may mean holding a multitude of agencies accountable to their fiduciary responsibilities in one enforcement action. In the pending federal case against the Obama administration challenging the US fossil fuel regime, youth plaintiffs named nearly a dozen federal agencies as defendants. In these cases, courts must innovate systems-wide,

---

22 *See, e.g.*, Gerald Torres and Nate Bellinger, *The Public Trust: The Law's DNA*, 4 Wake Forest J.L. & Pol'y 281, 288 (2014) (suggesting the public trust doctrine laid the foundation for the Constitution).

23 *Robinson*, 83 A.3d at 948.

24 *Juliana v. U.S.*, No. 6:15-cv-1517-TC, 2016 WL 1442435, at *11 (Or. Apr. 8, 2016).

macro-scale remedies in order to address trust mismanagement on a systemic level.

E. A Pan-Sovereign Global Instruction

Because trust duties infuse sovereignty, citizens may summon fiduciary obligations against government actors without reinventing statutory law (an impossible task given the urgency of a climate response and ecological restoration). The public trust exists in every state in the United States and is manifest in many nations world-wide. A growing number of legal thinkers urge the application of public trust principles to unprecedented problems of global ecology. As Ved Nanda and William Ris observe: "The principles of public trust are such that they can be understood and embraced by most countries of the world."[25]

Nature's Trust characterizes global environmental syndromes as matters of property law in which a set of discernible rules can promote a common, civilized plan to protect planetary life-systems such as the atmosphere and oceans – even in a world governed by multiple sovereigns with fragmented jurisdiction over the planet. The trust framework regards nations as sovereign trustees of natural resources, co-tenants with reciprocal and correlative duties towards each other in the conduct affecting the common Earth Endowment. By packaging problems of planetary ecology in property terms, the trust framework enables domestic courts of various nations to summon clear and enforceable fiduciary standards to hold political leaders accountable for global ecological duties. In theory, such standards could be enforced on the domestic level using principles that remain relatively uniform across jurisdictional sovereign borders.

IV. ATMOSPHERIC TRUST LITIGATION AS AN APPLICATION OF THE NATURE'S TRUST FRAMEWORK

To recap, the Nature's Trust paradigm would extend the public trust duty of protection to all life systems on Earth, and hold all governments, as trustees of shared resources, accountable for preventing "substantial impairment" to the function of such systems. The legal framework

---

[25] Ved P. Nanda and William K. Ris, Jr., *The Public Trust Doctrine: A Viable Approach to International Environmental Protection*, 5 Ecology L.Q. 291, 306 (1976).

connects directly to Nature's laws by seeking the best available science to determine appropriate actions.

The atmospheric trust litigation (ATL) campaign presently underway shows how the law can allocate collective responsibility calibrated directly to Nature's requirements for the atmosphere. In 2011, the non-profit, Our Children's Trust, launched a global campaign to force urgent carbon emissions reduction around the world.[26] Originally, this consisted of lawsuits and administrative petitions lawyers filed on behalf of children against all 50 states and the federal government. In September 2015, the children brought another federal lawsuit against the Obama Administration challenging the federal government's entire fossil fuel regime. The children's lawyers are bringing further actions and coordinating actions with partners in other countries as well. The campaign represents an unprecedented effort at forcing a coherent approach to a global crisis using the judicial system.

Invoking the public trust doctrine, all of the actions declare a uniform sovereign trust duty to protect the atmosphere needed by the youth and future generations for their long-term survival. They seek enforceable Climate Recovery Plans from government trustees to reduce carbon emissions at the rate called for by the scientific prescription formulated by the Hansen team of scientists (or best available science). Unlike prior climate litigation brought under statutory law or nuisance law – suits geared towards isolated parts of the climate problem – ATL presents a macro approach to the climate crisis by focusing on the atmosphere as a single public trust resource. As Dr James Hansen declared in an amicus brief in one atmospheric trust case, judicial relief in these cases "may be the best, the last, and, at this late stage, the only real chance to preserve a habitable planet for young people and future generations".[27]

The youth plaintiffs in the pending federal Oregon case (which combines a public trust claim with Constitutional due process and equal protection claims) gained a strong initial victory on 8 April 2016 when Magistrate Judge Thomas Coffin recommended denial of the government's and fossil fuel interveners' motions to dismiss in all aspects.[28] The court stated: "Given the allegations of direct or threatened direct harm, albeit shared

---

[26] Gabriel Nelson, *Young Activists Sue U.S. States Over Greenhouse Gas Emissions*, N.Y. TIMES (5 May 2011), available 23 January 2017 at http://www.nytimes.com/gwire/2011/05/05/05greenwire-young-activists-sue-us-states-over-greenhouse-64366.html?pagewanted=all.

[27] Amicus Brief for Dr. James Hansen at 7, *Alec L. v. Jackson*, No. C–11–2203 EMC, (Cal. Nov. 14, 2011), 2011 WL 8583134.

[28] *Juliana*, *supra* note 24, at *7.

by most of the population or future population, the court should be loath to decline standing to persons suffering an alleged concrete injury of a constitutional magnitude."[29]

V. THE FIDUCIARY CORPORATION

The Nature's Trust paradigm re-frames the corporate identity itself. Corporations, having no *actual personhood*, are legal entities created by state-issued charters, thus bound by the same public fiduciary responsibilities as the governments that created them. When the state enables a corporation through charter, its public trust duty to the citizens necessarily flows through the charter as a fiduciary limit, an inherent encumbrance, to constrain the acts of the corporation. It would be difficult to imagine otherwise, as the state cannot constitutionally abrogate its trust responsibility to the people. The state can give no more power to a corporation – a creature of the state – than it gained from the people. A Nature's Trust paradigm recognizes an embedded public trust limitation on the otherwise internally unconstrained power of corporations to destroy public resources. Out of this concept arises a transformational characterization: the fiduciary corporation.

In Speth's earlier chapter (Chapter 2), he urges a transformation of corporations to orient them towards benefiting stakeholders and not just shareholders. Revealing the corporation as a state-creature born within the cradle of sovereign fiduciary responsibility suggests an internal corporate obligation (already present but unrecognized) to protect Nature's Trust for future generations. Activating this fiduciary duty would change the decision making equation to incorporate environmental responsibility that corporations have been content to ignore in a single-minded pursuit of profit. Violation of public fiduciary duties should provide cause for corporate charter revocation.

VI. RE-ORIENTATION OF PROPERTY LAW

American property law is characteristically described as a highly individualistic regime giving landowners almost unfettered liberty to: (1) exert full dominion over all parts of Nature found within boundaries described on a deed; (2) destroy natural bounty with no concern for what remains

---

[29] *Id.* at *4.

for later landowners or future generations; and (3) assert monopolistic exclusion of others despite community need for resources such as water. In a climate-chaotic future with scarce resources, these features of private property law will threaten community welfare.

Private property rights remain inadequately limited by regulatory law (deriving from statutes) due to the political power that vested interests hold over regulatory agencies. A paradigm for a sustaining economy must include a formidable counterweight to private property rights – one that situates ownership in balance with the needs of the community (both the natural and human community) and protects vital resources for future generations. This counterweight must hold the force of a superior law, because once property rights have vested, governments such as the US cannot extinguish them without monetary compensation.[30]

The public trust doctrine represents the other, lesser known, side of property law – seemingly the only established legal doctrine that can adequately temper established private property rights. The *Illinois Central* test allows privatization of public trust assets only where: (1) the grant promotes the interests of the public; and (2) the grant does not *substantially impair* the public interest in the lands and waters remaining.[31] Even when trust lands and resources are properly alienated under this test, private property owners remain subject to the superior, antecedent rights of the public in such resources. The public rights (called *jus publicum*) combine with the private rights (called *jus privatum*) to form full title,[32] and the two sets of rights operate together within a frame of accommodation. The *jus publicum* may take the form of an easement allowing public access over the property (for example, areas along waterways below the high water mark) or a servitude protecting ecology.[33] Because the *jus publicum* forms a pre-existing and inalienable right that "inhere[s] in the title itself", a private property owner will not be entitled to compensation under the American takings clause when the public exercises its right.[34]

When government conveys property rights to a resource in violation of the alienation test above, the private property owner never legitimately acquires full private property rights to the trust property, because the legislature had no authority to alienate such property out of the trust. Therefore, the *Illinois Central* Court held that the railroad's title to

---

30 U.S. CONST. amend. IV.

31 *Ill. Cent. R.R. Co. v. Ill.*, 146 U.S. 387, 452 (1892).

32 *Marks v. Whitney*, 491 P.2d 374, 379 (1971).

33 *See, e.g.*, *Esplanade Properties, L.L.C. v. City of Seattle*, 307 F.3d 978, 985–6 (9th Cir. 2002).

34 *Stevens v. City of Cannon Beach*, 854 P.2d 449, 456 (Or. 1993).

the lakebed could be revoked without compensation where the private title conflicted with the purpose of the trust. This revocation authority finds modern affirmation in the American *Mono Lake* case, where the California Supreme Court declared that "the continuing power of the state as administrator of the public trust . . . extends to the revocation of previously granted rights".[35] Such public trust jurisprudence may prove indispensable to divesting fossil fuel corporations of their claimed rights to coal, oil and natural gas reserves.

In sum, the public trust principle presents a powerful and necessary accommodation between reserved public property rights and acquired private property rights by (1) limiting privatization of crucial resources; (2) empowering government to revoke, without compensation, private property rights to wrongfully alienated trust property (when doing so proves necessary for resource protection); (3) imposing a continuing restraint on private landowners to protect the public's interest in trust resources. It is vital to understand that the public trust principle holds its remarkable legal force precisely because it operates *within* the property rights framework. It is the only existing, anciently established doctrine that sets supreme, recognized limits on private property rights affecting ecology. And by presenting public property rights to protect natural ecosystems, the doctrine broadcasts the importance of ecology to human survival and community welfare.

The key mistake of the industrial legal tradition lies in the assumption that privatization could extend to the natural world as it does to any material object – allowing owners to alter and destroy Nature's parts at their whim. Operating within this realm of property law, the *ecological res* concept overrides industrial dominion in its totality, while still recognizing private rights to quiet enjoyment and usufructuary occupation of titled land. A Nature's Trust concept presents a fiduciary construct of private property ownership, subjecting the owner's use and privacy rights on boundary-defined land to superior community and generational rights to protect the *ecological res* within the claimed private lot. Nature's Trust broadly views all "property rights" to crucial ecology as usufruct rights or life-tenancies only, encumbered with the duty not to waste or cause substantial impairment to the rhythms of Nature, its life-systems, its communities, or its landscapes. Justice Christopher Weeramantry, former judge on the International Court of Justice, articulated this construct when he wrote, "[L]and is never the subject of human ownership, but is only held in

---

35 *Nat'l Audubon Soc'y v. Superior Court of Alpine Co.*, 658 P.2d 709, 723 (1983); *see also Illinois Cent. R.R.*, 146 U.S. at 453.

trust, with all the connotations that follow of due care, wise management, and custody for future generations."[36] The India Supreme Court similarly stated in a leading public trust opinion: "[E]very person exercising his or her right to use the air, water, or land and associated natural ecosystems has the obligation to secure for the rest of us the right to live or otherwise use that same resource or property for the long term and enjoyment by future generations."[37]

VII. BRIDGE TERMINOLOGY

The language traditionally invoked in public trust cases has both benefits and drawbacks. Because courts often use terms such as public trust "assets" or "resources" – terms that have no ready substitute in the English language – to indicate the coverage of trust protection, some may perceive the doctrine as anthropogenic. The critique is too simplistic. The trust construct deals not with the relationship of humans to Nature, but rather the relationship of citizens to the government they empower. The principle arises out of sovereignty, democracy and concern for human rights – all of which are presumably "anthropocentric" (dealing with human relations), but nevertheless legitimate and inspirational ideals of human society. The principle secures inalienable rights of citizens to force the government they empower to protect crucial resources for their survival and for future generations. As one justice of the Massachusetts Supreme Court explained in a tidelands case, "[T]he public trust doctrine stands as a covenant between the people of the Commonwealth and their government, a covenant to safeguard our tidelands *for all generations* for the use of the people."[38]

As a bridge towards a post-industrial law of stewardship, the public trust may reframe divisive ecological conflicts precisely because it brings human-held values (such as liberty, equality, human rights and democracy) into the discussion of environmental policy. For those many Americans who remain openly hostile to the environmental movement, having been fully alienated from its objectives by the fracturing narrative of "environment versus jobs", the description of ecological resources as public trust "assets" yielding "ecosystem services" may be a gateway

---

36 *Gabčíkovo-Nagymaros Project (Hung v. Slovk), Judgment*, 1997 I.C.J. Rep. 7, 108 (Sept. 25) (separate opinion by Weeramantry, J.).

37 *Fomento Resorts and Hotels Ltd. v. Minguel Martins*, (2009) Civ. App. No. 4154 of 2000 (India).

38 *All. to Protect Nantucket Sound v. Energy Facilities Siting Bd.*, 932 N.E.2d 787, 816 (Mass. 2010).

towards recognizing ecological stability as both essential to economic security and a linchpin to other values they cherish.

Nature's Trust moves beyond transition terminology, using the term *ecological res* to signify a full natural world beyond the grasp of private property exploitation and dominion. A Nature's Trust approach characterizes Earth as a full community of balance with both human and natural communities as beneficiaries of the trust. The holistic conception of an *ecological res* within Nature's Trust finds compelling synergy with an approach known as Earth Jurisprudence, which aims towards "expanding the legal consideration of nature".[39] Professor Judith Koons explains, "In this [Earth Jurisprudence] ethic, the role of humanity changes 'from conqueror of the land-community to plain member and citizen of it'."[40] A proposed public trust ordinance drafted (not enacted) for Portland, Oregon forges such ground by identifying both citizens and natural communities as beneficiaries of the public trust to which the sovereign duty of protection is owed, underscoring the "right of local ecology to exist and flourish".[41]

VIII. CULTURAL ENLIGHTENMENT: SYNERGY WITH MORAL, SPIRITUAL, AND RELIGIOUS APPROACHES

Law has the most powerful effect when it reflects deep moral and/or religious understandings in society. Indeed, one of the great weaknesses of environmental statutory law is its wholesale reliance on techno-jargon and procedural requirements that fail to inspire human protection of Nature. The Nature's Trust paradigm dovetails with powerful religious and moral conceptions of the duty to protect the natural world.

The paradigm taps the impulse of human beings to protect a natural legacy for children and the coming generations. As the Philippines Supreme Court stated in a landmark public trust decision, *Oposa v. Factoran*: "[E]very generation has a responsibility to the next to preserve

---

[39] Patricia Siemen, *Earth Jurisprudence: Toward Law in Nature's Balance*, 11 BARRY L. REV. 1, 2–3 (2008).

[40] Judith Koons, *Earth Jurisprudence*, 25 PACE ENVTL. L. REV. 263, 265, 339 (2008) (quoting Aldo Leopold, *The Land Ethic*, *in* A SAND COUNTY ALMANAC 204 (Oxford University Press 1949)).

[41] Portland Or., Draft Ordinance to Create the People's Water Trust (28 October 2013), available 23 January 2017 at https://www.portlandoregon.gov/auditor/59271?a=474699.

that . . . harmony [of Nature] . . . [The] right [to a balanced ecology] concerns nothing less than self-preservation and self-perpetuation[,] . . . the advancement of which may even be said to predate all governments and constitutions . . ."[42]

The world's major religions appear to observe a sacred trusteeship running parallel to the legal trust concept. In a Creation Address, Catholic Pope Benedict XVI declared that God's grant of "dominion" to humankind came entrusted with strong stewardship obligations:

> [N]ature is a gift of the Creator . . . Everything that exists belongs to God, who has *entrusted it to man*, albeit not for his arbitrary use . . . Man thus has a duty to exercise responsible stewardship over creation, to care for it and to cultivate it.[43]

Justice Weeramantry points to a similar trusteeship paradigm operating in the religions of Islam, Buddhism, and Hinduism. Describing Islamic notions of trust, he writes:

> [A] reason why, in Islam, humans are expected to protect the environment is that no other creature is able to perform this task. Humans are the only beings that God has "entrusted" with the responsibility of looking after the earth . . . The planet was inherited by all humankind and all its posterity from generation to generation . . . Each generation is only the trustee.[44]

A lengthy edict issued by Pope Francis, *Laudato Si*, describes a sacred trust by pronouncing Earth "a common home" that God "entrusted" to humans.[45] Focusing on the restraint imposed by a trust, Pope Francis writes: "A fragile world, *entrusted by God to human care*, challenges us to devise intelligent ways of directing, developing and limiting our power."[46] Iterating the same concern for future generations found in the public trust, he writes: "Intergenerational solidarity is not optional, but rather a basic question of justice, since the world we have received also belongs to those who will follow us."[47]

---

42 *Oposa v. Factoran*, G.R. No. 101083 (S.C., July 30, 1993) (Phil.).

43 Mary Christina Wood, *supra* note 1, at 279 (citing Pope Benedict XVI, Address For the Celebration of the World Day of Peace, *If You Want to Cultivate Peace, Protect Creation* (1 January 2010) (transcript available 23 January 2017 at https://www.pope2you.net/download/messaggio%20pace%20ENG.pdf).

44 *Id.* at 279–80 (quoting Justice Weeramantry).

45 Pope Francis, Laudato Si: On Care for Our Common Home ¶¶ 5, 13 (2015).

46 *Id.* ¶ 232.

47 *Id.* ¶ 159.

Ultimately, the Nature's Trust paradigm strives towards an indigenous concept. Traditional native cultures, while by no means generic, characteristically show reverence towards the Creator's gifts, concern for future generations, and an orientation towards the laws of Nature. But the native worldview is complex, refined by millennia of human experience and traditional ecological knowledge, passed down through oral history. In many native societies, law remains inseparable from religion, such that community restraints find inherent reinforcement with the spiritual and moral understandings of the community. This seamless fusion between law and religion forms a worldview utterly foreign to modern industrial society, which has detached humans from Nature, divorced environmental law from the moral pulse of humanity, and embarked on a wholly secular and technocratic course in dealing with the catastrophic environmental syndromes it has caused.

The Nature's Trust construct recognizes tribes as sovereigns having a legitimate and central co-trustee role in ecological management. In the Pacific Northwest, where native American people have lived for 10,000 years in dependence on salmon, the tribes now assert sovereign co-leadership in major ecological disputes of the region. Often voicing values and visions far outside the rhetoric of state and federal agents, tribal leaders have played a crucial role in bringing wolves back to the mountains and keeping salmon alive in the rivers. By recognizing a tribal co-trusteeship, the Nature's Trust paradigm may help society strive towards a new land ethic. As native American law author Rennard Strickland once wrote, "If there is to be a post-Columbian future – a future for any of us – it will be an Indian future . . . a world in which this time . . . the superior world view . . . might even hope to compete with, if not triumph over, technology."[48]

IX. CONCLUSION

The statutory law that has dominated the environmental field for 40 years has legalized colossal damage to life-sustaining resources. In face of looming ecological calamity to which the political branches have not responded, the judiciary's willingness to enforce the public trust doctrine could prove crucial to the endurance of society. The public trust may provide a bridge "across the abyss" towards a Nature's Trust paradigm that would re-orient law towards balanced and sustaining interactions with the natural world.

---

48 Rennard Strickland, *Afterword* to Tonto's Revenge: Reflections on American Indian Culture and Policy 130 (University of New Mexico Press 1997).

PART II

Practical applications

6. Three legal principles for organizations rebuilding the commons

Janelle Orsi

I. INTRODUCTION: ECONOMICS FOR LIFE

Social movements benefit from slogans, so here's one for the next economy: "Trees don't grow on money." The older conventional "wisdom" tells us that "money doesn't grow on trees", and, thus, we are urged to get to work, buy property, invest, and generate money. In industrial societies, wealth accumulation has become a popular strategy for survival. But if survival, or life, itself, is the ultimate goal, why not cut to the chase and simply focus on activities that contribute to the thriving of life? We can sell land and generate money. Or we can steward land and generate life. Trees don't grow on money. They grow on land and life. How do we make that the priority?

Life, itself, could be the basis for the next economy if we work, in earnest, to invert the predominant paradigms of business and markets. It's time to revisit, revise, or replace most of the laws, contracts and organizational structures on which our predominant economy is founded. It will be a task of epic proportions, requiring the assistance of countless legal minds.

Fortunately, this task will demand so much of our creativity, cultural knowledge, social instincts and attention to nature and ecosystems, that the moment we begin to undertake the task, we will feel more alive, joyful and human than we did even the moment before.

Inverting the predominant paradigms of business does not mean doing something *new*; it means applying to enterprise, work and consumption something that we find familiar and uncomplicated. At home, and with ease, we feed our families, tend to the plants, help a neighbor unload her car, smile and enjoy the moments we spend with others, and – incredibly – never send anyone an invoice for our efforts. Elsewhere in our lives, we vie to earn more and pay less, work our way up career ladders, accumulate credentials, strive to get ahead, "make a killing" in the stock market, hoard our assets, and we do all this – quite understandably – because the predominant economy has given no indication that we'll be provided for otherwise.

We go about distinct parts of our lives with those two different orientations, each with their accompanying social protocols, ethics and values. Yet, the same stewardship ethic with which we approach our households can, within carefully crafted organizations, expand into other areas of the economy – into our work, food systems, energy access, housing and land access, and far beyond. The very origin of the word "economy" validates this is a fitting goal. The Greek word "oikonomia" means household management.

Picture your future: You might derive a sense of joy from your participation in a community solar cooperative, a preschool cooperative, a local housing land trust, a neighborhood meal-sharing collective, a community garden, a community lending pool, and the democratic workplace where you work. Why do you derive joy? Because these activities have removed you substantially from the work and business structures that had you driven by a sense of scarcity and competition. Instead, you feel at home in your various communities. You secure your future, not by accumulating a surplus of wealth, but by deepening social ties that provide for you. Your own economy has taken on its true and original meaning of household management. You have also put the lively back into livelihood.

This chapter starts by describing what the commons is and why it is important. It discusses why we need legal structures tailored to enhance and protect the commons. Based on my law practice experience, the chapter then distills three legal principles for the commons: that it is important to cap individuals' ability to extract wealth, the commons are not on the market for sale, and the commons should have polycentric governance, spreading power and responsibility to all involved. Real life case studies provide examples of each of these principles in action.

II. BACK BY POPULAR DEMAND: THE COMMONS

Fortunately, throughout the world and throughout time, people have thrived in similar ways. In his book, *Stewarding the Earth*, Kabir Sanjay Bavikatte describes the works of economic historian Karl Polyani and anthropologist Marshall Sahlins, who show that, "until the nineteenth century, contrary to popular myth, the economy was embedded in social relations",[1] and it wasn't all about buying, selling, competing and accumulating. Since the latter has not worked out well for the majority of people or the planet, we are fortunate to be able to draw upon the examples and methods of the many who have built commons before us.

"Commons" has become an umbrella term for a wide variety of practices that look roughly like this: People work together to make decisions and allocate resources, with the goal of providing for and sustaining communities in the long-term.[2]

There isn't a perfect formula for identifying what is or isn't a "commons", but there is a certain frame-of-mind that accompanies the act of commoning. To borrow from Bavikatte's way of summing it up, this is an "ethic of sufficiency, sharing and caring".[3] In more detail, this means that in commons:

(1) caring – not competing – motivates our actions and decisions;
(2) sharing – not bidding and buying – is our mode of providing for our needs; and
(3) sufficiency (aka enough) – not as-much-as-we-can-get – is a primary goal.

Marjorie Kelly, author of *Owning our Future*,[4] frames this well. She describes generative enterprises ("creating economic architectures that are self-organized around serving the needs of life"), in contrast to extractive enterprises (which are designed for "maximum physical and financial extraction").

Other words and phrases, such as "new economy", "sharing economy", "sustainable economies" and "resilient communities" have been used to encapsulate the transition to generative and commons-based economies. However, I caution that those phrases sometimes get applied to activities that layer socially and environmentally beneficial activities over otherwise extractive business structures. Corporate social responsibility, B Corp certification, green business certification, and other trendy business practices

---

[1] Kabir Sanjay Bavikatte, Stewarding The Earth: Rethinking Property and the Emergence of Biocultural Rights (Oxford University Press 2014).

[2] There are many ways to define and describe "commons". My way of describing the commons is largely derived from the work of David Bollier. *See, e.g.*, David Bollier, Think Like a Commoner: A Short Introduction to the Life of the Commons (New Society Publishers 2014).

[3] Kabir Sanjay Bavikatte, *supra* note 1.

[4] Marjorie Kelly, Owning Our Future: The Emerging Ownership Revolution 10–11 (Berrett-Koehler Publishers 2012).

make a positive difference in the world, but do not necessarily challenge the underlying ownership structures of the predominant system. So long as individual shareholders are able to profit substantially or limitlessly by extracting resources or making resources scarce, attempts to affect positive social and environmental transformation will remain laden with the pressures of the market. Commons-based organizations, on the other hand, could offer a true paradigm shift.

III. WHY COMMONS NEED LAW . . . AND SO MUCH MORE

It may be hard to believe that something so cold, dry and distant as law could have anything to do with creating a culture of caring, sharing and sufficiency. But law can hold commons in place, even with destabilizing market forces swirling all around us. Law can also give us a sense of security, even with fears of rapid global change and scarcity troubling our minds. We can use legally enforceable agreements, bylaws, deed restrictions and other legal tools to make safe spaces for commons.

There's one snag: We can't just use rules and crafty legal structures to make something into a commons. Commons won't succeed without accompanying cultural, social, inter-personal, emotional and psychological transformation. It would be like trying to build a sofa with nothing but wood. It's no good without the soft parts. But without the solid frame, it would be a loose pile of pillows. Solid legal structures will support the flourishing of the softer parts of commoning.

And those are the *good* parts: the trust that we build with others, the use of our innate caring abilities, and the overall reduction of the sense of separation between ourselves and others. It's worth repeating: commons-based legal work is going to make us come alive. We'll build the legal structures and the cultural, social, interpersonal, emotional and psychological structures all at the same time. Sometimes we won't even perceive the place where law ends and life begins.

We can use the law to protect commons from the extractive tendencies of the predominant economic system. In the common grazing lands of England, the shepherds who shared responsibility for and access to the lands had a regular practice known as "beating the bounds".[5] Where other people had put up walls or hedges to enclose lands and exclude

---

[5] *Beating the Bounds*, WIKIPEDIA, available 24 January 2017 at https://en.wikipedia.org/wiki/Beating_the_bounds.

others, the commoners "beat back" those boundaries to keep the land open to the group. Today, we are beating back more than a hedge row. We are beating back one of the strongest, most oppressive, yet somehow most enticing forces in history: the market and potential for wealth accumulation. For commons to emerge, thrive and survive in the long term, we need to build strong legal foundations that hold commons in place, resisting the seduction of the market and the temptation to fall into old habits of operation. In particular, we'll need enforceable rules to keep the commons from being sold into the market or devolving into oppressive hierarchies.

We can use the law to build trust in the foundations of the commons. The agreements we make with one another become laws to the extent that they are enforceable by courts and other mechanisms of our legal system. Those agreements – whether formalized or not – create the necessary predictability and reliability within which commons may emerge. Within certain boundaries, people will relax and share with others. With long-term commitments, people can let go of the tendency to hoard for the future. With limits on the ability to satisfy our drive to accumulate, other motivations, like nurturing, can take over the helm. Caring, sharing and sufficiency can begin to flourish when they rest securely on solid legal foundations.

The next section outlines some cornerstones of those legal foundations: Practices and principles to embed into commons-based organizations that not only create a protective space in which commons may safely emerge, but also create the conditions in which a flourishing of new customs and social ties will become the real substance of the commons.

IV. METHODOLOGY: LESSONS FROM PRACTICE

Much of what I write about in this chapter is inspired by my experiences providing legal services to clients, both in private practice and through my nonprofit organization, the Sustainable Economies Law Center. I have worked with nearly 350 clients over almost a decade, including land trusts, worker cooperatives, energy cooperatives, housing cooperatives and lending circles. While observing their successes and challenges, I have been on a constant search for the legal strategies that make their initiatives powerful, transformative and sustainable in the long-term.

From that, I have begun to take seriously the potential for governance and financial structures to really make or break the success of our clients' work. The principles described below have now become essential considerations that we discuss with most clients. Further, we have also been working to subvert predominant paradigms within our law center, and have put many of these principles into practice in our governance and financial structure. Thus, I use these actual applications of the principles to serve as examples throughout.

A. Three Legal Principles for the Commons

There are three legal principles for the commons. These are that it is important to cap individuals' ability to extract wealth from the commons, the commons are not on the market for sale, and the commons should have polycentric governance providing many sources of power and responsibility. Each principle is introduced by noting how it can be viewed from both a positive/creative angle and a negative/preventive angle. This is followed by narratives providing examples of each principle. Each principle protects against the destructive forces of inequality, hierarchy, greed, and extraction; at the same time, they generate more equitable, participatory and sustainable organizations. Altogether, they create a stable foundation for commons and for the natural emergence of caring, sharing, and sufficiency as the driving values.

1. Principle: caps on extraction

- **To create:** A culture of sufficiency.
- **To prevent:** A drive toward maximum return.

In every commons-based enterprise and organization, it will be important to put a cap on the wealth that any private individual may extract. This means capping salaries, capping return on investment, capping sale price for assets such as land, and limiting the use or depletion of resources.

In this way, decisions are no longer driven by the question of: "How can we maximize our gain?" Rather, decisions are made with reference to other goals, such as: "What do we need to ensure that everyone has *enough*?" "How can we create a broad social or ecological benefit?" and "What will sustain this resource for us in the long-term?" The goals of sufficiency, outward benefit, and long-term sustainability more easily fill the gap left when we remove the profit-maximization imperative.

When extraction is capped, everyone's state-of-mind changes. Worker-owners of worker cooperatives don't concern themselves with the market value of their business. They focus on creating good livelihoods in the long-term. When extraction is capped, homeowners are less likely to make cosmetic improvements and time their home sale with the goal of gaining the maximum return in the market. Rather, they focus on creating a wonderful place to live and they sell when their life circumstances – not fluctuating housing prices – tell them it's time to do so.

(a) Example: capping home equity and living well together I have provided legal services to many "intentional communities", from urban cohousing communities to rural ecovillages. After I prepared the legal documents and helped with legal compliance to establish the communities, a handful of my clients have later sought my help to dissolve their communities, often after dramatic interpersonal conflict tore the community apart. The conflict-ridden communities had one characteristic in common: None of them used a limited equity model. Thus, they formed their communities with two conflicting motivations: (1) to have a wonderful home and community, and (2) to profit from their investment. These two motivations clashed when market value fluctuations made people nervous and put pressure on some to invest in unnecessary improvements and sell before others were ready. The chapter starts with the slogan that trees don't grow on money. Neither do love and community. The desire to profit off their investment often had a chilling effect on the warmth and mutual respect within the groups.

The Sustainable Economies Law Center is currently working with a client to implement what we are calling a Permanent Real Estate Cooperative (PREC). The vision is to form a large cooperative of individuals who work to create multiple limited equity housing projects in the San Francisco Bay Area. "Limited equity" refers to an ownership model that puts a cap on the rate of return received when a resident-owner sells a housing unit. That rate of return is usually modest and tied to an index such as the Consumer Price Index, thereby preventing owners from profiting due simply to area market conditions. This also stabilizes the price of the unit so desirable homes don't become too expensive and go to ever-wealthier households.

Unlike charities and other affordable housing developers that provide housing for low to moderate income households, PREC's goal is to perpetuate a culture in which everyone – not just low-income people – will come to expect that they should live in limited equity housing, treating homes as *homes*, and not as investment vehicles. If someone purchases a unit for USD$200,000 and knows they will get USD$220,000 if they vacate the unit 10 years later, they can relax and not worry that the activities or ethnic make-up of their neighbors will depress market values. The widespread perpetuation of limited equity models may break with historical patterns of redlining, "White flight", gentrification, displacement and other socio-economic dynamics driven by real estate markets that leave many people behind in pursuit of profits. The stabilization of housing prices can allow everyone to spend less on housing, and thereby build wealth in other ways, eliminating the current divide between people who build wealth (homeowners) and people who generally don't (renters).

Capping extraction creates a more stable environment, insulated from the pressures of the market; it allows more trusting relationships and stronger communities to emerge.

(b) Example: capping salaries and growing our collective benefit Even a nonprofit or cooperative can get swept up in the dynamic of limitless extraction if democracy breaks down and powerful stakeholders use their leverage to extract value from the organization. For example, the CEO of Recreation Equipment, Inc. (REI Cooperative) leveraged USD$3.6 million in compensation from the cooperative in 2015, up from USD$2.7 million in 2014.[6] Apparently no one, especially not the CEO, was asking whether 2.7 million was "enough". If enough were the goal, the cooperative wouldn't give the CEO a USD$900,000 raise while employees are still working at minimum wage. Each part-time Board member is paid USD$80,000 per year, an amount recently set by the Board. Further weakening democratic participation of cooperative members, the Board nominates candidates to run in Board elections. The cooperative members then vote to elect individuals from this narrow pool of candidates, leaving very little room for the exercise of democracy. Without compensation limits, without checks and balances on Board power by the cooperative members, it isn't too surprising that compensation has run amuck at this cooperative.

What would it look like if we stop viewing our time, labor, skills and credentials as commodities we leverage to climb a pay scale ladder? When people are not in a position to limitlessly grow their wealth, their likely impulse will be to grow in other ways. People grow personally and work to grow the wealth and vitality of the organizations and world around them. Already, more and more people are developing the self-awareness to know that money doesn't buy happiness. Daniel Pink's book, *Drive: The Surprising Truth About What Motivates Us*, cites countless studies demonstrating this.[7]

To shift from an extractive to a generative view of our time and labor, we need to shift the focus of compensation decisions from "as-much-as-we-can-get" to "enough". All staff members of the Sustainable Economies Law Center, which is based in the high-cost of living area of Berkeley, California, make USD$51,125 per year, plus health and childcare benefits. We use the MIT Living Wage Calculator as an objective measure of

---

6 Recreation Equipment, Inc., Executive Compensation (2015), available 24 January 2017 at https://www.rei.com/content/dam/documents/pdf/Financial%20 Statements/2015%20Executive%20Compensation%20Summary.pdf.

7 Daniel H. Pink, Drive: The Surprising Truth About What Motivates Us (Riverhead Books 2011).

"enough" for a parent and child to live on in our region. This is an experiment in progress, and we are finding that "enough" is even more context-specific than region-specific. This salary feels like more-than-enough to some coworkers and not-quite-enough to others, making it a source of tension, leading staff and the Board of the Sustainable Economies Law Center to consider paying some people more based on their need.

Regardless of whether the law center keeps equal salaries or creates a differential based on need, what's powerful from this example is that no staff member can push to raise their salary on the basis of their education level, experience, or contribution to the organization. Any energy that could have been spent on competition among coworkers is channeled into the purpose of the organization: to serve the community. My coworkers invest a good deal in personal growth and education and they contribute incredible work and passion to the organization, and it's not driven by a desire for a raise in pay. Without the potential for extractive work, we focus more fully on generative work.

Whether in home equity or salaries, capping extraction is challenging. It has interesting implications for the autonomy of commons because it requires that one or more parties be in a position to enforce the caps. Sometimes it will be wise to give an outside party, such as a separate organization, the ability to intervene if the caps are violated. Otherwise, the collective self-interest of decision makers, the break-down of democracy, or coercive patterns among commoners could lead to a disregard for any caps. In California, limited equity housing cooperatives are required by law to adhere to the caps, but even the law doesn't guarantee actual adherence. For this reason, community land trusts often obtain the right to enforce such caps by owning the land underlying the buildings and leasing the land to the cooperative with an enforceable requirement that residents maintain limited equity. With a land trust as a landlord, however, the cooperative may have less autonomy. Striking a balance between autonomy and enforceable restraints is a theme that will weave throughout the emergence of commons-based organizations.

2. Principle: the commons are not for sale: permanent removal from the market

- **To create:** Commons in perpetuity.
- **To prevent:** Being enclosed and sold into the market.

All of our efforts to build more localized, sustainable economies will be undermined if, down the road, someone has the power to sell off the assets on which such economies were built. If a cooperative establishes a small local farm on land it rents, the landowner may still one day sell the land to a large corporation. If we create worker-owned businesses, the workers could decide to sell the entire business to a larger company.

The profitable New Belgium Brewing company provides just such a cautionary tale. While the company brags that it is 100 percent worker-owned through an employee stock ownership plan (ESOP), there are rumors that the company is seeking a buyer.[8] Lately, the world's largest beer companies, such as Budweiser, are rapidly buying up smaller breweries. With an estimated valuation of one billion USD, it's possible that each of New Belgium's approximately 500 current worker-shareholders could cash out with an average of two million USD. This is a nice deal for current workers, but a terrible deal for future workers and potentially for the communities in which New Belgium is located. A large beer corporation could consolidate the operation with other holdings, move to where labor is cheaper, cut pay and benefits, or do any other number of things that profit-maximizing companies do to make money. The flaw of New Belgium's worker-ownership model is that it is designed for exit. It will guarantee very good livelihoods for the employees at the table at the time of sale, but only for a limited time.

(a) Example: the Loconomics Cooperative is not for sale Tech company Loconomics recently converted into a cooperative, owned primarily by independent or freelance workers who use the company's app to offer, schedule and receive payment for services such as house cleaning, home care, health care, dog walking and errands. Unlike similar companies, such as TaskRabbit, which takes a 30 percent cut of freelance workers' pay, Loconomics operates for the benefit of freelance workers and therefore takes no cut, opting instead to cover company costs with a USD$30 monthly fee for users.

In a world filled with multibillion-dollar tech giants, if Loconomics is to gain success by growing a large number of users, it will also likely gain the interest of potential buyers. To remove this future option, the Loconomics Bylaws include multiple safeguards against the sale of the company:

- There is a clear statement that Loconomics and its assets may not be sold for the purpose of operating as a conventional for-profit. There

---

[8] John Boyle, *Potential New Belgium Sale Worth Fretting Over?* Citizen-Times (7 January 2016), available 24 January 2017 at http://www.citizen-times.com/story/news/local/2016/01/07/potential-new-belgium-sale-worth-fretting-over/78326298/.

is also a statement to protect Directors who vote against sale and to prevent a court from undermining this decision:

> "It shall never be considered a violation of a Director's fiduciary duty to vote against a buyout of Loconomics. In the event that a court is asked to consider whether this section of the Bylaws creates an unreasonable restraint on alienation, the court should analyze this restraint in consideration of the values and mission of Loconomics, along with a view toward the current economic conditions in the world where the vast majority of wealth is controlled by a relatively small number of corporations and individuals. Loconomics aims to grow the wealth and economic stability of the many, and therefore consciously aims to restrain its ability to contribute to the consolidation of wealth by freely selling Loconomics to a high bidder."[9]

- In the event that a sale does take place, the members/owners may receive no more than an average of USD$1,000 each, and any remaining proceeds must go to nonprofit organizations.[10]
- Any attempts to sell the company or change the above would require approval by a majority of *all* member/owners (consider that there could be tens of thousands of them), a majority of the Board, and a majority of three individuals who helped create the cooperative (with the idea that the three individuals, if no longer involved, will likely vote to preserve the original intent to maintain a cooperative in the long-term).[11]

3. Principle: many centers of power; many centers of responsibility

- **To create:** A diverse, adaptable, and resilient commons, with communities of engaged participants to whom the system is responsive and accountable.
- **To prevent:** The concentration of power at the top of hierarchies.

Nobel Prize-winning economist, Elinor Ostrom, studied commons around the world and demonstrated that commons generally thrive – meaning they endure and do not easily fall victim to individuals acting in self-interest – when they exhibit certain characteristics and practices. These include that the rulemaking, decision making, and monitoring of the

---

[9] Loconomics Cooperative Bylaws (adopted 8 December 2015) paragraph 44(a), on file with author, and www.Loconomics.com.

[10] Loconomics Cooperative Bylaws (adopted 8 December 2015) paragraph 44(b).

[11] Loconomics Cooperative Bylaws (adopted 8 December 2015) paragraphs 44(c) and 53.

resources is participatory, adapted to local conditions, and conducted by the very same people who use and benefit from the resources.[12] A centralized top-down governance structure simply cannot achieve such a participatory and adaptive system.

Thus, polycentric governance is critical. This means creating many centers of power. A governance structure that actively cultivates many centers of power avoids the concentration of power in the hands of few. In a commons-based organization, ideally, every person would be a center of power, having a good deal of agency and any necessary autonomy to identify needs and meet them, come up with ideas and execute them, and spot opportunities and take them. The individual does so within the context of small groups that are also centers of power. Preferably, such groups are small enough that members can participate meaningfully and be highly accountable to one another in the exercise of their own autonomy.

I emphasize that power must be distributed to the level of the individual (as opposed merely to small groups) because of the necessity that participation in commons be voluntary and intrinsically motivated. In addition, I emphasize that it must happen within the context of small groups to create direct accountability and spur social motivation. The highly necessary "soft parts" of commons, such as trust and caring, emerge from quite deep within each person. They cannot be coerced out of people.

The more that power can be distributed down to the level of individuals working semi-autonomously in small groups, the more that intrinsic and social motivation become drivers of people's decisions and actions. In hierarchical organizations, people often do things because they have to. Coercion, however subtle, is present throughout organizations. In successful commons, people work together with others, build relationships and are motivated to act, voluntarily, in ways that sustain those relationships. It is within these centers of power that people begin to work well together, because they see each other, care about one another and trust one another.

Polycentricity has other benefits that are both obvious and subtle, but which are critical to the emergence of commons. Polycentric organizations are inviting of cultural diversity, and resist tendencies to become homogeneous. Another benefit of polycentricity is that semi-autonomous centers of power can sometimes break off and become fully autonomous. This makes commons resilient in the event that one part of the organization becomes corrupt or challenged in other ways. In addition, polycentricity enables rapid scaling, as I describe in the next example.

---

12 Elinor Ostrom, Governing the Commons: The Evolution of Institutions for Collective Action (Cambridge University Press 1990).

(a) Example: polycentric strategies for building a National Farmland Commons Polycentric structures help meet a timely need: To scale commons rapidly. With the help of the Sustainable Economies Law Center, the Agrarian Trust is developing a polycentric structure in order to scale up rapidly. With nearly half the US farmland expected to be sold by retiring "Baby Boomers" within the next 20 years, there are at least two choices: Build commons-based organizations everywhere to acquire that land soon or allow the wealthiest people and corporations to purchase and enclose this precious commons. By designing the Agrarian Trust to be polycentric, we enable groups of farmers, aspiring farmers and community members everywhere to come together locally, self-organize into teams, and then plug themselves into the Agrarian Trust for the purpose of acquiring and protecting land in the long term. The Board of the Agrarian Trust will not sit at the top of the hierarchy recruiting participants and deciding where to buy land and what to do with it. Rather, the Board will work to create a welcoming space into which groups of individuals may voluntarily enter and participate, as well as a container in which to hold legal title to land.

The client and legal team contemplated a more conventional representative democracy because it sounded good in theory: Different classes of Trust members (farmers, farmworkers and farm support organizations) would vote to elect representatives to the national Board of Directors, under the theory that the Board members would lead from the top while representing the interests of various member classes.

But we kept recalling a classic problem of membership-based organizations: It can be very hard to get a diversity of people to attend meetings, vote in elections, serve on the Board, or even serve on committees. When representative democracy doesn't actually feel representative of people's interests, people disengage, and lack of representation becomes self-reinforcing. Getting people to show up to meetings feels like pulling teeth. Governing from the top becomes a thankless job.

So we resolved that the entire structure of the Agrarian Trust should emphasize governance from the bottom. There will still be a representative Board elected by farmers, farmworkers and farm support organizations, but the Board's primary role is to oversee a system of polycentric governance, to push planning and decision making away from itself and into transparent and accountable groups working at the ground-level. The idea behind this legal design is to motivate people to show up and participate in meetings when the meetings involve small groups working together on projects involving their own land and their own community. It may be too soon to say whether the vision will succeed, but I have seen a glimpse of it in action. The Trust's founder, Severine von Tscharner Fleming, and I gave a joint keynote speech at an environmental law conference in Eugene, Oregon. After the speech, a group of young farmers immediately approached Severine to discuss how they could get organized to bring local land into the Agrarian Trust. That is exactly the kind of locally-initiated and self-motivated action that the Trust is aiming to set into autonomous motion everywhere.

(b) Example: worker self-management and staff trusteeship at the Sustainable Economies Law Center The Sustainable Economies Law Center has a unique governance structure compared to most 501(c)(3) nonprofit organizations. Instead of a Board delegating management to an Executive Director who administers a hierarchical structure, the Board has empowered all workers to manage the organization through a highly structured and accountable system of staff self-management. Apart from receiving equal salaries, all staff members participate in a system of governance largely borrowed from a model called Holacracy,[13] which distributes power to small semi-autonomous circles throughout the organization. The various facets of the law center's governance structure are detailed on our website, and it would be too much to describe here.[14] However, one of the effects of the structure is that each of the 12 staff members is a center of power and self-management, meaning that they are empowered to sense the needs of the organization and the constituents we serve, and respond to those needs by taking action, with input from coworkers. The Board of Directors serves primarily in an oversight role, having resolved that it is in the best interest of the organization and most effectively advances our mission to activate all staff members as leaders.

We call our model "staff trusteeship," by which we mean all staff members of the organization are trustees with a duty to manage the organization for its beneficiaries, the community and planet. In a staff trusteeship nonprofit, every staff member becomes a point of accountability for the organization, taking on responsibility to listen to the needs and ideas of its stakeholders. Each staff member has heightened duties to respond to those needs and ideas, and, as such, heightened influence within the organization. The self-management structure provides the necessary degree of agency for each staff member. In particular, staff will formally recognize a duty of care that requires that any staff person take action when they see a

---

13 Brian Robertson, Holacracy: The New Management System for a Rapidly Changing World (Holt 2015).

14 Sustainable Econ. Law Ctr., www.theselc.org (accessed 24 January 2017).

problem or room for improvement. Staff trusteeship creates many centers of responsibility by creating many centers of power.

Having practiced this self-management structure at the Sustainable Economies Law Center for three-and-a-half-years, I've come to believe that staff self-management can radically improve the efficacy of any organization working toward a public benefit. This goes against a great deal of conventional "wisdom" in the nonprofit sector, which posits that financially disinterested individuals should exercise careful control from the top, in order to keep the organization accountable to the public. This reflects a belief that people at every level could act in self-interest to the detriment of the organization and its mission.

What the world has now learned from people like Elinor Ostrom is that such a "tragedy of the commons" is not inevitable. Certain organizational characteristics, including participatory governance by interested stakeholders and high levels of autonomy for small groups, can cultivate a different pattern of behavior and go significantly beyond the tendency of people to maximize their self-interest to the detriment of the community. Thus, public benefit nonprofit organizations that adopt a commons-based structure and operate under guiding principles recommended by Ostrom, could very likely be more accountable to the public and more effective in advancing their missions than hierarchical organizations.

In other words, the nonprofit sector should be looking seriously at restructuring organizational governance. Further, if the 10 percent of people in the US who work in nonprofits were all to experience and practice work in a commons-based organization, we would be well-prepared to apply such experiences and skills to many other areas of life.[15] I have now experienced the trust, accountability and dedication that can emerge in a polycentric workplace: nonprofits with staff self-management can be powerful training grounds for leadership for a commons-based economy.

(c) Example: interpretive [cartoon] legal documents for a worker collective Writer and revolutionary, Frantz Fanon, wrote in his book, *The Wretched of the Earth*: "Of course, if we choose to use a language comprehensible only to law and economics graduates it will be easy to prove that the masses need to have their life run for them."[16]

---

[15] *Nonprofits Account for 11.4 Million Jobs, 10.3 Percent of all Private Sector Employment*, BUREAU OF LABOR STATISTICS, U.S. DEPT. OF LABOR (21 October 2014), accessed 24 January 2017 at http://www.bls.gov/opub/ted/2014/ted_20141021.htm.

[16] FRANTZ FANON, THE WRETCHED OF THE EARTH 130–31 (Richard Philcox trans., Grove Press 2004) (1963).

That quote resonates with my recent decision to abandon conventional legal document templates when drafting an Operating Agreement for an immigrant women-owned worker collective. An Operating Agreement represents the workers' mutual agreement about decision making processes, finances, distribution of responsibilities and other key matters in the running of a business. A staff member at a nonprofit organization that incubates such cooperatives recently told me: "In every cooperative we've worked with, this has always been the MOST difficult thing for everyone – getting cooperative members to read and understand the Operating Agreement."[17] It is true that, even when I have drafted documents in what I believed to be plain language, it has been a challenge for cooperative members to read and retain all of the information. Now, the more I grasp the absolute necessity of empowering every individual to participate meaningfully, express their autonomy, and know the impact their actions have on the collective, I see that the critical importance of cooperative members not being intimidated or confused by the very operating rules that govern them.

Thus, instead of a standard legal document, I drafted an LLC Operating Agreement consisting of 50 cartoon slides, each explaining an aspect of the organization's operations. The agreement begins with a statement that the cartoon slideshow is designed to be a legally-binding document and that any court interpreting the document should do so by deriving meaning from the perspective of a reasonable person in reading the combination of pictures and words. The cooperative members' ability to grasp the concepts in the Operating Agreement allowed us to deepen our conversations about the details of their operations, much more than I have experienced in any other worker cooperative. Figure 6.1 is one of the cartoon slides from this Operating Agreement of a worker-owned popsicle company. The Operating Agreement was executed in Spanish.[18] In the bottom right corner is a space for each Owner to write their initials to approve the page.

Graphic legal documents are likely to become the modus operandi at

---

[17] Janelle Orsi, Co-Founder, Sustainable Econ. Law Ctr., interview with anonymous (28 July 2015).

[18] This page translates:

Rotation of responsibilities

With the goal of empowering all Owners to understand various aspects of the business, and with the goal of avoiding the formation of hierarchies, the Owners will regularly rotate responsibilities. Every Owner can develop a particular area of skill and responsibility, but at the same time, also commits to training other Owners in that area. The yellow popsicle person is holding a bank statement and asking "What do I do with this?" The green person is holding a pineapple and asking "What do I do with this?"

Figure 6.1 Example of graphic legal document

the Sustainable Economies Law Center. I've begun to call these visual legal documents "interpretive legal documents", since they are designed to be interpreted by the users, themselves, and prevent the common situation where people must hire a lawyer to help them understand their own agreements. The Ristino chapter (Chapter 12) describes a similar process and calls this "Legal Design". Whatever the term, the end is to increase the accessibility of the law.

Our clients are building democratic organizations and every member should therefore be able to participate meaningfully in the democratic process. When we draft legal documents that people genuinely understand, everyone can become a creator and re-shaper of the law. We can craft rules and policies that are adapted to our circumstances, reducing a reliance on broad-sweeping top-down solutions imposed by unaccountable governments or boards of directors, and enabling the creation of a far more localized and adaptive legal system overall.

V. CONCLUSION

The three principles described in this chapter do not stand alone in creating the legal basis for the commons, although they are among the most important. Other principles and practices are critical, particularly as we begin to build the commons in the context of a world fraught with extreme ecosystem damage and racial and economic inequality. As such, it is paramount that organizations look beyond their immediate contexts and adopt practices that actively seek to restore ecosystems, redress the harms of historic racism, redistribute wealth, and regenerate the conditions for thriving local economies around the globe.

In addition, commons-based organizations must actively participate in building a commons movement, since the success of the commons is so dependent on the simultaneous emergence of a diverse ecosystem of commons organizations. We need financial cooperatives to fund software cooperatives that meet the needs of workers cooperatives that work on land cooperatives, and so on. Each new piece of this ecosystem will further strengthen the other, enabling organizations to evermore safely and powerfully step outside of the predominant economic system. How do we craft legal structures that support and drive organizations to build movements and seek widespread equity and justice? Answers lie ahead, as the legal life of the commons has only begun to take shape.

7. Reinventing law for the commons

David Bollier

I. INTRODUCTION

Although it is customary for mainstream economists and politicians to consider the commons a failed management regime – the "tragedy of the commons" – it is in fact a pervasive and highly generative system for meeting people's needs. Commons tend to function in more culturally satisfying, ecologically responsible ways, which is more than can be said for conventional markets and government systems. An estimated two billion people in the world depend upon various natural resource commons (water, forests, fisheries, farmland, wild game, and so on) to meet their everyday needs – and over the past 20 years, many people in modern, industrialized contexts have (re)discovered the commons as a new paradigm of self-provisioning.[1] It is producing everything from software, textbooks to farm equipment, and providing valuable stewardship for urban spaces, indigenous knowledge, natural resources and cooperative finance.

Historically, most commons have not needed nor sought formal protections of law. Their self-organized customs, socially negotiated rules and relative isolation from outside capital and markets, were enough to sustain them. This has changed dramatically over the past 30 to 40 years, however, as global commerce, technology and conventional law have relentlessly expanded, superimposing the logic and values of markets on nearly every corner of nature and social life. The resulting enclosures of the commons amount to seizures of common assets for private gain. They are also destroying culturally coherent, productive communities operating

---

[1] Fred Pearce, Int'l Land Coalition, Common Ground: Securing Land Rights and Safeguarding the Earth 7 (2016), available 25 January 2017 at http://www.landcoalition.org/sites/default/files/documents/resources/bp-common-ground-land-rights-020316-en.pdf. Since these commons do not generally involve market activity and do not contribute to GDP, they are ignored by conventional economists as insufficiently interesting or as a deficiency ("wastelands") to be remedied by "development".

outside of the market/state order, forcing people to become consumers and employees in order to meet their needs.

As enclosures have taken control of common assets – paradoxically acknowledging the actual value of commons – they have spurred new interest in using law to protect commons. This topic has a rich but interrupted history going back to the Magna Carta and its companion document, the Charter of the Forest, which provided commoners with explicit legal rights of access to forests, pastures, rivers and other natural resources.[2] In similar fashion today, commoners are increasingly devising new legal mechanisms to protect their access and use of shared resources from predatory market activity.

This is, in fact, a burgeoning new arena of political innovation – commoners devising their own forms of law. It can be seen in subsistence commons of the global South, digital commons on the Internet, and knowledge and design commons for physical production. New legal regimes are being created to manage public spaces, water systems and education as urban commons; provide social services, and introduce credit and barter systems through co-operatives.

These and other efforts brashly embrace a paradox – building a new social order of commoning through creative hacks of laws that have been predicated on the sanctity of individual rights, private property, markets and state authority. Remarkably, there are now many successful adaptations of laws dealing with contracts, trusts, co-operatives, municipal government, copyright and patents, among others, that aim to protect common assets and the social practices of commoning. One might say that this experimentation and exploration are producing a new, not-yet-recognized body of socio-legal-political innovation, "Law for the Commons".

Taken together, the efforts described in this chapter represent a bold attempt to move beyond the confines of conventional law, governance and bureaucracy, and to invent new legal forms for authorizing and enabling commoning. Rather than emphasize law as an instrument of external coercion and presumed legitimacy, this chapter highlights "commoning", a set of self-organized, living social practices and norms, as the critical force of governance and "law". From this perspective, state law is seen as an enabling tool for commoners – chiefly in dealing with the state and market enclosures – and not as a substitute for commoning itself. The chapter proceeds by laying the foundation for understanding the relationship between the state and the commons. Then it identifies eight fields of inno-

---

2 *See, e.g.*, PETER LINEBAUGH, THE MAGNA CARTA MANIFESTO: LIBERTY AND COMMONS FOR ALL (University of California Press 2008).

vations in commoning: (1) indigenous commons, (2) subsistence commons in the global South, (3) digital commons, (4) stakeholder trusts, (5) urban commons, (6) localism, (7) cooperative law, and (8) new organizational forms. Finally, it reflects on the "why" behind the chapter, the strategic value of developing law for the commons.

II. THE STATE AND THE COMMONS

As this introduction implies, the commons envisions a modified role for the state in meeting people's needs. Currently the state is committed to expanding markets and economic growth, and secondarily, to providing basic social services and environmental protections that markets do not or cannot provide. As neoliberal economic policies and politics have surged since the 1980s, these latter state functions have been relentlessly attacked through "austerity politics" (budget cutbacks, deregulation, privatization) and wishful dreams of achieving "sustainability" through a "green economy".

Many commons advocates believe that the commons provides many answers to vexing problems such as climate change, ecological destruction and wealth inequality, and that the larger agenda must be the pursuit of a post-capitalist vision of state power.[3] While familiar state functions such as social services and security will continue to be needed, commoners see affirmative value in new forms of self-provisioning that avoid the pathologies of markets. This tends to entail the development of new forms of social organization, more respectful relationships with particular ecosystems, and the relocalization of markets and self-governance.

Eventually, such changes require affirmative changes in law so that commoning is not criminalized, ignored or subordinated to market-based norms, especially in terms of recognized property rights, social organization and collective entitlements. As we will see below, commoners have responded to these lacunae in state law by developing creative improvisations. Commons-based law becomes a modus vivendi with a hostile state that has prior allegiances to capital and markets, and disdain for commoning as a competing nexus of power and moral authority.[4]

---

[3] *See, e.g.*, David Bollier, *New Report: State Power and Commoning* (22 July 2016), available 25 January 2017 at http://bollier.org/blog/new-report-state-power-and-commoning (exploring how state power is used to support markets and stymie commoning)

[4] *See, e.g.*, FRITJOF CAPRA AND UGO MATTEI, THE ECOLOGY OF LAW: TOWARD A LEGAL SYSTEM IN TUNE WITH NATURE AND COMMUNITY (Berrett-Koehler Publishers 2015).

Many commoners wish to change conventional state law because of the alarming gap they see between legality and legitimacy, a distinction made by French legal scholar Étienne Le Roy.[5] The state may have formal legality on its side, but often it does not have an earned social legitimacy. Law for the Commons seeks to bridge this gap between the formal strictures of state law and bureaucratic rules adopted by political and corporate elites – "legality" – and the experiences and vernacular norms and practices of ordinary people. Commoners often need to evade, hack or finesse this gap. "Vernacular law," as I call it, consists of the "unofficial" social norms, procedures and customary institutions that peer communities devise to manage their own resources, outside of the state and market. Vernacular law has a moral and social legitimacy that commoners are struggling to assert, not just through law but through political struggles and cultural expression.[6]

So in this sense, commons-based legal innovation is an attempt to overcome the structural limitations of the formal apparatus of market/state governance as now constituted. This is a vexing challenge because, with the exception of the public trust doctrine as explained in Wood's chapter (Chapter 5), state law is philosophically hostile to, or simply non-comprehending of, the very idea of commons and commoning. State-administered law is focused on individual, private property rights and market exchange; it is structurally focused on "things" in isolation from dynamic social relationships, history, culture and ecosystems. The struggle to inscribe a "commons-based law" within the edifice of conventional state law is therefore an ambiguous or paradoxical challenge; some say it is impossible.[7]

To be sure, the idea of the commons as a generative force independent of the state or market flies in the face of the "tragedy of the commons" parable popularized by Garrett Hardin in his famous 1968 essay.[8] Hardin

---

[5] Étienne Le Roy, *How I Have Been Conducting Research on the Commons for Thirty Years Without Knowing It*, *in* PATTERNS OF COMMONING 277, 277–96 (David Bollier and Silke Helfrich, eds., The Commons Strategies Group 2015).

[6] *See generally* BURNS H. WESTON AND DAVID BOLLIER, GREEN GOVERNANCE: ECOLOGICAL SURVIVAL, HUMAN RIGHTS AND THE LAW OF THE COMMONS 104–12 (Cambridge University Press 2013) (developing the idea of vernacular law).

[7] For example, Étienne Le Roy notes that the French civil code of 1804 broke with the old ideas of customary law, introducing new norms that quite deliberately do not recognize the social and resource-management practices of ancient commoners. The mismatch between contemporary law and commoning continues today, as seen in the juridical categories of international trade treaties, intellectual property laws and other legal regimes dedicated to neoliberal market exchange.

[8] Garrett Hardin, *The Tragedy of the Commons*, 162 SCI. 1243 (1968).

and countless economists, politicians and property-rights advocates see the commons as unowned resources – an open access regime that, like a shared pasture, for which everyone has a "rational" incentive to over-exploit. The inevitable result, said Hardin, is that each farmer will selfishly use as much of the common resource as possible, which will inevitably result in its overuse and ruin – the so-called "tragedy of the commons". The best solution, he argued, is to allocate private property rights to the resource in question.

In truth, Hardin was not describing a commons, but an open access regime or free-for-all in which everything is free for the taking. That is not a commons, however. In a commons, members negotiate their own rules of access and use, assign responsibilities and entitlements, set up monitoring systems to identify and penalize free riders, among other acts to maintain the commons. Commons scholar Lewis Hyde has puckishly called Hardin's "tragedy" thesis "The Tragedy of Unmanaged, Laissez-Faire, Commons-Pool Resources with Easy Access for Non-Communicating, Self-Interested Individuals".[9]

Professor Elinor Ostrom, a political scientist at Indiana University, helped rescue the commons from the memory hole to which mainstream economics had consigned it. Over the course of her career, from the 1970s until her death in 2012, Ostrom documented the many ways in which hundreds of communities, mostly in rural settings in poorer nations, do in fact manage natural resources sustainably. As an empirical matter, the commons can work, and work well. The central issue that Ostrom tried to address was "how a group of principals who are in an interdependent situation can organize and govern themselves to obtain continuing joint benefits when all face temptations to free-ride, shirk or otherwise act opportunistically".[10] Ostrom's landmark 1990 book, *Governing the Commons*, is justly renowned for identifying eight key "design principles" for successful commons. Her other books explored, among other things, ways to diversify and nest governance (that is, what she labeled "polyarchy") in order to empower bottom-up initiative and decision making.[11] For this work, Ostrom won the Nobel Prize in Economics in 2009, the first woman to be so honored.

---

[9] LEWIS HYDE, COMMON AS AIR: REVOLUTION, ART, AND OWNERSHIP 44 (Farrar, Strauss and Giroux 2010).

[10] ELINOR OSTROM, GOVERNING THE COMMONS: THE EVOLUTION OF INSTITUTIONS FOR COLLECTIVE ACTION 42 (Cambridge University Press 1990).

[11] ELINOR OSTROM, UNDERSTANDING INSTITUTIONAL DIVERSITY (Princeton University Press 2005); PROTECTING THE COMMONS: A FRAMEWORK FOR RESOURCE MANAGEMENT IN THE AMERICAS (Island Press Joanna Burger, et al. eds., 2001).

There are, of course, many different reasons for people creating commons. For much of the world, commons are a necessity for human survival. Forests, fisheries, farmland, water and other natural resources are managed as commons to meet basic needs. However, commons are not just about "resource management"; indigenous peoples are "born into" commons as a matter of cultural inheritance and identity, which are arguably essential to their flourishing as human beings. Still other commons, especially in industrialized countries or Internet contexts, are seen as discretionary choices, not systems for survival. Yet even here, where markets and the state may be highly developed, millions of people seek to build commons to escape the logic of expansive property rights, exploitative market dependencies, bureaucratic governance and unaccountable state power. Commons are seen as a way to secure greater personal autonomy, convivial (nonmarket) social relationships, healthier relations with ecosystems, and more stable local communities.

Many commoners are developing innovative types of commons law as a way to win legal recognition for these social practices, values and community norms. This propensity is particularly evident on the Internet, where millions of ordinary people have in effect decided that "representative" legislatures and centralized bureaucratic systems are not as responsive or effective as bottom-up, commons-based approaches used on open network platforms. Indeed, this is one important reason why the nation-state is suffering a decline in authority as a form of governance. More effective forms of self-governance, experienced as more legitimate, are emerging. Meanwhile, the nation-state's capacities to tame the growing power of global capital and deal with the distributed complexity of countless economic, social and ecological problems, are waning. Centralized bureaucracies, whether corporate or governmental, are often slow-moving, politically captive, corrupt or simply incapable of dealing with urgent problems.

Commoners are attempting to fill this void in politics and governance with new sorts of commons-based "law" that have not yet been recognized by the state. This strategic shift of focus away from government venues to self-organized DIY solutions reflects dwindling confidence in conventional politics and law as ways to address important needs. It also reflects growing interest in technology platforms and social norms as direct vehicles for "making law", which are seen as more likely to be participatory, effective, respected and legitimate.

Law for the Commons can help rehabilitate and transform mainstream politics and public policy by legitimizing values and social practices that are structurally marginalized by the neoliberal policy consensus – participation, inclusiveness, fairness, non-instrumental human relationships, transparency and accountability. Commons-based law attempts to declare that certain human relationships and resources must be insulated from market exchange; this is the "inalienability" aspect of the commons. It honors the sovereignty of people to devise their own forms of hands-on governance to meet their needs, especially in a local context. It recognizes the importance of bottom-up initiatives and engagement. It provides a philosophically coherent framework that is distinct from the governing ethos of the liberal market state, for meeting people's needs. And it does this without bureaucracy (politically corrupted, paralyzed by formalities, dominated by lawyers and credentialed experts, unable to address local complexities) or conventional markets (concentrated, predatory, often rigged and oligopolistic, ecologically harmful, winner-take-all). Thomas Jefferson would likely endorse this project of developing law for the commons because, as he once said, "laws and institutions must go hand in hand with the progress of the human mind".[12] The human mind and social circumstances have changed quite a bit in the last generation, not to mention the last 225 years. We need laws and institutions to reflect that.

Well beyond moral or political philosophy, the economic logic and appeal of commoning are rapidly increasing. As analysts such as Jeremy Rifkin, Paul Mason, Yochai Benkler, Michel Bauwens,[13] and many others argue, the world economy is undergoing a profound structural shift. The twentieth century economy of institutions based on strict, hierarchical systems of centralized control and mass production overseen by experts, are giving way to an economy based on open networks that depend upon self-organized, bottom-up participation in the manner of open source software. This shift in basic economic structures entails a move away from a logic of scarcity (for example, proprietary business models; copyright and patents on non-rival information) to a logic of abundance (where sufficiency is valued over maximum production, and information can be shared and re-used at virtually no cost).

In this new context, social, ethical and personal relationships are becoming more important in economic life. People are able to escape

---

[12] Letter from Thomas Jefferson, to Samuel Kercheval, (12 June 1816), available 25 January 2017 at http://teachingamericanhistory.org/library/document/letter-to-samuel-kercheval/.

[13] Jeremy Rifkin, The Zero Marginal Cost Society (Palgrave Macmillan 2014); Paul Mason, Post-Capitalism: A Guide to Our Future (Allen Lane 2015); Michel Bauwens, Network Society and Future Scenarios for a Collaborative Economy (Palgrave Macmillan 2014); Yochai Benkler, The Wealth of Networks (Yale University Press 2006).

from the fiction of the infinitely rational homo economicus as the default template for economic policies and social practice. Network infrastructures are inviting ordinary people to invent their own systems of provisioning tailored to their local needs and niche preferences; self-determination through commoning is providing the basis for a new, more resilient political economy.[14] By focusing more on stewardship than market-oriented ownership, people are able to instill greater regenerative capacities into production systems.

Unfortunately, the prevailing outdated legal regimes tend to ignore or criminalize commoning, thwarting a faster, fuller transition to the next economy. The next section surveys some of more promising innovations in commons-based law.

III. LEGAL INNOVATIONS TO ADVANCE COMMONING

A. Eight Promising Fields of Action

In this section I survey some of the more significant commons-based legal innovations occurring today. Besides providing a rough inventory of disparate projects and theaters of legal innovation, these initiatives can be seen as a new strategic and legal framing, "Law for the Commons", for the otherwise-ignored potential of commoning. The point of this section is to describe some of the more significant attempts to protect commons and transform the legal paradigm by carving out new "protected zones" of enforceable rights within existing legal frameworks. Here are eight major "clusters" of interesting experimentation and ferment:

1. Indigenous commons.
2. Subsistence commons in the global South.
3. Digital commons.
4. Stakeholder trusts.
5. Urban commons.
6. Localism.
7. Cooperative law.
8. New organizational forms.

---

[14] See The Internet of Ownership, http://internetofownership.net (accessed 25 January 2017), for dozens of examples.

Most of the examples involve attempts to secure new legal recognition, support or protection for various sorts of commons through statutes, court rulings, public policies, municipal ordinances, or private law "hacks" of existing bodies of law. This inventory of clusters and projects is not meant to be comprehensive, but suggestive of the wide variety of constructive alternatives to the neoliberal vision of economic growth and consumerism and their inevitable byproducts, ecological decline and wealth inequality. This review of emerging examples will be followed in the next section by some reflections on the transformative strategic value of developing Law for the Commons.

Elevating a new realm of inquiry known as Law for the Commons may seem visionary, but if we are serious about trying to imagine a "new economy", then the workings of law itself must change as much as the economy. Law for the Commons could provide a clearer, more muscular foundation for facilitating the creation of a new economy. It could provide a shared focal point for the Social and Solidarity Economy movement, co-operatives, the Transition Town movement, peer production networks, indigenous peoples, and many others to coordinate their post-capitalist activist strategies. These movements all seek to achieve systemic changes in production, state policies and governance. They all seek to move beyond the fetish of economic growth and the culture of consumerism, especially as they relate to the environment and the quality of everyday life. A new field of Law for the Commons could help consolidate and loosely coordinate the diverse initiatives now unfolding, and give them greater focus and visibility as kindred endeavors. It could also provide new forms of direct self-governance and access to resources for basic needs, thereby advancing the interests of women and marginalized minorities who disproportionately depend on commons,[15] and who tend to have limited access to the legal system.

This chapter makes the case for commons-based law as a distinct field of policy research, legal innovation and activism. It seeks to show how such a body of law could initiate transformational dialogues, collaborations and cross-movement fertilization of ideas. The many varieties of commons-based law described below are merely suggestive of a larger universe of similar examples.[16] Despite the obvious differences among these different

---

15 *See, e.g.*, SILVIA FEDERICI, CALIBAN AND THE WITCH: WOMEN, THE BODY AND PRIMITIVE ACCUMULATION (Autonomedia 2004).

16 See Memorandum from David Bollier on Reinventing Law for the Commons to The Heinrich Böll Foundation (16 September 2015), available 25 January 2017 at http://bollier.org/sites/default/files/misc-file-upload/files/Reinventing%20Law%20for%20the%20Commons%20memo.pdf; *Law for the Commons*, WIKIPEDIA,

fields of legal innovation, each is in some way focused on enabling commoning and/or preventing market enclosures, and to building a new type of political economy and culture.

1. Indigenous commons

The legal rights of the world's 300 million indigenous peoples[17] is of particular interest to commoners because both face similar philosophical and strategic challenges in coming to terms with (unresponsive, sometimes hostile) national and international law. In that sense, the legal fights of indigenous peoples may be a bellwether for commoners and a source of guidance. In general, indigenous peoples are seeking to protect their own distinctive identities, collective resources and cultural commitments to collective law (both formal and informal). They do not seek to "manage their resources", in the standard economic sense of that term, but to nurture their cultural identity, traditions and relations to a living Earth. Some of the more contested aspects of indigenous peoples law include conflicts with nation-states over self-determination (vs. state sovereignty); the preservation of cultural traditions (vs. western consumerism); the preservation of their languages and agroecological practices (vs. intellectual property rights); and compensation (or repatriation) for theft of collectively shared land and property (vs. conventional claims of individual property rights).[18]

Not surprisingly, the many initiatives that indigenous peoples are pursuing to protect their commoning generally have highly positive ecological impacts. One noteworthy innovation in this area is the Potato Park, a sui generis legal regime that empowers indigenous Quechua indigenous peoples in an area near Cusco, Peru. The Quechua are legally recognized as stewards of a rich biodiversity of more than 900 genetically distinct potatoes that they have managed on 12,000 hectares of traditional lands for millennia. The Quechua regard their stewardship of this "biocultural heritage area" as essential to the agrobiodiversity of the region and to preserving their traditional culture, knowledge and livelihoods.[19] The

---

http://wiki.commonstransition.org/wiki/Law_for_the_Commons (last updated 30 December 2015).

[17] Broadly defined as peoples whose societies and cultures predated the nation-states that have come to engulf them.

[18] See STEVEN C. PERKINS, RESEARCHING INDIGENOUS PEOPLES' RIGHTS UNDER INTERNATIONAL LAW (2013), available 25 January 2017 at http://intelligent-internet.info/law/ipr2.html#Present%20Activities, for an extensive overview of indigenous peoples' law.

[19] Alejandro Argumedo, *The Potato Park, Peru: Conserving Agrobiodiversity in an Andean Indigenous Biocultural Heritage Area, in* PROTECTED LANDSCAPES AND AGROBIODIVERSITY VALUES 45, 45–58 (Thora Amend et al. (eds), Kasparek 2008).

market-based alternatives, which would otherwise patent, brand and market potatoes from this region, would shift the focus from stewardship of these lands and potatoes, to economic "development".

Protecting stewardship of nature can also be seen in the Traditional Knowledge Digital Library (TKDL), an India-based database launched in 2001 that documents the knowledge and usage of traditional biomedical knowledge, plants and practices such as yoga, so that such knowledge cannot be patented.[20] The goal of the project, as its website explains, is to:

> give legitimacy to existing traditional knowledge and enable protection of such information from getting patented by the fly-by-night inventors acquiring patents on India's traditional knowledge systems. It will prevent misappropriation of Indian traditional knowledge, mainly by breaking the format and language barrier and making it accessible to patent examiners at International Patent Offices for the purpose of carrying out search and examination.[21]

Although defensive in character, aimed at preventing market enclosures of traditional knowledge, TKDL points toward more affirmative legal strategies for protecting useful agricultural or scientific knowledge as a commons.[22]

Beyond empowering indigenous people's political struggles with western law, commons-based law would help give legal recognition to the Earth as a living subject, and not just as an object of market exploitation. For westerners who dismiss environmentalists as "tree huggers", the idea that human beings are embedded in nature, and not separate from it, will likely be seen as lunacy. But this paradigm shift in belief and sensibility, backed by emergent scientific findings,[23] is precisely what is needed if we are going to deal effectively with climate change. This concept is explored in depth in Iorns and Sheehan's chapter, "Reframing Rights and Responsibilities to Prioritize Nature" (Chapter 4).

---

20 *About TKDL*, Traditional Knowledge Digital Libr., available 25 January 2017 at http://www.tkdl.res.in/tkdl/langdefault/Common/Abouttkdl.asp?GL=Eng.

21 *Id.*

22 Examples include the Open Source Seed Initiative; open-source-licensed technologies developed by the Australian nonprofit research institute CAMBIA and its BiOS project ("Biological Innovation for Open Society"); and the biohacking/DIY biology movement that is devising commons-based systems to oversee responsible, ethical and safe research in synthetic biology.

23 Andreas Weber, Biology of Wonder: Aliveness, Consciousness and the Metamorphosis of Science (New Society Publishers 2016).

2. Subsistence commons in the global South

There are many subsistence commons, not exclusively those managed by indigenous peoples, that rely upon self-governed access and use of forests, fisheries, farmlands, coastal lands, bodies of water, wild game, and other natural resources.[24] It is not only important to protect these vital subsistence commons from enclosure, but to improve their governance and functioning as eco-responsible, climate-friendly ways of meeting needs: an alternative vision of "development".[25] This goal may require certain legal frameworks or selective, light-touch state involvement to help regularize and support self-governance.

Here are two ways that law could help protect subsistence commons in the global South, which would not only stabilize the food sovereignty of millions of people, but help protect large tracts of land from ecological harm. Preserving local stewardship of agriculture has obvious benefits in contrast to fossil fuel-intensive industrial agriculture and the long-haul transport that it generally entails.

In Africa, Latin America and Asia, land tenure systems that recognize subsistence commons could help stop a massive global land grab that is destroying tens of thousands of commons – and an estimated 8.54 million hectares – that people have relied upon for generations. Fortunately, there are some efforts to formally recognize customary rights to land use, which could be helpful in resisting the investor-privileged terms of national laws and international treaties. Liz Alden Wily, a land reform expert and specialist based in Africa, reports:

> In light of the fact that most allocations to investors are in the form of renewable medium-term leases of up to 99 years, it may be expected that loss of common properties will remove these lands from meaningful access, use and livelihood benefit for at least one generation and potentially up to four generations.[26]

---

24 *See, e.g.*, INT'L FOOD POLICY RESEARCH INST., RESOURCES, RIGHTS AND COOPERATION: A SOURCEBOOK ON PROPERTY RIGHTS AND COLLECTIVE ACTION FOR SUSTAINABLE DEVELOPMENT (2010), available 25 January 2017 at http://capri.cgiar.org/files/pdf/Resources_Rights_Cooperation_full.pdf. See The Int'l Journal of the Commons, https://www.thecommonsjournal.org (accessed 25 January 2017), for a leading scholarly journal for the study of traditional subsistence commons as well as "new commons".

25 David Bollier, *Beyond Development: The Commons as a New/Old Vision of Development*, (21 June, 2016), http://bollier.org/blog/beyond-development-commons-newold-paradigm-human-flourishing.

26 LIZ ALDEN WILY, INT'L LAND COALITION, THE TRAGEDY OF PUBLIC LANDS: THE FATE OF THE COMMONS UNDER GLOBAL COMMERCIAL PRESSURE 5 (2011), available 25 January 2017 at http://www.landcoalition.org/sites/default/files/documen

This is a recipe for decades of famine, poverty, political turmoil and additional forms of unsustainable development. Wily and others are pushing for legal reforms of the sort adopted by some African and Latin American states, which no longer require property rights in land to be fungible, based on individual ownership, or formally registered, in order for the land to be recognized as real property.[27]

India is one nation in which state law has formally recognized commons qua commons. This stems from a landmark ruling by the Indian Supreme Court in 2012 that legally recognized subsistence commons and ruled against a real estate developer whose buildings had enclosed a village pond functioning as a commons.[28] The political and legal repercussions of this ruling are still reverberating in India, but it is symbolically and perhaps substantively an important legal victory for commoners trying to protect their traditional, collective uses of forests, farm land, bodies of water and other "unowned" resources long regarded by conventional law as "wastelands". India's landmark Forests Act of 1997 explicitly empowers village governance bodies known as panchayats to act as commons-based stewards of forests. Although this authority has not been faithfully respected by the government's Forest Department, many panchayats have mobilized to assert their authority to manage village forests, pitting participatory governance and local knowledge against conventional bureaucratic authority and expertise.[29]

3. Digital commons

It is not widely appreciated how tech platforms can alter ecological stewardship and production practices in positive ways. To be sure information and communications technologies (ICTs) have many negative ecological impacts, at least as deployed by capitalist enterprises today – lots of electricity, reliance on rare earths, transport costs, pollution and planned

---

ts/resources/WILY_Commons_web_11.03.11.pdf. *See also* Liz Alden Wily, *Communities and the State*, 33 ENVTL. F. 68, 68–71 (2016).

[27] Liz Alden Wily, *The Global Land Grab: The New Enclosures*, *in* THE WEALTH OF THE COMMONS: A WORLD BEYOND MARKET AND STATE (David Bollier and Silke Helfrich (eds), 2012), available 25 January 2017 at http://www.wealthofthecommons.org/essay/global-land-grab-new-enclosures. *See also* Liz Alden Wily, *supra* note 26.

[28] *Jagpal Singh v. State Of Punjab*, No. 3109/2011, (India 2011), available 25 January 2017 at http://judis.nic.in/supremecourt/imgs1.aspx?filename=37417.

[29] See, e.g., Soma K. P. and Richa Audichya, *Our Ways of Knowing: Women Protect Common Forest Rights in Rajasthan*, *in* PATTERNS OF COMMONING (*supra* note 5), available 25 January 2017 at http://patternsofcommoning.org/our-ways-of-knowing-women-protect-common-forest-rights-in-rajasthan.

obsolescence. But it is also true that these systems, when used in commons-based forms, could help usher in new, more ecologically benign forms of decentralized production and consumption. They can reorient people toward more cooperative, post-capitalist modes of life and culture while still hosting needed types of technological innovation.

It must be stressed that the open platforms often associated with the "sharing economy" are in fact standard capitalist enterprises that simply deal in micro-transactions and rentals; they are not committed to "sharing". A digital commons, by contrast, also uses open platforms to enable real sharing and collaboration because commoners retain the autonomy to manage the resources that they generate on their own terms. The social relationships are indirectly reciprocal, not a direct *quid pro quo* exchange, which fosters strong social bonds. Participants are not "sharecroppers" on a corporate-owned "digital plantation".

One notable digital commons that is advancing agroecological concerns is Farm Hack, a global design and manufacturing community that has applied open source development principles to agricultural equipment. To date, the Farm Hack network has produced designs for over 100 tools, such as an organic no-till roller, garlic planters, an "extinct" oat huller, greenhouse automation systems, sensor networks and business models for organic egg enterprises. As Dorn Cox, a founding member of Farm Hack, writes:

> Farm Hack is an emergent, networked culture of collaborative problem-solving . . . Building on models of voluntary reciprocity, Farm Hack implicitly challenges the prevailing norms of conventional agricultural economics and research. The Farm Hack community believes that the tools, seeds and techniques used in agriculture should both reflect and benefit those who intend to use them, not just those intent on selling them.[30]

Cox explains how the open, social collaboration of the Farm Hack community "creates the potential for every farm to become a research farm, and every neighbor to be a manufacturer, drawing upon a global library of skills and designs".[31] The preindustrial and modern are conjoined through a marriage of agrarianism and maker/hacker ideals.

Another potent eco-digital commons is the international network of farmers who practice a kind of open-source agronomy for rice cultiva-

---

[30] Dorn Cox, *Farm Hack: A Commons for Agricultural Innovation*, *in* PATTERNS OF COMMONING 145, 145–50 (*supra* note 5), available 25 January 2017 at http://patternsofcommoning.org/farm-hack-a-commons-for-agricultural-innovation.

[31] *Id.* at 145.

tion. The System for Rice Intensification (SRI) is a vast network of thousands of farmers in Cuba, Sri Lanka, Indonesia and dozens of other countries who share their ideas for improving the yield of rice without the use of GMO seeds, pesticides or herbicides.[32] With the help of Cornell University, farmers collaborate through an online platform on which they share lectures, seminars, emails, publications and other materials, on an international scale.[33] It is a bottom-up driven process without the sponsorship of government ministries or corporations. Even though SRI methodologies must be locally adapted, they are easy to understand and implement, and the impacts impressive: Crop yields are 20 to 50 percent more than conventional rice farming while using less seed, water and fewer chemical inputs.[34] SRI is an example of how open-source collaborations, when applied to agricultural challenges, can yield practical, ecologically benign answers that do not even occur to commercial vendors and state authorities, largely because SRI is a commons-based system that is not profit-driven or hierarchically governed.

SRI is but one of many examples of agricultural crowdsourcing. Using network platforms to aggregate data and interpret them, farmers in diverse localities around the world can apply their best judgment in selecting the most adaptive crops as they respond to climate disruption.[35] A similar idea animates the Open Ag Data Alliance, which is trying to help farmers access and control the data about the crop yields, open source style, instead of agribusiness vendors owning and controlling that data through their proprietary, non-interoperable platforms.[36] A data commons is a highly effective way for farmers to assess and improve their agricultural practices.

Since sharing knowledge about research, technology and social practices

---

[32] Erika Styger, *The System of Rice Intensification and Its International Community of Practice*, *in* PATTERNS OF COMMONING 108, 108–12 (*supra* note 5), available 25 January 2017 at http://patternsofcommoning.org/the-system-of-rice-intensification-and-its-international-community-of-practice.

[33] *SRI International Network and Resource Center*, COLL. OF AGRIC. AND LIFE SCIS., CORNELL UNIV., www.sririce.org (accessed 25 January 2017).

[34] *Frequently Asked Questions,* COLL. OF AGRIC. AND LIFE SCIS., CORNELL UNIV., available 25 January 2017 at http://sri.ciifad.cornell.edu/aboutsri/FAQs1.html.

[35] Jacob van Etten, *Farmers Become Citizen Scientists: Testing Wheat Crops for Climate Change Adaptation*, CLIMATE CHANGE AGRIC. AND FOOD SEC. (11 March 2013), available 25 January 2017 at https://ccafs.cgiar.org/blog/testing-wheat-crops-climate-change-adaptation.

[36] *About Open Ag Data Alliance*, OPEN AG DATA ALL., http://openag.io/about-us (accessed 25 January 2017).

is so important to addressing climate change and environmental problems swiftly, and in eliciting innovative new approaches, it is critical that law address the impediments of copyright and patents in promoting knowledge and technology-transfer. Fortunately, copyright-based licenses to authorize sharing and re-use are now commonplace, thanks to the General Public License that originally enabled free software, especially Linux, and the Creative Commons licenses launched in 2003. These licenses prevent businesses from treating the shared resources of commoners, such as code, information, images, videos, product design, and so on, as "free" feedstock for their proprietary market purposes.[37] However, these licenses do not necessarily prevent the free corporate exploitation of code, design, data, and creative works generated on open platforms. To help deal with this problem, the P2P Foundation and others are developing "commons-based reciprocity licenses", which are intended to allow no-cost sharing among members of a commons, but require payment by any commercial users of the protected work.[38] Unlike the Creative Commons NonCommercial license, which absolutely stops commercial development of a line of information or creative work, the CopyFair license would allow commercialization, but on the basis of mandatory monetized reciprocity with a given digital commons.

Building on open source principles, many open design, hardware and manufacturing communities are reinventing production value-chains so the benefits can be mutualized for collective benefit, and not privatized for investors. These collaborative networks – for building farm equipment, motor vehicles, furniture, houses and more – offer the rudiments of a commons-based production model. Inexpensive, nonproprietary, modular systems use FabLabs and makerspaces as infrastructures for local production. Preliminary estimates by the P2P Foundation suggest that the mutualization of knowledge and production infrastructures could produce an "80-80" improvement in ecological impact: 80 percent less physical matter and energy would be needed to produce 80 percent of what we produce right now.[39]

---

[37] See David Bollier, VIRAL SPIRAL: HOW COMMONERS CREATED A DIGITAL REPUBLIC OF THEIR OWN (New Press 2008), for a history of copyright licenses.

[38] *Commons-Based Reciprocity Licenses*, P2P FOUND. WIKI, http://p2pfoundation.net/Commons-Based_Reciprocity_Licenses (last updated 4 October 2016). *See also From the Communism of Capital to a Capital for the Commons*, P2P FOUND. WIKI, http://p2pfoundation.net/From_the_Communism_of_Capital_to_a_Capital_for_the_Commons (last updated 22 December 2016).

[39] Personal conversation with Michel Bauwens, Founder of the P2P Foundation (13 June 2016).

The blockchain ledger, a software innovation that lies at the heart of Bitcoin, is a breakthrough that could be of enormous importance to the future of commoning on open network platforms. Although Bitcoin itself has been designed to serve familiar capitalist functions, like tax avoidance and private accumulation through speculation, the blockchain ledger is significant because it can enable highly reliable, versatile forms of collective action on open networks. It does this by validating the authenticity of a digital object (for now, a bitcoin) without the need for a third-party guarantor such as a bank or government body. This solves a particularly difficult collective-action problem in an open network context: How do you know that a given digital object – a bitcoin, a legal document, digital certificate, dataset, a vote or digital identity asserted by an individual – is the "real thing" and not a forgery? Blockchain technology can help solve this problem by using a searchable "ledger" on a vast distributed peer network that keeps track of all transactions.

A recently released report suggests that blockchain technology could provide a critical infrastructure for building what are called "distributed collaborative organizations" or sometimes "distributed autonomous organizations."[40] These are essentially self-organized online commons. Such a distributed organization could use blockchain technology to give its members specified rights within the organization, which could be managed and guaranteed by the blockchain. This set of rights, in turn, can be linked to the conventional legal system to make those rights legally cognizable. A more generic aspect of this field of experimentation is smart contracts, which are dynamic software modules that may soon enable new types of group governance, decision making and rules-enforcement on open network platforms. As the power of collaborative sharing has become clear, some tech innovators have recognized that the real challenge is not how to lock up and privatize digital artifacts, using encryption or Digital Rights Management, but how to assure that digital resources can be shared on open platforms in legally enforceable ways. Hence the

---

[40] Peter Van Valkenburgh et al., Distributed Collaborative Organizations: Distributed Networks & Regulatory Frameworks (March 2015) (unpublished report), available 25 January 2017 at http://bollier.org/distributed-networks-and-law. *See also* Rachel O'Dwyer, *The Revolution Will (Not) Be Decentralized: Blockchains*, Commons Transition (11 June 2015), available 25 January 2017 at http://commonstransition.org/the-revolution-will-not-be-decentralised-blockchains. See, From Bitcoin to Burning Man and Beyond: The Quest for Identity and Autonomy in a Digital Society (John H. Clippinger and David Bollier (eds), Off the Commons Books 2014), for a broader introduction to this general topic.

many active efforts now underway to devise technical systems that would act as "smart" legal agents whose transactions would also be enforceable under conventional law.

While these technologies are still in fledging states, they could greatly empower local communities in managing ecosystem resources in more responsible, transparent and effective ways. For example, blockchain technology could establish the authenticity of data-streams from environmental sensors or information submitted by citizen-scientists, which could enable authorized commoners to manage a local body of water or fishery, or oversee forests or species populations.[41] The blockchain could empower individual farmers to reclaim control over their agricultural data via managed data commons – helping them to monitor and improve their farming practices – instead of ceding this data to larger agribusinesses that now claim such data as proprietary.[42] The blockchain could also help advance community solar; it can be used to establish an accounting system for the flow of rooftop solar energy among residents in a neighborhood energy grid, a micro-market based on a commons of shared infrastructure and terms of exchange.[43]

The point is that the blockchain ensures the authenticity and security of digital knowledge that originates from diverse online sources. This enables new forms of collective deliberation, decision making, network-driven data-analysis, participatory budgeting, sharing of sensitive group information, and collective interventions – all of which could be applied to more sustainable ecosystems and commoning projects.

---

[41] For example, Open Source Beehives is a global network of citizen scientists who are using sensor-enhanced beehives to try to determine why bee populations are declining around the world, and then to use their findings to inform regulatory decision making and beekeeping practices. OPEN SOURCE BEEHIVES, http://opensourcebeehives.net (accessed 25 January 2017).

[42] *See, e.g.*, Roxana Hegeman, *American Farmers Confront 'Big Data' Revolution*, TOPEKA CAPITAL JOURNAL (29 March 2014), available 25 January 2017 at http://cjonline.com/news/2014-03-29/american-farmers-confront-big-data-revolution. *See also Open Agriculture*, MASS. INST. OF TECH., http://openag.media.mit.edu (accessed 25 January 2017); OPEN AG TOOLKIT, http://openatk.com (accessed 25 January 2017).

[43] Aviva Rutkin, *Blockchain micro-grid gives power to consumers in New York*, NEW SCIENTIST (2 March 2016), https://www.newscientist.com/article/2079334-blockchain-based-microgrid-gives-power-to-consumers-in-new-york. *See also* Reed E. Hunt et al., *Green Coins: Using Digital Currency to Build the New Power Platform*, *in* FROM BITCOIN TO BURNING MAN AND BEYOND (*supra* note 40), available 25 January 2017 at https://idcubed.org/chapter-10-green-coins-using-digital-currency-build-new-power-platform.

4. Stakeholder trusts

The stakeholder trust, inspired by the Alaska Permanent Fund, is a species of large-scale commons that distributes revenues from a shared asset, typically a natural resource, and distributes it to citizens with a recognized "stake" in the resource. The archetypical example is the Alaska Permanent Fund, a state-chartered trust that is authorized to collect, manage and distribute revenues from oil drilled on state land, on behalf of Alaska residents. Each household gets a dividend of between USD$1,000 to $2,000 per year from corporations that extract oil on Alaska state lands. These revenues for individual citizens are praised by both progressives and conservatives as a welcome display of citizen sovereignty over "what we own" and a source of non-wage income for ordinary people that can reduce inequality. Stakeholder trusts are also touted as "common wealth trusts" that can safeguard natural and social resources that are our collective inheritance.

In his 2014 book, *With Liberty and Dividends for All*,[44] Peter Barnes has extended the idea of stakeholder trusts to a wide variety of "common assets" that could be responsibly monetized and revenues shared via common wealth trusts. The trusts would act as trustees for revenues collected from various commercial users of common assets, where monetization is appropriate. Some examples are industries that use the atmosphere for their wastes and thus must buy air pollution rights to use that scarce resource; banks and stock sellers who must pay a financial transaction tax, in recognition of public support for the financial regulatory infrastructure; and broadcasters' use of the public's electromagnetic spectrum.[45] Stakeholder trusts could be applied at the state or provincial level. In fact, a 2008 report outlined the various state assets in Vermont that could be managed via stakeholder trusts – forests, rocks and minerals, water used in bottling, broadcast spectrum, land, wind.[46] Versions of the stakeholder trust governance/management model have also been proposed for the atmosphere, oceans, and the human genome.[47]

---

44 PETER BARNES, WITH LIBERTY AND DIVIDENDS FOR ALL: HOW TO SAVE OUR MIDDLE CLASS WHEN JOBS DON'T PAY ENOUGH (Berrett-Koehler Publishers 2014).

45 Barnes recently published an essay on the Great Transition Initiative website, which includes numerous comments and criticisms. Peter Barnes, *Common Wealth Trusts: Structures of Transition*, GREAT TRANSITION INITIATIVE (August 2015), available 25 January 2017 at www.greattransition.org/publication/common-wealth-trusts.

46 CONOR CASEY ET AL., VALUING COMMON ASSETS FOR PUBLIC FINANCE IN VERMONT (2008).

47 Peter Barnes et al., *Creating an Earth Atmospheric Trust: A System to Control Climate Change and Reduce Poverty*, 319 SCI. 724, 724 (2008); Peter H.

Working with Peter Barnes, the Sustainable Economies Law Center[48] is currently exploring ways to extend and adapt the stakeholder trust idea to different contexts. For example, local commons trusts could serve as a steward of local forests, watersheds or open spaces. Interested citizens and legislatures could use model versions of government-chartered trusts as standard organizational forms for creating commons-managed trusts.[49] This is described more in Orsi's chapter, "Three Legal Principles for Organizations Rebuilding the Commons" (Chapter 6), which includes the Agrarian Trust, putting farm land into trusts as a strategy to help retiring farmers sell their farms while preserving the land for agricultural uses.[50]

5. Urban commons

While investors and developers have their own capital-driven models for how cities should be designed and managed, commoners have some very different ideas – ones that put a premium on "livability", accessible public spaces, commons-based models such as land trusts and platform cooperatives, and democratic participation. The burgeoning "city as a commons" movement is pioneering this new vision for cities, creating fascinating new legal forms to enable commoning.[51]

One of the most significant such experiments is the Bologna Regulation for the Care and Regeneration of Urban Commons.[52] This one-year-old

---

Sand, *Public Trusteeship for the Oceans*, *in* LAW OF THE SEA, ENVIRONMENTAL LAW AND SETTLEMENT OF DISPUTES 521(Tafsir Malic Ndiaye and Rudiger Wolfrum (eds), Martinus Nijhoff 2007); David E. Winickoff and Richard N. Winickoff, *The Charitable Trust as a Model for Genomic Biobanks*, 349 NEW ENGLAND J. MED. 1180 (2003); and David Bollier, *The Vermont Common Assets Trust*, BOLLIER.ORG (10 March 2011), available 25 January 2017 at http://www.bollier.org/Vermont-common-assets-trust. *See also* BURNS H. WESTON AND DAVID BOLLIER, GREEN GOVERNANCE: ECOLOGICAL SURVIVAL, HUMAN RIGHTS AND THE LAW OF THE COMMONS 245–48 (Cambridge University Press 2013).

[48] SOUTHERN ECONOMIES LAW CENTER, http://www.theselc.org (accessed 25 January 2017).

[49] In such a scheme, as Barnes explains, "Outwardly, the shells [of trusts] would be not-for-profit corporations with state charters, self-governance, perpetual life and legal personhood. Inwardly, they'd be coded to protect their assets for future generations and to share current income." Peter Barnes, *supra* note 45, at 2.

[50] Agrarian Trust, http://agrariantrust.org (accessed 25 January 2017).

[51] JOSE MARIA RAMOS, THE CITY AS A COMMONS: A POLICY READER (2016), available 25 January 2017 at https://www.academia.edu/27143172/The_City_as_Commons_a_Policy_Reader.

[52] See David Bollier, *Bologna, a Laboratory for Urban Commoning*, BOLLIER.ORG (4 June 2015), available 25 January 2017 at http://bollier.org/blog/bologna-laboratory-urban-commoning, for an overview. *See also Bologna Regulation on Public Collaboration for Urban Commons*, LABGOV (18 December 2014),

project in Bologna, Italy, is attempting to remake local government and transform standard bureaucratic process by inviting ordinary citizens and neighborhoods to come up with their own urban commons ideas, and then work with the government to make them real. The city now has more than 90 "pacts of cooperation" with self-nominated citizen groups, each of which works with the city in three areas: "living together, growing together and making together".[53] Examples include a neighborhood becoming a designated steward of certain public spaces or gardens; residents of a street removing graffiti with the city's help; parents who are managing a local kindergarten; and neighbors creating "social streets" that encourage socializing. The Bologna Regulation is now being emulated by dozens of Italian cities.

A broader, US-based initiative is seeking to promote "shareable cities". Two Bay Area organizations, Shareable and the Sustainable Economies Law Center, released an October 2013 report, "Policies for Shareable Cities: A Sharing Economy Policy Primer for Urban Leaders".[54] This report identifies scores of innovative, high impact policies that US city governments have put in place to help citizens share resources, co-produce and create their own jobs. Examples include participatory budgeting, car-sharing, bike-sharing and ride-sharing, as well as changes in local taxes and other policies to promote them. A number of cities have very aggressive sharing cities initiatives, including Seoul, Korea;[55] Lille, France;[56] and Barcelona, Spain.[57]

---

available 25 January 2017 at http://www.labgov.it/bologna-regulation-on-public-collaboration-for-urban-commons. See COMUNE DI BOLOGNA, REGULATION ON COLLABORATION BETWEEN CITIZENS AND THE CITY FOR THE CARE AND REGENERATION OF URBAN COMMONS (2014), available 25 January 2017 at http://www.comune.bologna.it/media/files/bolognaregulation.pdf, for the regulation itself.

[53] *The XXI Century as a Co-Century*, LABGOV (18 February 2015), available 25 January 2017 at http://www.labgov.it/2015/02/18/xxi-century-cocentury.

[54] SHAREABLE & SUSTAINABLE ECONS. LAW CTR., POLICIES FOR SHAREABLE CITIES: A SHARING ECONOMY POLICY PRIMER FOR URBAN LEADERS (2013), available 25 January 2017 at http://www.shareable.net/download-your-copy-of-policies-for-shareable-cities.

[55] Cat Johnson, *Sharing City Seoul: A Model for the World*, SHAREABLE (3 June 2014), available 25 January 2017 at http://www.shareable.net/blog/sharing-city-seoul-a-model-for-the-world.

[56] *Communs*, UN COMMUN, http://encommuns.org (accessed 25 January 2017).

[57] Michael Bauwens, *The Barcelona Fab City 5.0 Plan Outlined in Barcelona Metropolis Magazine*, P2P FOUND. (26 June 2015), available 25 January 2017 at http://blog.p2pfoundation.net/barcelona-metropolis/2015/06/26.

6. Localism

A subset of work on urban commons is specifically directed at fostering relocalization of the economy and governance. These initiatives could greatly reduce energy usage and transport costs, and thus greenhouse gas emissions, by transforming infrastructure and market structures for meeting needs. There are many notable legal initiatives attempting to expand the self-determination of local communities. One example is community ordinances that seek to empower local communities to resist fracking, the transport of hazardous materials, and other violations of local self-determination, especially on environmental matters.[58] The legality of such ordinances under state and federal law may be problematic, but in some ways that is the point – to dramatize how outsider investors, in collusion with state and federal governments, are riding roughshod over community sentiment, and to provoke test cases and political controversy about enclosures of local commons. This effort is based on work by the Community Environmental Legal Defense Fund (CELDF) in the US.

The community charters movement is a similar attempt by people in many countries to assert moral and legal rights to control certain local resources. Inspired in part by CELDF's "Community Bill of Rights", community charters have been drafted to protect neighborhoods in Dakar, Senegal; the entire city of Bologna, Italy; the venerated Teatro Valle in Rome, which the city government tried to sell to private investors;[59] and the Great Lakes.[60] There is a Falkirk City Charter in the UK,[61] and a charter developed by the self-managed cultural space, the Aqua Bene Comune, in Milan. Remix The Commons has recently begun a project to compile a compendium of community charters and mapping

---

58 Community Environmental Legal Defense Fund, http://www.celdf.org (accessed 25 January 2017).

59 Dario Gentili and Andrea Mura, *The Birth of a Theater Commons in Rome: Fondazione Teatro Valle Bene Comune*, *in* Patterns of Commoning (supra note 5). *See also* Ugo Mattei, *The Valle Theater Commons Foundation: How to Deploy the Law in Current and Future Struggles*, *in* Global Activism: Art and Conflict in the 21st Century (Peter Weibel (ed.), MIT Press 2014); David Bollier, *The Teatro Valle Occupation Ends – And a New Theater Commons Begins*, Bollier.org (11 August 2014), available 25 January 2017 at http://bollier.org/blog/teatro-valle-occupation-ends-and-new-theater-commons-begins.

60 *Great Lakes Commons: Charter Declaration*, Great Lakes Commons, http://www.greatlakescommons.org/charter-declaration/ (accessed 25 January 2017).

61 *Atlas des Chartes des Communs Urbains*, Hackpad, https://hackpad.com/Atlas-des-chartes-des-communs-urbains-T7DJe0ftdRJ (accessed 25 January 2017).

tool, an "Atlas of the Charters of Urban Commons".[62] The Remix database includes the players in each charter, the purpose of sharing, the goods and means being used, the fundamental rights asserted, the mechanisms for meeting user rights, as well as the types of shareholder organizations.[63]

7. Cooperative law

There are a number of legal and organizational innovations transforming cooperatives these days, making them more oriented to commoning and the common good than just marketplace success. However, these innovations are geographically dispersed and not necessarily widely known, even within the cooperative movement. Yet they are significant templates for using commons-based law to build new types of organizations for a new economy.

One of the most notable new organizational forms is the multistakeholder cooperative (or "social and solidarity cooperative"), which has been rapidly proliferating in recent years. First launched in Italy in 1963, this new entity collectivizes and centralizes basic overhead services (administration, personnel, accounting, and so on) and in this way empowers smaller social economy ventures dealing with social care, healthcare and education. Multistakeholder coops regularize governance for co-stewardship of commons spaces and move away from rigid bureaucratic methods that increasingly don't work.[64] In Italy, multistakeholder coops now employ more than 360,000 in paid jobs, including the disabled, the formerly imprisoned and marginalized people, and more than 40,000 volunteers, making it a significant sector of the Italian economy that is

---

62 Community Chartering, http://www.communitychartering.org (accessed 25 January 2017). *See also Atlas des Chartes des Communs Urbains*, Hackpad, https://hackpad.com/Atlas-des-chartes-des-communs-urbains-T7DJe0ftdRJ (accessed 25 January 2017).

63 *Ebauche de Categories de Description des Chartes (et Reglements)*, Remix the Commons Wiki, http://wiki.remixthecommons.org/index.php/%C3%89bauche_de_cat%C3%A9gories_de_description_des_chartes_%28et_r%C3%A8glements%29 (accessed 25 January 2017).

64 Cat Johnson, *Michel Bauwens on the Rise of Multistakeholder Cooperatives*, Shareable (5 November 2014), available 25 January 2017 at http://www.shareable.net/blog/michel-bauwens-on-the-rise-of-multi-stakeholder-cooperatives. *See also* Margaret Lund, Solidarity as a Business Model: A Multi-stakeholder Cooperatives Manual, (2011), available 25 January 2017 at http://community-wealth.org/content/solidarity-business-model-multi-stakeholder-cooperatives-manual; and see *Index of /Cooperatives/Multi-Stakeholder_Co-ops/*, United Diversity, available 25 January 2017 at http://library.uniteddiversity.coop/Cooperatives/Multi-Stakeholder_Co-ops, for a listing of articles and reports about multistakeholder coops.

neither market nor state-based. Today there are multi-stakeholder cooperative movements in Canada, France, Spain, Poland, Hungary, Finland and Greece.[65]

In recent years, there have also been a number of new strategies for implementing community land trusts and cooperative housing. Since land values typically account for 25 to 75 percent of house prices, a community land trust (CLT) can serve to remove land from the market and thus drastically reduce housing prices and keep homes permanently affordable. They can also be used for workspace development, community-owned energy generation, and new forms of urban agriculture and community gardens. There are now over 250 CLTs in the USA and about 50 established with more than 100 in the pipeline in the UK. The model is being developed in Canada and in Belgium, and interest is gaining in France and Portugal. The Schumacher Center for a New Economics is now developing a prototype for "community supported industry" that builds on the model of community support agriculture.[66]

Another new coop based model now being explored is platform cooperativism, which advocates the creation of cooperative structures on open network platforms to carry out crowdfunding, crowdsourcing of knowledge, and community self-governance.[67] A November 2015 conference at the New School in New York City explored how platform cooperativism facilitates self-selected participation, iterative innovation, knowledge-sharing and high-quality and low-cost self-provisioning.

8. New organizational forms

Beyond cooperatives, there is a great deal of experimentation going on with new organizational forms because old structures, whether for-profit or nonprofit, do not adequately recognize and support the types of commoning that people are doing or aspire to do. The old organizational structures, even in their variations (cooperatives, limited partnerships, charities, nonprofits) often reflect institutional orientations to markets and the economics of scarcity. How, then, to devise organizational forms

---

[65] PAT CONATY AND DAVID BOLLIER, TOWARD AN OPEN CO-OPERATIVISM: A NEW SOCIAL ECONOMY BASED ON OPEN PLATFORMS, CO-OPERATIVE MODELS AND THE COMMONS (2015), available 25 January 2017 at http://www.boell.de/en/2015/01/21/toward-open-co-operativism.

[66] SCHUMACHER CENTER FOR A NEW ECONOMICS, http://www.centerforneweconomics.org/content/community-supported-industry (accessed 25 January 2017).

[67] *See, e.g.*, TREBOR SCHOLZ, PLATFORM COOPERATIVISM: CHALLENGING THE CORPORATE SHARING ECONOMY (2016), available 25 January 2017 at http://www.rosalux-nyc.org/wp-content/files_mf/scholz_platformcoop_5.9.2016.pdf.

that can both serve the interests of commons while being legally recognized by the state?

One of the more interesting new organizational forms is the "omni-commons", which are enterprises that take on administrative, fiscal and legal tasks for collectives of small, artisanal enterprises with a commons orientation. The Omni Commons of Oakland, California, one notable example, hosts the Contemporary Art Museum of Oakland, a citizen-science and DIY bio space for open sourcing biology, a small book publisher, a food justice advocacy and support group, a radical film and video collective, a hackerspace, a worker-owned café, and a print shop. They share a political vision of "equitable commoning of resources and meeting of human needs over private interests or corporate profit".[68]

Another impressive omni-commons is Cecosesola in the Venezuelan state of Lara.[69] Cecosesola is a network of about 60 cooperatives and grassroots organizations, with about 20,000 members. It provides healthcare to 200,000 patients every year, funeral services, produce selling in local markets, and a variety of coops that are run on the basis of consensus, trust and egalitarian principles.[70]

Digital platforms are also incubating some innovative new organizational forms. One of the most intriguing is the Open Value Network (OVN), which consists of digital platforms that facilitate new modes of open, decentralized and self-organized social governance, production and livelihoods. While still fairly rudimentary, OVNs represent a new type of consensual governance/production regime, bound by contractual terms, that blends commons principles and market activity. Two of the leading OVN projects, Sensorica[71] and Enspiral,[72] are organized in ways that let anyone contribute to the project, and be rewarded based on their contributions, as measured by actual contributions, experience and other

---

[68] From a mission statement of the Omni Oakland Collective. *Governance/Proposal*, OMNI COMMONS WIKI, available 25 January 2017 at https://omnicommons.org/wiki/Governance/Proposal (last updated 9 September 2014).

[69] *Cecosesola*, WIKIPEDIA, available 25 January 2017 at https://en.wikipedia.org/wiki/Cecosesola (last updated 5 February 2016). *See also CECOSESOLA*, P2P FOUND. WIKI, available 25 January 2017 at http://wiki.p2pfoundation.net/CECOSESOLA (last updated 14 January 2013). *See also "We Are One Big Conversation": Commoning in Venezuela*, *in* PATTERNS OF COMMONING 258, 258–64 (*supra* note 5), available 25 January 2017 at http://patternsofcommoning.org/we-are-one-big-conversation-commoning-in-venezuela.

[70] *Id.*

[71] SENSORICA, http://www.sensorica.co (accessed 25 January 2017).

[72] EN SPIRAL, http://www.enspiral.com (accessed 25 January 2017).

collectively determined criteria.[73] OVNs stress that while they may be legally nonprofits or for-profits, they are not functionally either in that they have no retained earnings or fixed assets. They instead function as "a flow-through entity which is as formless as possible", but which functions as a trust for members, as outlined by a "nondominium" agreement.[74] Other OVNs include the projects iAGRI innovation portfolio, Greener Acres, metamaps and Guerrilla Translation.

IV. REFLECTIONS ON THE STRATEGIC VALUE OF DEVELOPING LAW FOR THE COMMONS

Law for the Commons attempts to open up new spaces through which commoners can have greater freedom and autonomy to devise governance forms of their own making, consistent with overarching principles of democracy and human rights. It is perhaps risky to stipulate a specific set of principles and purposes that a Law for the Commons seeks to uphold, but there are clearly affinities among the diverse examples described above. Each in its own way seeks to:

- provide structure for internal, participatory, bottom-up deliberation and governance;
- protect shared assets that are threatened by market enclosure;
- provide a legal identity and structure for commons so that they can be legally cognizable to the state or international law;
- secure state authority for commoning through legal "work-arounds" that modify or extend state law;
- openly challenge recognized boundaries of law as a way to provoke a political debate or validate a particular commons; and/or
- use digital technologies to create more effective alternatives to state law.

---

73 See *Main Page*, VALUE NETWORK WIKI, available 25 January 2017 at http://valuenetwork.referata.com/wiki/Main_Page (last updated 6 January 2017), for more information.

74 A new form of common property governed, in the words of Chris Cook, by "a consensual legal framework agreement within which value may be created, shared and exchanged (P2P) on credit terms by reference to a unit of account (note that a unit of account is NOT a currency)." *Nondomunium*, P2P FOUND. WIKI, available 25 January 2017 at http://p2pfoundation.net/Nondominium (last updated 29 March 2015).

The very idea of Law for the Commons constitutes a profound philosophical challenge to the liberal capitalist polity. After all, many commons seek to enact different ideals of human flourishing and governance than the formal, universal and rational/utilitarian ones of the modern liberal state and neoliberal economics. In this sense, Law for the Commons, as it expands, could help propel a paradigm shift because it asserts a different theory of value than that of conventional economics and the (formally) neutral apparatus of the liberal state. Law for the Commons generally rejects capital accumulation and market exchange as the default engine of social and economic progress, and in this sense proposes a very different vision of human development.

By asserting moral and legal claims on shared resources before markets allocate wealth, commoners challenge the liberal presumption that equality should be pursued through strategies of state redistribution only. Commons discourse instead asserts that communities of people have prior, original claims on resources and thus are entitled to a "predistribution" of equity. This perspective reverses the moral burden imposed on those whose vision of social justice is criticized for "interfering" with free market outcomes to "confiscate" "privately earned" wealth.

The forgoing polemic presumes that the commons is mostly about common assets, and that everyone accepts the premises of the conventional economic paradigm. But the commons, and the new species of commons-based law that is fitfully emerging, is generally based on some very different ontological premises of what human beings are and how they actually do (or could and should) relate to each other, the state and the Earth. To hark back to criticism of the Garrett Hardin "tragedy of the commons" story, the commons is not simply about unowned resources, it is about social systems for collectively managing shared wealth. This requires a very different ontological understanding of human beings than that of standard economics, which presumes that people should be understood as rational, selfish, materialist individuals without histories or community identities.

Hence the frisson that tends to erupt when commoners try to enshrine their ways of knowing, being and producing in state law, which is deeply entangled with free-market ideology and cultural assumptions. In this context, commoning ultimately poses philosophical and practical challenges to state law. It breaches our cultural narratives about the proper roles of markets and government; our beliefs in technology-as-progress and economic growth; and the liberal faith that government can reliably and fairly apply universal principles to highly diverse people and local contexts.

Yet Law for the Commons does not reject liberal principles outright. It is functionally compatible with the liberal polity in many respects because it admires and depends upon many core liberal principles such as human rights, individual conscience and initiative, transparency and democratic participation. But Law for the Commons seeks to actualize these principles in different ways than the modern industrial market/state, and it wishes to do so more effectively, equitably and in decentralized forms than the market/state system seems capable of doing.

The commons, in fact, aspires to enlarge many liberal principles by, for example, broadening the definitions of human rights and human flourishing, prioritizing the inalienability of natural resources, and more effectively addressing the complexities of local circumstances and natural ecosystems. In many instances, the Law for the Commons seeks to create new juridical categories such as "common assets" and "rights of commoning", which refer to the pertinence of social relationships, custom and collective moral authority that have no standing in conventional market/state law.

Law for the Commons can give us a new vocabulary to help us imagine and build a different legal foundation for new types of institutions, provisioning systems and social relationships. It provides a serious philosophical backbone for envisioning new systems of law, governance and politics. And withal, the Law for the Commons does not aspire to be a coercive, external imposition of governance, but rather to enable self-organized commoning as a living, evolving consensual process.

V. CONCLUSION

The vision of Law for the Commons is obviously ambitious. Yet it is not merely a notional abstraction; it is a logical field of convergence for dozens of active commons-based projects, successful legal hacks, and post-capitalist theaters of activism. This convergence could be hastened and enriched through the convening of strategy workshops, conferences and gatherings of people in the key "clusters" named above. New legal treatises on the topic, partnerships with forward-looking law schools and colleges and briefings for foundations would help. It may even be feasible to establish a new center or clearinghouse to catalyze Law for the Commons projects.

Two things are clear: existing bodies of western law and bureaucratic administration are limited in their ability to address urgent needs; and broad-based energies for a transformation of law to support commons lie just below the surface. It is time to take this idea to a new and richer level by inaugurating a new dialogue about Law for the Commons.

8. New hopes and hazards for social investment crowdfunding

Jennifer Taub[1]

I. INTRODUCTION

In his chapter on the "Joyful Economy" (Chapter 2), Gus Speth contends that building a new economy requires a redefinition of the corporation and its goals. He advocates for shifting it from an enterprise designed primarily to provide profits for shareholders to one concerned about a broader set of values and stakeholders. To develop what he deems a joyful economy, he suggests that people, place and planet must be prioritized. Perhaps those who bring leadership to businesses that focus on social and environmental concerns – social entrepreneurs[2] – can answer the call by reorienting the corporations that they create. Such efforts to transform individual firms could inspire widespread change.[3]

[1] The author thanks Melissa Scanlan and Gus Speth for their editorial guidance, and the participants, including host James Salzman at the "Law for the New Economy Workshop", held on 23–24 May 2016 at the University of California, Santa Barbara's Bren School for the Environment, co-sponsored by the Vermont Law School New Economy Law Center. In addition, the author is grateful for guidance from scholars including Joan MacLeod Heminway whose leading scholarship in investment crowdfunding and helpful feedback have been invaluable.

[2] The term "social entrepreneurs" refers to those who start up enterprises that serve a social need. Other definitions include, "entrepreneurs who serve the whole of society with solutions that are sustainable, fair and sufficient". Stephanie Dangel and Michael J. Madison, *Innovators, Esq.: Training the Next Generation of Lawyer Social Entrepreneurs* 83 UMKC L. Rev. 967, 967 n. 2 (2015) (citing Scott London, *How Do You Change the World? Become a Social Entrepreneur*, Scott London, available 25 January 2017 at http://www.scottlondon.com/interviews/drayton.html). See Andrew Samwick, *Social Entrepreneurship Syllabus*, Dartmouth Coll. (23 June 2015), available 25 January 2017 at http://www.dartmouth.edu/~samwick/PBPL%2043%20Syllabus%20Summer%202015%2020150623.pdf, for a broader study of social entrepreneurship, including in the US and developing world.

[3] Based on the work of Donella Meadows, interventions affecting the goals of a system and the mindset out of which a system arises are ranked as highly effective

The timing is good for such a transition, as social entrepreneurs have promising new options available for widely soliciting like-minded investors and organizing their business enterprises to include social goals. Yet, due to distrust of the existing system,[4] some may not explore these opportunities. Not attuned to mainstream matters, they may be unaware of the recent legal changes that make it easier for them to engage within the existing financial and corporate governance systems to fund their enterprises and to organize them with a social or environmental mission in mind.

These recent legal developments are significant. Now in the US, those seeking to fund an enterprise using securities offerings can forgo a complex, time-consuming full federal registration process with the Securities and Exchange Commission (SEC) while still reaching out to solicit a wide group of potential investors. This general solicitation can take place in a variety of media, including advertising online through crowdfunding portals and other platforms. The ability to bypass the full SEC registration process is the result of recent legal reforms that streamline how businesses can raise money through the offering and sale of securities. These legal reforms impact social entrepreneurs because the law covers the methods they might use to attract funding. Unlike a donation made through a site like Kickstarter or GoFundMe, which is not subject to the securities laws, investments made with an expectation of profit typically are subject to securities regulation at the federal or state levels (or both). This is because as a matter of law, securities include investments of money in a common enterprise with the expectation of profit as well as more common financial instruments like stocks and bonds.[5]

There are two key new methods to solicit investments from the general

---

leverage points. DONELLA MEADOWS, SUSTAINABILITY INST., LEVERAGE POINTS: PLACES TO INTERVENE IN A SYSTEM (1999), available 25 January 2017 at http://donellameadows.org/wp-content/userfiles/Leverage_Points.pdf.

[4] Bourree Lam, *Quantifying America's Distrust of Corporations*, THE ATLANTIC (25 September 2014), available 25 January 2017 at http://www.theatlantic.com/business/archive/2014/09/quantifying-americans-distrust-of-corporations/380713/ (finding according to the "Corporate Perception Indicator Survey". that included "data from 25,000 general public participants and 1,800 senior corporate executives . . . in North America and Western Europe only 44 percent of the public see corporations as a source of hope . . . The survey reports that 40 percent of millennials see corporations as a source of fear. They don't even think their good deeds are genuine—49 percent of millennials believe that corporations are only undertaking philanthropic efforts for tax benefits" . . . In contrast in China "84 percent of people consider corporations a source of hope").

[5] Joan MacLeod Heminway, *How Congress Killed Investment Crowdfunding: A Tale of Political Pressure, Hasty Decisions, and Inexpert Judgments that Begs for a Happy Ending*, 102 KY. L.J. 865, 865–6 (2014).

public without a full registration with the SEC that are likely to be used in financing socially conscious businesses. Both approaches can be used online (and one, in fact, must be used online) to attract funds to launch or support a social enterprise. The first of these options came into effect in 2013 with the SEC's Rule 506(c).[6] Under this recent rule, issuers of securities – including social enterprises – can now offer securities of unlimited value through general solicitations or advertisements to the public including online, so long as the actual sales of these securities are made only to verified "accredited investors". For a natural person to qualify as an accredited investor they must have annual income of at least USD$200,000 (or USD$300,000 for a couple) or net worth of at least USD$1 million, not including their primary residence.[7] No specific disclosures to the public are required under 506(c) and only a short four-page form, expected to take about four hours to complete, needs to be filled out with the SEC.[8] However, investors do expect disclosures, and typically issuers voluntarily provide a document that resembles the prospectus that investors would receive in a registered offering.

The most significant change with 506(c) is that general solicitation and advertising is now permitted. In the past, if securities were not registered with the SEC, they could not be advertised to the general public except under limited circumstances. For example, previously, general advertising was permitted for a state-registered offering capped at USD$1 million where substantive disclosures were provided to all investors or for a state-exempted offering capped at USD$1 million in which the securities were *only* sold to accredited investors.[9]

While 506(c) provides an easier path to raise capital for social entrepreneurs (and does not require state or federal registration), there are some restrictions. In addition to having to verify that all investors are accredited,[10] there is another important requirement. To avoid being treated as a "reporting company" which would require filing regular, detailed financial and other reports with the SEC, the issuer must limit the number of individuals that may hold the issuer's equity[11] securities.

---

[6] 17 C.F.R. 230.506(c) (2016).

[7] 17 C.F.R § 230.501(a) (2016).

[8] The form is four pages not including instructions. *Form D*, U.S. Sec. & Exch. Comm'n, https://www.sec.gov/about/forms/formd.pdf (accessed 25 January 2017).

[9] 17 C.F.R. § 230.504(b)(1) (2016). Regulation A (which has since been amended) also provided a path to avoid full registration with the SEC for offerings capped at USD$5 million, however this was not used very often and did require filing of an offering document with the SEC.

[10] 17 C.F.R. § 230.506(c)(2)(ii) (2016).

[11] For debt securities (such as a bond with semi-annual interest payments and

Specifically, an issuer that has more than USD$10 million in assets may have no more than a total of 1,999 equity holders or 499 non-accredited investors in order to avoid reporting company status.[12] This limit can be a challenge for local businesses that wish to attract a broad base of stock holders. As described below, however, there is another capital-raising path that lacks this limit.

The second new promising option that also avoids full SEC registration became available with new rules effective in May 2016. These rules were created to allow for investment crowdfunding. Investment crowdfunding is different from other types of similar capital raising, such as donation crowdfunding, which is used to receive charitable donations or pre-sale crowdfunding where money is paid in advance for a product or service. Investment crowdfunding, in which people provide money with the expectation of profit or purchase an instrument such as a stock or bond, involves the offering and sale of securities. So, in the absence of an exemption, full registration of the offering with the SEC would be required. The new rules, referred to as "Regulation Crowdfunding"[13] were adopted under Title III of the Jumpstart Our Business Startups Act (the JOBS Act) and allow raising up to USD$1 million online per year from an unlimited number of investors either through brokers or funding portals registered with the SEC. With Regulation Crowdfunding, issuers must file an offering document with the SEC that explains, for example, how the proceeds from the offering will be used. This document must also be available to investors on the web portal. This document is much less time-consuming to prepare than a full registration statement would be.[14] Unlike Rule 506(c) discussed above, with Regulation Crowdfunding, equity holders who purchase shares this way are not counted for "reporting company" purposes if certain conditions are met. However, under certain circumstances, these companies will have to file annual reports with the SEC.

In summary, both Rule 506(c) and Regulation Crowdfunding allow social entrepreneurs to promote and obtain securities-based investments online. Relying on Rule 506(c), social entrepreneurs can use the internet

---

a balloon payment of principal at the end of the term), this owner-limit would not apply.

[12] Securities Exchange Act, 15 U.S.C. § 78l(g) (2015).

[13] 17 C.F.R. 230.506(c) (2016).

[14] The estimated time to complete form is about 49 hours. *Regulation Crowdfunding: A Small Entity Compliance Guide for Issuers*, U.S. Sec. & Exch. Comm'n (13 May 2016), available 25 January 2017 at https://www.sec.gov/info/smallbus/secg/rccomplianceguide-051316.htm; *see also Form C*, Sec. & Exch. Comm'n, https://www.sec.gov/about/forms/formc.pdf (accessed 25 January 2017).

(as well as other media) to generally advertise and solicit investments without a full SEC registration. However, this may not be very attractive for two reasons. First, taking this method could require limiting the number of equity holders to no more than 1,999 or 499 non-accredited investors. Secondly, the 506(c) approach excludes non-accredited investors from purchasing the offered securities. This would shut out a large group of individuals who might be interested in financing the social enterprise, those who either do not earn at least USD$200,000 a year or have a minimum net worth of USD$1 million.

By comparison, Regulation Crowdfunding works better for those who want to attract a large number of ordinary investors. And, it works well for those who want to delegate the promotion to someone else. With investment crowdfunding, it is the operator of the funding portal, not the issuer, who does nearly all of the promoting. Yet, the Regulation Crowdfunding approach might be insufficient for those who want to advertise beyond the web portal itself or to raise more than $1 million in a given year. Addressing these tradeoffs, the SEC has made clear that simultaneous (known as "side-by-side") offerings via Regulation Crowdfunding and 506(c) even of the same type of securities are permissible.[15]

There is also a third recent development – the ability to structure an enterprise as for-profit but also with a social or environmental mission through a "benefit corporation" designation.[16] This change is happening on a state-by-state basis, as corporations must be chartered at the state level. In 2010, Maryland was the first state to offer a benefit corporation option. Maryland's statute provides that the purpose of a benefit corporation is to "create a certain specific public benefit". Among the list of seven public benefits set out in the law are benefits for society and the

---

15 *Regulation Crowdfunding Rules*, SEEDINVEST, available 25 January 2017 at https://www.seedinvest.com/blog/crowdfunding/regulation-crowdfunding-rules.

16 Hans Rawhouser, et al., *Benefit Corporation Legislation and the Emergence of a Social Hybrid Category*, 57 CAL. MGMT. REV. 13 (2015). Notably, in the United States, incorporation of an entity takes place at the state level only. In contrast, the offering and sale of securities is governed at the federal level and sometimes also the state level. *Also see* J. Haskell Murray, *Understanding and Improving Benefit Corporation Reporting*, BUS. L. TODAY (July 2016) ("Benefit corporations, which are for-profit entities meant to serve a social purpose beyond the financial interests of shareholders, are the most prominent of a plethora of recently created social enterprise legal forms. Social enterprise legal forms also include public benefit corporations, benefit LLCs, social-purpose corporations, and low-profit limited liability companies (L3Cs). Proponents of the benefit corporation form claim that the entity 'meets higher standards of corporate purpose, accountability, and transparency.'")

environment.[17] By 2016, more than 30 states and the District of Columbia had a benefit corporation type statute. By selecting this hybrid corporate structure, it is hoped that founders can help ensure that their enterprise can turn a profit while also serving a much broader social purpose.[18]

Taken together, these federal and state legal and regulatory updates make it easier for startups, including socially or environmentally-focused enterprises to raise capital and for members of the general public to channel their savings into such investments. These changes can provide space for those social entrepreneurs who believe they do not fit within the current system.[19]

With these hopeful legal developments, however, come hazards. The usual concerns around fraud and mismanagement[20] endure. Moreover, less sophisticated members of the public may not have the skills to assess the investment opportunities. And, they may not fully understand that the majority of startups fail and may invest more in individual startups or even in a diversified portfolio than they can stand to lose. Streamlining the offering process and eliminating traditional federal registration and disclosure requirements may result in investors not obtaining information essential to their investment decisions.[21] These streamlined offering

---

17 S.B. 690, Reg. Sess. (Md. 2010).

18 When Patagonia, Inc re-registered in 2012 and became the first benefit corporation under California law, founder Yvon Choinard said, "Benefit corporation legislation creates the legal framework to enable mission-driven companies like Patagonia to stay mission-driven through succession, capital raises, and even changes in ownership, by institutionalizing the values, culture, processes, and high standards put in place by founding entrepreneurs." Press Release, B Lab, Patagonia Registers as First California Benefit Corporation (3 January 2012), available 25 January 2017 at http://www.csrwire.com/press_releases/33565-Patagonia-Registers-as-First-California-Benefit-Corporation.

19 Mark Cheng, *Financing Social Entrepreneurs,* The Guardian (8 June 2012), available 25 January 2017 at https://www.theguardian.com/sustainable-business/social-entrepreneurs-corporates-finance-collaboration (concluding that "fledgling social enterprise looking for capital to grow can find itself falling between charitable and commercial funding, and appealing to neither. Our current financial system simply isn't designed to meet the needs of these hybrid organizations that are businesses serving a social mission").

20 Letter from David M. Cromwell to the U.S. Sec. and Exch. Comm'n, File No. S7-09-12 (27 October 2013), available 25 January 2017 at https://www.sec.gov/comments/s7-09-13/s70913-22.htm (finding that "[i]ncompetent management causes more failures in new business ventures than all of the other reasons, combined. Read any good textbook on venture capital investment or talk to some real VC firms – almost all of them will say exactly the same thing.").

21 Thomas Lee Hazen, *Crowdfunding or Fraudfunding? Social Networks and the Securities Laws—Why the Specially Tailored Exemption Must be Conditioned on Meaningful Disclosure*, 90 N.C.L. Rev. 1735, 1754 (2012).

processes may also attract the unscrupulous and reckless issuers seeking a quick buck without sufficient skill or realistic business plans. Indeed, in some cases, given the combination of the perceived virtue of or affinity with local and mission-driven enterprises and unsophisticated investors,[22] fraud could be even more prevalent.[23]

This chapter will first provide background on securities laws in the US to contextualize the legal changes. Then it will detail how the three, aforementioned recent legal developments at the federal and state levels can aid the startup or expansion of social, community and environmental business enterprises. Included among state law changes will also be one state's law to smooth the path for investing in local solar energy businesses. The next section will discuss and provide examples of potential hazards centered on inexperience, fraud and mismanagement. In conclusion, the chapter will suggest ways, such as a private certification or monitoring process,[24] to help guard against the incompetent issuers and fraudsters who could exploit a social label to fleece socially-minded, inexperienced investors.

II. NEW INVESTMENT OPPORTUNITIES IN CONTEXT

Some historical context is helpful toward appreciating how recent changes have expanded opportunities for social entrepreneurs to raise capital for their enterprises. The original federal regulatory scheme that governs US investments dates back to the 1930s. Focused on protecting investors

---

[22] Letter from Richard D. Greenfield to the U.S. Sec. and Exch. Comm'n, File No. S-7-09-12 (11 November 2013), available 25 January 2017 at https://www.sec.gov/comments/s7-09-13/s70913-47.pdf (concluding that "[t]he proposed rules, if enacted, will be for the principal benefit of proponents of largely unregulated securities sales . . . and to the detriment of the broad investing public, particularly unsophisticated investors, who have had, heretofore, no practical access to investments to which the proposed rules are aimed").

[23] Ben DiPietro, *The Morning Risk Report: Affinity Fraud Cases Point to Need for Proper Due Diligence*, Wall St. J., 1 August 2016 ("Recent high-profile fraud cases targeting members of a specific community—known as affinity fraud—can serve as a cautionary tale about the dangers of investing with a person or fund because of a religious, ethnic or other type of affiliation"), available 25 January 2017 at http://blogs.wsj.com/riskandcompliance/2016/08/01/the-morning-risk-report-affinity-fraud-cases-point-to-need-for-proper-due-diligence/.

[24] Special thanks go to Laurie Ristino who made this very entrepreneurial suggestion at the Bren Center conference.

as well as avoiding another stockmarket crash,[25] the prohibitions and requirements were designed to provide full and fair information to the public before making an investment decision. These laws and associated rules have been altered over the years. Well before this most recent round of changes, large exemptions from SEC registration existed. This section of the chapter provides a brief overview of the requirements and restrictions generally associated with raising capital.

A. Background on the Offering and Sale of Securities

Those new to the business world need to be wary of accidentally violating federal and state securities laws when they go out and ask others for money. Something as simple as phoning friends, sending an email solicitation, or posting an announcement on social media could suddenly subject a business operator to federal laws and related SEC regulations as well as state laws. In addition to facing government scrutiny, failing to abide by communications restrictions, disclosure obligations and registration requirements before, during and after a securities offering could subject a perfectly well intentioned and honest business and its operators to litigation from disgruntled investors.

Because this area of law is highly technical, fact specific and evolving, the purpose here should not be to commit these details to memory. Instead what follows provides context so those interested in transforming the corporate sector understand the key role played by the rules governing funding a business, why the new legal changes are advantageous, and for

---

[25] *See, e.g.*, Securities Act, 15 U.S.C. § 77b(b) (2012) ("Whenever pursuant to this subchapter the Commission is engaged in rulemaking and is required to consider or determine whether an action is necessary or appropriate in the public interest, the Commission shall also consider, in addition to the protection of investors, whether the action will promote efficiency, competition, and capital formation."), Securities Exchange Act, 15 U.S.C. § 78c(f) (2012) ("Whenever pursuant to this chapter the Commission is engaged in rulemaking, or in the review of a rule of a self-regulatory organization, and is required to consider or determine whether an action is necessary or appropriate in the public interest, the Commission shall also consider, in addition to the protection of investors, whether the action will promote efficiency, competition, and capital formation."); *see also* Securities Exchange Act, 15 U.S.C. § 78b(4) (2012) ("National emergencies, which produce widespread unemployment and the dislocation of trade, transportation, and industry, and which burden interstate commerce and adversely affect the general welfare, are precipitated, intensified, and prolonged by manipulation and sudden and unreasonable fluctuations of security prices and by excessive speculation on such exchanges and markets, and to meet such emergencies the Federal Government is put to such great expense as to burden the national credit.").

social entrepreneurs to have a sense of when it is a good time to call legal counsel for assistance.

At the federal level, the offering and sale of securities in interstate commerce is governed by laws and regulations dating back to the US stock market crash of 1929 and subsequent Great Depression. The threshold question for anyone seeking funding is whether what they are doing involves offering or selling a "security". For purposes of federal law, securities include a long list of instruments such as stocks, bonds and partnership interests.[26] However, under this law a security also includes any arrangement that is considered an "investment contract". For purposes of federal law, this term has been defined by the US Supreme Court and further refined by lower federal courts. Generally speaking, an investment contract is a contract, transaction or scheme in which a person invests their money, in a common enterprise, with the expectation of profits, predominantly from the efforts of others.[27] It is not uncommon for the inexperienced to gather funding in such a way that qualifies as an investment contract and thus to run afoul of the law by making offers to the public that they failed to properly register and that they pitched to the public in ways that violated the law.

Generally speaking, the federal securities laws require full and fair disclosure of material information about the business, its leaders, and the investment opportunity. And, these laws and rules provide for sanctions for fraud. These sanctions can include government criminal and civil actions and also civil lawsuits by investors as the law provides a private right of action. Specifically, the Securities Act of 1933 (the 1933 Act)[28] and associated regulations govern the offering and sale of securities in the primary market. The Securities Exchange Act of 1934 (the 1934 Act)[29] and related regulations cover secondary market sales. Also, public companies, meaning those that issued securities to the public through registered offerings (and other reporting companies, such as those with more than 1,999 equity holders) must make periodic financial disclosures to the Securities Exchange Commission (SEC) and comply with other requirements designed to keep investors informed. In addition, the 1934

---

26 15 U.S.C. § 77b(a)(1).

27 *See U.S. Sec. Exch. Comm'n v. Howey*, 328 U.S. 293, 298 (1946). Note that *Howey* originally used the "solely from the efforts of others" language but subsequent lower courts have changed this to mean predominantly, and the Supreme Court omitted the "solely" language in *United Hous. Found., Inc. v. Forman*, 421 U.S. 837, 852 (1975).

28 15 U.S.C. § 77.

29 15 U.S.C. § 78.

Act prohibits and punishes securities-related fraud in both the primary and secondary markets.

Under Section 5 of the 1933 Act,[30] in the absence of an exemption, public offerings and sales of securities need to be registered with the SEC. Prior to the preparing and filing of an extensively detailed registration statement, those involved in the offering and sale are subject to stringent restrictions on oral and written communications. Even after the registration statement is filed there are communication restrictions and disclosure requirements prior to the "effective" date of the offering and even beyond. False or misleading statements in the registration statement or sales documents, or communications before it is permissible (known as "gun jumping") can lead to liability for various parties involved. Moreover, even in the absence of fraud, shareholders who purchase securities as part of a public offering can sue certain individuals and entities involved in the offer and sale if the procedures were not properly followed.

Given the complex and time-consuming nature of the SEC registration process for public offerings, and the liability risks, issuers seeking capital have sought to use the various exemptions provided for in the statutes. And over time, they have successfully lobbied for additional exemptions to be granted through legislation and regulation.

B. Exemptions from Registration and Reporting Built-in to the Law

Built into the 1933 Act, well before the recent changes we will discuss, are numerous exemptions from the SEC registered offering process. Some provisions exempt certain types of securities from some aspects of the law, whereas other provisions exempt particular types of offerings from other provisions. The following is a general overview of those exemptions, and of course it is wise to consult with an attorney who is expert in these matters about the specifics of any investment solicitation plan.

Built-in exemptions were provided because, "Congress . . . recognized that in certain situations there is no practical need for registration or the public benefits from registration are too remote."[31] Statutory exemptions from registration appear, for example, in Section 4(a)(2)[32] (which exempts from registration transactions "not involving any public offering") and in

---

30 15 U.S.C. § 77e.

31 Sec. and Exch. Comm'n, Report on the Review of the Definition of "Accredited Investor" 1 (2015), available 25 January 2017 at https://www.sec.gov/corpfin/reportspubs/special-studies/review-definition-of-accredited-investor-12-18-2015.pdf (citing H.R. Rep. No. 73–85 (1933).

32 Originally, this was section 4(1) and later 4(2), but presently 4(a)(2). It

Section 3(b) (when the dollar value of the securities issued is small). The so-called "private placement" and "small issue" exemptions are relevant to social entrepreneurs. But their utility is largely due to SEC rules from the 1980s that clarified how to meet the exemptions. Prior to those rules, it was risky to rely on the private placement exemption, because language in the statute is quite vague. For example, the statute does not define what is meant by a transaction "not involving any public offering". The Supreme Court and lower federal courts provided some guidance early on and over the years, but it too created uncertainty. In 1953 with *SEC v. Ralston Purina*,[33] no bright line was provided based on the number of offerees. Instead, the Supreme Court held that an offering to those who do not need disclosure but who can "fend for themselves" would be a transaction "not involving any public offering". Thus, unless an issuer could be sure that those to whom they offered securities could fend for themselves, SEC registration was necessary. Subsequent cases by lower federal courts[34] provided various factors to consider but still no clear lines.

Help was on the way when in 1982, the SEC clarified these statutory sections through the issuance of Regulation D (or Reg D).[35] Reg D is a series of rules that create some exemptions and a "safe harbor". The safe harbor (under Rule 506) means if a business complies with the rule when it makes an offering of securities, there will be no violation of Section 5 of the 1933 Act for failing to register with the SEC. If a business fails to comply with the safe harbor, it would need to fall back on the less precise statutory language and the related case law interpreting it.[36]

The regulation, in addition to providing definitions of terms, has three main rules: 504 through 506. Rules 504 and 505 implement the

---

exempts from Section 5, "transactions by an issuer not involving any public offering". 15 U.S.C. § 77d(a)(2).

[33] *Sec. and Exch. Comm'n v. Ralston Purina Co.*, 346 U.S. 119, 125 (1953).

[34] *See, e.g., Doran v. Petroleum Mgmt. Corp.*, 545 F.2d 893, 899–900 (5th Cir. 1977) (including factors such as the number of offerees (not the number of purchasers), the sophistication of the offerees, disclosure and availability of information, the relationship of the offerees to the issuer, the manner of the advertisements, and limitations on resale).

[35] Proposed Revision of Certain Exemptions from the Registration Provisions of the Securities Act of 1933 for Transactions Involving Limited Offers and Sales, 46 Fed. Reg. 41,791 (1981). *See also Investor Bulletin: Private Placements Under Regulation D*, U.S. Sec. and Exch. Comm'n (24 September 2014), available 25 January 2017 at https://www.investor.gov/news-alerts/investor-bulletins/investor-bulletin-private-placements-under-regulation-d.

[36] *See* John C. Coffee Jr., et al., Securities Regulation 368 (13th edn., Foundation Press 2015).

small offering exemption found in section 3(b),[37] and currently apply to offerings capped at USD$1 million and USD$5 million respectively. Rule 506 is the "private placement" exemption and implements Section 4(a)(2) that exempts from registration a transaction "not involving any public offering". Prior to 2013 when Rule 506(c) became effective, Rule 506 limited the number of non-accredited investors in a private offering to just 35 people. To be an accredited investor, a person needs to earn either USD$200,000 per year or have USD$1 million in assets (not including equity in a home). While it did not cap the total number of accredited securities purchasers, as a practical matter, there was a cap, as the maximum number of equity securities holders for a Rule 506 offering was 499 record-holders. Now that figure is 1,999 (or 499 non-accredited). Businesses trying to avoid federal registration would avoid exceeding this limit of record-holders as doing so would transform the enterprise into a "reporting" company. Reporting companies need to file ongoing reports including financial statements and comply with other obligations under the 1934 Act.[38]

Another relevant statutory exemption from registering with the SEC applies to offerings of securities within a single state (intrastate offerings). The purpose of this built-in exemption is to support local financing of local businesses engaging in investment in the local community. The relevant language appears in Section 3(a)(11) of the 1933 Act. This provision limits the intrastate exemption to securities "offered and sold only to persons resident within a single State or Territory, where the issuer of such security is a person resident and doing business within or, if a corporation, incorporated by and doing business within, such State or Territory".[39]

The federal court decisions interpreting this language left some uncertainty as to when the exemption from SEC registration for intrastate offerings would apply. This was a problem as issuers could inadvertently run afoul of the law, and perhaps holdback from seeking local financing. To help clarify, in 1974 the SEC created a safe harbor under Rule 147. This rule helped to ensure that Section 3(a)(11) could be used for "the local financing of companies by investors within the company's state or territory". This safe harbor applied both to offers and sales. To be considered "resident" within the state, the issuer, if a corporation, must be incorporated or organized there. Under the safe harbor, to be treated as "doing business" within a state, the issuer must meet each of three tests.

---

[37] 15 U.S.C. § 77c(b).

[38] Securities Exchange Act, 15 U.S.C. § 78l(g) (2012).

[39] 17 C.F.R. 230.147(c)(2) (2016).

It must (1) derive at least 80 percent of its consolidated gross revenues in the state; (2) have at least 80 percent of its consolidated assets in the state; and (3) intend to use and actually use 80 percent of the net proceeds from the Rule 147 securities offering in connection with operating the business within the state or real property within the state. In addition, all securities purchasers must be residents of the state, and even an inadvertent offer or sale to a nonresident could result in undermining the safe harbor.[40] While new rules have been proposed to revise Rule 147 to have it rely on a new section of the statute and make it less restrictive, at the time of writing, they have not gone into effect.

Even intrastate offerings that do not need to register with the SEC may still be subject to federal reporting requirements under Section 12(g) if equity holders of record exceed 1,999 (or 499 non-accredited). In addition, the state in which the offering and sale takes place may have filing requirements.

In summary, prior to the recent changes in 2013 and 2016, subject to very limited exceptions, it was not possible for a business to reach out to potential investors through general advertisements whether online, via television, flyer, email, phone or otherwise without first registering with the SEC. And, such exceptions still required state registration with either substantial investor disclosures or state registration with no sales to non-accredited investors. While designed to protect investors, some observed that the existing regime create too many obstacles for small businesses (which would include those launched by social entrepreneurs) to use modern technology to reach interested investors. And, many contended that it was unfair to ordinary investors with average incomes and assets who could only donate via crowdfunding but not invest. Thus, somewhat ironically, giving away money without any expectation of profit was permitted, whereas investing money with an expectation of (and a potential for) a profit was not.

With these concerns in mind (as well as other unrelated deregulation goals which are separately subject to critique), JOBS Act was enacted in 2012.[41] Pursuant to authority under Title II of this legislation the SEC issued Rule 506(c) effective in 2013, expanding the private placement exemption and also pursuant to Title III, issued Regulation Crowdfunding, effective in 2016.

---

40 John C. Coffee Jr., et al., *supra* note 36.

41 Jumpstart Our Business Startups ("JOBS") Act, Pub. L. No. 112–106, 126 Stat. 306 (2012).

III. RECENT DEVELOPMENTS THAT CAN LINK SOCIALLY MINDED INVESTORS WITH SOCIAL ENTREPRENEURS TO TRANSFORM THE CORPORATE SECTOR

From a legal standpoint, it is now much easier for business enterprises to raise capital locally and for founders to organize a corporate entity that emphasizes values beyond profit maximization. This relative ease in soliciting investments and organizing this type of business stems from a series of very recent legal developments that occurred at both the federal and state level. Three developments at the federal level and two examples at the state level have expanded the opportunities for local capital raising from local communities to support a range of social-entrepreneurial efforts. This section will detail these changes.

At the federal level, there have been three significant developments over the past few years. First, as of 2013 enterprises can now use the SEC's Rule 506(c), which was adopted pursuant to Title II of the JOBS Act. This rule permits issuers to generally solicit the public including through online advertisements, while also bypassing the complex, time-consuming SEC registration process. Second, in late 2015, the SEC issued final rules implementing the Crowdfunding provisions of Title III of the JOBS Act. This law created a new Section 4(a)(6) of the Securities Act. The implementing rules known as Regulation Crowdfunding went into effect on 16 May 2016.

At the local level, certain state securities regulators have taken steps to encourage investment in community businesses. For example, in 2014, Vermont's Department of Financial Regulation (the DFR) created an exception to Vermont state securities registration for certain community solar energy enterprises. On the business organization topic, there are even more alternative enterprise structure options in light of the new benefit corporation statutes. And, even ordinary corporations can have a social purpose under traditional state corporate law, as reflected in a recent Supreme Court decision indicating that there is a more nuanced appreciation for organizations to serve a broad range of constituencies and purposes.[42]

---

42 *Burwell v. Hobby Lobby Stores, Inc.*, 573 U.S. 22 (2014).

A. General Solicitations of Unlimited Capital from Accredited Investors

As of 2013, pursuant to the SEC's new Rule 506(c), issuers can avoid filing a registration statement with the SEC yet still offer securities and raise unlimited amounts of money through a general solicitation to the public. The significance of this change cannot be overstated. Prior to 2013, other than a state-registered small offering of no more than $1 million, it was not generally possible to advertise a federally-unregistered securities offering through a general solicitation to the public. The exception was an offering up to USD$5 million via a Regulation A, however although this was exempt from full registration, an offering document did have to be filed with the SEC. And, even those small offerings under rule 504 had to be registered at the state level. With the state registration came either substantive disclosure to investors or a prohibition on allowing non-accredited[43] investors to buy securities. In other words, with this new rule 506(c), offerings to raise unlimited amounts of money are treated as "private placements" even though they are advertised widely to the public. This is a significant change further blurring the distinction between private and public offerings.[44]

From a social entrepreneur's perspective, the benefits of these 506(c) offerings are that they can be advertised, they do not have to be registered with the SEC and there are no specific disclosure requirements. There is a notice filing via Form D, but that is all. This notice filing involves spending about four hours filling out a very short form. This is substantially less time than the 972 hours estimated to complete the full registration form.[45] It is not difficult or time-consuming. Of course, those solicited may and should ask for information prior to investing. And, any information provided would be subject to the antifraud provisions of the securities laws, including Section 10(b) and related Rule 10b-5.[46]

There are a few limitations to a 506(c) offering, however. The actual purchasers must be verified as accredited. This is slightly different from the pre-existing 506 process, which is still available under Rule 506(b). Under the 506(b) process, which still forbids general solicitation,

---

[43] *See supra,* note 7 for a definition of accredited "investor".

[44] Joan MacLeod Heminway, *Crowdfunding and the Public/Private Divide in the U.S. Securities Regulation*, 83 U. Cin. L. Rev. 477, 479 (2014) ("Until the JOBS Act became law, the dividing lines between public and private offerings and companies had been well understood—even if somewhat under-studied.")

[45] *Form S-1*, U.S. Sec. & Exch. Comm'n, https://www.sec.gov/about/forms/forms-1.pdf (accessed 25 January 2017).

[46] 15 U.S.C. § 78j; 17 C.F.R. 240.10b-5 (2016).

unlimited amounts of money can be raised. However, no more than 35 non-accredited investors can purchase the securities. Yet, under that rule the accredited do not need to be verified. In contrast with this new process permitted under Rule 506(c), there can be a general solicitation to the public, but there cannot be sales to any non-accredited investor. There are also limitations on reselling the securities.

Even though Section 12(g) of the 1934 Act seems to limit even a 506(c) generally-solicited offering of securities to just a total of 1,999 accredited investors, there is a way to still take advantage of this approach while simultaneously reaching out to non-accredited investors. That can be done through investment crowdfunding, as discussed in the next section.

B. Investment Crowdfunding Including to Non-Accredited Investors

There are two types of crowdfunding. The first type is the original crowdfunding (referred to at times as "donation crowdfunding" or "charitable crowdfunding"). The second type is investment crowdfunding. Donation crowdfunding became popular with such sites as Kickstarter, GoFundMe and Indiegogo. Donors give money to a person, cause or entity without promise of any profit, though they might receive a product or service. In contrast, with investment crowdfunding a person would purchase an instrument such as a stock or bond or invest their money in a common enterprise with an expectation of profit, derived from the efforts of others. Because each of these can be considered a security, and because internet fundraising is a widespread general solicitation, generally speaking, it was unlawful to do this without registering with the SEC. An exception would be for a state-registered small offering sold only to accredited investors. However, even with a state-registered small-offering if more than 499 (now 1,999) individuals held the equity securities, then this would trigger ongoing reporting with the SEC.

This impediment to investment crowdfunding was removed in part with the passage and implementation of the JOBS Act. This part of the statute Title III of the JOBS Act is entitled Capital Raising Online While Deterring Fraud and Unethical Non–Disclosure Act (the CROWDFUND Act). It was implemented when the SEC issued final rules to permit investment crowdfunding, known as Regulation Crowdfunding.[47] Most of these rules only became effective on 16 May 2016 and because of this, there is very little information on how many firm are likely to participate.

Regulation Crowdfunding has several requirements. To begin, offers

---

[47] Crowdfunding, 80 Fed. Reg. 71388 (16 November 2015).

and sales must take place exclusively through a designated funding portal; if a registered funding portal is not used, then the securities must be sold by an SEC-registered broker. And, only US companies can use this exemptive rule. While teaser announcements can draw investors to the site, no oral offers or sales can occur outside the portal. Portal operators need to register with the SEC or otherwise need to be registered with the SEC as broker-dealers. Also required under Regulation Crowdfunding, businesses will need to complete a form and provide it to investors; the form includes information concerning the planned use of the proceeds, financial statements (to the extent there is a business track record), possibly an audit, but at least an accountant's review. And, annually within 120 days of the end of each fiscal year, a filing with the SEC is required.

Regulation Crowdfunding provides several benefits for startup social entrepreneurs. It removes some limits that have made it hard in the past for enterprises to raise a relatively small amount of capital (capped at $1 million per year) from a wide range of investors. It taps into the so-called wisdom-of-the-crowd mentality behind the popular charitable crowdfunding sites and is particularly significant as holders of crowdfunded securities are not counted toward either the 1,999 total or 499 non-accredited limits. Moreover, Regulation Crowdfunding allows for nationwide general solicitation and sale to any investors (subject to per-investor annual limits).

However Regulation Crowdfunding has limits. The crowdfunding exemption caps total capital raising at USD$1 million per year. It also places limits on the amount any given person can contribute to a single project as well as how much such person can contribute to all crowdfunding projects in any given year. For those who have a net worth of or earn less than USD$100,000 in any given year, the investment limits are the greater of USD$2,000 or 5 percent of annual income or net worth (whichever is lower). And those with a net worth of or who earn more than USD$100,000 per year are capped at the lesser of 10 percent of annual income or net worth (whichever is lower) or USD$100,000. The SEC has provided helpful, plain-English guidance on its website on how to comply with these income-related caps.[48]

One of the drawbacks of Regulation Crowdfunding is the USD$1 million cap. Many individuals submitted comment letters in which they opposed the limit.[49] However, this is not an obstacle to raising more, as

---

[48] *Regulation Crowdfunding: A Small Entity Compliance for Issuers*, *supra* note 14.

[49] *See, e.g.*, Letter from Ben Barnes, Director of Tribal Gaming, Miami Nation Enterprises, to U.S. Sec. & Exch. Comm'n, File No. S7-09-13 (25 October 2013) (finding that "[t]he proposed $1 million cap on crowd funded projects limits

enterprises may choose to use 506(c) instead of Regulation Crowdfunding. Or, as the SEC has made clear, both might be used together. The salient differences between the two approaches include the following. First, the limits of Regulation Crowdfunding from an issuer's perspective include that it must largely take place on an authorized platform (or through a licensed broker), it requires an audit or at least an accountant's review, it is limited to $1 million per year, it requires annual reporting, and individual's investments are capped, regardless of their financial well-being or sophistication, at USD$100,000 per year in total for all possible crowdfunded investments. However, its benefits include that the purchasers will not be counted as recordholders for purposes of Section 12(g), meaning that a business could have more than 1,999 investors. In contrast, the limits of 506(c) include that purchasers must be verified accredited, and they are counted for purposes of 12(g). By combining these types of approaches, an issuer can get the best of both worlds, but must be careful to comply with the separate requirements of each offering type.

C. State Law Changes

Two types of state law changes should help founders raise capital for environmentally or socially minded enterprises. One area relates to state securities regulation and the other relates to the selection of organizational structure under state law. While federal law applies to most large offerings and sales of securities, there is still a requirement to register small offerings at the state level. In addition, state securities laws govern purely intrastate offerings that are exempt from federal registration under Section 3(a)(11) of the 1933 Act. Recently, there have been tailored state law changes to create exemptions from state registration for particular types of businesses. For example, in 2014 in Vermont, the Department of Financial Regulation (DFR) created a self-executing exemption for community solar businesses. In addition, there are proposals to expand Rule 147 to allow for regional offerings.

---

public excitement for new innovations across a broad range of products . . . Please, reconsider the cap and either keep the hands off this emerging system or impose a much higher cap in the neighborhood of $10–$25 million to if you do decide to interfere with the public's desire for free trade."). See *Comments on Proposed Rule: Crowdfunding*, U.S. Sec. & Exch. Comm'n, available 25 January 2017 at https://www.sec.gov/comments/s7-09-13/s70913.shtml, for more comment letters.

1. Community solar

In Vermont, the DFR created an exemption from registering securities offerings for certain types of community solar businesses. The DFR issued an order called the Vermont Solar Utility No-Action Exemption (the S.U.N. exemption).[50] The order makes clear that it does not exempt issuers from requirements under federal law or other states' laws if applicable. Thus, a project using the S.U.N. exemption would need to have a federal securities law exemption (such as pursuant to the small offering exemption under 3(b) and the intrastate offering exemption under 3(a)(11), Rule 506(c), or under Regulation Crowdfunding).

The S.U.N. exemption applies to certain solar electric generation facilities with group net metering. Under the order, the DFR states that community solar projects can be "investment contracts" and thus a security under Vermont law. Referring to the Supreme Court's *Howey* decision, the order lists four elements that make an arrangement an investment contract in Vermont: an investment, in a common enterprise, with the expectation of profits, derived primarily from the efforts of another person, other than the investor. In the case of community solar, those arrangements where investors front much of the development money are subject to the closest scrutiny.

Instead of a "one-size-fits-all" exemption, the DFR recognized that individuals and residential projects should be subject to more careful attention. According to a DFR press release: "The S.U.N. Exemption categorically exempts transactions with businesses, schools and state or local governmental entities from Vermont's securities registration."

Exemptions are also provided for other projects outside of those categories, subject to specific conditions. As stated in the press release, the registration exemption also applies:

- If no upfront payments are required, the payments are evenly spread out over the life of the solar contract and the contract may be terminated with minimal expense or notice;
- If an upfront fee is required, then the Vermonter must receive the required disclosures before entering into the solar contract and the person is able to assign their interest or sell it back to the solar developer;
- If it involves 10 or fewer Vermonters who have a pre-existing relationship, such as neighbors, friends or relatives who decide to develop a solar project for their own use.

---

[50] The Vermont Solar/Utility No-Action ("SUN") Exemption, 2014 WL 3697670 (Vt. Sec. Div. July 21, 2014).

This exemption for community solar investments was thought to be the first of its type in the nation. Even with these conditions, it is not clear whether Vermonters will be fully protected. For example, it remains unclear what price the solar developer would pay if the investors chose to sell their interests. Will investors get their full upfront fee returned or a prorated version, and what would that valuation be based upon? Similarly if the firm is no longer solvent, this type of buyback would be of little comfort. Thus, one wonders whether financial statement information would also be relevant to the solar investor and whether it will be provided.

One wonders whether this model could be (or even should be) expanded to facilitate small community-minded business start ups. Before such an experiment were undertaken, however, more information should be gathered about how investors fare under the S.U.N. exemption as well as under the many new capital raising options nationwide so that investor fraud and abuse are prevented. Given that full and fair disclosure is the bedrock of investor protection, the more we move away from this at the federal and state level, the greater the need to gather data to discern whether this move delivers the economic and other community development as promised or instead, greater perils.

2. Benefit corporations

In addition, at the state level, a variety of new business structures have been introduced to supplement the more traditional "for-profit" and nonprofit corporation structures. This includes the benefit corporation option. The purpose of this new type of corporate charter is to put shareholders on notice that the enterprise will have a mission that includes a public purpose not just profit seeking. In addition it is designed to help preserve the public-private character of the enterprise into the future. Maryland was the first state to enact a law creating this hybrid corporate structure. Under the Maryland statute, the purpose of a benefit corporation is to further a certain public benefit. The seven enumerated public benefits under Maryland law are: (1) providing individuals or communities with socially beneficial products or services; (2) promoting economic opportunity for individuals or communities beyond the creation of jobs in the normal course of business; (3) preserving the environment; (4) improving human health; (5) promoting the arts, sciences; (6) increasing the flow of capital to entities with a public benefit or purpose; or (7) the accomplishment of any other particular benefit for society or the environment. Under the law, the shareholders can elect to end the benefit corporation status and decide to become a regular for-profit corporation.

More than 30 states now have benefit corporation statutes. The case law interpreting these laws is developing. And, the scholarship examining how they are faring is also emerging. Some observers question whether these entities will provide benefits to society.[51] It is also important to note, though, that many scholars consider, as the US Supreme Court clarified in 2014, that a regular business corporation can serve a variety of purposes beyond shareholder profit maximization. In the otherwise controversial *Hobby Lobby* decision, the Supreme Court made clear that corporate purpose can include a range of focuses beyond profit maximization.[52]

IV. FRAUD AND MISMANAGEMENT

With innovation and ease of access to capital more broadly will come additional opportunities for fraud. Unfortunately overly optimistic or downright cynically corrupt individuals could gravitate to new economy aspirational projects. And, investors in environmentally, socially-minded enterprises may be less informed about the economic risks due to the limited required disclosures. Moreover, local regulators may have conflicting goals of developing economic or environmental opportunities and lose sight of the dangers of fraud and mismanagement.

Supporters of investment crowdfunding often oppose regulation, perhaps not appreciating the investor protection concerns lead to the securities laws in the first place. Some supporters take on a populist tone suggesting that investment crowdfunding helps "Main Street" investors access opportunities as alternatives to Wall Street investments.[53] However, others do recognize that many enterprises that select this route may have been justifiably turned down for funding from banks small and large. Investors need to understand that startups are speculative in nature and often fail. The SEC has published a bulletin to investors on its website concerning such risks,[54] but whether it will be widely read is not clear.

---

[51] Daryl Koehn, *Why the New Benefit Corporations May Not Prove to Be Truly Socially Beneficial,* Bus. & Prof. Ethics J. (2016).

[52] *See e.g.*, Jennifer Taub, *Is* Hobby Lobby *a Tool for Limiting Corporate Constitutional Rights?*, 30 Const. Comment. 403, 414 (2015).

[53] Letter from Matt R. Morse Sr., to U.S. Sec. & Exch. Comm'n, File No.S7-09-13, (3 December 2013), available 25 January 2017 at https://www.sec.gov/comments/s7-09-13/s70913-79.htm.

[54] *Investor Bulletin: Investment Crowdfunding for Investors*, Sec. and Exch. Comm'n (16 February 2016), available 25 January 2017 at https://www.sec.gov/oiea/investor-alerts-bulletins/ib_crowdfunding-.html (finding that "[i]nvestments in startups and early-stage ventures are speculative and these enterprises often fail. Unlike an investment in a mature business where there is a track record of revenue and income, the success of a startup or early-stage venture often relies on the

There is a risk, then, that honest social entrepreneurs become associated with a platform used by the unscrupulous or unwise. Moreover, there is a risk to investors with good hearts being insufficiently cautious about the seemingly sustainable, socially-beneficial opportunities presented to them online.

Comment letters submitted to the SEC in response to the then-proposed investment crowdfunding rules reveal these concerns. The Consumer Federation of America (CFA) submitted a 36-page letter detailing concerns about the proposed rule.[55] The CFA warned that based on a study cited by the SEC, "of more than 2,000 companies that received at least $1 million in venture funding from 2004 through 2010, almost three-quarters subsequently failed".[56] In addition to failure, the CFA noted the liquidity risk investors will face as they may not sell for a year and even after that it is not clear there will be willing buyers or a "suitable trading venue" where a fair price can be obtained. Similarly, Americans for Financial Reform (AFR) noted that it hoped to "ensure that steps promoted as encouraging capital formation did not come at the expense of reasonable protections for investors".[57] AFR argued that the proposed rule allowed for too much money to be put at risk by ordinary investors in startups. While the SEC had contended that this approach allowed for necessary diversification, AFR argued that:

> The percentage of the population for whom an investment of ten or even five percent of their net worth in individual stocks of start-up companies would be deemed suitable or prudent is extremely small . . . even if crowdfunding avoids becoming a mecca for fraud, the risks to investors are enormous. And it is naïve to suppose that the "wisdom of the crowd" will be sufficient to address all those risks.[58]

Other less formal, sometimes one-paragraph or one-page submissions to the SEC concerning the proposed investment crowdfunding rule were

---

development of a new product or service that may or may not find a market. ***You should be able to afford and be prepared to lose your entire investment.***").

[55] Letter from Barbara Roper, Director of Investor Protection, Consumer Federation of America, to Elizabeth M. Murphy, Secretary, U.S. Sec. & Exch. Comm'n (2 February 2014), available 25 January 2017 at http://www.consumerfed.org/pdfs/CFA-crowdfunding-comment-letter.pdf.

[56] Id.

[57] Letter from Americans for Fin. Reform to Elizabeth M. Murphy, Secretary, U.S. Sec. & Exch. Comm'n (5 March 2014), available 25 January 2017 at https://www.sec.gov/comments/s7-09-13/s70913-295.pdf.

[58] Id.

also revealing. An expert who submitted a comment letter contended that mismanagement is the most pervasive cause of business failure and that it is not possible to judge management skills via the internet.[59] An investor and entrepreneur raised fraud concerns and suggested requiring a process where issuers have their identities authenticated.[60] Others decried the way in which permitting investment crowdfunding would damage donation-crowdfunding and also attract fraud.[61]

V. CONCLUSION: BALANCING FRAUD PREVENTION AND FACILITATING ACCESS TO CAPITAL FOR LOCAL AND SOCIAL-MISSION ORIENTED BUSINESSES

Social entrepreneurs have tools to, in the words of Gus Speth, prioritize people, place and planet while also operating a business. Organizing as a benefit corporation under state law and reaching out broadly to find investors is easier now than ever before. But with this ease comes tremendous responsibility. Not everyone who uses these new methods, including investment crowdfunding, will be competent or honest. Moreover, even the highly qualified and best-intentioned will not always succeed. Unexpected failures and frauds could erode trust and undermine efforts to support worthy enterprises.

At the outset investors need to appreciate the risk in investing in start-ups and learn to look out for hallmarks of fraud. With respect to crowdfunding to unaccredited investors, it is essential to begin gathering data on

---

59 Cromwell, *supra* note 20 (finding that "[a]s an venture investor, you cannot judge the abilities of the management team over the Internet. Real venture capitalists do not make their investments over the Internet – they spend hours and hours interviewing the founders / management team, in person. Small investors cannot successfully invest over the Internet, either.").

60 Letter from Leo M. Bullock, IV, to the U.S. Sec. & Exch. Comm'n (10 November 2013), https://www.sec.gov/comments/s7-09-13/s70913-46.htm (finding that "[i]n considering the safeguards against frauds on Investors, I would propose that we incorporate in the Issuer vetting process, some type of very substantive measure to guarantee that the purported Principal(s) associated with any prospective Issuer be required to prove his or her respective identity conclusively").

61 Letter from Heather Duke, to the U.S. Sec. & Exch. Comm'n (3 December 2013), https://www.sec.gov/comments/s7-09-13/s70913-77.htm (concluding that "you are opening up a whole new window of opportunity for fraud. My mailbox is already full of SPAM and internet fishing requests. Giving fraudsters a legitimate leaping off point will only hurt the people the crowd funding was created to help").

issuers and outcomes. This will help scholars and investors in the future. Moreover, it could be helpful to establish a third-party certifier that would acknowledge having met with the founders, performed background checks on their identities and legal histories. This might grow on its own like the various customer-rating services have on TripAdvisor, Yelp! and even marketplaces like Amazon or eBay. The problem, however, with establishing such an opinion forum is that it could also be subject to manipulation and fraud by those who are trying to manipulate prices such as pumping up the price of issued crowdfunded securities in order to sell them off once the one-year restriction on resale runs. Nevertheless, some sort of system will need to grow alongside these portals as the wisdom of the crowd can only flourish if the crowd's wisdom can be expressed and seen. A model might be emerging now through the nonprofit entity B Lab, which offers certification of "B Corporations".

Hopefully, on balance these new legal changes that facilitate capital formation will help creative leaders find and fund solutions to the critical social and environmental problems we face.

9. Distributed renewables in the new economy: lessons from community solar development in Vermont

Kevin B. Jones and Mark James

I. INTRODUCTION

This chapter analyzes the factors driving solar development in the US. With the climate imperative in mind, it focuses on transforming US electric generation because this is the largest source of greenhouse gases in the world, second only to China in total emissions.[1] The chapter begins with a discussion of the current solar energy market in the US, explores how solar fits into the changing electric utility landscape, provides an overview of current federal and state policies, and then presents the Boardman Hill Solar Farm case study. Based on this case study, the chapter concludes with an assessment of how the community owned solar model could be scaled up to build local economic wealth and reduce carbon emissions.

II. DISRUPTIVE GENERATION: DISTRIBUTED GENERATION VERSUS UTILITY-OWNED GENERATION

The US electric industry, with the combination of aging infrastructure, increasing penetration of renewable energy, and an outdated business model is on the precipice of dramatic change. Significant investment is needed to reliably meet long-term energy goals. The nation's electrical grid is estimated to require USD$1.5–2 trillion of investment by 2030 in order

[1] *Global Greenhouse Gas Emissions Data: Global Emissions by Gas*, ENVTL. PROT. AGENCY, available 26 January 2017 at https://www3.epa.gov/climatechange/ghgemissions/sources.html (last updated 10 June 2016); *Sources of Greenhouse Gas Emissions*, ENVTL. PROT. AGENCY, available 26 January 2017 at https://www3.epa.gov/climatechange/ghgemissions/global.html (last updated 26 May 2016).

to preserve and maintain reliability and security standards and prepare for new renewable sources of generation.[2] This is an opportunity to implement substantive changes to how energy is generated and delivered across the electrical grid; changes that will alter the relationship between the roles of consumers and electric utilities.

For most of the twentieth century, roles in the electricity sector were clearly defined. A changing regulatory structure and technology innovations are now blurring the formerly bright lines defining the roles of utility and consumer. Historically, vertically integrated utilities owned and operated every piece of the electricity sector: generation, transmission and distribution. Electricity generated by large central station power plants was transported on high voltage transmission lines to the distribution grid that connected to the end-user. End-use customers connected to the grid and paid the utility for the electricity they received.

The dominance of the vertically integrated utility model began to erode at the end of the twentieth century through a series of state and federal actions. At the state level, the deregulation of retail energy markets started the move towards a distributed utility by giving customers more freedom in their energy purchasing decisions.[3] Buoyed by concerns of anti-competitive behavior, Congress and the Federal Energy Regulatory Commission (FERC), opened up the grid to wholesale competition.[4] Subsequent initiatives are fundamentally altering the relationship between utility and end-use consumer.

The role of consumer has been recast by improvements in technology and the introduction of federal and state incentive programs for small-scale generation. A new system is emerging where customers are "prosumers", acting as both energy producers and consumers depending upon the time of day. Reduced solar photovoltaic (PV) panel costs, net metering and federal tax incentives are encouraging homeowners to generate their own power. Between 2009 and 2014, the installed cost of

---

2 Johannes Pfeifenberger, et al., *Investment Trends and Fundamentals in US Transmission and Electricity Infrastructure*, Brattle Grp. (15 July 2015), available 26 January 2017 at http://www.brattle.com/system/publications/pdfs/000/005/190/original/Investment_Trends_and_Fundamentals_in_US_Transmission_and_Electricity_Infrastructure.pdf?1437147799.

3 *See, e.g.,* Competitive Opportunities for Electric Service, 168 P.U.R.4th 515 (1996).

4 Public Utility Regulatory Policies Act, 16 U.S.C. §§ 2601–2645 (1978); Promoting Wholesale Competition Through Open Access Non-Discriminatory Transmission Services by Public Utilities; Recovery of Stranded Costs by Public Utilities and Transmitting Utilities, Order No. 888, 61 FR 21540 (10 May 1996), 18 C.F.R. pts. 35, 385 (2015).

a solar panel dropped by more than 50 percent, from USD$6.3/Watt to USD$3.1/Watt.[5]

Faced with these changes, state governments have begun the process of revamping the traditional utility model.[6] The New York State Public Service Commission's Renewing the Energy Vision (REV) process is an example of how states are addressing the challenges facing their electricity sectors.[7] REV is exploring an energy modernization effort that could "fundamentally transform the way electricity is distributed and used".[8] The Commission understands that "the customer side of the grid represents an enormous and largely untapped resource to improve the value of the system".[9] Distributed energy resources, smaller scale, often renewable, resources interconnected to the local distribution grid, will play a major role in providing both improved reliability and efficiency for customers.

Other states, including California and Hawaii, are reviewing their utility regulatory models in response to technological advancements and environmental concerns to both support increased adoption of renewables and improve reliability.[10]

---

[5] Jon Weiner, *Price of Solar Energy in the United States Has Fallen to 5¢/kWh on Average*, LAWRENCE BERKELEY NAT'L LAB. (20 September 2015), available 26 January 2017 at http://newscenter.lbl.gov/2015/09/30/price-of-solar-energy-in-the-united-states-has-fallen-to-5%C2%A2kwh-on-average/.

[6] *See, e.g.*, E21 INITIATIVE, PHASE 1 REPORT, CHARTING A PATH TO A 21ST CENTURY ENERGY SYSTEM IN MINNESOTA (2014), available 26 January 2017 at https://www.betterenergy.org/sites/www.betterenergy.org/files/e21; Order Instituting Rulemaking Regarding Policies, Procedures and Rules for Development of Distribution Resources Plans Pursuant to Public Utilities Code Section 769, 2014 WL 4248588 (Cal. Pub. Util. Comm'n 2014); Proceeding to Investigate Distributed Energy Resource Policies, 2014 WL 4258315 (Haw. Pub. Util. Comm'n 2014).

[7] Press Release, Governor Andrew M. Cuomo, Governor Cuomo Announces Fundamental Shift in Utility Regulation (24 April 2015), available 26 January 2017 at https://www.governor.ny.gov/news/governor-cuomo-announces-fundamental-shift-utility-regulation.

[8] Press Release, Governor Andrew M. Cuomo, Governor Cuomo Announces Fundamental Shift in Utility Regulation (24 April 2015), available 26 January 2017 at https://www.governor.ny.gov/news/governor-cuomo-announces-fundamental-shift-utility-regulation.

[9] Order Adopting Regulatory Framework and Implementation Plan, 2015 WL 862119, *10 (N.Y. Pub. Serv. Comm'n 2015).

[10] Kevin B. Jones, Taylor L. Curtis, Marc de Konkily Thege, Daniel Sauer and Matthew Roche, *Distributed Utility: Conflicts and Opportunities between Incumbent Utilities, Suppliers, and Emerging New Entrants*, *in* FUTURE OF UTILITIES, UTILITIES OF THE FUTURE: HOW TECHNOLOGICAL INNOVATIONS IN DISTRIBUTED ENERGY RESOURCES WILL RESHAPE THE ELECTRIC POWER SECTOR 399, 405–12 (F. P. Sioshansi (ed.), 2016).

III. TRENDS IN RENEWABLE ENERGY: PAST, PRESENT, FUTURE

America's distributed energy revolution is literally shining down upon us. For the past decade, American solar energy production has experienced unprecedented growth. Since 2008, American solar power has grown from 1.2 GW to more than 20 GW of installed capacity.[11] Between 2013 and 2015, annual solar generation grew from 9 GWh to 26 GWh, with 7.3 GW of solar generation capacity being installed in 2015.[12] In 2015, 29.5 percent of all new electricity-generating capacity was solar.[13] The growth rate is impressive but there is significant room for expansion and significant flexibility to expand in a manner that provides enhanced economic and environmental benefits.

Despite this new growth, there is a long way to go to move the US electricity sector off of fossil fuels and onto renewables. As of September 2015, utility-scale PV, distributed PV, and thermal solar generation was equivalent to only 1 percent of total reported electric generation.[14]

Meanwhile, electricity usage has stabilized in the United States. From 2005, US energy consumption increased by 0.2 percent per year.[15] Electric sector carbon emissions peaked in 2007, and have now declined to 1995 levels.[16]

---

[11] Parth Shah, *Gas, Wind Contribute 82% of Capacity Additions in 2015*, S&P Global Market Intelligence (7 January 2016), available 26 January 2017 at https://www.snl.com/InteractiveX/Article.aspx?cdid=A-34950800-13103.

[12] Mike Munsell, *US Solar Market Sets New Record, Installing 7.3GW of Solar PV in 2015*, Greentech Media (22 February 2016), available 26 January 2017 at http://www.greentechmedia.com/articles/read/us-solar-market-sets-new-record-installing-7.3-gw-of-solar-pv-in-2015.

[13] *U.S. Solar Market Sets New Record, Installing 7.3GW of Solar PV in 2015*, Solar Energy Industries Ass'n (22 February 2016), available 26 January 2017 at http://www.seia.org/news/us-solar-market-sets-new-record-installing-73-gw-solar-pv-2015.

[14] *Today in Energy: EIA Electricity Data Now Include Small-Scale Solar PV Capacity and Generation*, U.S. Energy Info. Admin. (2 December 2015), available 26 January 2017 at https://www.eia.gov/todayinenergy/detail.cfm?id=23972.

[15] Pat Knight, *Synapse Electricity Snapshot: A Review of the U.S. Electric System Through December 2015*, Synapse Energy Econ. (3 March 2016), available 26 January 2017 at http://www.synapse-energy.com/sites/default/files/Synapse_Electricity_Snapshot_2016.pdf.

[16] This transition started prior to either the Clean Power Plan or the Paris Agreement. *Total Energy: Carbon Dioxide Emissions from Energy Consumption: Electric Power Sector*, U.S. Energy Info. Admin., available 26 January 2017 at http://www.eia.gov/beta/MER/index.cfm?tbl=T12.06#/?f=A&start=1973&end=2015&charted=0-1-6.

Solar power's transformation of the US energy system is only just beginning. The potential generation available from solar resources dwarfs current installed capacity. America has a solar generation potential of almost 300,000 TWh/yr and a solar capacity potential in excess of 190,000 GW which is more than 80 times what the US currently consumes for electricity.[17] In fact we could meet 39 percent of our electricity needs by placing solar panels on existing rooftops alone and we could meet all of our needs by placing solar on only 0.6 percent of our land area.[18]

The solar revolution is being fueled by new installations of large utility-scale and smaller distributed generation facilities.[19] In 2015, utility-scale generation produced 23,232 GWh, an increase of 52 percent over 2014. In 2015, distributed generation facilities produced 12,141 GWh, an increase of 27 percent over 2014.[20] Distributed generation is split between industrial, commercial, and residential sectors. Industrial sector generation produced 1,190 GWh, commercial sector distributed generation produced 5,024 GWh, and residential sector distributed generation produced 5,927 GWh. Residential sector distributed generation increased by almost 40 percent between 2014 and 2015. It is important to understand the drivers behind these increases.

A. Federal and State Policies Advancing Solar

Federal and state policies are fueling the dramatic expansion of ground-mounted solar, rooftop solar, utility-scale solar and community solar projects. Federal policies are concentrated in supporting research programs and providing tax credits. State policies have taken a more varied approach to creating opportunities for solar generation.

---

17 ANTHONY LOPEZ ET AL., NAT. RENEWABLE ENERGY LAB., U.S. RENEWABLE ENERGY TECHNICAL POTENTIALS: A GIS-BASED ANALYSIS 10-12 (2012), available 26 January 2017 at http://www.nrel.gov/docs/fy12osti/51946.pdf.

18 PIETER GAGNON, ET AL., NAT. RENEWABLE ENERGY LAB., ROOFTOP SOLAR PHOTOVOLTAIC TECHNICAL POTENTIAL IN THE UNITED STATES: A DETAILED ASSESSMENT 34 (2016), available 26 January 2017 at http://www.nrel.gov/docs/fy16osti/65298.pdf; U.S. DEPT. OF ENERGY, SUNSHOT VISION STUDY 4 (2012), http://www1.eere.energy.gov/solar/pdfs/47927.pdf.

19 *Electric Power Monthly: Net Generation from Solar Photovoltaic*, U.S. ENERGY INFO. ADMIN., available 26 January 2017 at http://www.eia.gov/electricity/monthly/epm_table_grapher.cfm?t=epmt_1_17_b.

20 *Id.*

1. Federal programs

The federal government has two major programs: the SunShot research program and the Investment Tax Credit (ITC). Launched in 2011, SunShot research programs seek to reduce the hard and soft costs of installing residential solar PV panels, utility-scale solar PV panels, and concentrating solar.[21] Since the inception of the program, the average price of a utility-scale PV project dropped from approximately $0.21/kWh to $0.11/kWh, more than halfway to the goal of $0.06/kWh by 2020.

The federal ITC altered the landscape for renewable energy development. Introduced in 1992, the ITC provides a 30 percent tax credit for renewable energy commercial and residential projects, including solar PV.[22] The ITC was renewed in December 2015[23] and is phasing down to only 10 percent for commercial and 0 percent for residential projects after 2021.[24] The ITC renewal is expected to produce $40 billion of investment in solar between 2016 and 2020.[25]

For a brief period of time following the 2008 financial crisis but expiring at the end of 2011, solar developers could claim their ITC credits in the form of a one-time Section 1603 Treasury program cash grant payout.[26] The program freed developers from having to rely upon tax equity investors to capitalize on all of the available financial incentives. The program expired on 31 December 2011.[27]

---

[21] U.S. Dept. of Energy, *supra* note 18, at xix–xx.

[22] *Business Energy Investment Tax Credit (ITC)*, Dept. of Energy, available 26 January 2017 at http://energy.gov/savings/business-energy-investment-tax-credit-itc (last visited 15 July, 2016).

[23] Consolidated Appropriations Act of 2016, Pub. L. No. 114-113, § 181, 129 Stat. 2242, 3073 (2015).

[24] Dept. of Energy, *supra* note 22.

[25] Mike Munsell, *Investment Tax Credit Extension Would Increase US Solar Installations 54% Through 2020*, Greentech Media (16 December, 2015), available 26 January 2017 at http://www.greentechmedia.com/articles/read/investment-tax-credit-extension-will-increase-solar-installations-54-throug.

[26] *Recovery Act: 1603 Program: Payments for Specified Energy Property in Lieu of Tax Credits*, U.S. Treasury (30 September 2015), available 26 January 2017 at https://www.treasury.gov/initiatives/recovery/Pages/1603.aspx; *See also* Michael Mendelsohn, Nat'l Renewable Energy Lab., §1603 Treasury Grant Expiration: Industry Insight on Financing and Market Implications 22 (2012), available 26 January 2017 at http://www.nrel.gov/docs/fy12osti/53720.pdf.

[27] The program continued to make payments after 31 December 2011 to individuals who met the qualification requirements.

2. State policies: renewable portfolio standards, solar carve outs and net metering

State incentive programs have largely focused on retail electricity procurement mandates, solar carve-out policies and net metering programs. A state renewable portfolio standard (RPS) is a mandate imposed on utilities to sell a specified percentage of renewable energy. Twenty-nine states, three territories, and the District of Columbia have an RPS.[28]

State governments determine how much renewable energy they will require their regulated utilities to procure and when they will be required to meet the standard. RPS amounts can range between 10 percent and 100 percent of retail electric sales. State-imposed schedules can require compliance by 2020 or as far away as 2050. The established pattern for RPS is one of increasing ambition. For example, California's RPS has increased from 20 percent in 2012 to 33 percent by 2020 to 50 percent by 2030. Hawaii's RPS has increased from 10 percent in 2010 to 100 percent by 2045.

State RPS programs vary in the renewable energy procurement requirement, the length of time for compliance, which resources are eligible for inclusion in the program, whether existing or only new resources qualify and which utilities must comply with the standard. Most state standards are measured by percentage of kilowatt hours of retail electric sales. A few states require specific amounts of renewable energy capacity or a percentage of peak demand.[29] States also control which resources are eligible for inclusion in the RPS. The inclusion of renewable resources like wind and solar resources is standard; some states exclude large-scale hydropower, while others only allow resources developed after a certain date. Other states permit non-renewable resources like the incineration of municipal solid waste and coal gasification technology.[30]

Given the cost advantage of utility scale wind, most utility RPS procurements have been dominated by wind power. To create a balanced portfolio of resources, many states carve out capacity for specific resource types such as solar. A solar carve-out can take a couple of forms: a resource-specific requirement to purchase a minimum amount of energy from

---

[28] Jocelyn Durkay, State Renewable Portfolio Standards and Goals, NAT'L CONF. OF STATE LEGIS.'s (23 March, 2016), available 26 January 2017 at http://www.ncsl.org/research/energy/renewable-portfolio-standards.aspx.

[29] *Id.*

[30] JENNY HEETER AND LORI BIRD, NAT'L RENEWABLE ENERGY LAB., INCLUDING ALTERNATE RESOURCES IN STATE RENEWABLE PORTFOLIO STANDARDS: CURRENT DESIGN AND IMPLEMENTATION EXPERIENCE 1 (2012), available 26 January 2017 at http://www.nrel.gov/docs/fy13osti/55979.pdf.

in-state solar facilities or credit multipliers to increase the value of solar energy in meeting the RPS mandate.

Net metering is the most widely adopted state program to incentivize small-scale renewable energy development. Net metering programs have become a standard component of renewable energy programs. As of February 2016, there are 45 jurisdictions (41 states, District of Columbia, and three territories) with state-developed mandatory net metering rules for some or all of their utilities.[31] Seventeen states allow aggregated net metering.[32] Sixteen states have virtual net metering policies.[33]

Net metering allows a solar system owner to receive credit for the electricity produced from their solar panels and fed into the grid, which can then be used to offset their electricity bill. Solar is not an on-demand generation facility; energy is produced when the sun shines. The pattern of energy production rarely matches the pattern of energy consumption. Net metering allows for a customer to deliver energy to and take energy from the grid. Customers accrue monthly credits at the retail rate during periods of excess generation that can be applied to the months when consumption exceeds demand. Unused credits often have an expiration date limiting a customer's ability to carry them forward.

Net metering can take multiple forms: conventional net metering, aggregated net metering, and virtual (also known as group) net metering. Conventional net metering occurs when the solar PV system is located behind the meter, which is when the electricity generated from the panels runs back through the meter allowing the meter to be rolled back during periods of production. Conventional net metering is confined to the single meter. Aggregated net metering allows for customers with multiple meters to offset their energy use with production from a single solar array located on their property. Virtual net metering cuts the link between "behind the meter" generation and net metering credits. Customers who do not have an array physically located on their property can offset their generation by taking a share in an array located off-site. The energy from the array is normally shared in proportion to the ownership in the system. Furthermore, multiple parties can receive net metering credits from a

---

[31] *Net Metering*, Database of State Incentive for Renewables & Efficiency (February 2016), available 26 January 2017 at http://ncsolarcen-prod.s3.amazonaws.com/wp-content/uploads/2016/02/Net_Metering_022016.pdf.

[32] John Farrell, *Aggregate Net Metering*, Inst. for Local Self-Reliance (5 June 2015), available 26 January 2017 at https://ilsr.org/aggregate-net-metering/.

[33] John Farrell, *Updated: States Supporting Virtual Net Metering*, Inst. for Local Self-Reliance (4 November 2015), available 26 January 2017 at https://ilsr.org/virtual-net-metering/.

single array provided they are located within the same utility zone as the array.

States normally develop specific rules for virtual net metered projects. States can limit the number of participants in a project, cap the overall size of a project, and limit the aggregate capacity of projects connecting onto a distribution grid. Virtual net metering is a key factor in the rapid expansion of community solar projects.

B. The Problem of Separating the Environmental Attributes from the Solar Electricity

Historically, net metered solar was additive to other state policies, such as RPS programs. Increasingly, the incentives and mandates for these programs are being comingled and thus net metering is no longer driving additional solar development nor is it producing additional greenhouse gas reductions. The stripping of Renewable Energy Credits (RECs) from third-party owned projects creates a false promise of more solar. Companies promote to consumers that they can "go solar" with their project, but the reality is that these projects are not providing solar in addition to other states existing mandates. Since two solar consumers cannot consume the same green kWh of electricity, these practices have both led to false green claims to the consumer and resulted in producing much less solar than if the consumer had been sold an additional kWh of solar energy.

In Vermont, particularly, current net metering program design inefficiencies promote the transfer of the environmental benefits of solar energy to other regions in New England. The RECs from the vast majority of the solar developed in Vermont, which recently exceeded the state's 15 percent net metering cap, are being sold into the RPS programs in Massachusetts and Connecticut.[34] As a result, Vermont's net metering program is not producing additional solar development, but instead is subsidizing the existing RPS mandates in other New England states.[35]

---

[34] *New Energy Clinic REC Report: Solar and Wind Provide Zero Percent of Vermont Electric Supply*, INST. FOR ENERGY AND THE ENV'T (29 February 2016), available 26 January 2017 at http://wordpress.vermontlaw.edu/energy/new-energy-clinic-rec-report-solar-and-wind-provide-zero-percent-of-vermont-electric-supply/.

[35] About 125 MW of Massachusetts RPS Class 1 RECs are from solar facilities with 84 MW of those from Vermont projects. MASS. DEPT. OF ENERGY RES., MASS. RPS & APS ANNUAL COMPLIANCE REPORT FOR 2014, MASS. DEPT. OF ENERGY RES. 17 (2016), available 26 January 2017 at http://www.mass.gov/eea/docs/doer/rps-aps/rps-aps-2014-annual-compliance-report.pdf.

Meanwhile many community solar participants who believe they have reduced their carbon footprints have not, since developers of both third-party owned projects, as well as projects where direct ownership interests in the arrays have been sold to customers, have been stripping RECs from projects and not including them in the sales to the customers. As a result of this practice the Vermont attorney general's office in 2015 issued guidance to solar companies on deceptive claims.[36] The guidance warned solar companies not to make deceptive claims that they were selling solar energy to a customer if they had separately sold the RECs.

Additionality is an important component in designing a renewable energy program. Additionality means that a solar project produces carbon emission reductions in excess of those mandated by law. If the owners of the project retain and retire the RECs, their renewable energy cannot be used by a utility to meet its state renewables goal or toward any other requirement. Instead, the RECs are retired in the name of the customer, allowing them to make appropriate green claims and their purchases resulting in an additional mWh of renewable energy. The utility will still have to generate or procure additional RECs to meet its state RPS mandate.

Pacific Gas and Electric's (PG&E) community solar tariff is an example of how a properly designed utility owned program can result in the construction of additional distributed solar. PG&E retires the solar RECs from the project on behalf of the customers and does not count the solar RECs toward the California RPS. As a result the PG&E community solar arrays scale up additional solar beyond the previous mandates. Advocating for more transparency, as well as regulatory and policy action on this issue, will ensure that community solar is in addition to existing mandates and scales up the national development of solar.

C. The Growth of Third-Party Solar Ownership

The presence of the federal investment tax credit, as well as stable revenues available from state net metering programs, attracted significant sources of outside capital to the solar industry. As a result, distributed solar, which

---

[36] *State Advises Solar Companies About Deceptive Advertising*, Vt. Office of the Attorney Gen. (Dec. 8, 2015), available 26 January 2017 at http://ago.vermont.gov/focus/news/state-advises-solar-companies-about-deceptive-advertising1.php.

was once almost exclusively owned by the customer, is now dominated by third-party ownership. In 2014, third parties owned 72 percent of the 1.2 GW of residential solar installed that year.[37]

Third-party ownership is where outside investors own the solar panels that supply solar energy to the customer. The solar panels can be located on the customer's property or offsite.[38] Third-party ownership models are structured in a variety of ways: with little to no upfront costs to the consumer, with partial down payments, or with the option to purchase the system in the future. As of April 2016, at least 33 states allow third-party power purchase agreements for solar PV.[39]

Third-party ownership has proliferated because solar projects have high initial capital costs and low operating costs. Third-party ownership takes advantage of the considerable federal tax incentives available for renewable energy resources. As discussed above, the federal investment tax credit (ITC) is a major driver of the growth of solar. To claim the tax credits an individual or business or third-party developer must have sufficient taxable income. Solar developers partner with tax equity investors, individuals or companies with available tax appetite, in a financial arrangement to access the ITC. Tax equity investors provide capital for solar projects and in return they are given the right to claim the ITC. These investors rely on both the interconnection rights and steady stream of revenues from solar net metering customers in order to be able to take advantage of the ITC, since otherwise they would have to negotiate a contract directly with the utility.

D. Third-Party Versus Direct Ownership

The reliance on third-party tax equity investors has pushed the marketplace away from community-owned solar projects. As a result, significant economic value has flowed to the investor rather than remaining with the solar consumer. Tax equity investing also increases the overall cost of

---

37 Mike Munsell, *72% of US Residential Solar Installed in 2014 was Third-Party Owned*, Greentech Media (29 July 2015), available 26 January 2017 at http://www.greentechmedia.com/articles/read/72-of-us-residential-solar-installed-in-2014-was-third-party-owned.

38 Third-party ownership include models including leases and partnership flip models.

39 *3rd Party Solar PV Purchase Power Agreement (PPA)*, Database of State Incentives for Renewables & Efficiency (Mar. 2015), available 26 January 2017 at http://ncsolarcen-prod.s3.amazonaws.com/wp-content/uploads/2015/01/3rd-Party-PPA_0302015.pdf.

capital as compared to debt financing which reduces the economic benefits available to consumers who want solar energy.[40]

Tax equity investors pursue projects to maximize their economic returns, often, at the expense of community and environmental benefits. For example, in addition to diverting economic value away from the energy consumer, many third-party owned systems are also selling off the environmental benefits. Third-party owned solar systems often strip the environmental attributes called Renewable Energy Credits (RECs) from the energy that they provide to net metering customers and sell the RECs to a different customer for additional revenue. Utilities and nonutility energy service companies purchase RECs in order to comply with their state RPS requirements.

The third-party developer needs the utility customer to interconnect, access the federal ITC, and gain a consistent revenue source through net metering credits. If the developer then sells the RECs to another third party as well, rooftop and community solar net metering customers engaged with these developers do not receive the solar energy they thought they were purchasing. Consumer complaints are increasing over the financial savings and green environmental claims made in regards to the provisions of these multi-year customer agreements.[41]

Fortunately, the direct ownership model is making a comeback. Direct ownership of solar panels is predicted to overtake third-party ownership by 2020.[42] One reason is the declining cost of installed solar with an average sized residential array of 5 kW now costing approximately USD$15,000 instead of close to USD$35,000.[43]

Local financing options are also increasing in some regions. As the number of solar installations has increased, financial institutions gained more information on their performance, which has in turn created a lower risk profile for people seeking loans to finance solar. Additionally, customers are seeking assurances that they are keeping the environmental

---

40 Scott Fisher, et al., U.S. P'ship for Renewable Energy Fin., Tax Credits, Tax Equity and Alternatives to Spur Clean Energy Financing 2 (2011), available 26 January 2017 at http://uspref.org/wp-content/uploads/2011/09/Tax-Credits-Tax-Equity-for-Clean-Energy-Financing.pdf.

41 *See, e.g.,* Barbara Alexander, Solar Power on the Roof and in the Neighborhood: Recommendations for Consumer Protection Policies 19–20 (2016), available 26 January 2017 at http://www.opc.state.md.us/Portals/0/Publications/BAlexander.FINAL%20Solar%20Power%20Consumer%20Protection%20Report.March2016.pdf; Vt. Office of the Attorney Gen., *supra* note 36.

42 Munsell, *supra* note 37.

43 The cost of a solar array is calculated using the figures provided by the SunShot Initiative.

attributes of their projects by not selling the RECs to a third party. With the declining cost of solar and local financing increasingly available, community solar offers a meaningful alternative to the problematic third-party ownership model.

IV. THE CASE FOR COMMUNITY SOLAR

A. Community Solar Opens Solar Ownership Opportunities to More People

Half of America's population cannot participate in the solar revolution because they either live in a home that cannot support a solar array or rent an apartment. NREL's Shared Solar report estimates that only half of American residences and businesses are able to support their own solar arrays.[44] Rental agreements, lack of access to a roof, and insufficient roof space are some of the reasons why hosting an array is not possible.

Community solar is an opportunity to provide access to solar to those who have missed out on the boom. The Department of Energy defines community shared solar as "a solar-electric system that provides power and/or financial benefit to multiple community members".[45] Community solar arrays allow individuals and businesses to receive the economic and environmental benefits of solar without locating an array on their property.

Community solar is an untapped opportunity to bring more residential and commercial customers into the solar revolution. NREL estimates that shared solar could represent "32–49% of the distributed market in 2020", an additional 5.5–11 GW of generating capacity worth USD$8.2–USD$16.3 billion of investment.[46]

As discussed in the preceding chapter, the ability to host an array is also a socio-economic issue as access to solar power overwhelmingly favors the middle and upper classes. A 2013 study showed that more than 60 percent of solar installations occur in zip codes with median annual

---

[44] DAVID FELDMAN ET AL., NAT'L RENEWABLE ENERGY LAB., SHARED SOLAR: CURRENT LANDSCAPE, MARKET POTENTIAL, AND THE IMPACT OF FEDERAL SECURITIES REGULATION v (2015), available 26 January 2017 at http://www.nrel.gov/docs/fy15osti/63892.pdf.

[45] U.S. DEPT. OF ENERGY, A GUIDE TO COMMUNITY SHARED SOLAR: UTILITY, PRIVATE AND NONPROFIT PROJECT DEVELOPMENT 3 (2012), available 26 January 2017 at http://www.nrel.gov/docs/fy12osti/54570.pdf.

[46] FELDMAN ET AL., *supra* note 44, at v.

incomes ranging from USD$40,000 to USD$90,000 and less than 10 percent of installations occur in zip codes with median annual incomes below USD$40,000.[47]

Community solar lowers the financial barriers to solar energy, both in hard and soft costs, and can provide affordable renewable power and financial benefit to many, including renters and low-income households previously excluded. The NREL participation estimates for community solar do not capture households that currently cannot afford to invest in a solar PV system as individuals, but would be able to consider a community solar option.

B. Overcoming the Barriers to Community Solar

Community solar has the potential to significantly scale up renewable energy production in the US, helping communities and individuals meet their energy needs with clean, resilient, locally owned energy production.

Tapping into the community solar market will require new models and business arrangements to divide ownership of arrays between multiple parties. One of the greatest challenges to broad adoption of community solar is the legal hurdles that potential customers encounter.

Each state has different laws, regulations and incentives, and each utility has policies that help or hurt community solar. These policies exist in a constant state of flux due to ongoing legislative and regulatory changes. Additionally, there is uncertainty as to whether off-site community solar is eligible for the 30 percent federal residential investment tax credit and whether investments in community solar facilities are considered securities under state and federal laws. Having to register an offering for community solar as a security adds significant development costs and legal complexity to a project and can be enough to deter community groups from getting involved in a project.

Community-owned solar is also hindered by the lack of clarity on how to structure a shared solar program; the legal and business structures needed to support and implement community-owned renewable energy projects are not fully formulated in many states. Consequently, guidance in determining which ownership model will provide the greatest economic and environmental benefit can be hard to find – and the tools and

---

47 Mari Hernandez, *Solar Power to the People: The Rise of Rooftop Solar Among the Middle Class*, Ctr. For Am. Progress (21 October 2013), available 26 January 2017 at https://www.americanprogress.org/issues/green/report/2013/10/21/76013/solar-power-to-the-people-the-rise-of-rooftop-solar-among-the-middle-class/.

resources that do exist are developed for one location, and may not apply in another jurisdiction.

What is sometimes being promoted as community solar, even in states that have strong policies in place, does not necessarily best serve the interests of the community or individual participants. A solar deal which appears low cost may unnecessarily transfer significant economic value to third-party investors, utilize inferior equipment, result in costs beyond those anticipated, and not even provide renewable energy to the consumer. These models, promoted by utilities, developers, and even some organizations seeking to scale up solar energy, may allow or encourage the selling of renewable energy credits, which does not reduce additional GHG pollution.

Expanding the number of GW of solar energy generated is important, but it is also important to do this while also creating more local owners of solar projects, and thus enhancing greater wealth equity across society. By helping community members expand solar ownership opportunities, people can make decisions to support local suppliers, improve local siting, and increase the economic value for local community members.

Policy changes are needed to address existing challenges at the state, federal and local level for community owned solar. In some states, legislation guiding community solar is vague, which leaves the state agencies that regulate energy to make policy in conjunction with public utility regulatory authorities. Simultaneously, public utilities are pushing back against financial incentives for renewable power that they deem as harmful to their existing business models. In addition, many states have met their net metering caps and are not authorizing new projects. The federal government has not clarified how the residential tax credit applies to off-site community solar or how federal securities laws apply to community-owned solar. Municipalities, schools and other not-for-profit organizations continue to be punished by their inability to qualify for the federal investment tax credit.

C. Community Solar Case Study – Boardman Hill Solar Farm: A Success Story for the New Economy

1. Genesis of the project

The genesis for the project was two-fold: the owners of Boardman Hill Farm, Greg and Gaye Cox, were interested in hosting a solar farm because a number of solar development companies had approached them. But the farmers were skeptical of these proposals and concerned about the developers' selling the RECs. The farmers wanted the solar developed on their land to contribute to the economic and environmental health of the community in the same manner as their community supported agriculture and local farmers market (see Figure 9.1).

Meanwhile, a group of community members in Mount Holly, Vermont, were looking for a project site to build a community owned array. Led by Marcy Tanger and Roland Marx, two long-time residents who had been previously involved in town solar and efficiency projects, the group talked with multiple entities proposing various project structures for solar projects.

Ultimately the group determined that working directly with a project developer who would construct a turn-key project for them, which the community members owned, would provide the best economic and environmental value for the community.

A local solar developer, Nils Behn, President of Aegis Renewable Energy, connected the two parties and developed the Solar Farm. At this point, summer was quickly transitioning to fall. To complete the project during the limited construction season the project plan would need to be developed and implemented in short order.

Following some preliminary discussions, the parties agreed on a basic concept. Aegis Renewable Energy would construct a turnkey solar system and sell it directly to the community members at a competitive price, given the economy of scale benefits available from community solar. Aegis was responsible for obtaining necessary permits and constructing the Solar Farm.

Members of the community group, largely comprised of residents from Mount Holly, Vermont, would contract directly with Aegis to purchase the quantity of solar panels each individual required. Since the members directly own their shares of the array, they applied to receive the federal 30 percent residential investment tax credit.

2. Key elements of the community solar model

Boardman Hill Solar Farm (Solar Farm) is a community-owned solar project that serves as a model for the new economy. The key features of this model are appropriate land use and siting, community ownership of solar array and solar energy, affordable cost with growing member equity in the project, and a member-managed organizational structure.

(a) Land use and proper siting of a renewable energy project The community chose a site for the project in a manner that respected the agricultural and residential nature of the neighborhood in which it was located. They constructed the 150 kW AC Solar Farm on an acre of the homestead portion of a 70-acre organic farm the Vermont Land Trust had conserved. The sunny location, in West Rutland, Vermont, is neighborhood and

Figure 9.1 *Boardman Hill Farm community solar participants*

environmentally friendly because it is sited with adequate setback from the property's boundaries and is located on the homestead rather than conserved agricultural land.

(b) Community ownership of the solar array and RECs Community members own the solar array, receive all revenues available from the project, and directly participate in the governance and management of the project. The RECs from the project remain bundled with the net metered energy credits from the utility, ensuring that the electricity purchased by the members can legally be called solar electricity. As a result, the Solar Farm feeds additional local solar energy into the grid and reduces the community's greenhouse gas emissions.

As part of the agreement, the Solar Farm land lease required that the RECs remain bundled with the net-metered electricity in order to legally preserve the local nature of the greenhouse gas reductions. In essence, it is a solar farm owned by local participants where the solar energy is both generated and consumed – locally. From the point where the basic proposal for the Solar Farm was conceived, it took only four months to permit and construct the array and finalize the membership and organizational structure.

(c) Affordable cost Under Vermont's group net metering program, the solar electric energy output from the array is directly fed into the grid operated by Green Mountain Power (the utility). The utility monitors production and purchases the output at a premium price. The utility pays the retail rate for the electricity plus a "solar adder" of approximately 4.5 cents per kWh for a total of 19 cents per kWh. State law guarantees the solar adder to the group net metered customer for a ten-year period following construction. Under Vermont's group net metering rules, each individual owner of the community solar array has the revenue produced by their share of the array credited against the amount of electricity they use on their residential electric bill.[48]

The community owned solar model brings economy of scale savings to a project without having to rely on third-party financing. The model brings community members together in a project that is structured similarly to rooftop solar in that the member-owners purchase their share of the

---

[48] Group net meter customers in Vermont can only utilize the monthly credit to offset a positive balance on their bill. If the monthly credit is larger than their current bill then the excess balance can be carried over for up to a 12-month period. After 12 months any excess credit goes to the utility. VT. STAT. ANN. tit. 30, § 219a(e)(3)(C) (2016).

system directly from the solar developer as if they were installing a small array on their property. Because of the reduced customer acquisition costs and other economy of scale savings, the model is attractive to local solar installers who have been able to build these projects for over a dollar per watt less than residential rooftop projects. The Solar Farm members paid USD$2.87/W before tax.[49] In addition to the construction and financing costs, the Solar Farm members pay annual operation and maintenance costs, taxes and insurance.

The Solar Farm's direct ownership model addresses a major problem for community solar, the federal residential investment tax credit. Previously, the IRS tax guidance was unclear on whether offsite community solar owned by an individual is eligible for the investment tax credit. Proponents of the direct ownership model found modest support in IRS guidance that the residential ITC was available to member/owners, as long as the community solar was net metered for their home residential account and they did not purchase substantially more solar than what they needed for their own use.

In 2015, the IRS provided a Private Letter Ruling that supported one member's right to take the residential ITC for their investment in the project. The IRS concluded that:

> a particular owner of PV panels in an offsite, community-shared solar array is eligible for the residential tax credit under section 25D of the US tax code. While the IRS's ruling is only legally applicable to the individual taxpayer in question—a solar panel owner in Boardman Hill Solar Farm, a member-managed 150 kW off-site solar array in Vermont—the ruling may open up project opportunities for direct ownership of community-shared solar systems by multiple individuals.[50]

The Solar Farm's direct ownership model has proven to be a very cost effective means to support locally owned solar development. The Solar Farm's direct ownership model requires member-owners to finance their upfront investment in the solar array. Access to affordable local financing helps keep the economic benefits within the local community. The combination of a guaranteed revenue stream from net metering and the direct investment from individual member-owners can overcome this

---

[49] The $2.87 per watt costs includes the cost of the land lease, which allocates 5% of the output to the land owner.

[50] *Private Letter Ruling on the Eligibility of an Individual Panel Owner in an Offsite, Net-Metered Community-Shared Solar Project to Claim the Section 25D Tax Credit*, Clean Energy States All., available 26 January 2017 at http://www.cesa.org/assets/2015-Files/IRS-Community-Shared-Solar-PLR.pdf.

hurdle. A participant purchasing a typical 5 kW share of the array had a USD$15,000 pre-tax investment, and then received 30 percent of that back as a federal tax credit. A variety of local credit unions and community banks now view solar investments as low risk and they have been willing to finance these solar investments at reasonable rates without requiring additional collateral.

(d) Legal organization: member managed LLC A distinguishing feature of the project is that it is managed by its member-owners. The members formed their own organization to directly manage the affairs of the solar array, such as paying taxes and maintaining the array. The community owners investigated a variety of ownership structures seeking an option that was simple, and provided liability protection for its members. The member-owners selected a member-managed LLC to manage financial and administrative matters due to the simplicity of LLC formation. The member developed BHSF LLC Operating Agreement creates a democratic forum for addressing the management, business purpose, membership, contributions, voting and other organizational matters.[51]

The BHSF LLC does not own the solar array; the LLC members individually own the solar panels and associated equipment. Given this structure, BHSF LLC earns no profit; it only collects enough revenue from its members to pay the operating expenses of the solar array.

The owners of Boardman Hill Farm leased the land to the LLC for the community solar farm and the landowners receive 5 percent of the output of the array and had the opportunity to purchase an additional share of affordable community solar located on their farm.

3. Solar for the community not just solar in the community

The Solar Farm model brings clear environmental benefits to the process of developing and operating a community solar array. The siting process addressed landowner concerns and included the landowner as a project partner. The members' direct ownership and management of the solar array retains control of the array in the community and builds members'

---

[51] The Vermont Law School Energy Clinic, which advised the landowner on aspects of this project, has further refined the BHSF Operating Agreement into a model document that can be adapted by future community solar projects seeking to utilize this community-owned project structure. In addition the VLS Energy Clinic has also developed a model land lease and guide that informs new groups on the seven steps to community solar development. See *Energy Clinic*, Vt. Law School, available 26 January 2017 at http://vermontlaw.edu/academics/clinics-and-externships/energy-clinic for these resources.

wealth. The environmental benefits are not diluted by double dipping of companies deceptively attempting to sell solar to one customer and simultaneously selling the RECs to the another party.[52] This model reduces the carbon footprints of the participants.[53] Member-owners pay for and receive solar energy.

V. CONCLUSION: A COMMUNITY SOLAR SUCCESS SCALABLE FOR THE GLOBAL CLIMATE CHALLENGE?

The Boardman Hill Solar Farm is an encouraging success story for those who believe that renewable energy for the new economy must embrace greater local ownership of our energy resources in a manner that is both sustainable for the local and global environment. Boardman Hill Solar Farm has been deemed successful by its member-owners, the landowners and the developer. This unique partnership produced a cost-effective, locally owned and supported, and environmentally sustainable energy resource. The project gained national notice for directly conferring the tax benefits to the local owners and the model has been promoted by EPA's Green Power Partnership.[54] The Vermont Energy and Climate Action Network (VECAN) recognized the project as the Best Solar Project in 2015 and on 28 April 2016 it was awarded a Vermont Governor's Environmental Excellence Award.

The community-owned solar model is scalable. Under the right conditions, the model can promote meaningful community ownership that builds local economic wealth and reduces carbon emissions. As discussed, achieving scalability requires addressing the limitations of tax policy, federal and state security laws, constantly changing state net metering laws, and access to affordable financing. Specifically, it would be beneficial to clarify that the residential ITC is available for offsite solar that is net metered to individual residences. Additionally, it would be helpful

---

52 It would not be counted toward existing Vermont or other state mandates and could thus be claimed as additional solar by the owners of the array.

53 Both the operating agreement and land lease require for the RECs to remain bundled with the net-metered energy. A recent report by Vermont Law School's Energy Clinic addresses the conflicts of REC sales in Vermont with the states renewable and greenhouse gas reduction goals.

54 *An Introduction to Community Solar Programs*, Envt. Prot. Agency Green Power P'ship (9 March 2016), available 26 January 2017 at https://www.epa.gov/sites/production/files/2016-03/documents/webinar_20160309_kent.pdf.

to balance out the distorting impact of the ITC with direct cash grant program, similar to the previous Section 1603 Treasury program, that allowed solar project developers to receive a direct cash payment in lieu of the ITC. Similarly, creating broader exemptions from state and federal securities laws for community-owned solar would reduce some of the transactions costs for developing the legal structures for these projects. As the size and quantity of similar projects increases there will be a greater need for upfront capital to support more comprehensive siting and development considerations.

Fortunately, nothing from our analysis of these laws or experience in studying Boardman Hill Solar Farm suggests the challenges in scaling up community solar are insurmountable. This modest 150 kW community solar project could be increased to the megawatt level and replicated many times across the country. Community solar is an essential element of the new economy. It is paramount that this free, ubiquitous and renewable resource should be locally owned and developed in a manner that respects the local landscape, enhances community wealth, and brings the community together regularly in celebration of the magnificence of the sun.

10. Unlocking the energy commons: expanding community energy generation

Shalanda H. Baker

I. INTRODUCTION

In 2016, in at least 14 states around the United States, legislators have provided viable pathways to community participation in "community solar" and "community energy" programs.[1] Paradoxically, just as the market for energy generation expands to allow for broader community participation, the country is simultaneously witnessing the sweeping retrenchment of net energy metering (NEM) programs, which allow ordinary consumers of electricity to receive economic benefits by generating their own electricity and providing electricity to other consumers connected to the electrical grid.[2] To add further complexity to this emerging dynamic, utilities and regulators frequently cite the negative economic impacts of net energy metering programs on low-income communities to justify the curtailment, capping, or suspension of NEM programs. Such programs, according to utilities, harm low-income rate payers because NEM removes

---

[1] The statutes of Maine, Vermont, New Hampshire, Massachusetts, Connecticut, New York, Delaware, Maryland, Minnesota, Colorado, Washington, Oregon, California and Hawaii all feature some form of shared renewables which allow multiple utility customers to participate in the ownership of renewable energy. The state programs, in various stage design and regulatory stages, incorporate unique features. *USA Shared Energy Map*, Shared Renewables HQ, available 26 January 2017 at http://sharedrenewables.org/community-energy-projects (last visited 24 July, 2016).

[2] *See generally Issues and Policies: Net Metering*, Solar Energy Indus.'s Ass'n, available 26 January 2017 at http://www.seia.org/policy/distributed-solar/net-metering (citing Database of State Incentives for Renewables and Efficiency, available 26 January 2017 at http://www.dsireusa.org/) (describing net metering as "a billing mechanism that credits solar energy system owners for the electricity they add to the grid" and noting that 43 states, the District of Columbia, and four territories have adopted a net metering policy).

customer-generators from the rate base and leaves the fixed cost of maintaining the grid to low-to-moderate income ratepayers.[3] In response, states and utilities have offered a suite of community energy models to provide expanded opportunities for individuals to participate in renewable energy generation.[4] Unfortunately, none of the proposed programs truly levels the energy playing field for low-income and vulnerable communities.

This chapter evaluates the existing model of community energy development emerging around the United States. The aim is to provide lessons learned to reform the US market and inform the development of community solar programs in other countries. The analysis reveals that the predominant model relies on outdated understandings of the nature of energy that could actually undermine community resilience and energy independence. The chapter suggests that, if equity really forms the heart of the debate concerning NEM, the law must provide more radical opportunities for community engagement in energy generation, distribution, and ownership. In essence, the theoretical underpinnings of energy development must fundamentally shift. Authentically equitable opportunities for community energy development only emerge, however, within a New Energy Commons.

The chapter proceeds in three parts. First, it provides an overview of the current and emerging community energy development landscape, particularly in light of shifting rules surrounding NEM. This offers a glimpse into the US Department of Energy's (DOE's) existing community energy model (and its underlying theoretical assumptions), which states are currently deploying with varying degrees of success.

Then the chapter introduces the emerging energy justice theoretical framework and subsequently uncovers the ways that the narratives surrounding the energy transition fail to advance energy justice. Utilizing the energy justice lens, it then evaluates the DOE-based community energy models to reveal that these approaches to community energy development fail to fully advance transformative energy justice.

---

[3] *See, e.g.*, Benjamin Inskeep et al., NC Clean Energy Technology Center, The 50 States of Solar: A Quarterly Look at America's Fast-Evolving Distributed Solar Policy Conversation 5 (2015), available 26 January 2017 at https://nccleantech.ncsu.edu/wp-content/uploads/50-States-of-Solar-Q3-FINAL_25.pdf (citing Peter Kind, Edison Elec. Inst., Disruptive Challenges: Financial Implications and Strategic Responses to a Changing Retail Electric Business 17 (2013), available 26 January 2017 at http://www.eei.org/ourissues/finance/documents/disruptivechallenges.pdf).

[4] *See* Inskeep et al., *supra* note 3, at 5 (noting that as of "August 2014, there were 57 active or proposed utility-offered community solar programs in 22 states", and that such "utility programs range significantly in design and size").

Finally, the chapter offers a new set of practical and theoretical tools for community energy development, rooted in energy justice, which should guide the migration away from the existing utility model and foster increased low to moderate income community energy participation in energy development. This provides a normative development framework that borrows from the existing community energy models, but goes further by situating community energy development within a New Energy Commons.

II. COMMUNITY ENERGY DEVELOPMENT

A. Net Energy Metering Wars

The discussion begins with a brief overview of the current energy landscape. Since 2010, the country has witnessed a dramatic increase in distributed energy generation, primarily through rooftop solar generation.[5] As states adopted more aggressive renewable portfolio standards that required increased renewable energy generation on the electricity grid, they began to offer economic incentives to early adopters of rooftop solar photovoltaic (PV) units.[6] Given the expense of solar PV units, most early adopters were homeowners with the means to purchase rooftop solar panels.[7] In addition to the federal 30 percent investment tax credit,[8] such

[5] *Solar Market Insight Report 2016 Q2*, SOLAR ENERGY INDUS.'S ASS'N, available 26 January 2017 at http://www.seia.org/research-resources/solar-market-insight-report-2016-q2 (noting that at the end of the first quarter of 2016 there were over 1 million operating solar photovoltaic installations, and that 90% of the installations were brought online in the last decade).

[6] INSKEEP ET AL., *supra* note 3, at 5.

[7] GALEN BARBOSE ET AL., LAWRENCE BERKELEY NAT'L LAB., TRACKING THE SUN VII: THE INSTALLED PRICE OF RESIDENTIAL AND NON-RESIDENTIAL PHOTOVOLTAIC SYSTEMS IN THE UNITED STATES 15 (2015), available 26 January 2017 at https://emp.lbl.gov/sites/all/files/lbnl-188238_1.pdf (illustrating that in 1998 the median installed price of residential solar hovered around $12 per watt, and by 2014 the cost per watt was $4 per watt).

[8] The federal tax code provides a one-time 30% tax credit to businesses for the installation of solar and small-scale wind developments. This tax credit has facilitated the rise of third party ownership of solar installations installed in residential homes. *See* Energy Credit, 26 U.S.C. § 48(a)(2)(a) (West 2015). The federal residential renewable energy tax credit provides a 30% tax credit for renewable energy systems installed on a home owned by a tax payer and that is used as the tax payer's primary residence. Residential Energy Efficient Property, 26 U.S.C. § 25D (West 2015).

adopters received a state tax benefit and a credit on their monthly electricity bill.[9] This bill credit forms the crux of net energy metering (NEM).[10]

As the bill credit was originally conceived, NEM allows an ordinary ratepayer to generate electricity through a rooftop solar panel, feed it into the electricity grid, and receive a credit for the net electricity the ratepayer generates in excess of the ratepayer's energy use. NEM programs provided necessary financial incentives to increase renewable energy generation; however, they challenged the economics of the utility industry.[11] In most states, the regulatory compact between the state and investor-owned utilities allows utilities to receive a guaranteed rate of reasonable return on investments, and pass along to ratepayers the cost of maintaining the grid.[12] With increased "behind-the-meter" generation by solar PV unit owners, however, fewer ratepayers comprise the base for collecting payments, which means that these ratepayers, according to utilities, bear a disproportionate burden of sustaining the utility business model.[13]

NEM policies sparked a solar revolution. According to the North Carolina Clean Energy Technology Center, by the end of 2014 over 600,000 homes and businesses around the country had installed some form of onsite solar generation, and between 2012 and 2014 the residential market for rooftop solar had increased by 50 percent annually.[14] In the aggregate, these systems produce around a third of the country's solar electricity.[15]

---

[9] *See generally Programs*, DATABASE OF STATE INCENTIVES FOR RENEWABLES AND EFFICIENCY, available 26 January 2017 at http://programs.dsireusa.org/system/program (providing a comprehensive overview of the various incentives and programs available in each state).

[10] *See, e.g.*, JASON COUGHLIN ET AL., NAT'L RENEWABLE ENERGY LAB, A GUIDE TO COMMUNITY SHARED SOLAR: UTILITY, PRIVATE, AND NONPROFIT PROJECT DEVELOPMENT 4 (2012), available 26 January 2017 at http://www.nrel.gov/docs/fy12osti/54570.pdf (describing the heart of net metering: "[w]henever the customer's system is producing more energy than the customer is consuming, the excess energy flows to the grid and the customer's meter 'runs backwards'.").

[11] INSKEEP ET AL., THE 50 STATES OF SOLAR: 2015 POLICY REVIEW: Q4 QUARTERLY REPORT 9 (2016), available 26 January 2017 at https://nccleantech.ncsu.edu/wp-content/uploads/50sosQ4-FINAL.pdf (discussing utility death spiral and impact of distributed energy resources on the utility business model).

[12] JIM LAZAR ET AL., REGULATORY ASSISTANCE PROJECT, ELECTRICITY REGULATION IN THE US: A GUIDE, 40–1 (2nd edn, 2016), available 26 January 2017 at http://www.raponline.org/wp-content/uploads/2016/07/rap-lazar-electricity-regulation-US-june-2016.pdf.

[13] KIND, *supra* note 3, at 5.

[14] INSKEEP ET AL., *supra* note 3, at 5.

[15] *Id.*

Unfortunately, the revolution did not treat all ratepayers equally. According to a 2008 analysis by the National Renewable Energy Laboratory (NREL), only 22–27 percent of residential rooftops provide a viable location to host an on-site solar PV system.[16] Those left out of NEM programs – renters, condominium dwellers, moderate and low-income residents – comprised the ratepayer base and, until very recently, were unable to participate in the renewable energy revolution.[17]

This imperfect system led to two dynamics. First, the proliferation of rooftop PV threatens and undermines the utility business model. As more and more customers generate their own electricity, the utility's ability to recover costs and its return on investment decreases.[18] Second, based on the potential for this so-called "utility death spiral" and the looming economic threat created by distributed energy resources, utilities began to advocate, vociferously, for retrenchment of NEM policies, increase of fixed charges on utility bills, and reduced compensation for NEM customers.[19]

Throughout this rocky time, utilities deftly used the poor as scapegoats in the broader electricity transition landscape. Utilities argued that the poor and low-income ratepayers were left to subsidize more affluent rooftop solar adopters. These retrenchment tactics are ongoing, but seem to have met some success. Indeed, in 2015 alone, "regulators, lawmakers, or utilities in at least 46 states studied, proposed or enacted policy changes pertaining to net metering, valuation of distributed solar, fixed or solar charges, third-party or utility-led solar ownership, or community solar".[20] These efforts include the initiation of studies to understand the "true value" of rooftop solar, tinkering with fixed rate charges, and enacting aggregate caps on NEM programs.

Community energy programs emerged within this complex renewable energy policy soup as an answer to the equity issues embedded within the

---

[16] Paul Denholm and Robert Margolis, Nat'l Renewable Energy Lab., Supply Curves for Rooftop Solar PV-Generated Electricity for the United States 4 (2008), available 26 January 2017 at http://www.nrel.gov/docs/fy09osti/44073.pdf.

[17] Coughlin et al., *supra* note 10, at 3.

[18] Kind, *supra* note 3, at 13 (noting that although utilities are granted a return on investment, with fewer customers in the rate base it will become more difficult, from a political standpoint, for utility shareholders to receive a return).

[19] Stephen Lacy, *This is What the Utility Death Spiral Looks Like*, Greentech Media (4 March 2014), available 26 January 2017 at http://www.greentechmedia.com/articles/read/this-is-what-the-utility-death-spiral-looks-like; William Boyd, *Public Utility and the Low Carbon Future*, 61 UCLA L. Rev. 1614, 1676 (2014).

[20] Inskeep et al., *supra* note 3, at 11.

renewable energy transition. Community energy programs offered states a way to expand opportunities for participation in renewable energy projects, and were initially seen as a way to increase generation opportunities for vulnerable populations, including low and moderate-income ratepayers. Community generation also offered a way for utilities to continue to control the narrative for electricity generation.

B. Community Energy Models

In the United States, the DOE, through its SunShot Initiative and the National Renewable Energy Laboratory (NREL), has taken the lead in developing a community energy framework.[21] The DOE launched the SunShot Initiative in 2011 as a part of a collaborative effort within the DOE Solar Energy Technologies Office to create grid parity between solar and other grid resources, and ultimately, to drive the cost of solar down.[22] The myriad aggressive technology and regulatory efforts of SunShot reflect this goal.

At the outset, the SunShot Initiative concerned itself with the technological aspects of solar energy and integrating solar energy within a traditional, utility-operated electrical grid. For example, the DOE marked the initiative's formation in 2011 with three grants totaling $112.5 million to support solar photovoltaic developments within SunShot Advanced Manufacturing Partnerships.[23] Moreover, the stated goal of the program is to reduce the costs of solar PV systems by 75 percent within ten years of the program's formation to make solar more cost-competitive when viewed alongside other potential grid resources.[24] Implicit in these goals and initial projects is a commitment to large-scale development largely reliant on the incumbent utility system. A review of the key community energy program advanced by the initiative through its partner, the NREL, bears this out.

According to NREL, community "shared solar projects allow customers

---

21 *Community and Shared Solar*, Office of Energy Efficiency & Renewable Energy, U.S. Dept. of Energy, available 26 January 2017 at http://energy.gov/eere/sunshot/community-and-shared-solar.

22 *Sunshot Initiative Mission,* Office of Energy Efficiency & Renewable Energy, U.S. Dept. of Energy, available 26 January 2017 at http://energy.gov/eere/sunshot/sunshot-initiative-mission.

23 *History,* Office of Energy Efficiency & Renewable Energy, U.S. Dept. of Energy, available 26 January 2017 at http://energy.gov/eere/sunshot/history.

24 *Sunshot Initiative*, Office of Energy Efficiency & Renewable Energy, U.S. Dept. of Energy, available 26 January 2017 at http://energy.gov/eere/sunshot/sunshot-initiative.

that do not have sufficient solar resource, that rent their homes, or that are otherwise unable or unwilling to install solar on their residences, to buy or lease a part of a shared solar system".[25] In addition, the "participant's share of the electricity generated is credited to their electricity bill, as if the solar system were located at their home".[26] Although NREL lauds this business model as helping to "expand the distributed solar market", this model is essentially designed to promote centralized, utility-scale generation.[27]

Three types of ownership models comprise the community shared solar approach to community energy development: utility or third-party owned projects; special purpose entity-owned projects; and non-profit owned projects.[28] In all three models, a solar generation facility is constructed; a promoter, or sponsor, solicits subscriptions for the project; and once the project is fully subscribed, the promoter receives any relevant tax or renewable energy credits and the electricity generated is credited to subscribers.[29] A cottage industry of sorts has emerged to capitalize on new models of customer-owned generation;[30] however, NREL emphasizes that utilities should take the lead in developing such projects.[31]

In many ways, the community shared solar model is more of the same approach to development, but by a different name. The predominant models advanced by NREL remove the locus of control for generation away from the consumer, focus on utility-scale generation and economies of scale, and do little to foster more distributed models of generation.

The following section introduces energy justice into the discourse concerning the global renewable energy transition. The section then utilizes the energy justice frame to evaluate the proposed community energy model, exposing several shortcomings.

---

[25] Nat'l Renewable Energy Lab., Community Shared Solar Policy and Regulatory Considerations 1 (2014), available 26 January 2017 at http://www.nrel.gov/docs/fy14osti/62367.pdf.

[26] *Id.*

[27] *Id.* at 5.

[28] Coughlin et al., *supra* note 10, at 7.

[29] *Id.*

[30] *Id.* at 53 (providing a short list of toolkits).

[31] *Id.* at 8–12.

III. THE ENERGY JUSTICE FRAME

Stakeholders, scholars and industry observers frequently frame the global renewable energy transition as a technical and technological transition that merely invites the opportunity to develop a "smarter", faster, grid.[32] This technology focus obscures the true opportunities for structural transformation that lie at the heart of the transition. The integration of more renewable energy resources onto the electrical grid; the proliferation of smarter technologies that allow for enhanced distributed energy resources; and the opportunities for storage all implicate energy justice. Energy justice is an umbrella term that captures three core concepts embedded in related discourses: climate justice, environmental justice and energy democracy. Subsection B addresses the energy transition dialectic, and illustrates how the current renewable energy transition underway provides an opportunity for a more transformative transition of energy systems and models than currently contemplated by energy policymakers and stakeholders. The last subsection returns to the default community energy development model promoted by states and the US DOE and explains how it falls short of the larger opportunity to structurally transform power.

A. What is Energy Justice?

Although energy justice is an emerging field of study, two distinct strands emerge from the existing literature. As a model for understanding global energy issues concerning the most vulnerable populations, Professor Lakshman Guruswamy has argued that energy justice primarily addresses access to energy for "the Other Third", the 2.8 billion people around the world who lack access to energy.[33] Professors Michael Dworkin and Benjamin Sovacool have staked out considerably broader territory, arguing that energy justice includes procedural and substantive justice.[34]

---

32 *See, e.g.*, *Smart Grid*, Office of Energy Efficiency & Renewable Energy, U.S. Dept. of Energy, available 26 January 2017 at http://energy.gov/eere/sunshot/sunshot-initiative.

33 Lakshman Guruswamy, Global Energy Justice: Law and Policy 87 (West 2016) (noting that around the world, "around 2.8 billion people . . . have little or no access to beneficial energy to meet their needs for cooking, heating, water, sanitation, illumination, transportation, or basic mechanical power").

34 Benjamin K. Sovacool and Michael H. Dworkin, Global Energy Justice: Problems, Principles, and Practices 13 (Cambridge University Press 2014) (defining energy justice as "a global energy system that fairly disseminates both the benefits and costs of energy services, and one that has representative and impartial energy decision-making").

In their book, *Global Energy Justice*, Sovacool and Dworkin begin with the philosophical underpinnings of justice to posit that justice requires opportunities for participation in energy decisions, as well as beneficial outcomes.[35]

While these scholars provide useful tools to grapple with the moral and philosophical bases on which to argue for energy justice, they do not expressly acknowledge that energy justice, as a set of principles, builds upon, encompasses and expands the existing justice discourses surrounding climate change and the environment. Thus, as we move into the renewable energy transition, we must acknowledge that the energy transition is not ahistorical. It is taking place within a broader socio-economic and historical context. Energy justice thus must encapsulate existing principles and areas of study, so that these justice lessons are not forgotten or relegated to separate academic silos. For these reasons, energy justice must allow space for the theoretical and practical tools of environmental justice and climate justice within its analytical umbrella. In addition, energy justice introduces the concept of energy democracy into the energy development lexicon.[36]

As discussed in Purdy's chapter (Chapter 3), environmental justice provides for the remediation of harm within communities that have historically borne the brunt of polluting activities and have lacked access to environmental amenities, such as parks and wilderness.[37] Environmental justice communities experience vulnerabilities at multiple axes. Such communities exhibit larger amounts of environmental-related illnesses, such as asthma and lead poisoning.[38] They also tend to be members of historically disenfranchised groups, including the poor, indigenous communities, and communities of color.[39] Scholars advancing environmental justice have traditionally focused on procedural remedies that remediate vulnerability and, more recently, the identification of "hot spots" prior to engaging in development activities.

---

35 *Id.* at 5, 191–222, 223–55 (discussing energy and due process concerns, as well as energy poverty, access and welfare).

36 *Id.* at 13 (discussing imperative for "impartial energy decision-making").

37 Scott Lawrence, et al., *Global Inequity in Energy Consumption from 1980 to 2010*, 15 Entropy 5565, 5565–77 (2013), available 26 January 2017 at http://arxiv.org/pdf/1312.6443.pdf.

38 *See, e.g.*, Sovacool and Dworkin, *supra* note 34, at 230; Alan H. Lockwood et al., Physicians For Social Responsibility, Coal's Assault on Human Health v (2009), available 26 January 2017 at http://www.psr.org/assets/pdfs/psr-coal-fullreport.pdf.

39 *Environmental Justice*, U.S. Envtl. Prot. Agency, available 26 January 2017 at https://www.epa.gov/environmentaljustice/learn-about-environmental-justice.

Climate justice expressly builds on the important work of environmental justice scholars, and uses vulnerability as a key starting point for the analysis.[40] Climate justice suggests that climate change mitigation and adaptation policies should begin in those communities that will face the most devastating impacts of climate change.[41] Developing countries, as well as low-income communities, fit within this framework. Scholars have also argued for reparations to communities who will not only face the harshest impacts of climate change, but who did very little to contribute to the problem of climate change.[42]

Energy democracy, like energy justice, is a newly developing field of scholarship. As Sovacool and Dworkin suggest, energy justice requires that communities have a say in shaping their energy systems.[43] Energy democracy provides avenues for adequate processes to affect meaningful change regarding energy development, as well as opportunities to substantively shape the outcomes associated with energy planning.[44] In addition to these procedural components, energy democracy incorporates the important substantive outcome of economic justice. Economic justice provides that communities may derive economic benefits from energy development projects.[45] Energy democracy, though still gaining legibility within the broader energy discourse, provides a crucial component of the energy justice intellectual and theoretical framework.

As a unifying framework that ties together all three components – environmental justice, climate justice, and energy democracy – energy justice provides a powerful analytical tool with which to evaluate the justness renewable energy transition. Indeed, with energy justice as a guiding framework, energy development must enhance community resiliency rather than exacerbate existing vulnerability. Energy development should also remediate vulnerability to climate change and, where possible, contribute to a community's ability to adapt to climate change. Finally,

---

[40] Randall S. Abate, *Comment on Maxine Burkett's Rehabilitation: A Proposal for a Climate Compensation Mechanism for Small Island States*, 13 Santa Clara J. Int'l L. 125, 126 (2015).

[41] *Id.*

[42] Maxine Burkett, *Climate Reparations*, 10 Melbourne J. of Int'l L. 509 (2009).

[43] Sovacool and Dworkin, *supra* note 34, at 214–22.

[44] Owen Zinaman et al., *The Power Systems of the Future*, Electricity J. 113, 123–4 (2015) (discussing "bundled community energy planning" to allow communities to develop new grid resources in a context-specific way and to scale according to community needs).

[45] Raina Wagner, *Adapting Environmental Justice: In the Age of Climate Change, Environmental Justice Demands A Combined Adaptation-Mitigation Response*, 2 Ariz. J. Envtl. L. & Pol'y 153, 154 (2011).

communities should be engaged in determining their energy future and have access to participatory economic rights, which requires that they engage in energy democracy. The next section animates this tool by focusing on the aspect of the renewable energy transition that has received the most regulatory and popular attention – distributed energy generation.

B. Failed Opportunities for Structural Transformation

Along with efficiency, distributed energy generation provides low-hanging fruit for the renewable energy transition. Distributed energy generation, in the form of rooftop PV, once existed outside of reach to most Americans. As discussed, between 2010 and 2014, rooftop solar technology vastly improved to allow more individuals to participate in the generation of their own electricity. States, for their part, assisted with the distributed generation boom by creating policy and tax incentives for participation. For example, many states provided investment tax credits on top of the existing federal tax credit, which effectively reduced the real cost of solar panels for residential homeowners. In addition, legislatures and public utilities commissions around the US enacted policies to incentivize residents to generate electricity on their rooftops and sell such energy back into the grid.[46] In exchange, solar adopters earned NEM credits, effectively turning back the electricity meter for owners of rooftop PV. The solar industry also played a role, eventually offering a suite of attractive financing packages for homeowners unwilling or unable to front the initial capital for rooftop solar panels. Indeed, according to NREL, approximately 72 percent of rooftop solar systems are managed via third-party agreements.[47]

All of the foregoing led to the widespread adoption of distributed energy generation. Beginning in 2015, however, the economic boom for solar companies and early adopters of solar energy began to slow down. Hawai'i,[48] then Nevada,[49] effectively ended their NEM policies. The curtailment of

---

[46] See *Summary Tables,* Database of State Incentives for Renewables & Efficiency, available 26 January 2017 at http://programs.dsireusa.org/system/program/tables (provides a summary of the various incentives and policies enacted throughout the United States with respect to renewable energy and energy efficiency).

[47] Travis Lowder et al., Nat'l Renewable Energy Lab., Historical and Current U.S. Strategies for Boosting Distributed Generation 16 (2015), available 26 January 2017 at http://www.nrel.gov/docs/fy16osti/64843.pdf.

[48] Instituting a Proceeding to Investigate Distributed Energy Resources Policies, Decision and Order No. 33258, 2015 WL 9258143 (Haw. Pub. Serv. Comm'n 12 October 2015).

[49] Application of Nevada Power Company d/b/a/ NV Energy for Approval of a Cost-of-Service and Net Metering Tariffs, 2015 WL 9590781 (Nev. Pub. Utils.

NEM was in large part due to strong (and effective) advocacy on the part of utility companies who claimed that NEM harmed low-income ratepayers.[50] Utilities argued that the fixed costs of maintaining the grid, which included an embedded guarantee for a reasonable return on utility investments in infrastructure, would be borne by those least able to afford rooftop solar panels, namely, low to moderate-income ratepayers. Solar companies responded with their own counterattacks. They argued that policymakers should take a broader view of the value of rooftop solar programs, and that any costs borne by non-participating ratepayers should effectively come out in the wash, since rooftop solar allowed states to reach aggressive renewable energy goals and cut down on greenhouse gas emissions.[51]

Lost within this debate were actual low to moderate-income ratepayers, for whom the integration of distributed renewable energy generation within their communities could provide an opportunity for unprecedented structural transformation of existing environmental and social relationships, leading to a lasting environmental, climate, and economic justice. With the exception of voices like the National Association for the Advancement of Colored People (NAACP),[52] low-income communities and communities of color largely accepted the narrative offered by both the utility and solar companies.[53]

Comm'n 23 December 2015) [hereinafter Nevada Public Utilities Commission Order].

[50] *See, e.g.*, Jon Wellinghoff and James Tong, *Wellinghoff and Tong: A Common Confusion of Net Metering is Undermining Utilities and the Grid: 'Cost-shifting' and 'not Paying Your Fair Share' Are Not the Same Thing*, UtilityDive (22 January 2015), available 26 January 2017 at http://www.utilitydive.com/news/wellinghoff-and-tong-a-common-confusion-over-net-metering-is-undermining-u/355388/ (finding the debate on this issue is lively and frequently involves competing formulations of the nature of the equity issues).

[51] *See, e.g.*, Nevada Public Utilities Commission Order; *See also* Snuller Price et al., Energy and Environmental Economics, Inc., Nevada Net Energy Metering Impacts Evaluation, (2014), available 26 January 2017 at http://puc.nv.gov/uploadedFiles/pucnvgov/Content/About/Media_Outreach/Announcements/Announcements/E3%20PUCN%20NEM%20Report%202014.pdf?pdf=Net-Metering-Study.

[52] Nat'l Ass'n for the Advancement of Colored People, Promoting Equitable Access to Clean Energy Alternatives (2015), available 26 January 2017 at http://action.naacp.org/page/-/RESOLUTION--Promoting%20Equitable%20Access%20to%20Clean%20Energy%20%20Alternatives%20FINAL%20February%2021%202015.pdf (discussing the nexus between the failure to transition to energy efficiency and clean energy and the impact on communities of color and low-income communities, and resolving to support clean energy development).

[53] *See, e.g.*, Michael T. Burr, *Reverse Robin Hood Declaring War on Non-Utility PV*, Fortnightly (July 2013), available 26 January 2017 at http://mag.fortnightly.

What if the adoption of distributed energy resources is not, as the polarization of this debate would suggest, zero sum? Rather, the operative question is: How might low-income communities also participate in renewable energy generation, ownership and distribution? Neither side appears fully willing to embrace this query, as incumbent utilities struggle mightily to hang on to market share and increasingly regressive solar companies fight to maintain their bread and butter business: providing solar panels to relatively affluent and middle-class homeowners.

As the battle lines have deepened, these constituent groups have become ever more wedded to their business models and program designs. It is no surprise that the community energy model developed to serve communities bears no real resemblance to energy justice.

C. Community Energy Limitations

Community shared solar, the community energy model advanced by NREL and the majority of the states that have adopted community energy programs, leaves "community" out of the equation. By design, the community solar model essentially allows individuals to buy into a larger project or enterprise located away from the end user.[54] While this flexible structure has some merit, it can be implemented in a way that undermines the resiliency and democratic aspects of community-controlled development. Community shared solar programs that involve utility-scale generation (over one MW), located away from project subscribers, replicate an approach to scale and siting that maintains the paradigm of utility-oriented energy development.[55] This approach does very little to advance core tenets of energy justice.[56]

---

com/display_article.php?id=1440995&_width= (discussing the "robbing the poor to pay for rich people's fancy solar systems" narrative adopted in some communities of color).

[54] In order to remedy potential scale concerns with community scale solar projects, the Interstate Renewable Energy Council Model Rules for Community Solar place a two-megawatt cap on the size of community shared solar projects. Coughlin et al., *supra* note 10, at 68.

[55] For example, in Hawaii, the community-based renewable energy development model proposed by the state's utility provides three tiers for community-based energy development. In Tier 1 relates to projects under 20 kW; Tier 2 concerns projects between 20 kW and 1 MW, and Tier 3 relates to projects over 1 MW. The utility's proposal caps Tier 1 and Tier 2 projects for solar and wind at 8 MW, but caps Tier 3 solar and wind projects at 24 MW, effectively incentivizing the development of large-scale projects. Hawaiian Electric Company, Inc., 2016 WL 3480609 (Haw. Pub. Utils. Comm'n 2016).

[56] Hannah J. Wiseman and Sara C. Bronin, *Community-Scale Renewable Energy*, 4 San Diego J. Climate & Energy L. 165, 169 (2013).

Some exceptions to this can be found, for instance, in the state of Washington, whose Community Renewables Enabling Act requires projects to be sited on community-owned property, such as schools, parks or government buildings and caps community owned solar projects at 75 kilowatts.[57] Further, as described in Jones and James's chapter (Chapter 9), well designed community solar projects may avoid many of the concerns that accompany traditional, utility-scale energy development. For example, the Boardman Hill Solar Farm involves key features that sketch a new model for community solar: appropriate land use and siting, community ownership of solar array and solar energy, affordable cost with growing member equity in the project, and member-managed organizational structure. These features, however, are not commonplace.

Despite an auspicious origin story, forged in the crucible of the NEM wars, community energy programs tend to fail low-income communities because they marginalize or render "additive" low-income participants. Community solar advocates often point to efforts in Colorado, New York and California to illustrate how community energy development models can include low-income residents. These jurisdictions, however, also fall short of achieving energy justice.

In Colorado, for example, developers are required to ensure that a mere 5 percent of subscribers to Solar Garden projects are low-income ratepayers.[58] The state's Public Utilities Commission set this fairly modest threshold through a rulemaking, given the broad and discretionary language provided in the statute itself.[59] New York's community solar program, created in connection with the state's Reforming the Energy Vision regulatory reform efforts, carves out 20 percent for low-income participation;[60] however, the 20 percent requirement only endures for Phase 1 of the reform, slated to last approximately six months.

California is much further along in its efforts to incorporate low-income ratepayers into the renewable energy transition. The state's promising Green Tariff Shared Renewables Program provides ratepayers with the

---

57 Wash. Rev. Code Ann. § 82.16.110(2)(a)(i) (West 2016).

58 Colo. Rev. Stat. Ann. § 40-2-127(5)(IV)(B) (West 2016); Development of Solar Gardens, 2011 WL 3634216 (Colo. Pub. Utils. Comm'n 25 July 2011) (statute directed Colorado PUC to adopt rules regarding LMI allocation and Commission set allocation to 5%).

59 § 40-2-127(5)(IV)(B).

60 Order Establishing A Community Distributed Generation Program and Making Other Findings, 322 P.U.R.4th 113 (N.Y. Pub. Serv. Comm'n 17 July 2015).

option to choose among several developer-led green energy projects.[61] Unfortunately the program is expected to increase the cost for users by two to three cents per kilowatt-hour, which cuts against the inclusive intent of the program.[62] California's Multifamily Affordable Solar Housing program goes further than its shared renewables program, offering financial incentives to affordable housing customers to install onsite solar systems on residential dwellings.[63] According to one analysis of the program, however, residents of the subsidized housing where such projects are located will never see financial benefits. Even if the overall building's electricity bills are lowered, subsidized housing residents pay a combined utility and rent amount that is locked into a percentage of total income, which means that the proportion of rent may increase to cover the shortfall created by the onsite electricity generation.[64]

In low-income communities that could benefit from the economic opportunities that accompany community-scale renewable energy generation, the reliance on utility scale energy generation continues the injury of fossil-fuel extraction and energy generation. Given its footprint, the siting of utility-scale renewable energy generation requires many of the same difficult land-use decisions that encumber dirtier energy development.[65] Moreover, the additive nature of current policies that require low-income participation – Colorado and New York, for example – fail to transform the material conditions of entire communities due to narrow participatory requirements. And, even with policies that require nominal low-income participation, the subscription requirements for community solar require initial capital investments largely unavailable in low-income households.[66] Ultimately this approach to energy development, even if it is renewable, fails to promote the environmental justice and energy democracy aspects of energy justice.

Further, the design of the community shared solar model does little to advance distributed, behind-the-meter generation controlled by an on-site

---

[61] *See* 28 Cal. Pub. Util. Code § 2833 (West 2016).

[62] Interstate Renewable Energy Council, Shared Renewable Energy for Low- to Moderate-Income Consumers: Policy Guidelines and Model Provisions 13 (2016), available 26 January 2017 at http://energy.gov/sites/prod/files/2016/04/f30/IREC-LMI-Guidelines-Model-Provisions_FINAL.pdf.

[63] Cal. Pub. Util. Code § 2870 (West 2016).

[64] Interstate Renewable Energy Council, *supra* note 62, at 14.

[65] Uma Outka, *The Renewable Energy Footprint*, 30 Stan. Envtl. L.J. 241, 242–53 (2011).

[66] Indeed, low- to moderate-income ratepayers already pay a disproportionately high amount of income on energy. Interstate Renewable Energy Council, *supra* note 62, at 4.

user, which misses an opportunity to increase climate change resiliency in low-income and vulnerable communities. As noted by many who witnessed the destruction of Hurricane Sandy, the storm left New York City's low-income communities the most vulnerable within a city that boasts a sophisticated financial sector and diverse population.[67] The lack of electricity in the weeks following the storm led to losses of food supplies, dangerous medical conditions and, in some cases, a lack of water.[68] The reliance on incumbent utilities and utility infrastructure embedded in the current energy model exacerbates climate injustice and misses a critical opportunity to promote energy justice. What is needed are programs that focus specifically on community-sited generation and create genuine markets for participation by the most vulnerable communities. This will require the development of creative financing mechanisms, such as on-bill financing, as well as "green" banks created by states to provide cheap capital to residents seeking to develop community solar projects.

Finally, the inflexibility of community solar leaves little room for innovations that allow communities to take control of their energy production. The complexity of the program, including the regulatory and securities issues the program invites,[69] locks the program into limited designs. Although behind-the-meter generation offers a suite of potential regulatory challenges, the locus of control is closer to the community, which means that communities can design energy systems that work with their usage patterns and capacity requirements.[70] The approach to community energy currently promoted does not offer space for true energy democracy, a key principle within the energy justice framework.

In many ways, the early design of community energy programs falls prey to the same limitations of early NEM programs, where only middle-class and affluent homeowners fit within the solar panel market. The programs do little to remediate vulnerability. In addition, the programs maintain the locus of control for energy far away from communities. Rather than carve out opportunities for limited participation by early

---

[67] Furman Center, N.Y. University, Sandy's Effects On Housing in New York City 8 (2013), available 26 January 2017 at http://furmancenter.org/files/publications/SandysEffectsOnHousingInNYC.pdf.

[68] *Id.* at 5; Editorial, *Where Hurricane Sandy Still Hurts*, N.Y. Times (8 November 2012), available 26 January 2017 at http://www.nytimes.com/2012/11/09/opinion/where-hurricane-sandy-still-hurts.html.

[69] *See e.g.*, Samantha Booth, *Here Comes the Sun: How Securities Regulations Cast a Shadow on the Growth of Community Solar in the United States*, 61 UCLA L. Rev. 760, 780 (2014).

[70] Zinaman et al., *supra* note 44, at 123–4.

adopters, policymakers should look for opportunities to mitigate the financial burdens of low-income ratepayers who will most certainly be left to pay the utility's fixed cost of grid maintenance if not provided with an equal opportunity to generate power using renewable energy resources.

These types of opportunities might transform the customer-utility relationship. They may also further disrupt the utility business model. Policymakers should not turn away from such innovations in fear for such disruption, but should look for opportunities to create new models to replace the old. Community energy carried an implicit promise to provide an opportunity to bring the most vulnerable ratepayers into the renewable energy transition. As currently conceptualized, however, the dominant model falls far short of energy justice.

The following section offers a set of tools to resolve these concerns and reposition community solar programs within a new theoretical frame: the New Energy Commons.

IV. THE NEW ENERGY COMMONS

In a community meeting concerning energy development, a community elder approached me, looked me in the eye, and asked, "What is energy?" A smile curled up the corners of her mouth, and her eyes flickered. As a scholar of energy justice, I equivocated, responding, "I think the answer is changing". Although my response in that moment felt incomplete to both of us, it does appear that the nature of energy is changing. Indeed, what energy meant in 1900 is quite different from its 2016 meaning. This section provides some clues to what could be emerging: the New Energy Commons.

A. Out with the Old

The old energy paradigm conceptualized energy as a commodity to be extracted, refined and burned in centralized locations to create electricity. In the old paradigm, we needed extensive networks of wires to bring electricity to end-users. We built vast energy systems in reliance on this understanding of energy. In the renewable energy transitional moment, energy is reframed.

Individuals, communities and, yes, even utilities, see energy as something much more accessible and connected to nearly every aspect of life. Energy surrounds all beings, and is no longer necessarily a commodity to be extracted, refined and burned to create electricity. With a relatively minimal capital investment, individuals can now access energy to create electricity. Indeed, communities can also create electricity. In this new energy paradigm, energy is an abundant gift easily seen in the waves that surround island communities, the air that moves through breezes in windy places, and the sun that shines each day without fail.

Once accessed, energy allows for efficient pumping of water to irrigate crops,[71] and provides increased equality and safety for women who have carried water in rural communities.[72] It facilitates safer cooking methods to avoid using antiquated cook stoves.[73] It allows for the lighting of homes and community streets after sunset to foster human development,[74] and cooler classrooms for more engaged learning.[75] Very few subjects exist with such abundance and possess such broad connective links.

These new understandings of the abundance and accessibility of energy should yield to new business and economic models to support energy development; however, disrupting the old energy paradigm poses the potential to disrupt existing social, environmental and economic relationships. In the old paradigm, capitalists were made wealthy through the extraction of oil, gas and coal from the earth's crust. Utilities, in partnership with the oil and gas industry, benefited from the centralized structure of energy production, as well as the ongoing investments in energy infrastructure.

The move to develop a truly transformative energy development model has necessarily encountered a steady resistance from those who have long benefited from the old paradigm. Incumbent energy interests that remain wedded to the old paradigm of centralized energy production have advanced their interests in the renewable energy sphere by introducing renewable energy development models that continue to rely on large-scale infrastructure investment. The models that have arisen to facilitate the renewable energy transition are locked into the old paradigm, which requires a centralized producer, vast transmission networks of wires, as well as a sophisticated entity to manage the system, often across multiple jurisdictions.

Even technological and policy innovations, such as smart grids and community solar programs, when implemented poorly, prolong reliance on utility scale, expensive infrastructure, and complexity. These innovations also allow utilities to continue to make investments that can be recouped in reliance on ratepayers. Such ongoing investments are

---

71 GURUSWAMY, *supra* note 33, at 87.

72 *Id.* at 98.

73 *Id.* at 87.

74 *Id.* at 105.

75 *See, e.g.,* Molly Solomon, *Hawai'i Classrooms: How Hot is too Hot?* (16 September 2015), available 26 January 2017 at http://hpr2.org/post/hawaii-classrooms-how-hot-too-hot.

necessary to sustain the utility business model. Further, such investments lock communities into a utility vision of energy development, which contradicts the embedded simplicity and resilience that more decentralized energy development invites.

Distributed energy generation located within homes or scaled up to the community level inverts the classic economic relationship embedded in the old energy paradigm. Distributed energy transforms energy. It introduces into the modern energy system the idea that energy can be controlled by an individual user who is also a producer of energy, or a community of users and producers (prosumers). In this new energy paradigm, customers derive the bulk of financial benefits by cheaply harnessing the energy in the sun, wind and water. The new energy paradigm also raises the participatory stakes by deepening community bonds and providing space for civic engagement and financial literacy in order to facilitate community energy development. Reactions to this transformative moment ignore this new reality. The responses generated both within the utility industry and solar industry swim against the transformative current and attempt to fit the new paradigm within the old model, which has led to continued reliance on antiquated physical infrastructure; outdated policy and regulatory regimes; and imperfect financial models.

B. Defining the New Energy Commons

Arguably, the limitations and policy tensions that have surfaced during the renewable energy transition could be resolved by a theoretical repositioning of the transition. Explicitly framing the new energy paradigm within a commons theoretical frame invites the development of business and economic models more closely aligned with the principles of energy justice. This new theoretical framing could also help policy makers to avoid the pitfalls of the current polarized energy debates and create space for a range of policy approaches to the energy transition. The following discussion begins by establishing the theoretical underpinnings of the commons and then explores the ways in which the new energy paradigm could be repositioned within a commons resource management frame.

Elinor Ostrom, Nobel laureate and political economist, defines common-pool resources as possessing two key characteristics. First, common-pool resources are rival, in that an individual's use of the resources subtracts from the ability of another to use the resource.[76] Second, common-pool

---

[76] THE COMMONS IN THE NEW MILLENNIUM: CHALLENGES AND ADAPTATION 7 (Nives Dolsak et al. (eds), MIT Press 2003) [hereinafter THE COMMONS IN THE NEW

resources are prone to free-riding or overexploitation because they are not excludable; individuals who benefit from the resources are not incentivized to share the cost of maintaining the resource.[77]

Ostrom's work rebuts the presumption that to counter these challenges to common-pool resources they must be privatized. Some of her research draws on examples of commons management within traditional communities. Relying on case studies, Ostrom asserts that communities can properly manage common-pool resources through community rules and a community-based system of resource management.[78] In Ostrom's view, privatization does not necessarily provide the best pathway to sustainability, and common-property management regimes, though a form of private property, involve the allocation of rights to groups rather than individuals.[79] Moreover, communities are best positioned to determine the highest and best use for common pool resources.[80]

Turning back to energy, energy resources are themselves common-pool resources. They are rivals, in that the exploitation of the resource by one party limits opportunities for exploitation by another party. They are also non-excludable and subject to free-riding if not properly managed. Traditionally, and under the old paradigm of energy development, non-renewable fossil-fuel resources such as oil, gas and coal were managed through the allocation of private rights to avoid overexploitation and facilitate the efficient management of such resources. So far, the policy approaches to the renewable energy transition have largely fallen in line with this traditional approach. Energy policies allocate private rights to exploit renewable energy resources and send electricity to the grid. Even as energy resources shift towards renewable energy resources more easily accessed and converted to electricity by individuals and community members, this development paradigm and accompanying regulatory approach persists. Arguably, this insistence on an outdated development model and regulatory approach has given rise to much of the tension between individual energy customers and utilities, as well as effectively

MILLENNIUM]. Ostrom's lifetime of work provides a full account of the commons in response to the work of Garret Hardin, *The Tragedy of the Commons*, 162 SCI. 1243 (1968).

77 THE COMMONS IN THE NEW MILLENNIUM, *supra* note 76, at 7.

78 Elinor Ostrom, *Constituting Social Capital and Collective Action*, *in* LOCAL COMMONS AND GLOBAL INTERDEPENDENCE: HETEROGENEITY AND COOPERATION IN TWO DOMAINS 130 (Robert O. Keohane and Elinor Ostrom (eds), Sage 1995).

79 THE COMMONS IN THE NEW MILLENNIUM, *supra* note 76, at 8.

80 *Id.* at 22. *See also* DAVID BOLLIER, SILENT THEFT: THE PRIVATE PLUNDER OF OUR COMMON WEALTH 183–84 (Routledge 2002).

excluded community voices from the energy discourse. Fortunately, the nature of renewable energy invites a reexamination of these approaches.

Renewable energy resources lend themselves more easily to Ostrom's framing of commons resource management than traditional fossil fuels, such as coal, oil, and gas. As discussed, traditional fossil fuels require complex centralized facilities for extraction, refinement, and generation. In many ways, the most efficient way to exploit and manage these resources was through the allocation of private rights. Renewable energy resources, on the other hand, invite alternative approaches to resource management. Within the New Energy Commons, renewable energy is readily accessible to all community members and easily lends itself to management and development at the household or community level. Moreover, the economics of developing distributed energy resources relying on renewable energy provide a rare opportunity for communities to plan, initiate and develop resources in ways unimaginable within the old energy development paradigm, which relied on large, centralized generation facilities and complex networks of wires.

Despite the relative ease with which communities may now engage in energy resource management and energy system design, the overwhelming policy incentives to invest in new infrastructure by investor-owned utilities could limit opportunities for community participation in energy resource management and crowd out opportunities for renewable energy generation at the community level, thus limiting the potential of the New Energy Commons. Further, such aggressive investments could create a pathway dependency that limits renewable energy development by low-income people, in effect plundering the commons and curtailing opportunities for communities to benefit from cheaply accessing renewable energy. These "rival" features of the New Energy Commons require vigilance by policy makers to ensure the creation of opportunities for community planning and participation in the renewable energy transition.

Starting the policy discussion from the New Energy Commons theoretical orientation could open pathways for communities to plan, initiate, and develop energy resources in ways that correct the embedded inequalities within the old energy development paradigm. This new orientation could help to facilitate energy justice.

With respect to environmental justice, much like the communities within Ostrom's studies, communities engaged in commons-based energy development may determine the correct scale of energy needed within their community, based on adequate information and technical assistance. Examples of this can already be found throughout North America, where communities from Alaska to California, often with the technical assistance of utilities, have developed comprehensive community energy plans.

Communities engaged in community energy planning might determine that utility scale development would better meet the community needs, or community scale development, coupled with storage and other energy innovations such as microgrids will allow the community to meet its energy needs while preserving their local environment – and their rights to manage the energy commons. The New Energy Commons frame invites the opportunity for community energy planning.

Climate justice would also be advanced within a New Energy Commons. Reframing energy policy making from within a commons theoretical frame could increase pathways to community resilience as communities, assisted by technical experts develop plans to increase their resilience to major weather events and protect their most vulnerable citizens. Relying on resilience and vulnerability rather than profit or return on investment as the starting place of community-energy development presents a radical shift in energy development. This shift is needed to help facilitate climate justice.

Finally, the New Energy Commons supports the procedural and substantive components of energy democracy, given that community energy planning and meaningful civic engagement form essential cornerstones of the management of the New Energy Commons. Such planning efforts could also give rise to opportunities for economic engagement in energy development projects. Indeed, within a New Energy Commons, opportunities for participation abound, as it is the collective management and stewardship of the common energy resources that facilitate the community's thriving.

If policy makers place renewed focus on the commons and communities begin to envision renewable energy resources as a part of the New Energy Commons, the existing policy tensions presented by the renewable energy transition could more easily give way to solutions rooted in energy justice. Mining the theoretical contributions of the commons literature could help to facilitate a just energy transition. This chapter now concludes with a vision for the future based on early manifestations of commons-based community energy development.

V. CONCLUSION: ENVISIONING AN ENERGY COMMONS

This chapter invites policy makers, scholars, and community members to consider repositioning the renewable energy transition within a commons frame. This new frame, the New Energy Commons, provides a space for new thinking, bottom-up approaches, and energy system designs that render energy accessible and controllable by communities, especially low income communities that have been missing out on the renewable energy revolution. The old energy structure, reliant on centralized management of community-held resources, fades into the background, creating space for innovation, appropriate scaling, and community resilience. Although the dominant community energy discourse in many ways fails to deliver on its transformative promise, some communities have already begun to orient their energy systems within a New Energy Commons framework.

Vermont's model for community energy offers a hint of what is possible. Its Group Net Metering program originates within the community and allows community members, separate generators of behind-the-meter electricity, to combine their accounts to receive an offset for electricity produced. This program relies on community decision-making regarding the collective energy resource, thus creating a range of opportunities for energy democracy.

In the New Energy Commons, communities may elect to combine their respective generation as in Vermont's model, or convert existing distribution lines into microgrids, where renewable energy generated in a common area serves as anchor to the grid, and homeowners maintain smaller power systems and batteries to stabilize the grid. In this scenario communities may stand apart from a centralized utility, or elect to sell electricity back to the utility through a power purchase agreement. This approach to generation is truly decentralized. For vulnerable communities that face the prospect of electricity instability in the climate change era, this approach to development also promotes the key energy justice principle of climate justice.

The New Energy Commons also provides opportunities for creative financing. The Resilient Power Project, developed by the Clean Energy Group (also of Vermont), provides concrete analytical tools that illustrate how, after an initial capital investment in onsite renewable energy generation and batteries, low-income ratepayers can utilize such generation and storage to lower the cost of or eliminate electricity bills. Within an even more disruptive frame, the same low-income ratepayers might convert the displaced economic burdens of energy costs to other means of human development. As well documented in the environmental justice literature, low-income communities face a battery of energy development-related harms. In the New Energy Commons, low income communities that produce their own clean, locally sited energy are less likely to be burdened by the environmental hazards of non-renewable energy development, thus promoting environmental justice and energy justice.

As discussed, within the New Energy Commons, electricity moves away from its status as a pure commodity to be sold, toward a good to be manipulated within a community, at a community scale, and for the enjoyment of the community. Even within the current flawed approach to community energy development, the fortuitous move toward community-based energy development offers great promise. The importance of this moment, where communities can become generators and distributors of their own energy, cannot be overstated.

Framing community energy development within a New Energy Commons theoretical paradigm will dissolve existing limitations, promote energy democracy and, arguably, transform socio-economic relationships.

And so, what is energy?

Energy is power.

11. The decentralization of food policy and building a stronger food system

Diana R. H. Winters

I. INTRODUCTION

Recently, several state and local governments in the United States passed laws to address gaps in and perceived problems with federal food policy. These laws were focused on the public health, the humane treatment of animals, the transparency of the food system, the sustainability of food production, and the access to and distribution of safe and healthy food.

This decentralization of food regulation allows smaller governmental units to experiment with policy solutions, permits food policy to be responsive to local populaces, and promotes accountability for officials in charge of implementing the food system, thus demonstrating the benefits of the American federalist system.

The chapter on legal design and technology (Chapter 12) presents tools for citizens to participate in and enact food systems change. This chapter looks at the interplay between national standards and local decision-making in the food policy context. Both chapters discuss how law can respond to local concerns and facilitate democratic engagement. A system that permits decentralized policymaking, such as the American one, diffuses power. As discussed in Scanlan's chapter (Chapter 1), the power to add, change, evolve or self-organize system structure can be a powerful leverage point for system change. If the diffusion of power to local levels fosters public participation, it allows for greater system change potential.

Despite, or perhaps because of, their transformative potential, these state and local actions on food policy raise questions about where lies the proper balance between the uniformity and predictability of a national system and the flexibility and responsiveness of local regulation.

This chapter discusses some of the problems with the food systems of the United States and the repercussions of these failures, and then explores several more local solutions by looking at this recent state legislation.

These laws include a (now preempted) Vermont law that mandated the labeling of genetically engineered ingredients, a California law regulating the use of medically important antibiotics in animal feed, the strictest in the country, and several California humane treatment laws. There have been legal challenges to some of these laws in areas where these state actions encroach upon another regulatory authority, whether that of another state or of the federal government. These areas of tension highlight questions about the decentralization of food policy in the United States, including who gets to make policy decisions and the content of these decisions, but these spaces of conflict can also be sources of productivity for the development of food policy. While focused on the United States, the interaction between national and subnational regulatory units in the field of food policy is a matter of relevance to the global community. Brought into sharp relief by recent events in the United Kingdom, the negotiation of membership in political communities involves an interrogation of the specifics of where the boundaries of regulatory authority lie.[1]

II. PROBLEMS WITH THE AMERICAN FOOD SYSTEM: HEALTH AND SUSTAINABILITY

A. Nutrition and Health

The United States is one of the wealthiest countries in the world;[2] it produces more than enough food to feed its domestic population.[3] The sheer production of calories, however, does not speak to the overall success of the American food system.[4] If measured by the health of the population

---

[1] In June 2016, the United Kingdom voted to leave the European Union. The terms of this withdrawal, and the continued involvement of the UK with the EU remain to be negotiated. Brian Wheeler and Alex Hunt, *Brexit: All You Need to Know About the UK Leaving the EU*, BBC NEWS (21 July 2016), available 30 January 2017 at http://www.bbc.com/news/uk-politics-32810887.

[2] *See, e.g.,* Erik Sherman, *America is the Richest, and Most Unequal, Country*, FORTUNE (30 September 2015), http://fortune.com/2015/09/30/america-wealth-inequality/.

[3] *See, e.g., Food Availability (per Capita) Data System*, U.S. DEPT. OF AGRIC., available 30 January 2017 at https://www.ers.usda.gov/data-products/food-availability-per-capita-data-system/ (last updated 23 November 2016).

[4] *See generally* Stephanie Tai, *Food Systems Law from Farm to Fork and Beyond*, 45 SETON HALL L. REV. 109, 158–9 (2015) (quoting Polly J. Ericksen, *Conceptualizing Food Systems for Global Environmental Change Research*, 18 GLOBAL ENVTL. CHANGE 234, 234 (2008) (defining food systems as "the inter-

as related to diet, and by the health of the environment in relation to food production, the American food system is ailing.[5]

Malnourishment, which includes both obesity and hunger,[6] has a significant effect on the health of the American population, and this effect is greater on lower-income populations. As of late 2015, almost 35 percent of adults in the United States and 17% of children were obese.[7] The United States has the thirteenth highest prevalence of obesity in the world, only preceded by a variety of island and Middle Eastern nations.[8]

Although obesity affects all groups of people, it affects some more than others: in the US, non-Hispanic blacks have the highest rates of age-adjusted obesity, followed by Hispanics, non-Hispanic whites, and non-Hispanic Asians; middle age adults have higher obesity rates than seniors or children.[9] For men, obesity rates are slightly higher at higher income levels, while for women, a decrease in income correlates with an increase in obesity. Education level does not matter for men, while obesity rates increase as education levels decrease for women.[10] Obesity and related diseases cost the US $177 billion a year in medical costs.[11]

---

actions between and within biogeophysical and human environments, which determine a set of activities; the activities themselves (from production through to consumption); [and] outcomes of the activities (contributions to food security, environmental security, and social welfare)")).

[5] *See, e.g.*, Mark Bittman et al., *How a National Food Policy Could Save Millions of American Lives*, Wash. Post (7 November 2014), available 30 January 2017 at https://www.washingtonpost.com/opinions/how-a-national-food-policy-could-save-millions-of-american-lives/2014/11/07/89c55e16-637f-11e4-836c-83bc4f26eb67_story.html (noting that "[t]he food system and the diet it's created have caused incalculable damage to the health of our people and our land, water and air.").

[6] Mark Bittman, Opinion, *Don't Ask How to Feed the 9 Billion*, N.Y. Times (11 November 2014), available 30 January 2017 at http://www.nytimes.com/2014/11/12/opinion/dont-ask-how-to-feed-the-9-billion.html?_r=0.

[7] *Adult Obesity Facts*, Ctrs. for Disease Control and Prevention, https://www.cdc.gov/obesity/data/adult.html (last updated 1 September 2016); *Childhood Obesity Facts*, Ctrs. for Disease Control and Prevention, available 30 January 2017 at https://www.cdc.gov/obesity/data/childhood.html (last updated 22 December 2016); *Focus on Obesity*, 34 Health Affairs 1808, 1808–09 (2015).

[8] *Prevalence of Obesity*, World Health Org., available 30 January 2017 at http://gamapserver.who.int/gho/interactive_charts/ncd/risk_factors/obesity/atlas.html.

[9] *Adult Obesity Facts*, *supra* note 7.

[10] Cynthia L. Ogden et al., Obesity and Socioeconomic Status in Adults: United States, 2005–2008 3 (2010), available 30 January 2017 at http://www.cdc.gov/nchs/data/databriefs/db50.pdf.

[11] *Focus on Obesity*, *supra* note 7, at 1808–09.

Obesity is a form of malnourishment, and the other facet of malnourishment is hunger. The Department of Agriculture defines "food insecurity" as being uncertain of having or being able to acquire enough food to meet the needs of all members of the household.[12] This is measured by questions asked as part of the Census Bureau's Current Population Survey.[13] Census data from 2014 revealed 14 percent of American households and 19 percent of households with children were food insecure, mainly comprising low-income households with incomes below 185 percent of the poverty threshold.[14] In a survey of selected recent research on the relationship between food insecurity and health outcomes, the authors "show that the literature has consistently found food insecurity to be negatively associated with health".[15]

The effects of malnourishment on health and the disparate effect that this has on lower-income populations compound health inequality in the United States. A recent study in the Journal of the American Medical Association (JAMA) analyzed the relationship between income and longevity, confirming that in twenty-first century United States, "higher income was associated with greater longevity", and for the poor, average life expectancy varied significantly by locality.[16] Public health, like politics,[17] must be viewed through lenses of income inequality, locality and microclimate.

B. Environmental Sustainability of Food Production

As to sustainability, agricultural production has an enormous effect on water, soil and air. As of the early 2000s, 52 percent of all land in the

---

12 *Food Security in the U.S.*, ECON. RES. SERV., U.S. DEPT. OF AGRIC., available 30 January 2017 at http://www.ers.usda.gov/topics/food-nutrition-assistance/food-security-in-the-us/key-statistics-graphics.aspx (last updated 11 October 2016).

13 Craig Gundersen and James P. Ziliak, *Food Insecurity and Health Outcomes*, 34 HEALTH AFFAIRS 1830, 1831 (2015).

14 *Food Security in the U.S.*, *supra* note 12.

15 Gundersen and Ziliak, *supra* note 13, at 1830 ("For example . . . studies found that food-insecure children are at least twice as likely to report being in fair or poor health . . . and food-insecure seniors have limitations in activities of daily living comparable to those of food-secure seniors fourteen years older.").

16 Raj Chetty et al., *The Association Between Income and Life Expectancy in the United States, 2001–2014*, 315 J. AM. MEDICAL ASS'N 1750, 1762–63 (2016).

17 *See, e.g.,* Reid Wilson, *Which of the 11 American Nations Do You Live In?,* WASH. POST (8 November 2013), available 30 January 2017 at https://www.washingtonpost.com/blogs/govbeat/wp/2013/11/08/which-of-the-11-american-nations-do-you-live-in/.

United States (almost 2.3 billion acres) was used for agricultural purposes, and two-thirds of this was used for grazing (comprising grassland pasture and range, cropland pasture, and grazed forests).[18]

Agricultural uses of land have been, and continue to be, excepted from many of the nation's environmental laws, such as the Clean Water Act.[19] "Agriculture is the leading contributor to water quality problems in streams and rivers, making nutrients and sediments the most common pollutants fouling US waters."[20]

Attempts to bring farms and meat production facilities more directly under the purview of the environmental laws have faced organized opposition.[21] JB Ruhl wrote almost two decades ago that, "[t]o acknowledge that farms pollute and degrade the environment should neither indict farming as a way of life nor denigrate the ideals farmers hold",[22] and we cannot ignore the challenges posed by industrial farming.

Agriculture is, for example, a large contributor of greenhouse gas emissions. Emissions from agriculture, including from livestock digestion, livestock manure management, and soil management, amounted to 10 percent of the European Union's total greenhouse gas emissions in 2012 and 9 percent of the United States' total in 2014.[23]

In the European Union, the greenhouse gas emissions of the agricultural sector dropped by 24 percent between 1990 and 2012 due to "[a] significant

---

18 Econ. Res. Serv., U.S. Dept. of Agric., Major Uses of Land in the United States, 2002 (2006), available 30 January 2017 at https://www.ers.usda.gov/webdocs/publications/eib14/12980_eib14_reportsummary_1_.pdf.

19 J.B. Ruhl, *Farms, Their Environmental Harms, and Environmental Law*, 27 Ecol. L.Q. 263, 293–315 (2000).

20 Melissa K. Scanlan, *Adaptive Trading: Experimenting with Unlikely Partners*, 62 Kan. L. Rev. 971, 972 (2014) (citing U.S. Envtl. Prot. Agency, National Water Quality Inventory: Report To Congress: 2004 Reporting Cycle 16 (2009), available 30 January 2017 at https://www.epa.gov/sites/production/files/2015-09/documents/2009_01_22_305b_2004report_2004_305breport.pdf.

21 *See, e.g.*, Susan A. Schneider, *Food, Farming, and Sustainability, Readings in Agricultural Law*, Carolina Acad. Press (2016) (discussing Congress' attempt to expand the Environmental Protection Agency's authority over confined animal feeding operations (CAFOs), under the Clean Water Act, which faced multiple challenges and was altered and narrowed by the Second Circuit).

22 Ruhl, *supra* note 19, at 266.

23 *Agriculture and Climate Change*, European Env't Agency, available 30 January 2017 at http://www.eea.europa.eu/signals/signals-2015/articles/agriculture-and-climate-change (last modified 16 December 2016); *Sources of Greenhouse Gas Emissions: Agricultural Sector Emissions*, U.S. Envt'l Prot. Agency, available 30 January 2017 at https://www3.epa.gov/climatechange/ghgemissions/sources/agriculture.html (last updated 26 May 2016).

decline in livestock numbers, more efficient application of fertilisers, and better manure management", but increased by 11 percent over the same time period in the United States.[24] This impact is such that the future of agriculture is inextricably tied with climate change – not only must agriculture adapt to continue food production in a warming world,[25] but it must adapt so as to mitigate its impact on climate disruption.

III. STATE ACTION TO ADDRESS GAPS IN FEDERAL FOOD POLICY

While federal agencies, including the Food and Drug Administration (FDA), the United States Department of Agriculture (USDA), and the Environmental Protection Agency (EPA), take a large role in regulating food production, distribution, labeling and product safety, this federal regulation has always been in conjunction with state and local authority over certain aspects of food systems. For example, although the USDA has broad authority over the production, processing, and sale of meat in the United States, and the "inspection activity [over meat] claims a larger share of federal food safety resources than any other activity",[26] the USDA also enters into cooperative agreements with states to administer their own meat and poultry inspection services.[27] State and local agencies also have the main regulatory authority over "retail food establishments" such as restaurants, hospitals and grocery stores.[28]

The vigorous coexistence of federal, state, and local regulatory author-

---

24 *Id.*

25 U.S. Dept. of Agric., Climate Change and Agriculture in the United States: Effects and Adaptation 35–52 (2013), available 30 January 2017 at http://www.usda.gov/oce/climate_change/effects_2012/CC%20and%20Agriculture%20Report%20(02-04-2013)b.pdf.

26 Richard A. Merrill and Jeffrey K. Francer, *Organizing Federal Food Safety Regulation*, 31 Seton Hall L. Rev. 61, 100 (2000).

27 *See, e.g., Inspection*, Food Safety and Inspection Serv., U.S. Dept. of Agric., available 30 January 2017 at http://www.fsis.usda.gov/wps/portal/fsis/topics/inspection/state-inspection-programs/state-inspection-and-cooperative-agreements (last modified 3 June, 2014).

28 Merrill & Francer, *supra* note 26 at 110–11. The term "retail food store" varies by state, but for instance, the Texas Dept. of Health defines it as "Bed & breakfasts with more than 7 rooms, restaurants, bars, cafes, snack bars, hospitals that serve food to the general public, correctional facilities (jails) that contract with professional food management corporations for food preparation, and privately-owned correctional facilities are all considered to be retail food establishments. A retail food store is a food establishment or section of an establishment where

ity over some aspects of food systems does not, however, mean that there is a seamless sharing of regulatory authority over all of these aspects. There have been several state actions in the food policy context over the last few years that have attempted to make the American food system healthier or more sustainable, but have touched on areas traditionally within the purview of the federal government. Most of these actions have been challenged as overstepping state authority by infringing on another authority's sphere of power, whether the federal government's or another state's. The suits brought against these actions assert either that the state action is preempted by federal law or that the state action violates the US Constitution's Commerce Clause. This chapter examines three of these state actions to explore whether the decentralization of food policy can lead to system change – in the food policy context, and more generally. An improvement in our food system has the potential to affect the dual problems of climate change and economic inequality, and in the process, decentralization's promise to bring government closer to the people has the potential to allow for "democratic ideals [to be] more fully realized".[29]

A. California Senate Bill 27 – Restricting the Use of Antibiotics in Animal Feed

In October 2015, California passed a law restricting the routine use of antibiotics in animal feed. This law, the strictest animal antibiotics law in the country, prohibits the use of antibiotics in animal feed for growth promotion purposes and routine disease prevention purposes, mandates the collection of data about the use of antibiotics in animal feed, and requires veterinary oversight for the prescription of medically important antibiotics to livestock.[30]

Meat producers have been giving antibiotics to animals to promote growth since the 1950s, but, as a deputy director for science policy at FDA's Center for Veterinary Medicine noted, "it is not entirely understood how these drugs make animals grow faster".[31] The overuse of antibiotics in animal feed is a human health problem, and an enabler of

food and food products are offered to the consumer and intended for off-premise consumption."

[29] Samuel Issacharoff and Catherine M. Sharkey, *Backdoor Federalization*, 53 UCLA L. Rev. 1353, 1355 (2006).

[30] Cal. Food & Agric. Code §§ 14400–408 (West 2016).

[31] *Phasing Out Certain Antibiotic Use in Farm Animals*, U.S. Food and Drug Admin. (11 December 2013), available 30 January 2017 at http://www.fda.gov/ForConsumers/ConsumerUpdates/ucm378100.htm.

a sustainability problem. Antibiotics may be given to animals to treat disease, which is a therapeutic use, and which is not the main concern here. Human health concerns arise when meat producers use antibiotics to prevent disease and promote growth, which are subtherapeutic uses. It is the "stressful conditions of modern industrial agriculture" that encourage and support raising many animals in very close proximity to each other, which then necessitates the use of antibiotics to prevent infection.[32]

For decades, scientists have known that the overuse of certain medically important antibiotics can lead to antibiotic resistance in humans.[33] In 2013, the Centers for Disease and Prevention released a report on antimicrobial resistance, finding that 23,000 people die annually in the United States from antibiotic-resistant infections, and that antibiotic use in animal feed was one cause of this resistance.[34] In his bill signing message, the Governor of California wrote, "SB 27 addresses an urgent public health problem. The science is clear that the overuse of antibiotics in livestock has contributed to the spread of antibiotic resistance and the undermining of decades of live-saving advances in medicine."[35]

The California law followed decades of federal inaction regarding regulating the use of antibiotics in animal feed in the face of strong evidence of harm.[36] Although a district court had ordered the FDA to move forward on the withdrawal of approval for several antibiotics used in animal feed that were medically important to humans, the Second Circuit reversed the order in 2014.[37]

During the litigation, the FDA had been developing and implementing a voluntary program with drug manufacturers to reduce and eventually eliminate the use of these drugs. The agency released a draft guidance

---

[32] Lisa Heinzerling, *The FDA's Continuing Incapacity on Livestock Antibiotics*, 33 Stan Envtl. L.J. 325, 327 (2014).

[33] *See, e.g.*, Heinzerling, *supra* note 32, at 327.

[34] Ctrs. for Disease Control and Prevention, Antibiotic Resistance Threats in the United States, 2013 6 (2013), available 30 January 2017 at https://www.cdc.gov/drugresistance/pdf/ar-threats-2013-508.pdf; Heinzerling, *supra* note 32, at 327.

[35] Letter from Edmund G. Brown Jr., Governor of California, to the Members of the California State Senate (10 October 2015), available 30 January 2017 at https://www.gov.ca.gov/docs/SB_27_Signing_Message.pdf.

[36] *See* Heinzerling, *supra* note 32, at 327; Diana R. H. Winters, *Intractable Delay and the Need to Amend the Petition Provisions of the FDCA*, 90 Ind. L.J. 1047, 1060–65 (2015).

[37] *Natural Resources Defense Council, Inc. v. U.S. Food and Drug Admin.*, 760 F.3d 151, 176 (2d Cir. 2014).

document and a final rule on this plan in late 2013.[38] And in late 2014, the President released an Executive Order and a National Strategy document on combating antibiotic-resistant bacteria, which had an agricultural component.[39] While resting heavily on FDA's voluntary plan, these executive actions nevertheless acknowledged the depth of the problem and began to work toward a solution.

In addition, at the time of California's bill signing in 2015, there had been, and continues to be, significant activity in the private sector against the use of antibiotics in the US meat supply. For example, Chipotle and Panera have committed to using meat raised without the use of antibiotics,[40] and McDonald's stated it will not serve chicken raised with medically important antimicrobials.[41]

California's law, however, goes further than any of these other public or private initiatives because it prohibits the use of antibiotics not only for growth promotion, but also for routine disease prevention,[42] although the law does allow for prophylactic use to address an elevated risk of contraction

---

[38] U.S. Food and Drug Admin., Guidance for Industry #213: New Animal Drugs and New Animal Drug Combination Products Administered in or on Medicated Feed or Drinking Water of Food Producing Animals: Recommendations for Drug Sponsors for Voluntarily Aligning Product Use Conditions with GFI #209 (2013), available 30 January 2017 at http://www.fda.gov/downloads/AnimalVeterinary/GuidanceComplianceEnforcement/GuidanceforIndustry/UCM299624.pdf.

[39] Exec. Order No. 13676, 3 C.F.R. § 217 (2015); White House, National Strategy for Combating Antibiotic-Resistant Bacteria (2014), available 30 January 2017 at https://obamawhitehouse.archives.gov/sites/default/files/docs/carb_national_strategy.pdf; *see also* Diana R. H. Winters, *So Much, But Yet Not Enough—The Administration's Plan to Combat Antibiotic Resistance*, Bill of Health Blog (19 September 2014), available 30 January 2017 at http://blogs.harvard.edu/billofhealth/2014/09/19/so-much-but-yet-not-enough-the-administrations-plan-to-combat-antibiotic-resistance/ (discussing and critiquing the President's Executive Order and National Strategy on combating antibiotic-resistant bacteria).

[40] *See, e.g.*, Geoffrey Mohan, *On Antibiotics Fast-food Report Card, Panera, Chipotle get an A Grade*, L.A. Times (15 September 2015), available 30 January 2017 at http://www.latimes.com/business/la-fi-fast-food-antibiotics-20150914-story.html.

[41] Lisa McComb and Terri Hickey, *McDonald's USA Announces New Antibiotics Policy and Menu Sourcing Initiatives*, McDonald's (4 March 2015), available 30 January 2017 at http://news.mcdonalds.com/US/releases/McDonald%E2%80%99s-USA-Announces-New-Antibiotics-Policy-an.

[42] Lydia Zuraw, *California Governor Signs Bill Regulating Animal Antibiotics*, Food Safety News (10 October 2015), available 30 January 2017 at http://www.foodsafetynews.com/2015/10/california-governor-signs-groundbreaking-bill-regulating-animal-antibiotics/#.V4ZQ6WfVzL8.

of a particular infection. The law also mandates that "medically important antimicrobial drug(s) shall not be administered to livestock unless ordered by a licensed veterinarian through a prescription or veterinary feed directive, pursuant to a veterinarian-client-patient relationship".[43] FDA's voluntary plan also calls for veterinary oversight, but it relies on state practice requirements, which vary greatly. California's veterinarian client-patient relationship regulation, however, mandates that the vet has at the very least, seen the animal, or visited the premises, which is no longer required by the FDA.

As of yet, no one has brought a legal challenge to California's law.[44] This law demonstrates how, even in an area traditionally regulated by the federal government, a state can take stronger action in the face of federal inaction, or weak federal action, for the purpose of protecting public health. This state action in conjunction with private action is moving the conversation about the use of antibiotics in animal feed in the United States out of the purview of the federal government to different, and smaller, policymaking units.

B. The Humane Treatment of Animals

California has also passed several laws that regulate the humane treatment of animals in food production. First, in 2004, California prohibited the sale of products that are "the result of force feeding a bird for the purpose of enlarging the bird's liver beyond normal size",[45] which is the process used to produce foie gras. And second, in 2009, the California legislature strengthened an existing law to prohibit slaughterhouses from buying or selling animals that could not walk or processing or selling meat from such animals. The law also required slaughterhouses to immediately humanely euthanize any non-ambulatory animals on their premises.[46]

---

43 Cal. Food & Agric. Code §§ 14400–408 (West 2016).

44 The lack of legal challenge is somewhat surprising, because California's law does place stricter use restrictions on the use of antibiotics than does FDA policy. It is probable, however, that the law would survive challenge regardless. *See* Emilie Aguirre, *Contagion without Relief: Agency Action and State Antibiotics*, 64 UCLA L. Rev. (forthcoming 2017).

45 Products Resulting from Force-Feeding of Birds to Enlarge the Liver; Prohibition on Sale in California, Cal. Health & Safety Code § 25982 (West 2016), *invalidated by Ass'n des Éleveurs de Canards et D'Oies du Québec v. Harris*, 79 F. Supp. 3d 1136, 1147 (Cal. 2015); s*ee generally* § 25980(b) (defining "force feeding" as "a process that causes the bird to consume more food than a typical bird of the same species would consume voluntarily").

46 Cal. Penal Code § 599f (West 2016), *invalidated by Nat'l Meat Ass'n v. Harris*, 132 S. Ct. 965, 975 (2012).

Third, California worked to improve the conditions in which egg-laying hens were kept. Well ahead of the United States, where the vast majority of egg-laying hens are confined to battery cages, the European Union banned battery cages for chickens in 1999, effective as of 2011.[47] A battery cage provides less space than a single sheet of letter-sized paper.[48] In 2010, the California legislature passed AB 1437, which amended the California Health and Safety Code to prohibit the sale of an egg in the state if it "is the product of an egg-laying hen that was confined on a farm or place that is not in compliance with those animal care standards [of Proposition 2]".[49] Proposition 2 was a ballot proposition that passed in 2008 and requires that egg-laying hens (among other animals) "be confined only in ways that allow these animals to lie down, stand up, fully extend their limbs and turn around freely".[50]

The humane treatment of animals impacts public health and environmental sustainability. Humanely raised and slaughtered animals are less likely to carry foodborne pathogens that can make people sick.[51] Moreover, attention to the humane treatment and slaughter of animals necessitates an acknowledgement by producers, consumers, and regulators, that nonhuman lives have value apart from that inherent in food production.

Federal law regulates certain aspects of the production and slaughter of meat and poultry, and the production of eggs. Litigants challenged each of the California laws on the basis that federal law pre-empted state action: The foie gras law by the Poultry Products Inspection Act (PPIA), the slaughterhouse law by the Federal Meat Inspection Act (FMIA), and the Egg Laws by the Egg Products Inspection Act (EPIA). In 2012, the US Supreme Court found the federal FMIA expressly pre-empted California's slaughterhouse law.[52] In January 2015, a federal district court found that because the foie gras law "imposes an

---

[47] *Id.*

[48] *Cage-Free versus Battery-Cage Eggs: Comparison of Animal Welfare in Both Methods*, Humane Society, available 30 January 2017 at http://www.humanesociety.org/issues/confinement_farm/facts/cage-free_vs_battery-cage.html.

[49] Cal. Health & Safety Code § 25996 (West 2016).

[50] *Proposition 2: Standards for Confining Farm Animals, State of California*, Smart Voter (24 January 2009), available 30 January 2017 at http://www.smartvoter.org/2008/11/04/ca/state/prop/2/.

[51] *See, e.g.* Kathy Holliman, *More Humane Treatment of Farm Animals Tied to Food Safety*, Food Quality and Safety (15 May 2015), available 30 January 2017 at http://www.foodqualityandsafety.com/article/more-humane-treatment-of-farm-animals-tied-to-food-safety/.

[52] *Nat'l Meat Assoc. v. Harris*, 132 S. Ct. 965, 969 (2012).

ingredient requirement in addition to or different than the federal laws and regulations", the federal PPIA expressly pre-empted it.[53] The case is currently on appeal.[54] In early 2014, six states sued California alleging that the federal EPIA pre-empts California's Egg Laws and these state laws violate the Constitution's Commerce Clause.[55] The district court dismissed the case, finding that the plaintiffs lacked standing,[56] and it is now on appeal.[57]

These state humane treatment laws represent attempts by California to improve the sustainability of the food system beyond what is mandated by the federal government. The challenges to these laws demonstrate the resulting conflicts as other jurisdictions challenge California's authority to take these actions. These policy attempts and their ensuing conflicts, however, involve more voices in conversations about food policy and allow food policy to develop along various axes.

C. Labeling Transparency

Though there had been a significant amount of state legislative activity concerning the labeling of foods with genetically engineered (GE) ingredients,[58] Vermont became the first state to pass a "no strings attached"

---

53 *Ass'n des Éleveurs de Canards et D'Oies du Québec v. Harris*, 79 F. Supp, 3d 1136, 1144 (Cal. 2015). Defendants argued that the California law regulated a process rather than an ingredient, and that the process took place before the bird entered an official establishment, which triggered the pre-emption provision, but the court disagreed. *Id.* Plaintiffs did not challenge a separate provision of the California code that actually banned force feeding, but only § 25982, which prohibited the sale of products that are produced through force feeding. *Id.* at 1138.

54 *State Appeals Court Ruling that Overturned Foie Gras Ban*, CBS Radio Inc. (4 February 2015), available 30 January 2017 at http://sacramento.cbslocal.com/2015/02/04/fois-gras-ban/.

55 *Missouri v. Harris*, 58 F. Supp. 3d 1059, 1065 (Cal. 2014). This was not the only challenge to the law. Suit was also brought by a California citizen, alleging that the suit was void for vagueness. The Ninth Circuit affirmed the dismissal of his case in early 2015, finding that the egg-laying hen standards in Proposition 2 could be "readily discerned using objective criteria." *Cramer v. Harris*, 591 Fed. Appx. 634, 635 (9th Cir. 2015).

56 *Harris*, 58 F. Supp. 3d at 1079.

57 *Id.*, *appeal docketed*, No. 14-17111 (9th Cir. Oct. 28, 2014).

58 *See* Ross H. Pifer, *Mandatory Labeling Laws: What Do Recent State Enactments Portend for the Future of GMOs*, 118 Pa. St. L. Rev. 789, 790–91 (2014) (finding that "[a]ccording to the National Conference of State Legislatures, 110 bills on this subject were introduced in 32 different states in 2013. In the early months of 2014, this trend continued as at least 67 bills were introduced in 25 different states.").

labeling law, in 2014.[59] The Vermont law mandated that, with certain exceptions,[60] all food offered for sale in Vermont that is "entirely or partially produced with genetic engineering", must be labeled as such.[61] Foods that fall under the labeling requirement may not be labeled with "natural", "all-natural", "or any words of similar import that would have a tendency to mislead a consumer".[62]

Several trade associations, including the Grocery Manufacturers Association and the Snack Food Association, brought suit arguing that aspects of Act 120 violated the First Amendment and the Commerce Clause, and were pre-empted by the FDCA, the Nutrition Labeling and Education Act (NLEA), the FMIA, and the PPIA.[63] A district court dismissed several of plaintiffs' Commerce Clause claims and the allegations that the Act was pre-empted by the FDCA and the NLEA. The court permitted claims asserting that the law's provision prohibiting manufacturers to advertise their products as "natural" in any state would have discriminatory effects under the Commerce Clause, that the law's disclosure requirement is pre-empted by the FMIA and the PPIA, and that the Act violated the First Amendment to move forward.[64] The case was dropped in late summer 2016, after a federal labeling bill was passed.[65]

In July 2016, a national genetically engineered ingredients disclosure law was passed. The law gives the USDA's Agricultural Marketing Service the authority to establish rules for the disclosure standard within two years, which will include determinations regarding the threshold for triggering the requirement, the process of determining whether a product falls under the requirement, and options for disclosure. These options, according to the bill, must include a "quick response" code, so that the information will only be available to people with smartphones

---

[59] VT. STAT. ANN. tit. 9, § 3041 (2016). Connecticut and Maine have passed "strings attached" labeling laws: Connecticut's law will become effective when four additional states, including one that borders Connecticut, enact mandatory labeling laws consistent with Connecticut's, and the population of the states located in the northeast United States that have passed such laws exceeds 20 million people. CONN. GEN STAT. § 21a-92c(a) (2016). Maine's law goes into effect when at least five contiguous states, including Maine, enact mandatory labeling legislation. ME. REV. STAT. ANN. tit. 22, § 2593 (2016).

[60] VT. STAT. ANN. tit. 9, § 3044 (2016).

[61] *Id.* § 3043(a)(2) (2016).

[62] *Id.* § 3043(c).

[63] *Grocery Mfrs. Ass'n. v. Sorrell*, 102 F. Supp. 3d 583, 594 (Vt. 2015).

[64] *Id.* at 648.

[65] *Id.*, *appeal docketed*, No. 15-1504 (2nd Cir. May 6, 2015).

who make the effort to scan the code,[66] which makes the information less accessible and dampens the transparency purpose of the disclosure requirement.

The initiative toward labeling genetically engineered ingredients is to give consumers more information about the food they eat. Although it is questionable whether the labeling of genetically engineered ingredients will actually provide consumers with meaningful information about these aspects of food production – numerous scientific organizations have found no evidence that GMOs are harmful to human health,[67] nor does a label regarding whether a product contains GMOs indicate whether the product was produced using monoculture, pesticides or herbicides – the Vermont law was written for the purpose of allowing them to choose foods that are perceived to be healthier, or that are grown in a more sustainable way.[68] The federal law dilutes this purpose by allowing manufacturers to use codes instead of providing information on the label and preempting stricter state laws, but represents a compromise between consumer advocates and industry. We see here an example of national policy responding to state action, which resulted in benefits to national uniformity, but at the cost of a certain degree of consumer protection.

IV. CHALLENGES TO STATE ACTION AND THE POTENTIAL FOR SYSTEM CHANGE

With their policy innovations and their responsiveness to local populations, these state initiatives described above demonstrate the benefits of a tiered federal system with national and subnational governments.[69] For

---

66 *See* Peggy Lowe, *Senators Reach Deal on National GMO Labeling Bill*, NAT'L PUB. RADIO (23 June 2016), available 30 January 2017 at http://www.npr.org/sections/thesalt/2016/06/23/483290269/senate-unveils-a-national-gmo-labeling-bill; Riette van Lack and Ricardo Carvajal, GMO Labeling Bill is a Pen Stroke Away From Becoming Law: What Comes Next? FDA Law Blog, Hyman, Phelps & McNamara, P.C., 20 July 2016.

67 *E.g.*, William Saletan, *Unhealthy Fixation: The War Against Genetically Modified Organisms is Full of Fearmongering, Errors, and Fraud. Labeling Them Will Not Make You Safer*, SLATE GRP. (15 July 2015), available 30 January 2017 at http://www.slate.com/articles/health_and_science/science/2015/07/are_gmos_safe_yes_the_case_against_them_is_full_of_fraud_lies_and_errors.html.

68 VT. STAT. ANN. tit. 9, § 3041 (West 2016) (finding that genetically engineered foods have potential health and environmental risks).

69 *See, e.g.*, Samuel Issacharoff and Catherine M. Sharkey, *Backdoor Federalization*, 53 UCLA L. REV. 1353, 1354 (2006) (citing *New State Ice Co.*

example, Vermont's GE labeling law was the first of its kind to go into effect. Its performance against legal challenge was watched by other states, and it inspired the federal law.[70] California's Egg Laws inspired other state initiatives, including a Massachusetts law prohibiting the sale of eggs, veal, or pork of a farm animal confined in spaces that prevent the animal from lying down, standing up, extending its limbs, or turning around approved in November 2016.[71]

As to responsiveness, the California law banning the force-feeding of birds to enlarge their livers was passed in 2004.[72] The Egg Laws were passed by ballot initiative in 2008 and legislatively amended in 2010.[73] The law restricting the slaughter of non-ambulatory animals was passed in 2008, in direct response to a video released by the Humane Society of the United States "showing workers at a slaughterhouse in California dragging, kicking, and electro-shocking sick and disabled cows in an effort to move them".[74] This spate of laws reflects a preference in the local population to use the power of the marketplace to change methods of food

---

v. Liebmann, 285 U.S. 262, 311 (1932) (Brandeis, J., dissenting) (noting "Justice Brandeis's famous invocation of the states as laboratories of democracy in which 'a single courageous State' may blaze new paths by trying 'novel social and economic experiments'")); William Baude, *State Regulation and the Necessary and Proper Clause*, 65 Case W. Res. L. Rev. 513, 516 (2015) (citing Michael W. McConnell, *Federalism: Evaluating the Founders Design*, 54 U. Chi. L. Rev. 1484, 1493–1500 (1987) (discussing how "decentralized decision making . . . [is] better able to further the interests and general welfare of the people")).

70 *See, e.g.*, Puneet Kollipara, *Opposition stalls U.S. Senate bill aimed at blocking GMO labels*, Science (17 March 2016), available 30 January 2017 at http://www.sciencemag.org/news/2016/03/opposition-stalls-gmo-food-labeling-bill-us-senate; Chris Moran, *Senators Trying to Strike Down Vermont GMO Labeling Law at Last Minute*, Consumerist (27 June 2016), available 30 January 2017 at https://consumerist.com/2016/06/27/senators-trying-to-strike-down-vermont-gmo-labeling-law-at-last-minute/; John Herrick, *Vermont Will Be the First State in the Nation to Require GMO Labeling*, Vt. Bus. for Soc. Resp. (24 April 2014), available 30 January 2017 at http://vbsr.org/news/news_vermont_will_be_first_state_in_nation_to_require_gmo_labeling/cat/vbsr_in_the_news/P35/, ("'I do think that this is a model that other states can look to in passing other legislation,' said Falko Schilling, a lobbyist for the Vermont Public Interest Research Group. 'This is really a start to a much larger movement across the country.'").

71 *See* New York Times, Massachusetts Question #3, Feb. 10, 2017, available at http://www.nytimes.com/elections/results/massachusetts-ballot-measure-3-improve-farm-animal-confines.

72 Russ Parsons and David Pierson, *Foie Gras Ban Is Overturned*, L.A. Times (7 January 2015), available 30 January 2017 at http://www.latimes.com/business/la-fi-foie-gras-ban-lifted-20150108-story.html.

73 *Missouri v. Harris*, 58 F. Supp. 3d 1059, 1063 (Cal. 2014) (citation omitted).

74 *Nat'l Meat Ass'n v. Harris*, 132 S. Ct. 965, 969 (2012).

production,[75] and a continued willingness to elect legislators that support the passage of legislation regarding the humane treatment of animals.

These state laws are efforts towards systems change – the attempts to provide healthier food and to improve the sustainability of food production push back against industrialization and consumerism. For example, a restriction on the use of antibiotics in animal feed for subtherapeutic purposes leads to a necessary change in production practices and against a "bigger is always better" mindset. Humane treatment laws may result in less robust profit margins, at least initially, for producers, with a difficult to measure benefit in animal comfort and consumer good will. And in this diffusion of power, there is the potential for a "more robust democratic accountability by which 'government is brought closer to the people, and democratic ideals are more fully realized'".[76]

A. Challenges

Opponents of these state laws in the food policy context argue, however, that the uniformity of a national market is more important than responsiveness to a local populace or policy innovation, that Congress has enacted national legislation to further this purpose, and that this legislation pre-empts the state regulation.[77] For example, we can look to the truncated litigation against Vermont's labeling law.[78] In that suit, as well as those against the California humane treatment laws, the petitioners argued that Congress passed federal legislation to facilitate the movement of goods and services in a national market. The controversial state action threatened to destroy the uniformity necessary to sustain such a market and would thereby thwart the purpose of the relevant federal legislation.

Some of the challenges to these state laws also involved allegations of Commerce Clause violations. For example, in their suit against the

---

[75] *See* Transcript of Oral Argument at 51, *Nat'l Meat Assoc. v. Harris*, 132 S. Ct. 965 (2012) (No. 10-224), 2011 WL 5402757, at *51 ("California's purpose . . . was twofold, to one, protect public health but also to prohibit animal cruelty in an area where – where California legislators were concerned about the humane treatment of nonambulatory animals").

[76] Issacharoff and Sharkey, *supra* note 69, at 1355 (citing David L. Shapiro, Federalism: A Dialogue 91–2 (Northwestern University Press 1995)).

[77] *See generally* Diana R. H. Winters, *The Magical Thinking of Food Labeling: The NLEA as a Failed Statute*, 89 Tul. L. Rev. 815, 833–4 (citations omitted) (discussing "the Supremacy Clause of the Constitution", which states that federal laws are "the supreme Law of the Land", the Supreme Court recognizes that "state laws that conflict with federal law are 'without effect.'").

[78] *Grocery Manuf. Assoc. v. Sorrell*, 102 F. Supp. 3d 583, 593 (Vt. 2015).

California Egg Laws, Missouri, Nebraska, Oklahoma, Kentucky, Iowa and Alabama explained that with the laws' passage, they "became concerned that '[our] econom[ies] and status within the federal system will be irreparably injured if the California Legislature—who were not elected by, and are not answerable to, the people of [our states]—is allowed to regulate and increase the cost of egg production in [our own territory]'."[79] They alleged that the egg laws violate the Commerce Clause for three reasons: "(a) they were enacted solely to protect California egg producers from out-of-state competitors, (b) they have the purpose and effect of discriminating against interstate commerce, and (c) they regulate commercial activity occurring entirely within the Plaintiff States".[80]

These challenges assert that the actions the states have taken are not the states' to take, and that the acting state has harmed either the federal interest or another state's interest. In these allegations of overreach lie fundamental issues involved in the decentralization of food policy, including which decision-making body is appropriate to make these decisions, and what the substance of the decisions entails.

B. Questions of Who and What

There was extensive national discussion in each of the areas of legislative action discussed above – antibiotics in animal feed, the humane treatment of animals, and GE ingredient labeling – but federal action proved elusive. California passed the Egg Laws (in 2008 and 2010) while national awareness about the use of battery cages for egg-laying hens was increasing.[81] It seemed as if there was going to be a nationwide change in 2011, when the United Egg Producers, a trade group for egg farmers, and the Humane Society of the United States, an activist organization, agreed to work together towards a national law that would improve conditions for egg-laying hens, but this law failed.[82]

---

79 Brief for the State of Utah as Amici Curiae Supporting Appellants at 15, *Missouri v. Harris*, No. 14-7111 (9th Cir. Mar. 4, 2015).

80 *Id.*

81 *See, e.g.*, Laura Reddy, *Activists Call for End to 'Cruel' Battery Cages for Chickens*, ABC News (19 November 2011), available 30 January 2017 at http://abcnews.go.com/Blotter/activists-call-end-cruel-battery-cages-chickens/story?id=14989778 (discussing ABC News' 20/20 investigation of egg farms).

82 Dan Charles, *How Two Bitter Adversaries Hatched a Plan to Save the Egg Business*, Nat'l Pub. Radio (10 February 2012), available 30 January 2017 at http://www.npr.org/sections/thesalt/2012/02/10/146635596/how-two-bitter-adversaries-hatched-a-plan-to-change-the-egg-business; *see also* Pamela Vesilind, *Did the Dismissal of Missouri v. Harris Have an Unanticipated Effect?*, Agric. Law

Before the federal labeling bill was passed, "more than 70 bills ha[d] been introduced in over 30 states to require GE labeling or prohibiting genetically engineered foods",[83] including in Vermont, and Maine and Connecticut had passed laws that were to go into effect when other states pass similar laws. And as discussed, California's animal feed antibiotics law was passed in the midst of renewed national attention to antibiotic resistance and a failed legal challenge aimed at forcing federal regulation.[84] For various reasons, however, whether because a national solution was not reached (as with the treatment of egg-laying hens), or because federal action was weak (as with antibiotics in animal feed), there was room for state action to go farther.

What has become increasingly clear is that, because our food systems cross many borders, from state to national and international, state action taken in these areas of food policy will not remain confined to the enacting state. Instead, state policy, whether passed by the most populous or the second to the least populous, drives national policy. We see this when food manufacturers began changing their labels universally to comply with Vermont's law,[85] and as egg producers in various states change their practices to comply with California's. The states' Commerce Clause challenge to California's egg law, where the states complain of a violation of their rights under a federalist system, where their citizens must comply with a law passed by legislators they did not elect and that they have no ability to change, demonstrates that California's law is driving broad change.

Food manufacturers, which serve national and global markets, spent resources to label food containing GE ingredients because Vermont voted that it be so, which may exhaust the energy of the industry and the public to enact meaningful change to food labels. Here, decentralization enhanced

---

BLOG (7 October 2014), available 30 January 2017 at http://aglaw.blogspot.com/2014/10/did-dismissal-of-missouri-v-harris-have.html; Dan Flynn, *Despite Ruling, Midwest Egg Producers Unlikely to Give Up California Market Without Big Fight*, FOOD SAFETY NEWS (6 October 2014), available 30 January 2017 at http://www.foodsafetynews.com/2014/10/midwest-egg-producers-arent-going-to-give-up-california-market-without-a-fight/#.V4ba3pErLIU.

83 *State Labeling Initiatives*, CTR. FOR FOOD SAFETY, available 30 January 2017 at http://www.centerforfoodsafety.org/issues/976/ge-food-labeling/state-labeling-initiatives#.

84 *See supra*, at III.A.

85 *See, e.g.,* Chris D'Angelo, *The Tiny State Of Vermont Is Forcing GMO Labeling Nationwide*, HUFFINGTON POST (30 March 2016), available 30 January 2017 at http://www.huffingtonpost.com/entry/vermont-forces-nationwide-gmo-labeling_us_56f30ac2e4b0c3ef5217dafd.

democratic participation for those within the enacting state's geographic boundaries, while cutting off avenues of change for many others. This, however, is a result of the federalist system, and does not necessarily represent a problem because of the presence of other regulatory mechanisms, both public and private. For example, the reaction to Vermont's labeling law was a renewed appetite for a national solution. And even though the national bill will make further state experimentation impossible through its strong pre-emption clause,[86] this will not be the last say – consumer demand for more GE ingredient labeling than provided for in a federal law may drive private labeling efforts and voluntary certification regimes. Food policy and food systems will be altered, and bettered, in this nuanced interaction between different spheres of regulatory authority: national, subnational, public, and private.

V. CONCLUSION

Food systems, and hence food policy, are inherently complex, with multiple and interdependent moving parts. This kind of structure necessitates a multilayered regulatory authority, which may mean inconsistency and conflict at times, as we see with the state-based solutions and the challenges thereto. In the evolution of food system regulation and the challenges to regulation are benefits for food policy – which must reflect both local preference and national needs, and must incorporate profound scientific uncertainty – and for our democracy more generally.[87]

There is value in the decentralization of food policy not just because it diffuses power, but precisely because it causes friction between regulatory authorities. State-federal friction can check the power of the federal government and create a space where dissenters from national policy can manifest ideas and solutions at the state level.[88] State-federal friction also alerts policymakers to important gaps in federal regulation and

---

[86] Sometimes, of course, federal solutions are not ceilings, but are floors, allowing for stronger state laws. For example, the Privacy Rule of the Health Insurance Portability and Accountability Act (HIPAA) establishes a federal floor, upon which states can adopt additional privacy safeguards. A federal floor in the context of battery cages for egg-laying hens would mean that millions of animals would be treated more humanely than they are now.

[87] *See* Diana R. H. Winters, *The Benefits of Regulatory Friction in Shaping Policy*, Food & Drug L.J. (2016).

[88] Heather K. Gerken and Ari Holtzblatt, *The Political Safeguards of Horizontal Federalism*, 113 Mich. L. Rev. 57, 81–2 (2014).

illuminates which of these gaps are most salient to the general public.[89] These frictions can help get issues on the national policymaking agenda, and spur movement in the federal government.[90]

Moreover, state action that entails spillover into the realm of other states can spark dialogue that can help the country reach compromise on divisive issues.[91] This compromise may not necessarily be uniform, "[b]ut 'checkerboard policies' . . . should be adopted only after we've had the type of debate that national politicking alone can drive".[92] For example, it remains to be seen whether there will be a nationwide resolution on the labeling of GE ingredients, or whether a "patchwork" of state regulations will persist, but the ultimate outcome will be the product of much policy discussion.

Any discussion of decentralization must take into account the resulting friction between regulatory authorities and the need to move products across many borders while maintaining responsiveness to local populations. These ongoing public discourses are valuable to the maintenance of a healthy democratic environment. Within the interaction between these multitudes of authority will be the development of a new, and better, food system.

---

89 *See* Patti Zettler, *Pharmaceutical Federalism*, 92 IND. L.J. 1, 58–63 (forthcoming 2017) (discussing how state regulation in the field of drug policy can "force the FDA [or Congress] to account for state regulatory interests").

90 Gerken and Holtzblatt, *supra* note 88, at 89–93.

91 *Id.* at 86.

92 *Id.*

12. Legal democracy: using legal design, technology and communications to reform food and agriculture systems

Laurie Ristino[1]

> "Technology is nothing. What's important is that you have faith in people, that they're basically good and smart, and if you give them tools, they'll do wonderful things with them." Steve Jobs

I. INTRODUCTION

The US food system has undergone staggering changes since the 1970s. Farm consolidation and vertical integration have resulted in agricultural production that is increasingly controlled by fewer actors.[2] These changes, largely in rural America, have impacted local economies with negative externalities occurring beyond, such as water pollution, habitat loss and greenhouse gas emissions. The public's renewed interest in food and food systems has given rise to social movements that aim to address its pervasive ills.

[1] The author wishes to thank Amber Leasure-Earnhardt, research fellow extraordinaire, for her research assistance on this chapter and Sarah Danly for her urban farm graphic as well as Bren mini-colloquium attendees and Leslie Lagomarcino for their helpful comments on the manuscript. Of course, all opinions and any errors are the author's own.

[2] James M. MacDonald, *Cropland Consolidation and the Future of Family Farms*, Econ. Res. Serv., U.S. Dept. of Agric. (3 September 2013), available 31 January 2017 at https://www.ers.usda.gov/amber-waves/2013/september/cropland-consolidation-and-the-future-of-family-farms/; *see also Processing & Marketing: Manufacturing*, Econ. Res. Serv., U.S. Dept. of Agric., available 31 January 2017 at https://www.ers.usda.gov/topics/food-markets-prices/processing-marketing/manufacturing/ (last updated 30 December 2016); James M. MacDonald, et al., Econ. Res. Serv., U.S. Dept. of Agric., Consolidation in U.S. Meatpacking (2000), available 31 January 2017 at https://www.ers.usda.gov/webdocs/publications/aer785/18011_aer785_1_.pdf?v=41061.

The rich history of the current food movement is rooted, in part, in 1960s counter culture, which sought to reclaim the means of production by empowering citizens through access to tools. Similarly, this chapter explores how people may be empowered to use law and policy more effectively to improve the food system. While Winters's chapter (Chapter 11) probes the tensions between federal and state power when these movements result in more stringent local controls of the food system, this chapter focuses on the tool of legal design and technology to increase public access to and use of food law and policy.

This chapter begins by exploring threads of transdisciplinary, innovative thinking that cross-pollinated during the 1960s and from which the idea of democratizing the law springs. This narrative models the connect-the-dots thinking that informs social innovation and solution creation. This chapter then builds on these historical origins and discusses how law and policy may be reimagined as a tool through design and system thinking, empowering citizens to make positive change in their communities in food systems and beyond. By democratizing the law and policy through legal design and systems thinking, we can, and must, more fully harness its power to create a more sustainable future.

II. ACCESS TO TOOLS: NAIVES AND VISIONARIES[3]

In the late 1960s, the serial innovator Stewart Brand self-published a periodical called Whole Earth Catalog.[4] The idea behind Whole Earth was summed up in its subtitle "Access to Tools". The catalog was the ultimate do-it-yourself guide for the counter-culture movement. Although the publication, by design, existed only a few years, it was highly influential. Years after its celebrated demise, Steve Jobs recounted in his 2005 Stanford commencement address how Whole Earth had inspired him as a young man:

> When I was young, there was an amazing publication called *The Whole Earth Catalog*, which was one of the bibles of my generation. It was created by a

---

[3] Special appreciation to Greg Watson, an Alchemy Institute "alum", the first African American Secretary of Agriculture of Massachusetts, and currently Director of Policy and System Design at Schumacher Center for a New Economics, for this turn of phrase as well as his remembrances about New Alchemy, Buckminster Fuller, Stewart Brand, Donella Meadows and others.

[4] Whole Earth Catalog, available 31 January 2017 at http://www.wholeearth.com/index.php.

> fellow named Stewart Brand not far from here in Menlo Park, and he brought it to life with his poetic touch. This was in the late 1960s, before personal computers and desktop publishing, so it was all made with typewriters, scissors and Polaroid cameras. It was sort of like Google in paperback form, 35 years before Google came along: It was idealistic, and overflowing with neat tools and great notions.[5]

It might seem ironic that Jobs, who made his fortune on consumer technology, was enamored by this low-tech touchstone of 1960s counter-culture. In actuality, the personal computing (PC) revolution in which Jobs played an iconic role was an act of democratizing technology, of individual empowerment. Computers had previously consisted of large mainframes taking up entire rooms, usable and affordable only by large corporations and institutions. The PC was a defiant act, an inevitable child of the counter-culture movement, literally cooked-up in a suburban garage.

Seemingly in stark counterpoint, the modern environmental movement, also rising from 1960s foment, is often understood as a reaction against industrialization and its evils and, therefore, fundamentally anti-modern. However, Whole Earth Catalog embodied a line of thinking and practice informed by systems thinking (hence, "whole" in the title) that wove technology, science and counterculture together with environmentalism.[6] This current of the environmental movement saw its physical manifestation in the New Alchemy Institute.

New Alchemy was founded by John Todd, Nancy Jack Todd and William McLarney in 1969[7] on Cape Cod "[t]o protect the seas, restore the earth, and inform the earth's stewards". An "eco-technical" utopia,[8]

---

5 *Steve Jobs' 2005 Stanford Commencement Address,* Stanford News (14 June 2005), available 31 January 2017 at http://news.stanford.edu/news/2005/june15/jobs-061505.html.

6 Henry Trim, *A New Alchemy on the Land: Scientists, Hippies, and an Ecological Society*, Network in Canadian History & Env't (10 April 2012), available 31 January 2017 at http://niche-canada.org/2012/04/10/a-new-alchemy-on-the-land-scientists-hippies-and-an-ecological-society/; *see also* Andrew Kirk, *The New Alchemy: Technology, Consumerism, and Environmental Advocacy, in* The Columbia History of Post-World War II America 352 (Mark C. Carnes (ed.), Columbia University Press 2007); see Whole Earth Catalog, *supra* note 4, in which Stewart Brand explains that the Catalog was inspired by the insights of Buckminster Fuller, who referred to himself as a "comprehensive anticipatory design scientist", in a section of the Catalog entitled, *Understanding Whole Systems.*

7 *New Alchemy Institute*, Spatial Agency, available 31 January 2017 at http://www.spatialagency.net/database/why/ecological/new.alchemy.institute.

8 Trim, *supra* note 6.

the New Alchemists were inspired by, and engaged with, Stewart Brand as well as other iconic thought leaders such as Buckminster Fuller, E. F. Schumacher, Wes Jackson, Wendell Berry and Donella Meadows. The New Alchemists held that American society was ecologically unsustainable, but could be sustainable if managed consistent with ecological science. The New Alchemists used the model of Earth (and thereby nature), the ultimate closed loop system,[9] as a model for researching and practicing sustainability. In particular, they researched methods of intensive organic agriculture, eschewing petroleum inputs such as industrial fertilizers, pesticides, and large, mechanical infrastructure. Similar to Whole Earth Catalog, they published their research as manuals and guides so that others could use and replicate their work.[10]

John Todd explained the influence of E. F. Schumacher's ideas on the philosophy and practice of New Alchemy Institute,

> I owe a debt of gratitude to E.F. Schumacher for helping me see economics as if people and nature mattered.
>
> ***
>
> We started with food and agreed that the contemporary mechanistic agricultural model would in the long run fail to feed the planet. We looked for other models to guide us. The larger workings of nature provided us with clues. We sought out several places where nature is extremely bountiful and made a shopping list of the attributes unique to those places. As patterns gradually emerged, this effort proved directly fruitful. We also sought out places that, under the guiding hand of humans, have been bountiful for millennia. This was significant because humans normally destroy their biological capital. We wanted to learn what stable cultures know about caring for their lands.[11]

E. F. Schumacher, initially a protégé of the economist John Maynard Keynes, was an internationally recognized economic thinker. His highly influential 1973 book, a collection of essays, *Small is beautiful: a study of economics as if people mattered*,[12] argued that the modern economy is unsustainable, challenging the pervasive paradigm of economic growth

---

9 A closed loop system is one in which no waste is generated, and therefore, its operation is sustainable.

10 In fact, New Alchemy's journals are still available online. *New Alchemy's Journals*, The Green Ctr., available 31 January 2017 at https://newalchemists.net/publications/new-alchemy-1971-1991/.

11 John Todd, An Ecological Economic Order, Schumacher Ctr. for a New Economics (Hildegarde Hannum (ed.), 1985), available 31 January 2017 at http://www.centerforneweconomics.org/publications/lectures/Todd/John/An-Ecological-Economic-Order.

12 E.F. Schumacher, Small is Beautiful, a study of Economics as if People Mattered (Harper & Row 1973).

based upon our destructive use of natural resources, while arguing for sustainable development and the appropriate use of technology. His ideas inspired a cluster of organizations, including the Schumacher Center for a New Economics, which was founded to preserve his personal library and continue his work.[13]

The Schumacher Center promotes the "new economy", including related concepts of community self-sufficiency, buying locally and local currency. Like New Alchemy, the Center puts these ideas into practice in its community of Great Barrington, Massachusetts, with the goal of educating the public about sustainable economies. For example, the Center helped pioneer the idea of community land trusts, in which the community purchases land and related natural resources, returning these resources to the commons. A related organization, Community Land Trust of Southern Berkshires preserved Indian Line Farm, the first community supported farm in North America. The Indian Line project addresses "the critical connections between ecology, economy, and community" by "protecting habitat, preserving agricultural property, and keeping small-scale, organic farming viable".[14] The ideas that inform this chapter, the New Economy Law Center at Vermont Law School, and similar efforts can also be traced back to Schumacher.

In 2013, not long after I became the first Director of the Center for Agriculture and Food Systems at Vermont Law School, I met with Scott Stokoe, farm manager at the Dartmouth College Organic Garden. What started out as a farm tour turned into a lesson on "closed loop" production systems, the Holy Grail, if you will, of sustainability – with Stokoe explaining the elegant mechanics of a tilapia aquaculture system in the garden's greenhouses. As it turns out, he learned these principles of sustainability decades before at the New Alchemy Institute.

III. THE FOOD MOVEMENT: THE PROBLEMS OF SCALE, ACCESS AND TRANSPARENCY

Americans' renewed interest in food, variably called the food movement, good food movement, local food, or slow food, and so on, was hatched from the fabric of these experiments in sustainability, born of its

---

13 *See generally* SCHUMACHER CENTER FOR A NEW ECONOMICS, http://www.centerforneweconomics.org/ (accessed 31 January 2017) (seeking "to educate the public about the economics that support both people and the planet").

14 *Indian Line Farm,* SCHUMACHER CTR. FOR A NEW ECONOMICS, available 31 January 2017 at http://www.centerforneweconomics.org/content/indian-line-farm.

confluence of ideas. The CEO of Stonyfield Yogurt, Gary Hirschberg, served as the executive director of the New Alchemy Institute in the late 1970s and explained how New Alchemy would later shape his role in the organics movement:

> Luckily, what began as a philosophical fondness for dishes like brown rice and seaweed eventually matured into a tasty cuisine that attracted talented chefs, notably my friend Alice Waters, who called organics "the delicious revolution."
>
> How I found myself swept away by this revolution is a story that began in the late 1970s, when I was executive director of the New Alchemy Institute. We built a solar-heated greenhouse that used no fossil fuels, herbicides, pesticides or chemical fertilizers. Yet it produced enough food to feed 10 people three meals a day, 365 days per year.[15]

Similarly, popular author and food politics commentator, Michael Pollan, has traced the food movement to the counter-culture 1960s and the seminal act of Alice Waters opening the Berkeley restaurant Chez Panisse in 1971.[16] The fact that it took organics decades to go from the hippie fringe to big business fueled by consumer demand obscures its roots in the counter-culture movement, which sought to reclaim our relationship with food by knowing how and who produces it. Having an understanding of these antecedents helps illuminate a generative path forward – our actions should build on or re-examine these ideas, not recreate them.

A. Symptoms of an Ill Food System

Now that demand for "good food" has achieved a critical mass, American society is again grappling with the multiplicity of interrelated food system challenges. In particular, how can we ensure good food access to all people and, in the first instance, how can we ensure food produced is actually "good" for people, farmed animals and the planet? Despite the 1960s back-to-the-land movement, current challenges spring from our remove from agriculture and food production, coupled with the increasing consolidation and industrialization of the food system.

---

15 Gary Hirshberg, *Organics – Healthy Food and So Much More*, *in* FOOD, INC: HOW INDUSTRIAL FOOD IS MAKING US SICKER, FATTER AND POORER – AND WHAT YOU CAN DO ABOUT IT: A PARTICIPANT GUIDE 47 (Karl Weber (ed.), Public Affairs 2009).

16 *Michael Pollan on How Reclaiming Cooking Can Save Our Food System, Make Us Healthy & Grow Democracy*, DEMOCRACY NOW! (6 May 2013), available 31 January 2017 at http://www.democracynow.org/2013/5/6/michael_pollan_on_how_reclaiming_cooking.

To give a few examples of the systemic food system challenges:

- agriculture is the primary source of non-point source pollution, resulting in a dying Chesapeake Bay and the enormous dead zone in the Gulf of Mexico;[17]
- 35 percent of adults in America are obese, and obesity-related illnesses are epidemic and disproportionally impact minorities;[18]
- the meat industry has become dramatically consolidated and integrated over the last 30 years;[19]
- genetically modified corn and soy dominates American production with seeds being controlled by a handful of companies like Monsanto and Dow;[20]
- pollinators necessary for food production have suffered startling declines;[21] and
- a system of laws and anti-laws such as state "ag-gag" laws,[22] information restrictions in the farm bill, and insufficient Food and Drug Administration labeling requirements create a de facto black box around the food system.[23]

At the heart of many of our food system problems are issues of economies of scale, transparency, and access. The interrelated forces of federal

---

[17] David A. Dzombak, *Nutrient Control in Large-Scale U.S. Watersheds*, 41 BRIDGE ON SUSTAINABLE WATER RESOURCES 13, 13–22 (2011).

[18] *Special Report: Racial and Ethnic Disparities in Obesity*, ST. OF OBESITY, http://stateofobesity.org/disparities/.

[19] James M. MacDonald and Michael E. Ollinger, *Consolidation in Meatpacking: Causes and Concerns*, ECON. RES. SERV., U.S. DEPT. OF AGRIC. (2000), available 31 January 2017 at https://www.meatinstitute.org/index.php?ht=a/GetDocumentAction/i/7072.

[20] *The World's Top 10 Seed Companies: Who Owns Nature?*, GMWATCH, available 31 January 2017 at http://www.gmwatch.org/gm-firms/10558-the-worlds-top-ten-seed-companies-who-owns-nature.

[21] *Honey Bee Health and Colony Collapse Disorder*, AGRIC. RES. SERV., U.S. DEPT. OF AGRIC., available 31 January 2017 at https://iapreview.ars.usda.gov/News/docs.htm?docid=15572.

[22] "Ag-gag" is a term used to refer to state laws that forbid the undercover filming of agriculture operations to expose animal welfare abuses and harmful industrial agriculture practices in general. *See, e.g.*, Mark Bittman, *Who Protects the Animals?*, N.Y. TIMES (26 April 2011), available 31 January 2017 at http://opinionator.blogs.nytimes.com/2011/04/26/who-protects-the-animals/?_r=0.

[23] *See, e.g.*, Lisa Heinzerling, *The Varieties and Limits of Transparency in U.S. Food Law*, 70 FOOD AND DRUG L.J. 11 (2015); Justin F. Marceau, *Ag Gag Past, Present, and Future,* 38 SEATTLE U.L. REV. 1317 (2015).

policies, downward pressure on food prices, and high farm infrastructure costs have resulted in extreme consolidation of many aspects of agricultural production, squeezing out small and mid-sized farms, especially. At the same time, the food system is highly opaque because of a complex regulatory system fractured among many agencies, often with conflicting missions,[24] and a system of laws, such as state ag-gag laws, preventing transparency in the way food is produced. The food system is further plagued by access hurdles along several dimensions, including a lack of access to healthy food for many citizens, disproportionally impacting communities of color, and a lack of access to the tools of food production.

In short, the sick food system is a "wicked problem", a concept described in 1973 by Horst Rittel and Melvin Webber, design and urban planning professors at University of California Berkeley,[25] to describe problems resistant to solution because of complex interdependencies. Wicked problems are hard to address because they have multiple causes, are challenging to define, and have no single solution. In other words, wicked problems are born of complex systems.

B. Systems Thinking and Design to Solve Wicked Problems

Consequently, creating solutions to wicked problems requires thinking systemically. Systems thinking is "a discipline for seeing wholes. It is a framework for seeing interrelationships rather than things, for seeing patterns of change rather than static 'snapshots' . . . Today systems thinking is needed more than ever because we are becoming overwhelmed by complexity."[26] As detailed in Scanlan's chapter (Chapter 1), systems thinking arose from multiple disciplines post-World War II as a result of advances in science and social sciences requiring a more holistic understanding of things in contrast to reductionism, which reduces wholes into parts. Systems thinking saw its apotheosis in the work of Jay Forrester, founder of system dynamics, and Donella Meadows while both were at MIT, followed by Meadows's publication of the ground-breaking book *Limits to Growth* in 1972.

---

[24] Lisa Heinzerling, *Divide and Confound: The Relationship Between Transparency, Public Health, and Regulatory Authority in the National Food System*, *in* Food and Drug Regulation in an Era of Globalized Markets 125–34 (Sam F. Halabi (ed.), Academic Press 2015).

[25] John C. Camillus, *Strategy as a Wicked Problem*, Harv. Bus. Rev. (2008), available 31 January 2017 at https://hbr.org/2008/05/strategy-as-a-wicked-problem.

[26] Peter Senge, The Fifth Discipline: The Art & Practice of The Learning Organization 68–9 (Doubleday/Currency 1990).

Despite the potential of systems thinking to foster sustainable approaches to wicked problems, we have failed to embrace such an approach, as our fractured food regulatory system continues to illustrate.[27] Legal scholar Richard Lazarus has argued that the structure of the US government was intentionally designed to confound such a holistic approach.[28] In particular, the drafters of the Constitution, influenced by Enlightenment philosophy which emphasized reason and challenged authoritarian governance, decentralized power and provided for incremental law making with an emphasis on private rights, not public goods.[29] Given these structural hurdles, achieving national, holistic reform of the food system is a challenging prospect.

Rather, changes to the food system at the federal level will likely be made incrementally and slowly through the accretion of case law and in a piecemeal manner through legislation like the Farm Bill. Although one should not abandon federal reform efforts because of the entrenched role national policy plays in perpetuating the system's dysfunction,[30] one should not solely rely upon these traditional law and policy means to create progressive food system change. The reasons for this are multifaceted. There may be a greater potential to innovate and leverage change at more local points in the food system, as articulated in Winters's chapter (Chapter 11). Relatedly and critically, it is the imperative of a democracy that citizens are empowered to create social progress.

Despite the fractured federal approach to food and agriculture policy, it is in the realm of agriculture, as the New Alchemy Institute experience reflects, that the application of systems thinking has been most successful and from which we continue to learn about sustainability.

> Much of what we have learned about managing real systems began in agriculture, notably the work of horticulturist Liberty Hyde Bailey, agronomist Albert Howard in India, forester Aldo Leopold, agroecologists Miguel Altieri and Stephen Gliessman, plant geneticist Wes Jackson, range management expert

---

27 Heinzerling, *supra* note 23.

28 Richard J. Lazarus, *Super Wicked Problems and Climate Change: Restraining the Present to Liberate the Future,* 94 Cornell L. Rev. 1153, 1153–234 (2009).

29 *Id.*

30 See Andrea Freeman, *The 2014 Farm Bill: Farm Subsidies and Food Oppression*, 38 Seattle U.L. Rev. 1271 (2015); William S. Eubanks II, *Paying the Farm Bill: How One Statute Has Radically Degraded the Natural Environment and How a Newfound Emphasis on Sustainability is the Key to Reviving the Ecosystem*, 27 Envtl. F. 56 (2010) for examples of the harms perpetuated by federal agriculture law and policy.

Alan Savory, and ecologically savvy farmers like Joel Salatin. The most important lesson from their collective work is that the land is an evolving organism of interrelated parts soils, hydrology, biota, wildlife, plants, animals, and people. If sustainability is the goal, the land can neither be managed as a factory nor the profit it generates measured by its short-term yield.[31]

Notably, the term "wicked problem" was coined by the aforementioned Horst Rittel, an influential design thinker. Broadly, design theory, an umbrella term under which many permutations have flourished from different disciplinary perspectives, is the concepts and ideas that try to explain creative work.[32] Used in this sense, the term "design" is not a one dimensional concept meaning the way things look, but multidimensional, including methods, strategies, and research.[33] "Design thinking", which is part of the evolution of ideas and practices related to design, is a process for creating solutions to problems.[34]

In 1992, leading design thinker and academic, Richard Buchanan published his seminal article, "Wicked Problems in Design Thinking",[35] in which he argued for the application of design thinking to solve persistent and difficult challenges. In fact, as discussed above, this idea had already been put into practice in the context of agricultural production at places like the New Alchemy Institute where problem solving was based on design principles, that is, using nature and its whole systems as a template for designing sustainable solutions.[36] Thus, systems thinking and design thinking are complementary frameworks, which used together can help us generate sustainable solutions to complex problems.[37]

---

31 David Orr, *Systems Thinking and the Future of Cities*, POST CARBON INST. (30 May 2014), available 31 January 2017 at http://www.postcarbon.org/systems-thinking-and-the-future-of-cities/.

32 *See, e.g.,* Armand Hatcheul, *Towards Design Theory and Expandable Rationality: The Unfinished Program of Herbert Simon*, 5 J. MGMT. AND GOVERNANCE 260, 260–73 (2001).

33 *Id.*

34 Kaan Turnall, *What is Design Thinking?,* FORBES (10 May 2015), available 31 January 2017 at http://www.forbes.com/sites/sap/2015/05/10/what-is-design-thinking/#7cb196a03c18.

35 Richard Buchanan, *Wicked Problems in Design Thinking*, 8 DESIGN ISSUES 5, 5–21 (1992).

36 The Schumacher Center as well as The Land Institute, founded by Wes Jackson, also employed these ideas in their experiments on the land. LAND INSTITUTE, https://landinstitute.org (accessed 31 January 2017).

37 *See, e.g.*, Tim Brown and Roger L. Martin, *Design for Action*, HARV. BUS. REV. (2015), available 31 January 2017 at https://hbr.org/2015/09/design-for-action.

We cannot count on national solutions to address our "wicked" food system problems in a holistic way, although we should continue to advocate for holistic approaches. At the same time, we do not want to abdicate our agency, community self-reliance, and our capacity for creativity and innovation to generate progressive change. Fortunately, the food movement has generated innovative solutions at the local, state, national and international levels. Some examples are food hubs, fair trade cooperatives, third party certifications, farm to school, and urban farming. The question is, how to take these innovations, and where appropriate, translate and communicate them in order to scale (meaning grow) food system change. Next this chapter discusses access to tools to scale up food system change.

C. Scaling Change: Food, Design and the Law

> "When I am working on a problem, I never think about beauty. I think only how to solve the problem. But when I've finished, if the solution isn't beautiful, I know it's wrong." Buckminster Fuller

Law is a critical tool to create, scale, and sustain change. At its essence, law is a set of rules about how we treat each other and the environment. Unfortunately, as traditionally taught and practiced, law is a dry affair communicated in a form generally only lawyers understand. This systematically limits society's access to the tools law can create. Another negative result of this exclusivity is that because law is communicated within a limited construct, lawyers and non-lawyers alike tend to only see its limitations, not its possibilities. Consequently, we under-utilize the law's power to scale change by failing to empower others and ourselves.

However, by using systems thinking and applying design principles to the problems we want to solve, we can make legal tools that people can and will want to use. By creating legal tools in this way, we are able to empower individuals and communities to make positive food system changes, overcoming hurdles of economies of scale, transparency and access pervasive in the dominant food system. Applying design thinking to law and policy is a fundamentally different and creative approach than traditional lawyering and policymaking. Marrying a design approach to technology, we can help many people at the same time. In contrast, when we advocate using the traditional legal paradigm, lawyers are only able to help one client at a time.

Using legal design (see Figure 12.1), we democratize the law in two fundamental and complementary ways. First, we are robustly facilitating citizen-stakeholder (farmers, food producers, community members, and

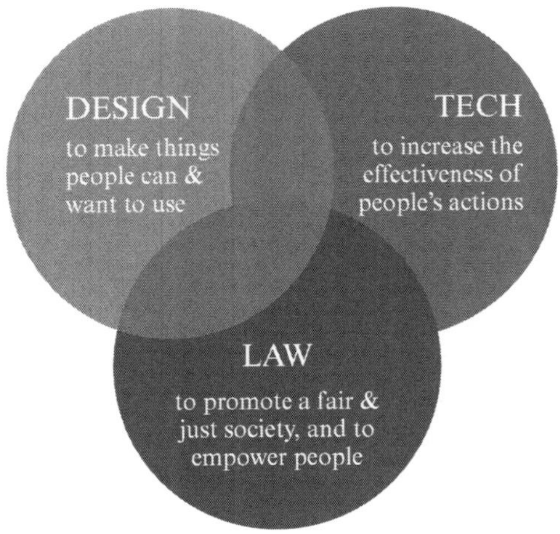

Source: Margaret Hagan (©2013), http://www.legaltechdesign.com (accessed 31 January 2017).

Figure 12.1 Legal design

so on) access to legal resources to which normally the cost of access is prohibitively high. Second, because we are creating resources from the users' perspective, we engage stakeholders in the design process itself, requiring designers to be reflective of the potential for their values and privilege to distort the ultimate tools created.

In addition, design thinking helps us see the multi-functionality of law. Law is not just about litigation or regulation. Law is about how we order society – it's everywhere. Coincidentally, legal designers are needed not just in traditional lawyering in government agencies or law firms, but in any enterprise aimed at engaging or mobilizing groups of people. Providing access to this fundamental information empowers citizens to create the relationships and environmental outcomes they need and want.

What do law and policy tools look like when they are created using design thinking? Figure 12.2 gives an example created by the Center for Agriculture and Food Systems at Vermont Law School as part of its partnership with the National Farm to School Network. Farm to school legislation accomplishes multiple, interrelated goals, including improving children's access to fresh fruits and vegetables while supporting local economies.

This infographic condenses and translates nation-wide legal research on the progress of farm to school state legislation adoption. The design communicates to a wider public the farm to school research in order to

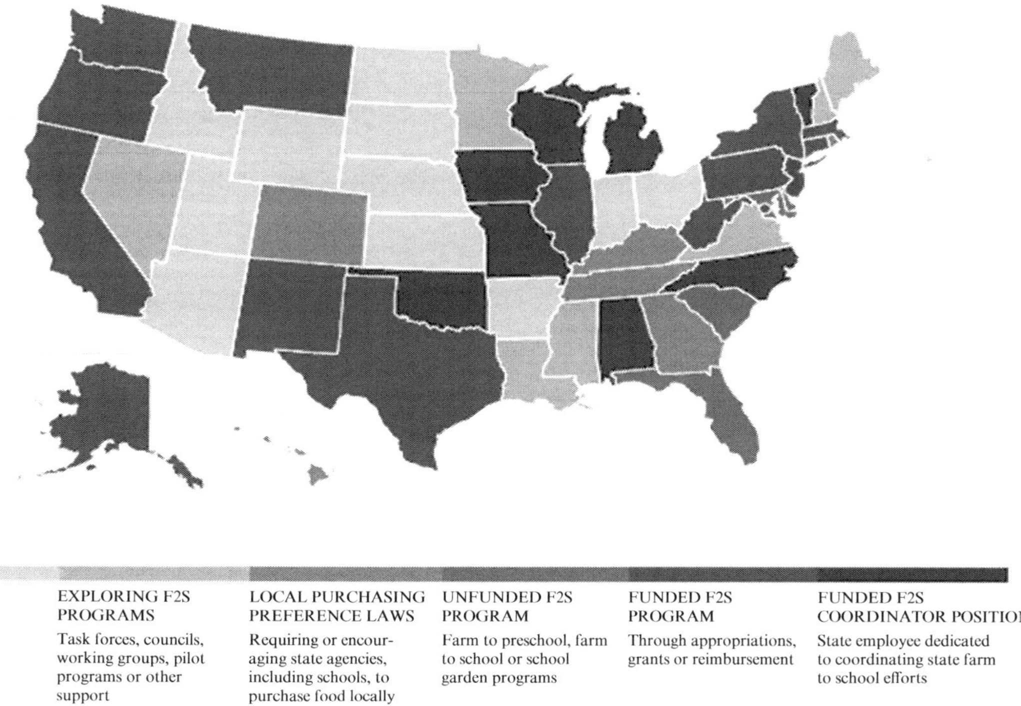

Source: National Farm to School Network & Vermont Law School's Center for Agriculture and Food Systems, State Farm to School Legislative Survey 2002–2014 (March 2015), available 31 January 2017 at http://www.farmtoschool.org/Resources/F2S-Survey-2014.pdf.

Figure 12.2 State farm to school legislation: 2002–2014

facilitate adoption of these policies. In particular, the form lends itself to social media and, therefore, broad dissemination, providing a more accessible entry point for many stakeholders (farmers, school teachers, state legislators) than the accompanying, extensive written report.

To further explore how design thinking can be used to solve problems in the food system, let's consider a hypothetical: how might we create legal tools to help farmers convert to organic agriculture production? We want to facilitate organic conversion because it supports environmental and economic sustainability by reducing the use of environmentally harmful synthetic pesticides and fertilizers while providing farmers access to premium organic markets. However, farmers who want to convert from conventional to organic, which is regulated by the United States Department of Agriculture (USDA) under the National Organic Program, face several barriers.

To create legal tools to address these barriers, we engage in a process of legal design that might look like this. First, we conduct research to determine key hurdles to organic conversion. This research includes not only researching the law, but developing an understanding of the needs of farmers and other potential stakeholders for whom we are creating the tools. In talking with farmers, we might find that a threshold barrier to conversion is understanding the legal requirements for organic certification set forth in the Code of Federal Regulations (CFR).

For a non-lawyer, the process of simply accessing the CFR is daunting. As legal designers, our task is to not only lower this initial access barrier, but also to figure out how to translate relevant information in the CFR in a way our intended audience can use. In other words, we create the legal tool from the farmer's perspective, not ours. This approach, called "empathy" in design thinking, is a staple of communication theory.[38] How we ultimately present the information is a multidimensional consideration, including the form(s) of the tool (visual, checklist, diagram), the medium in which the tool is developed (digital, paper, video), and the tool's relation or connection to other tools in the organic conversion toolbox.

Designing the tool (or legal product) is inherently creative because it is an iterative, interactive and transdisciplinary process. For example, when designing legal tools, we will likely work with others who bring different skill sets and perspectives to the process, such as a web designer, graphic

---

38 *See, e.g.*, *An Introduction to Design Thinking, Process Guide*, INST. OF DESIGN AT STANFORD, available 31 January 2017 at https://dschool.stanford.edu/sandbox/groups/designresources/wiki/36873/attachments/74b3d/ModeGuideBOOTCAMP2010L.pdf?sessionID=e29682c7569e583344b123a7116d9172e65e8531 (last visited 22 July, 2016).

artist, subject matter expert or communications professional. Further, we will test the beta of this legal "product" with the target audience to refine the tool. We may find that one approach to the legal tool works better than another or that we need to start over. Through the design process we are continuously learning and refining our approach to problem solving. We take the risks that creating truly useful products requires.

The design thinking process is visualized in Figure 12.3.

The end user will not necessarily see the legal analysis that supports the products we create (unless such information is relevant to the design). Similarly, we do not see the code that makes the iPhone work; most consumers simply want their phone to work, for it to be multifunctional and easy to use. This approach to problem-solving, refined by the Hasso Plattner School of Design ("D School") at Stanford University, is called "human-centered design" and is integral to design thinking.[39] When we design legal tools in this manner, they are more relevant to the intended user and, therefore, more useful. This is key because the over-arching goal is to facilitate systems change.

In our hypothetical, a tool that lowers the information barrier regarding the legal process for organic certification is not the end of the story. We can use legal design to do more than "translate" law and policy. Barriers to organic certification are likely multifactorial. Consequently, we also need to apply principles of systems thinking in order to more fully see and understand the barriers to conversion. We may use different techniques to help see more fully in systems.[40] For example, in our research, we may approach the problem from another perspective, for example, identify the factors that help farmers *successfully* convert to organic food production in addition to researching the barriers. By coming at the issue from multiple directions, we are better able to visualize the system that influences organic conversion. We will diagram our evolving understanding in order to reveal more connections.

As part of this visualization process, we may also draw the barriers and their relationship to each other to help discern ways that tools may be optimized, possibly addressing multiple barriers. For example, one barrier to conversion is cost because of the lost farm revenue during the required

---

[39] Institute of Design at Stanford, http://dschool.stanford.edu/ (accessed 31 January 2017); *see also* IDEO, https://www.ideo.com/ (accessed 31 January 2017).

[40] *See generally Systems Thinking Resources*, Donella Meadows Inst., available 31 January 2017 at http://donellameadows.org/systems-thinking-resources/ (discussing various ways to develop thinking skills).

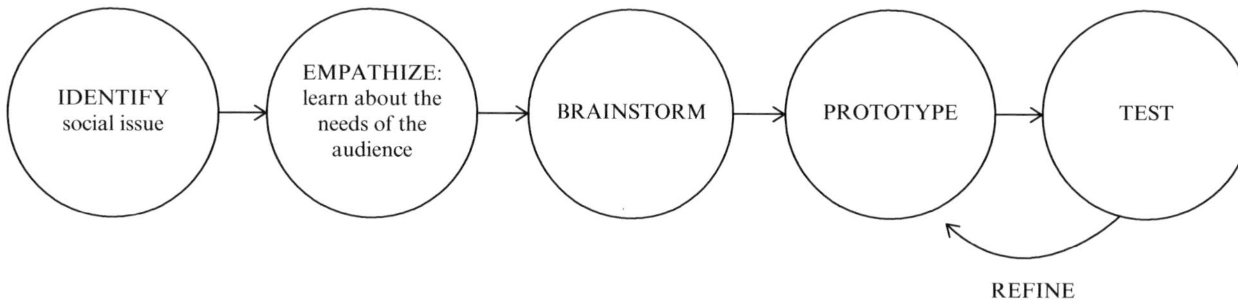

Source: Created by Sarah Danly at the Center for Agriculture and Food Systems, Vermont Law School 2016.

Figure 12.3 Visualization of design thinking process

three-year conversion period. We may decide to build a funding tool if we determine through the design process that inclusion of the tool would be particularly useful for farmers. During our research, we identify several financial resources, including federal financial assistance programs and non-governmental innovations such as the work of Farmland LLP, which invests in the conversion of conventional farmland to organic.[41] We may use design thinking to perform legal "forensics" on successful real-life conversion stories, creating templates from these case studies. When we use legal design in this manner, we are going beyond simply translating the law: we are making a blueprint of innovations so that others may adopt them. This scales the impact of what would otherwise be "one-off" success stories, thereby facilitating systems-based change.

If the organic conversion toolbox takes the form of a website, we will design the site linking "pages" in an intuitive manner based upon the end user's needs. For example, we might link the CFR requirement for the three-year conversion period to successful case studies financing the transition. On a deeper level, we want to design the digital space so that the architecture itself facilitates the user/farmer's understanding of the "system" (in this case, all the steps that must occur in order to successfully convert from conventional to organic). By helping the user "connect the dots", we create more powerful tools.

When we approach problem solving using design thinking, we see the law as part of the fabric of solutions – not as the solution itself – which more accurately mirrors life and the law's relevancy in it. It also means, as noted above, that legal design is inherently transdisciplinary. If we wanted to make a city's building code related to rooftop gardening more accessible to encourage urban farming in order to reduce food deserts, we might work with zoning officials, tradespeople and building owners, among others, to help us ground the abstraction of the code in the physical world. In designing a legal tool, we could, for example, collaborate with a web designer to "build" a digital building with a rooftop garden where users can scroll over parts of the building revealing relevant code sections translated for the target audience as in the hypothetical visual in Figure 12.4.

Designing legal products takes longer than the traditional individual client-centered legal approach of a legal memorandum, brief, or contract, for a variety of reasons. When we use design thinking to solve problems we are typically considering the interests of groups or multiple stakeholders.

---

41 *See, e.g.*, FARMLAND LP, http://www.farmlandlp.com/ (accessed 31 January 2017).

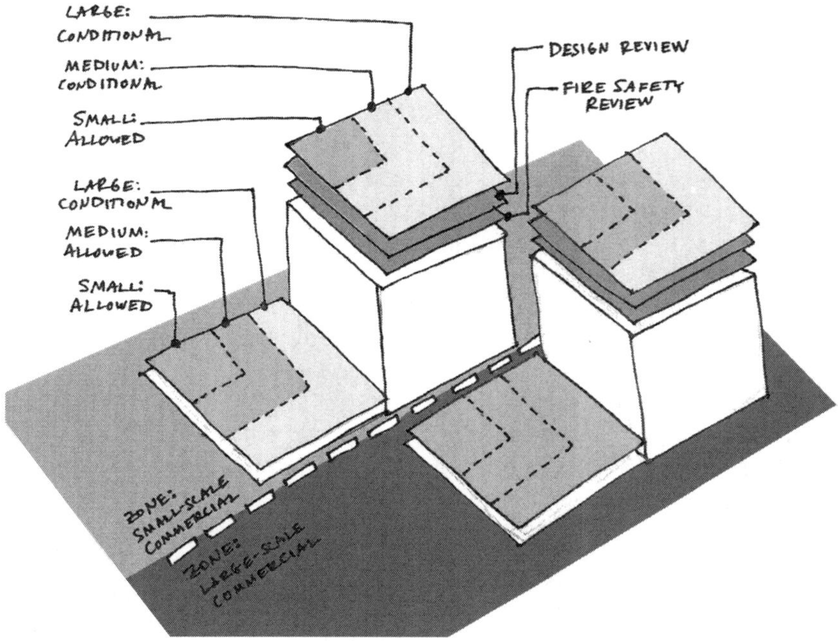

Source: Created by Sarah Danly, Center for Agriculture and Food Systems, Vermont Law School 2016.

Figure 12.4 Example design of a legal product

In addition, the form and the function of the tool determines the contours of legal research, analysis and writing and, therefore, both tool creation and research are done simultaneously. Because we develop a more intuitive product, another benefit to this problem solving approach is that we may discover additional legal questions that need consideration because design thinking is generative.

To use another tech analogy, when Apple developed the iPad, slavishly prototyping and testing, the code and design were done together so they not only function seamlessly as one, but they are one. The focus on design at Apple is integral to the company's success. Consumers want to own and use Apple products. Steve Jobs, known for obsessively laboring over the smallest details of Apple's products, was driven by design.[42] And, as evidenced in Apple's product evolution, his design focus was not simply

[42] Walter Isaacson, Steve Jobs (Simon & Schuster 2011).

aesthetic. Jobs's friend and collaborator was Stanford D (Design) School co-founder, David M. Kelley. Kelley is well-known for being part of the team that brought us Apple's mouse, now a ubiquitous computing tool.[43] However, as the Center for Agriculture and Food Systems at Vermont Law School demonstrates, the design thinking approach to problem solving is not just about creating products people will want to buy: the Center uses design thinking to solve social and environmental problems by making products people will want to use. Thus, this approach to solving wicked problems using legal design owes as much to the innovators at the New Alchemy Institute as to those in Palo Alto.

By marrying systems and design thinking to law and policy, we are able to harness the law's full potential to empower individuals and groups to make progressive change in their communities. Experimentation and innovation are necessary to create progress, and law and policy are necessary to scale and institutionalize that progress. Using legal design thinking, we may address the confounding issues that plague our food system, such as the pressure of farm consolidation, lack of transparency, and the high cost of access to resources and information. We create transparency by aggregating, translating, analyzing and disseminating information like statutes, regulations, case law and litigation resources. We build legal solutions that allow farmers to create infrastructure and access capital without necessarily getting bigger, all by designing legal tools with the end user in mind.

IV. CONCLUSION: CODA

The classical form of the sonata has three parts: the beginning or exposition, development, and then, recapitulation. By knowing the form and period of the piece, a listener may understand the whole of the work. Innovation in this system comes by deviating from the form itself. In his classic Children's Concerts, Leonard Bernstein explained the sonata form by playing portions of Mozart's Jupiter Symphony:

> Of course Mozart, like all geniuses is full of surprises. He doesn't always play the game according to the rules. In fact he often gives us more musical pleasure by breaking rules than by obeying them. In this C-major Sonata of his, where

---

[43] Amar Toor, *David Kelley Talks About Steve Jobs and 'Design Thinking' in '60 Minutes' Interview*, VERGE (6 January 2013), available 31 January 2017 at http://www.theverge.com/2013/1/6/3844604/david-kelley-talks-design-thinking-steve-jobs-60-minutes.

> the recapitulation should be in the tonic in the key of C, Mozart holds out on us; he is still resisting that magnet of the tonic; and so he gives us the recapitulation in the unexpected key of F.[44]

Similarly, nothing in this chapter is entirely new. Legal design has its roots in systems thinking and design theory, ideas which evolved over decades from multiple disciplines. This chapter sets forth a variation of the form, arguing for the use of legal design to create tools people can use to make progressive change. Moreover, legal design could be applied to a variety of wicked social problems, not just unsustainable food systems.

The idea of creating tools to push humans farther is, of course, as old as our species, and the drive to constantly improve them, our defining characteristic. The Cooper Hewitt Smithsonian Design Museum in Manhattan, the only museum in the nation dedicated to design, celebrated its reopening in 2014 with the show "Tools: Extending Our Reach". The book for the exhibition explains the criticality of tools:

> Tools are intended to bring about change. They exist so we may do more, see better, gather information, transform things, make decisions, investigate new frontiers, interact more fluidly and precisely, achieve higher forms of aesthetic satisfaction—extend our reach.[45]

Law and policy are critical tools to scale change. It is the scaffolding upon which our social relationships are built. But, it is woefully under-utilized. By increasing access to and understanding of law and policy, we are democratizing the law. We do this through legal design, and when we do, we empower citizens to use food system innovations in law and policy to create a more sustainable society.

---

44 *Young People's Concerts*, LEONARD BERNSTEIN OFF., available 31 January 2017 at http://www.leonardbernstein.com/ypc_script_what_is_sonata_form.htm.

45 CARA MCCARTY AND MATILDA MCQUAID, TOOLS: EXTENDING OUR REACH 14 (Cooper Hewitt Museum 2014).

Index